The Globalization of U.S.–Latin American Relations

Democracy, Intervention, and Human Rights

Edited by Virginia M. Bouvier

 PRAEGER

Westport, Connecticut
London

Library of Congress Cataloging-in-Publication Data

The globalization of U.S.–Latin American relations : democracy, intervention, and human rights / edited by Virginia M. Bouvier.
   p. cm.
Includes bibliographical references and index.
ISBN 0–275–97250–X (alk. paper)
1. Latin America—Foreign relations—United States. 2. United States—Foreign relations—Latin America. 3. United States—Foreign relations—20th century.
4. United States—Military relations—Latin America. 5. Latin America—Military relations—United States. 6. Globalization. 7. Democracy. 8. Human rights.
I. Bouvier, Virginia Marie, 1958–
F1418.G58 2002
327.7308—dc21   2001054584

British Library Cataloguing in Publication Data is available.

Library of Congress Catalog Card Number: 2001054584
ISBN: 0–275–97250–X

First published in 2002

Praeger Publishers, 88 Post Road West, Westport, CT 06881
An imprint of Greenwood Publishing Group, Inc.
www.praeger.com

Printed in the United States of America

The paper used in this book complies with the
Permanent Paper Standard issued by the National
Information Standards Organization (Z39.48–1984).

10 9 8 7 6 5 4 3 2 1

Copyright Acknowledgments

The editor and publisher gratefully acknowledge permission for use of the following material:

Excerpts from Carrie A. Foster. *The Women and the Warriors: The U.S. Section of the Women's International League for Peace and Freedom, 1915–1946.* Syracuse, NY: Syracuse University Press, 58–73.

Extracts from David A. Crocker. "Reckoning with Past Wrongs: A Normative Framework." *Ethics and International Affairs* 13 (1999): 43–64.

Excerpts from Records of the Women's International League for Peace and Freedom, U.S. Section, Swarthmore College Peace Collection; and National Council on the Cause and Cure of War, Swarthmore College Peace Collection.

We are capable of progress only to the degree that we become capable of adapting our acts to conditions that are increasingly distant from us in space and time. The certainty that we are contributing to work that will survive us, work that will benefit the future, enhances our sense of human dignity, helping us to triumph over the limitations of our nature.

—José Enrique Rodó, *Ariel*

Contents

Acknowledgments

I am indebted to John Cavanagh, Margaret E. Crahan, Edgar J. Dosman, Douglas Farah, Julio Ramos, Lars Schoultz, and Michael Shifter for the lucid and insightful papers they presented at the "Challenges to Peace, 1898–1998: Visions from the Past, Lessons for the Future" conference held at the Library of Congress in October 1998. Their papers formed the basis for this book. Likewise, I acknowledge herein the valuable contributions of Sarah Anderson, David Crocker, Carrie A. Foster, Ana Patricia Rodríguez, and Molly Todd, whose chapters round out this volume. It has been an intellectually and spiritually enriching process to work with these colleagues, many of whom have engaged in considerable rewriting and editing to add luster to the final product. I am grateful for their efforts.

About twenty units and departments from more than eight universities and organizations supported the conference, including the Department of Spanish and Portuguese and the Latin American Studies Center at the University of Maryland, College Park (UMCP); the Hispanic Division of the Library of Congress; the Consortium of Universities of the Washington Metropolitan Area; the Embassy of Spain; American University; Georgetown University; George Washington University; Catholic University of America; Howard University; Johns Hopkins University; and Trinity College. Additional support for the conference was provided by the following departments and individuals at UMCP: Charles S. Rutherford, associate dean for the College of Arts and Humanities; the College Academic Planning Advisory Committee; the Committee on Africa and the Americas; the Department of Women's Studies; the Department of Comparative Literature; the Sociology

Department; the University Honors Program; College Park Scholars program; and the Department of American Studies. Within those and other units, I wish to thank John Caughey, Regina Harrison, Carla Peterson, Martha Geores, Claire Moses, Lois Vietri, Patricio Korzeniewicz, and Sandy Mack, for their support. I would also like to acknowledge the generous collegiality of Barbara Weinstein, Evelyn Canabal-Torres, Christina Guidorizzi, Roxana Patiño, and Soledad Bianchi, and the good-natured participation in the event from my undergraduate and graduate students in the Honors Program, the Latin American Studies program, and the Department of Spanish and Portuguese at UMCP.

I acknowledge herein the collaboration of Georgette Dorn and Barbara Tenenbaum of the Hispanic Division at the Library of Congress; Philip Brenner, from the American University Latin American Studies Program; Cynthia McClintock, of the George Washington University Latin American Studies Center; Arturo Valenzuela, from the Center for Latin American Studies at Georgetown University; Michael Foley from the Catholic University of America; Mary Hayes from Trinity College; and Amelia Mondragón from Howard University. Bill LeoGrande, at the American University School of Public Affairs, was a particularly generous intellectual collaborator. Many thanks also for the gracious hospitality of Spain's Ambassador Antonio Oyarzábal and his wife, Beatriz; cultural affairs officer Juan Romero de Terreros; and the staff at the Embassy of Spain.

Others who contributed to the conceptualization of the conference include Mark Sullivan, Nina Serafino, and Larry Minnear of the Congressional Research Service; Fernando Cepeda, former Colombian Ambassador to the Organization of American States (OAS); Lou Goodman, of the School of International Studies at American University; Eileen Findlay, of the history department at American University; Peter Kornbluh of the National Security Archives; Wayne Smith of the Center for International Policy; Carlos Portales, Chilean Ambassador to the OAS; Kelly McBride of the Unit for the Promotion of Democracy at the OAS; Cynthia Arnson and Joseph Tulchin of the Woodrow Wilson International Center for Scholars; Dana Priest at the *Washington Post*; Mark Schneider at the Agency for International Development; Margaret Keck, at Johns Hopkins University; and Eusebio Mujal-León, of Georgetown University. Thank you for logistical help to Judith Weir at the Institute for Policy Studies; Doug Reilly at the Center for International Policy; Hugh Byrne, Coletta Youngers, and Rachel Nield at the Washington Office on Latin America; and Joy Olson, of the Latin American Working Group.

At Greenwood Press, I would like to thank my editor, Jim Sabin; my copyeditor, Joanne Freeman; my production editors, Jennifer Debo and Kristen Eberhard; my product manager, David Wilfinger; my indexer, Tom Broughton-Willett; and Marcia Goldstein for their fine work and their patience. Sue Goodwin, Marta Tanenhaus, Joseph Eldridge, Jo Marie Griesgraber, Heather Foote, Leyda Barbieri, Reggie Norton, Dana Martin, Cynthia Buhl, Jim McGovern, Bill Goodfellow, Cheryl Morden, Kathy Gille, Doug Tanner, Chris Krueger, George Rogers, John Cavanagh, and an entire generation of new activists continue to inspire me to search for ways to engage in scholarship that is relevant to the public policy debates. I thank my parents, Jane M. and Edouard S.P. Bouvier, and my siblings and their families for their ongoing support and faith in me. And finally, I thank my husband, Jim Lyons, and our daughter, Maya, for the sustenance that has allowed me to bring this project to fruition.

Introduction: The Globalization of U.S.–Latin American Relations: Past, Present, and Future Directions

Virginia M. Bouvier

Anniversaries provide auspicious occasions for taking stock of the past, present, and future directions of relationships. This volume is part of a project that began as a conference to analyze U.S.–Latin American relations in the century following the War of 1898.[1] The primary goal of the conference was to bring together academics and policymakers to reflect upon the context and impact of U.S. military intervention in the Caribbean in 1898, the subsequent development of international and regional conflict resolution mechanisms, and the current and future status of U.S.–Latin American relations. This book includes edited papers presented by seven of the presenters at that conference.[2] It also includes new essays that address other dimensions of U.S.–Latin American relations, such as the role of the nongovernmental organization (NGO) sector in U.S. foreign policy-making, the human rights and military dimensions of U.S.–Latin American relations, and the changing role of Latin American intellectuals vis-à-vis the shifting borders of national and global identities.

In addition to being the 100th anniversary of the first U.S. overseas intervention in Latin America, 1998 marked multiple anniversaries in the relationship between the United States and Latin America. That year was the 150th anniversary of the signing of the Treaty of Guadalupe Hidalgo that ended the Mexican–American War (known in Mexico as the Mexican War or the War of the United States against Mexico), by which the boundary between the United States and Latin America shifted northward and the United States annexed some 525,000 square miles of Mexican territory (currently occupied by California, Texas, Arizona, New Mexico, Utah, Nevada, and the western part of Colorado). It signaled fifty years since the founding of the United Nations and the Organization of American States (OAS), as well as the signing of the United Nations Universal Declaration of Human Rights. It also marked the twenty-fifth anniversary of military coups in Uruguay and Chile, where dictatorships supported by the U. S. government came to power, interrupting the historic tradition of democratic rule in each of those countries. Taken together, these multiple anniversaries underscore the shifts in the terrain of inter-American relationships, and remind us that the seeds of globalization were sown and took root long ago.

Since the Spanish conquest of the New World in the late fifteenth century, the Americas have become increasingly integrated into a world system. When the United States rebelled against England in the eighteenth century and after Latin Americans won their independence from Spain, Portugal, and France in the following century, the ties between the former colonies and their mother countries were enhanced by new economic, political, and social relations with the rest of the world.[3] In 1826, the Latin American independence hero Simón Bolívar convened a congress in Panama that sought (unsuccessfully) to create a confederation of Latin American nations to protect the sovereignty and independence of each of its members. In 1889, leaders at the first International Conference of American States (precursor to today's Organization of American States) promoted efforts to establish free trade among countries of South America. Since that time, Latin American struggles for political and economic independence from foreign domination have been increasingly accompanied by moves toward greater economic and political integration at both the regional and international levels. In the second half of the twentieth century, a variety of pan-American, inter-American, and Latin American institutions and agreements were created which formalized such ties. The most prominent of these include the Inter-American Development Bank (originally called the Latin American Integration Bank, 1959), the Central American Common Market (CACM, 1960), the Latin American Free Trade Association (1960), the Alliance for Progress (1961), the Cartagena Agreement (1969), the Andean Community (CAN, 1969), the Andean Development Fund (CAF, 1969), the Caribbean Free Trade Area (CARIFTA, 1969—later transformed into the Caribbean Community, CARICOM, 1973), the Latin American Integration Association (ALADI, 1980), the Common Market of the South (MERCOSUR, 1991), the North American Free Trade Agreement (NAFTA, 1992), and the Association of Caribbean States (ACS, 1994). Between 1992 and 1997, nations of Asia and Latin America signed some twenty new trade agreements.[4] This trend toward regional integration continues to be seen in efforts in the first years of the twenty-first century to create a South American Free Trade Area (SAFTA) and a Free Trade Area of the Americas (FTAA).[5]

The current landscape within Latin America offers a political environment that is propitious for this trend toward hemispheric cooperation and unity.

Democracy and human rights have become the watchwords for the hemisphere. Government-sponsored human rights abuses are on the decline in most countries of the Western Hemisphere. While throughout the 1970s and 1980s, dictatorial rule and civil war were sustained, by the 1990s negotiated solutions were prevailing over guerrilla warfare and armed conflicts in Central America and elected civilians had replaced authoritarian governments throughout South America. In 2000, the monolithic Institutional Revolutionary Party (PRI), which had held power in Mexico for more than 70 years, stepped aside to let Vicente Fox, candidate for the conservative National Action Party (PAN), assume the presidency. In January 2000, Guatemalan President Alfonso Portillo took power with an electoral promise to solve the murder of Guatemalan human rights advocate Bishop Juan Gerardi, who was killed in 1998 shortly after releasing a report charging the military with responsibility for most of the 200,000 deaths that occurred during Guatemala's thirty-six-year-old civil war.[6] That same year, Peruvian President Alberto Fujimori stepped down following disputed elections fraught with contradictions, and an internal crisis that prompted national and international outcries as well as the intervention of the Organization of American States. Likewise, in 2000 citizens of the Dominican Republic elected a new president, consolidating the recent hemispheric trend away from strongmen such as former president Joaquín Balaguer, who had sidestepped the Congress to rule his country for seven non-consecutive terms.[7]

As dictatorships have yielded to elected governments, many U.S. policymakers have challenged the Cold War mindset that insisted on viewing Latin American nations as Soviet pawns and dictatorial regimes as offering the best protection for U.S. interests.[8] By the early 1990s, political analysts Jonathan Hartlyn, Lars Schoultz, and Augusto Varas had documented an "emerging bipartisan consensus that the promotion of democracy and the protection of human rights should be goals of U.S. policy in Latin America."[9] The extent and tenure of this consensus grew stronger and became clear in the early months of 2001, when conservatives called upon President George W. Bush to make human rights, democracy, and religious freedom priorities for U.S. foreign policy.[10] Clearly, the discourse of human rights and democracy has become the political tender of current U.S. foreign policy debates.

However, bipartisan consensus has yet to be reached on exactly what these terms mean, how they should be achieved, and on the role of the United States in fostering respect for human rights and democratic practices. Debates over U.S. military aid to Colombia are imbued with a strange Wonderlandesque quality that posits a dichotomy between opponents of military aid who favor peace and human rights on the one hand, and sectors that favor military aid to help Colombia fight against drugs and defend democracy on the other. Likewise, U.S. policy toward Cuba seems trapped between two sectors that couch their positions on the trade embargo in terms of the desire to promote democratization in that country. Within these and other policy debates related to Latin America, the nature of and rationale for U.S. interventions have yet to be adequately explored, and the relationship between democratic practices at home and interventions abroad has yet to be reconciled. In the latter regard, President George W. Bush's choice of Otto J. Reich for assistant secretary of state for the Western Hemisphere, the top post on Latin American policy, embodies a century-old contradiction between U.S. actions at home and overseas. As head of a covert program to assist the Contra rebel forces in Nicaragua under President Ronald Reagan, government investigators found Reich to have engaged in illegal activities, including unlawful manipulation of the mass media to gain support for his cause.[11] His support for antidemocratic forces in Nicaragua, as well as his violation of democratic practices at home—all in the name of democracy—is symbolic of current appropriations of the word that are semantically bankrupt. It is time for a reexamination of the meanings of such basic concepts as democracy, human rights, and intervention.

Such issues and debates must occur within a new inter-American and global context. U.S.–Latin American relations have become more complex as the definition of U.S. security interests has broadened to include a wide range of political and economic concerns related directly or indirectly to human rights—debt, trade, democracy, civil–military relations, drug trafficking, environment, sustainable development, and migration.[12]

U.S.–Latin American relations are now marked by the proliferation of multiple linkages across national borders, as well as increased cooperation between nations throughout the hemisphere. Within this context of greater political convergence and democratization, and spurred by the carrot of free-trade arrangements, a series of summit meetings have provided important forums for the development of stronger relationships among Latin American political elites. In 1994, U.S. President Bill Clinton hosted the Miami Summit of the Americas, which committed all of the region's countries (minus Cuba) to negotiating a free-trade agreement for the Americas by 2005. In a follow-up summit in 1998, Latin American presidents and prime ministers gathered in Santiago to launch the Free Trade Area of the Americas (FTAA) to expand neo-liberalism throughout the hemisphere.[13] In 1999, Miami hosted a Mayors' Summit of the Americas with the participation of some 200 mayors from the hemisphere. The 2000 summit meeting of the twelve democratically elected presidents of South America, called by Brazilian President Fernando Henrique Cardoso, underscored the convergence of interest among these leaders in working together. An Interparliamentary Forum of the Americas was inaugurated in early 2001 in Ottawa, and a third summit of Latin American leaders took place in April 2001 in Quebec City.

Such gatherings may foster the consensus needed at the elite level to enable Latin American leaders both individually and collectively to exert stronger leadership in the Western Hemisphere. Stronger ties among Latin

America's political elites should enable this generation of leaders to meet the United States as more of an equal partner than was possible under earlier authoritarian regimes, and should make it more difficult for the United States to exert unilateral political, military, and economic hegemony over individual Latin American nations.[14]

The shifting dynamics in U.S.–Latin American economic relations in general, as well as new economic and political alliances within Latin America, have allowed Latin Americans more political space than they have had in some years. U.S. exports to the region in the 1990s grew more quickly than to any other region of the world, making Latin America currently the third largest market for U.S. investments and exports. From 1993 to 1996, U.S. exports to the South American Common Market countries (Mercosur) increased by 72 percent. In 1998, Mexico became America's second-largest trading partner after Canada, and total North American trade grew to $475 billion in 1997—a 76 percent increase from the volume traded in 1993.[15]

Such shifts may allow greater Latin American independence vis-à-vis the United States than in the past. Puerto Rico's new governor Sila M. Calderón is taking a hard line against ongoing U.S. Navy bombing exercises on Vieques Island. In the aftermath of the accidental killing by two off-target bombs of civilian guard David Sanes in 1999, Puerto Ricans began a campaign to reject the decades-long agreement that permitted U.S. military exercises on that island.[16] Venezuela, Brazil, Mexico, and Ecuador have expressed concern about the U.S. decision to give the Colombian military $1.3 billion for their counterinsurgency cum counter-narcotics efforts in Colombia. These countries are militarizing their borders, in part with the help of the United States, to counter the actual and potential spillover of Colombia's civil war.[17] Because Venezuela is now the United States' fourth-largest supplier (after Canada, Iraq, and Mexico) of oil and has the largest oil reserves outside of the Middle East, Venezuelan President Hugo Chávez, who came to power in February 2000, has thus far been able to chart a course that is at odds with some U.S. policies. He not only publicly criticized U.S. military aid to Colombia, but he has also provided oil to Cuba despite the U.S. embargo of that country, has rejected U.S. flood aid, and has broken the international isolation of Iraq by a state visit to that country in August 2000.[18] Whether Chávez's actions and rhetoric will be interpreted as a threat to U.S. interests under the Bush presidency in the 2000s and will incur the kinds of hostility suffered by other independent nationalist leaders of earlier decades remains to be seen.

Despite a general trend toward democratization, there is evidence of what Samuel Fitch has called "a slippage in the legitimacy of democracy" within Latin America itself.[19] The vast majority of Latin American populations have not benefited from democracy or from neo-liberal models that have failed to address adequately fundamental problems of extreme poverty, unemployment and underemployment, tremendous income disparities and maldistribution of wealth, and restricted access to land and resources.[20] In 1992, many Peruvians applauded when President Alberto Fujimori closed down the Congress there. U.S. intervention in Haiti in 1994 to return Jean-Bertrand Aristide to power following his overthrow by a military regime has hardly secured a democratic future for that country. In 1996, Paraguay narrowly averted a military coup, and its proponents are widely believed to have been responsible for the subsequent assassination in 1999 of Paraguay's Vice President Luis María Argaña. In 1997, Bolivia, one of Latin America's poorest countries, elected former dictator General Hugo Banzer to the presidency. In Venezuela, former Army lieutenant General Hugo Chávez, who participated in a failed coup attempt in 1992, assumed the presidency in 1998, and met little opposition when he appointed dozens of senior officers to important civilian posts and transferred congressional authority to a new Constitutional Assembly dominated by Chávez supporters. On 21 January 2000, a junta representing disgruntled colonels and indigenous leaders seized power in a bloodless coup against the unpopular Ecuadorian president Jamil Mahuad before turning power back to Vice-President Gustavo Novoa.[21] Ecuador has had five governments in the last five years, and highly organized indigenous sectors (about one-third of Ecuador's 12.5 million residents are of indigenous descent) are calling for the dissolution of the Congress to protest the increases in fuel and public transportation costs decreed as part of the dollarization of the Ecuadorian economy.[22] At the beginning of 2001, Argentina stands on the brink of economic collapse with volatile social pressures accruing in opposition to the requisite demands of international financial institutions.

Poverty and corruption may in fact pose the greatest threats to democratic trends in Latin America. A recent study by the World Bank found that, "Poor people's experiences with government institutions are largely negative, even when government programs were rated as important. Corruption, rudeness and poor quality services seemed to be the norm, whether in health care or in programs of social support."[23]

According to the United Nations' Economic Commission for Latin America and the Caribbean (ECLAC), poverty in Latin America and the Caribbean grew from 35 percent of the population in 1980, to 40 percent in 1990, to nearly 50 percent in 2000.[24] Two out of every five Latin Americans live on under two dollars a day, and some 75 million more Latin Americans are poorer today than in 1980.[25] Such poverty means that millions of people are unable to satisfy basic human needs of food, clothing, shelter, water, sanitation, and access to education and health. Those living in poverty are more vulnerable to ill health, malnutrition, economic dislocation, natural disasters, violence, and crime. They often lack a political voice or legal protection, and suffer more frequent attacks on their freedoms than other sectors of the population.

Latin America continues to be plagued by some of the greatest disparities of wealth in the world. Brazil ranks among the most skewed. There, 1 percent of the landowners control 44 percent of the land, the top 20 percent of the population receive 63.8 percent of the national income and the poorest 20 percent receive only 2.5 percent of the income.[26] The maldistribution of income in Guatemala and Paraguay is similarly severe. In Guatemala, the lowest one-fifth of the population earns only 2.1 percent of the national income while the richest fifth of the population earns 63 percent of the national income. In Paraguay, the poorest 20 percent of the population earns only 2.3 percent of the national income, while the wealthiest 20 percent receives 62.4 percent of the national income.[27] Furthermore, in countries such as Argentina, Chile, and Paraguay, income distribution worsened and unemployment rose during the 1990s.[28]

In addition to social problems related to poverty and the maldistribution of income, the trend toward democratic governance is threatened by military impunity and weak institutional guarantees. Societies that experienced years of dictatorial rule and human rights abuses in the past are torn between what Priscilla Hayner has called the "need to remember and the need to forget," and are seeking to find the delicate balance between holding the military accountable for past abuses and ensuring that they are not provoked into retaliation.[29] In such circumstances, a range of national and international mechanisms—including among other things trials, amnesties, peace accords, compensation, and truth commissions—have been set up to deal with abuses of the past. Numerous governments, both civilian and military, have decreed general amnesties. Truth commissions—called to provide a forum for denouncing, documenting, and ultimately preventing the recurrence of such abuses—appear to have been the most favored recourse in Latin America.[30] In 1982, Bolivian President Hernán Siles Suazo established the National Commission of Inquiry into Disappearances, which documented 155 cases of disappearances during the 1967–1982 period, including the period ruled by Bolivia's current president, General Hugo Banzer. In 1983, Argentina established a National Commission on the Disappeared, which produced the report *Nunca Más: Informe de la Comisión Nacional sobre la Desaparición de Personas,* that documents some 9,000 disappearances during the period of military government from 1976 to 1984. In 1990, Chile's newly elected President Patricio Aylwin established a National Commission for Truth and Reconciliation to investigate human rights abuses under the previous military government of General Augusto Pinochet from 1973 to 1990. In 1992, the United Nations mandated an international truth commission for El Salvador to report on the abuses enacted during twelve years of civil war in that country since 1980.[31] Peace agreements between the Guatemalan government and the National Guatemalan Revolutionary Unit (URNG) provided for the creation of the Historical Clarification Commission (CEH) in 1994 that published *Guatemala: Memory of Silence,* a report on human rights abuses during Guatemala's thirty-six-year-old armed conflict. In 1994, Haitian President Jean-Bertrand Aristide ordered the establishment of a National Truth and Justice Commission to probe human rights violations committed in the wake of the 1991 coup that pushed him out of office. In 2001, following the discovery of the remains of human skeletons at a former military base in Panama, Panamanian President Mireya Moscoso called for a truth commission to probe abuses under the military governments of Generals Omar Torrijos and Manuel Noriega between 1968 and 1989. In 2001, Peru is setting up a truth commission to investigate 3,190 cases of individuals who "disappeared" after their detentions by the military or police in the years from 1982 to 1996. Mexico is also discussing the establishment of such a commission. Citizens' groups, parliamentary and presidential bodies, religious groups, and labor unions have set up similar investigations, commissions, and even trials in Brazil, Honduras, Paraguay, and Uruguay. Some sectors are suggesting the need to form such a commission in the United States to analyze the U.S. role in supporting former governments that have engaged in gross violations of human rights.

Such efforts are being shaped in part by new configurations of local, national, and international actors. Whereas past national amnesty laws have excused violators of human rights and domestic remedies for injustice have been found inadequate, redress is increasingly being sought abroad, and the calls to end impunity are finding echoes across national borders. In this regard, national moves to ratify a statute (approved in July 1998) to create a permanent International Criminal Court with jurisdiction over crimes against humanity, genocide, and war crimes when domestic remedies have been exhausted are significant.[32]

In some instances, these international efforts are now creating new political space within the Latin American countries themselves. In October 1998, Spanish judge Baltasar Garzón issued a warrant for the arrest and extradition of Chilean General Augusto Pinochet from England to stand trial in Spain for human rights violations. Likewise, Belgium, France, and Switzerland filed extradition requests against the former dictator. Britain's highest court, the House of Lords, ruled that Pinochet did not have immunity from the charges against him, but after sixteen months under house arrest in London, British Home Secretary Jack Straw ordered Pinochet's release to Chile on medical grounds. New political space has opened within Chile as a result of the international indictments. Chilean Judge Juan Guzmán secured a decision from the Santiago appeals court, ratified by the Chilean Supreme Court in August 2000, to remove Pinochet's immunity as senator for life so that he might stand trial. In January 2001, Judge Guzmán ruled that Pinochet's dementia was "exceptionally normal" and would not impede a trial from taking place in a Santiago appeals court.[33] Within three months, Pinochet was placed under house arrest and the Santiago Court of Appeals agreed that Pinochet should stand trial as an accessory to the deaths and disappearances of some seventy-five political prisoners in the "Caravan of Death" following the coup that brought him to power in 1973.[34]

The Spanish judge Baltasar Garzón is also investigating close to ninety-eight Argentine military men, including heads of state, for genocide, torture, and terrorism.[35] Of these, he requested the extradition from Mexico of the Argentine former Lieutenant Commander Ricardo Miguel Cavallo, a request which Mexico's foreign ministry granted on 2 February 2001, pending appeals. This is a landmark decision for a number of reasons. It marks the first time that a country has agreed to extradite an indicted person for prosecution in a third country where the crimes were not committed based on international treaties against genocide and terrorism. Likewise, the decision strengthens the principle of universal jurisdiction for human rights violations. As Oscar González, the head of the Mexican Academy of Human Rights, noted, the decision "constitutes the exercise of a state's internal jurisdiction to uphold the universal character of human rights."[36] Furthermore, the finding also affirms a precedent for overruling national laws or amnesties in the case of offenses such as crimes against humanity, where no statute of limitations applies and, in effect, exposes suspected rights violators to extradition outside of their home countries.

In what is now being widely recognized as the "Garzón effect," judges and politicians throughout the world are being emboldened by the courage and independence of the Spanish judge's efforts. The shape of what is possible has shifted dramatically, and this has provided a new context within which domestic debates about the past are being reformulated and reconfigured. In July 2000, the President of the Human Rights Committee of Brazil's National Assembly called for the prosecution of former Paraguayan dictator Alfredo Stroessner, who is currently living in Brazil.[37] The Italian government has conducted trials and, on 6 December 2000, sentenced members of the Argentine Armed Forces to life imprisonment for the murder of Italian citizens in Argentina during the military dictatorship there.[38] In March 2001 in Argentina, a federal judge declared unconstitutional Argentina's amnesty laws of 1986 and 1987 (the so-called "due obedience" and "full stop" laws) that pardoned hundreds of such army officers accused of human rights violations during that country's "dirty war" against leftists during the military dictatorship that lasted from 1976 until 1983.[39] The March ruling could lead to the resumption of hundreds of lawsuits blocked by the earlier amnesty laws.

The international environment in general has become less hospitable for dictators. Panama, an earlier haven for dictators from Iran, Haiti, and Guatemala, refused to provide political asylum to Vladimiro Montesinos, Peru's intelligence chief under ex-President Alberto Fujimori, who fled Peru in September 2000 following revelations of his involvement in a high-profile bribery scandal.[40] Switzerland, long a protected oasis for corrupt dollars of dubious provenance—including those of the former Philippine president

Ferdinand Marcos and the late Nigerian dictator Sani Abacha—took the unusual step of freezing $50 million in bank accounts linked to Montesinos.[41] Likewise, encouraged by the private German anti-corruption organization Transparency International and the anti-corruption working group of the Paris-based Organization for Economic Co-operation and Development, twelve major international banks signed onto the Wolfsberg Anti-Money Laundering Principles in November 2000 in an effort to halt the laundering of illicit funds through financial institutions. The principles demand "heightened scrutiny" for "individuals who have or have had positions of public trust, such as government officials, senior executives of government corporations or politicians and their families or close associates."[42]

Such moves on the part of judges and institutions involved in these and other cases have found a resonance within an international human rights community that has grown exponentially in the recent past. In the twentieth and twenty-first centuries, a growing number of non-state actors have become increasingly engaged in the policy-making process.[43] Transnational alliances have historic precedents in the earlier struggles of groups and individuals to create inter-American alliances and to effect U.S. policies toward Latin America. When Francisco de Miranda sought to liberate South America from Spanish colonial rule, he recruited some 200 North American citizens from New York for his revolutionary project, some of whom died on their unsuccessful expedition in 1806 off the coast of Venezuela.[44] The U.S. war against Mexico in the mid-nineteenth century aroused considerable opposition in Congress, as did subsequent U.S. efforts to annex the Caribbean islands of Cuba and Hispaniola.[45] At the end of the nineteenth century, José Martí and the Cuban cause for independence found a groundswell of support among a North American public anxious to fight for human rights and justice.[46] The Anti-Imperialist League, which was formed in 1898 and by the following year counted some 50,000 members (including Samuel Clemens—a.k.a. Mark Twain—ex-President Grover Cleveland, William Jennings Bryant, and Jane Addams), was one of the first and largest NGOs to challenge U.S. foreign policies abroad.[47] The Mexican Revolution of 1910 and the Spanish Civil War (1936–39) generated tremendous public support throughout the hemisphere for revolutionary and republican forces in those two countries.[48] U.S. military and economic interventions in Central America and the Caribbean throughout the twentieth century were often met with resistance from concerned individuals and organizations, of which the Women's International League for Peace and Freedom is just one example.

In the wake of current trends toward greater ties worldwide, new nongovernmental organizations, configurations, and global relationships have become an essential component in any analysis of hemispheric relations. The establishment of new human rights bodies, conflict resolution mechanisms, and both governmental and non-state relationships are forming the basis of a new international human rights regime that may help to diminish, although not preclude, the likelihood of unilateral military intervention of the sort experienced a century ago. These new alliances are quantitatively and qualitatively different from those of the past. Fostered in part by the revolution in information and communications technologies and building upon relationships established in earlier years, horizontal and vertical relationships between NGOs across national borders today are capable of creating a more immediate, sustained, and extensive globalized solidarity than has heretofore been possible. The sheer numbers of NGOs are a quantitative departure from the past. In 1995, the semi-autonomous Inter-American Foundation, funded by the U.S. Congress, produced a guide to some 20,000 NGOs in Latin America—a sign of the tremendous vibrancy of civil society at the close of the twentieth century.[49]

If intervention was the watchword of NGOs in the early 20th century, human rights and democracy form the foundational basis for many of the new alliances of recent years. The cycle of dictatorships from the 1960s through the 1980s inadvertently spawned the growth of a trans-hemispheric NGO sector—including human rights groups like Amnesty International, the Washington Office on Latin America, the Lawyers' Committee for Human Rights, the International Human Rights Law Group, Americas Watch, and hundreds of country-specific organizations throughout the hemisphere—which has been increasingly active in documenting human rights abuses, monitoring foreign policies, educating the public, and advocating for alternative approaches.[50] The existence of such institutions and the proliferation of NGOs have undoubtedly been instrumental in fostering an environment in which human rights concerns are central, or at least given lip service, in the debates over U.S. foreign policy.

Since 1975, when Rep. Donald Fraser (D–Minn.) convened the first hearings on human rights and U.S. foreign policy in the U.S. Congress, U.S. policymakers have increasingly sought to link U.S. foreign aid to human rights conditions in the South. The human rights reports issued annually by the U.S. State Department since they were first mandated by Congress in 1976 have grown steadily in length and scope.[51] By 2001 they covered not only political and civil rights, labor rights, and the integrity of the person, but also the rights of women, children, refugees, and the disabled, and addressed repression and discrimination against indigenous populations as well as that against national, racial, ethnic, and religious minorities.

In the current era, globalization itself is becoming both a catalyst to and a theme unifying significant sectors across national borders.[52] Subcomandante Marcos of the Zapatista Army for National Liberation (EZLN) has used modern technologies to keep international public opinion informed of the conditions, rebellion, and government response or lack thereof to the indigenous uprising launched on 1 January 1994 in the Chiapas region of Mexico. The EZLN hosts an official website that boasts more than one million hits. Ironically, a digital divide that deepens the gap between the wealthy and the poor and creates a virtual reality where many are left behind is also bringing the Americas closer together. Technology has enabled many NGOs to forge new links with each other and with governmental bodies to challenge the direction and consequences of globalization.[53]

In the late 1990s and early 2000s, major economic and political conferences were frequently marked by alternative nongovernmental conferences or by extensive prior consultations with NGO counterparts. The People's Summit of the Americas held in Santiago in 1998 attracted some 1,000 participants from nearly every nation of the Western Hemisphere to formulate alternative approaches to the neo-liberal economic model encouraged by the NAFTA and similar free-trade alliances. The NGO presence was particularly noteworthy at the World Trade Organization ministerial conference in late 1999 in Seattle, Washington, and at the World Economic Forum in Mexico in February 2001, where an alternative forum highlighted the need for a globalization of justice, a global distribution of wealth, and for addressing the ways in which globalization favors the few and excludes the majority. NGOs have also voiced their concerns about the power of the global market to control national decisions without adequate regulation or disclosure and the lack of democratization and transparency in the process by which local, regional, and national forces are succumbing to the pressures of the free market.

The experiences of the past may enable us to navigate the intensified neo-globalization that has become increasingly dominant since the end of the Cold War. This volume examines the multiple impacts, legacies, and nature of the globalization of U.S.–Latin American relations, particularly as it concerns human rights, democracy, and intervention. This book takes as its point of departure relations established during the birth of the American republics, especially in the wake of the War of 1898, when U.S. intervention in Cuba's war for independence from Spain—what historians in the United States call the Spanish–American War—indelibly marked the future of inter-American relationships and initiated a deeper engagement between the northern and southern hemispheres.

U.S. intervention in the War of 1898, marking as it did the first U.S. military intervention overseas, effectively put in place the paradigm for U.S.–Latin American relations during the next century. For better or for worse, the worlds of Latin America and the United States—impinging on one another through a range of military, diplomatic, economic, social, and cultural interventions—are closer today as a result of that experience of empire one hundred years ago.

The chapters in this book analyze various aspects of the relations between these worlds during the past century. They are organized thematically in roughly chronological order, and they address the different U.S. experiences and experiments in hemispheric intervention and the diverse responses to such intervention. The authors of this book analyze the changes and continuities of U.S.–Latin American relations over the past century through a broad cross section of disciplinary and interdisciplinary perspectives. Literary scholars, historians, political scientists and policy analysts, economists, and philosophers herein chart the legacies of the past, the complexities of the present, and the challenges for and visions of the future of inter-American relations. Policymakers should pay heed to such multidisciplinary perspectives and academic reflections. The impact of globalization in the economic, political, military, social, philosophical, environmental, and cultural realms is too complex to be understood with the tools, questions, or frameworks provided by a single discipline. As Roland Barthes has noted, "Interdisciplinary work . . . is not about confronting already constituted disciplines (none of which, in fact, is willing to let itself go.) To do something interdisciplinary, it's not enough to choose a 'subject' (a theme) and gather around it two or three sciences. Interdisciplinarity consists in creating a new object that belongs to no one."[54] The disintegration and merging of borders between regions and nations not only finds an echo in the obfuscation of borders between disciplines, but demands the very process of innovative realignments in order to create new understanding and knowledge.

Part I of this volume deals with questions of democracy and intervention raised within the context of U.S.–Latin American relations since the birth of the American republics throughout the hemisphere. In the first chapter, Lars Schoultz analyzes today's shifting meanings of democracy and the changing patterns of U.S. intervention in Latin America in light of earlier practices. He notes that U.S. military intervention in Latin America over the past century constitutes an extreme form of intervention and that current U.S. efforts to promote democracy abroad seek to restructure Latin American societies in a far more ubiquitous way. Drawing on primary sources from the U.S. independence era until the present, Schoultz analyzes past patterns of U.S. intervention in Latin America, particularly in Nicaragua in the first two decades of the twentieth century. He documents the attitudes and mindset of multiple generations of U.S. policymakers, who historically have considered Latin Americans to be inferior to their U.S. counterparts, and cautions that policies based on such negative images and attitudes are more likely to impede than to promote the development of democracy in Latin America. Schoultz notes nonetheless that the emergence of new nongovernmental organizations that transcend the earlier boundaries between national and international politics has created a new inter-American space within which U.S. governmental agencies are no longer the sole, dominant actor.

In the second chapter, Julio Ramos discusses the changes and continuities in Latin American identities as he moves us with fluidity across the borders of time and space to probe the meanings of globalization for Latin American culture and democracy. The construction of the Panama Canal at the beginning of the twentieth century initiated an era of U.S. hegemony in Latin

America. Following U.S. intervention in Cuba's war for independence, the United States sought a way to link the East and West coasts via a waterway that would connect the Atlantic Ocean with the Pacific Ocean, a modern version of the fabled Straits of Anián. Colombian resistance to such a trans-isthmian canal led U.S. officials to intervene in the region, where they backed the creation of a separate, independent, and more amenable state in Panama, which declared its independence from Colombia in 1903. Ramos presents us with the powerful metaphor of the Panama Canal—that trans-national zone, that "profound cut in the earth" which simultaneously sep-arated and united North and South, and East and West, that "marvelous emblem of the new articulations between the North and South." Ramos discusses how the shifting forces that led to U.S. interventions a century ago in Cuba, Puerto Rico, the Philippines, and later Panama, gradually re-configured the geopolitical boundaries between the North and South and produced the beginnings of a transnational reordering with resounding cul-tural and political effects that can still be felt in the multiple border crossings that characterize current hemispheric relations. The transfer of the canal back to Panama at the close of the twentieth century, Ramos suggests, sym-bolizes the beginning of a new era in the relationships between the North and South, in which the residue of the past, symbolized by the abandoned buildings and military equipment, must be reconstructed and imbued with new usages and meanings.

Ramos's essay reflects the struggles of generations of Latin American in-tellectuals to come to terms with questions of "internal" democracy and the need for inclusion and participation. He argues that the earlier validations of a Latin American vernacular appear to be inadequate in the face of glob-alizing forces. Within this new context, the historic role of public intellec-tuals in Latin America as voices for the voiceless and as translators of both local and global realities is challenged. Earlier dichotomies between me-tropolis and periphery, global and local, and what is authentic or not are now inadequate tools for protecting and affirming cultural identities. Ramos documents the erosion of previous models of cultural integration that le-gitimated the production of knowledge in terms of the construction of cit-izenship and national identity. He examines the marginalization of public intellectuals and humanists from an increasingly global, consumer-oriented society where even intellectual production is subject to the demands of the marketplace, and he raises provocative questions about the future role of the humanities, intellectuals, and Latin American studies in the new millen-nium. Such questions are critical to current debates about globalization, representation, and democracy.

The third chapter by Carrie A. Foster examines an often-overlooked as-pect of U.S. foreign policy-making in the first part of the twentieth century and an important aspect of U.S. democratic practices at home, namely, the role of nongovernmental organizations. The War of 1898 sparked controversial debates in the U.S. Congress over the nature of U.S. democratic practices and the role of the United States overseas, and inadvertently fostered the emergence of a series of nongovernmental organizations dedicated to peace activism, nonintervention, and anti-imperialism. In the decades following the war, many of the activists who cut their teeth on the debates over U.S. intervention in Cuba and the Philippines, including leaders and members of the Anti-Imperialist League, continued to lay claim to democratic traditions that demanded respect for the sovereignty of other nations. On this point, historian Jim Zwick has documented elsewhere the continuities between officers of the League and U.S.-based groups formed in the first three decades of the twentieth century, including the Haiti–Santo Domingo Independence Committee (1921), the American Fund for Public Service Committee on American Imperialism (1924), the All-America Anti-Imperialist League of the Workers (Communist) Party (1925), and the Fair Play for Puerto Rico Committee created by the American Civil Liberties Union in the late 1930s. Zwick mentions as well the role of female Anti-Imperialist League officers, such as League vice-president Jane Addams, in establishing the Women's International League for Peace and Freedom.[55]

The NGOs formed in the wake of the War of 1898 and their successors laid the foundations for the critical role that NGOs play in today's foreign policy-making environment. As U.S. financial and political control over Latin American countries increased in the early decades of the twentieth century, these advocates moved beyond a mere antiwar stance to examine, challenge, and change the nature of U.S.–Latin American relations. In her chapter, Carrie A. Foster analyzes this important aspect of the globalization of U.S. policy-making as she studies the U.S. peace movement in the period between the two world wars. She documents the roots and trajectory of the U.S. section of the Women's International League for Peace and Freedom (WILPF), a nongovernmental women's organization formed in the first third of the twentieth century with a peak membership in 1936 of some 16,000 members. Foster provides a significant case study of an early NGO that sustained a gendered intervention in favor of more democratic U.S. foreign policies, particularly in Latin America. Foster's chapter, excerpted from her book on the history of the WILPF, is an important contribution to the recuperation of the history of nongovernmental organizations, progressive movements, and women in effecting U.S. policies, and it addresses directly the dynamics between democracy at home and intervention abroad.[56]

In Part II of this volume, we turn to the context leading up to shifts in U.S.–Latin American relations in the years following World War II. During this period, NGOs in the inter-American sphere became more global, as new standards, norms, and organizations were established to focus on questions of human rights, intervention, and conflict resolution. In his chapter, Michael Shifter takes us back in time to explore the complex and often contradictory dimensions of the inter-American system's relationship to the promotion of democracy. His chapter analyzes the origins of the inter-American system and provides a case study of the Organization of American States and its changing roles in the shifting international context within which it has operated since the inter-American system emerged in the late nineteenth century. Shifter critiques both the limitations and successes of that body, noting in particular the difficulties of securing international cooperation in a hemisphere characterized by a tremendous asymmetry of power and the tensions inherent in enforcing concepts of international human rights law while still respecting the principle of national sovereignty.

The roots of the OAS run deep into the late nineteenth century, when its predecessor, the Pan American Union, was formed as a vehicle for U.S. hegemony and Pan-Americanism in the hemisphere; the United Nations (UN), in contrast, emerged in the post-World War II period, when concerns about sovereignty were given a back seat to human rights. In the next chapter, Margaret E. Crahan documents the move toward codifying a covenant of international rights, which gained support in the wake of the Holocaust and World War II and culminated in the creation of the League of Nations, the UN, the OAS, the OAU (Organization of African Unity), and the approval of the UN Universal Declaration of Human Rights. Crahan discusses the progressive internationalization of human rights principles and organizations, particularly since the 1940s, the increasing consensus on core universal human rights and standards, and the proliferation of human rights NGOs in both the North and South. Crahan also addresses the formulation of the current criteria that define when military intervention is or is not appropriate, and shows how such standards have set the stage for the resolution of long-standing domestic and regional conflicts.[57] Her chapter underscores the movement toward global consensus on a number of basic human rights issues, as well as the national and regional tensions still present within this general global consensus. Such tensions concern questions of cultural relativism, differing priorities given to clusters of socioeconomic or civil–political rights, collective rights of self-determination and development, questions of sovereignty, and the demands of nonintervention versus human rights guarantees. Where Shifter analyzes the interventionist tendencies and democratic rhetoric of the OAS, Crahan stresses the prevalence of the principle of nonintervention among international bodies other than the OAS. Each of these chapters raises questions about the motivations, ethical implications, and efficacy of state-sponsored interventions, as well as the emergence of new kinds of global interventions that challenge scholars to rethink traditional definitions of intervention and democracy and develop new paradigms for global engagement.

Part III of this book analyzes the evolution of relationships between the U.S. and Latin American militaries—sectors that have been key to understanding U.S.–Latin American relations, particularly since the beginnings of the Cold War. The chapters in this section underscore the polemics regarding the involvement of the United States in training Latin American militaries. First, Molly Todd provides a brief history of the School of the Americas (SOA) and the SOA Watch—the oppositional movement to which it gave rise. Todd analyzes the transnational nature of the inter-American military relations fostered by the SOA, which have constituted an "historical and present-day instrument of U.S. foreign policy in Latin America." Likewise, she analyzes the emergence and growth of the SOA Watch and its efforts to close the SOA. In her chapter, Todd hones in on the global dimensions of U.S. foreign policy and its links to domestic democratic practices.

In the next chapter, Douglas Farah writes about current U.S. military engagement in Latin America based on interviews he conducted as an investigative reporter for the *Washington Post*. Farah raises provocative questions about the changing nature of military intervention in Latin America, the continued involvement of the U.S. military in training its Latin American counterparts in the new post-Cold War era, and the difficulties in reporting on and achieving accountability for U.S. funding of Latin American militaries. Farah calls for an examination of the role of U.S. military training and assistance and its relationship to the promotion of democracy in Latin America—a region where the military have traditionally exerted great power and often undermined democratic institutions. Farah argues implicitly that the making and execution of U.S. foreign policies must be consistent with democratic practices of disclosure and accountability. His findings that Latin American militaries continue to be funded through legal loopholes and surreptitious channels present a challenge to U.S. policymakers to tighten the human rights language instituted earlier in the 1970s to distance the United States from militaries which were linked to violations of internationally recognized standards of human rights.

The authors in Part IV look beyond earlier U.S.–Latin American paradigms to situate Latin America within a greater world context. Bilateral relationships between the United States and individual Latin American countries are infinitely more complex within today's globalized economy than they were 100 years ago, making it incumbent upon us to analyze and imagine new alternative configurations and paradigms that might provide the missing ingredients for a new recipe for international relationships. In his chapter, Edgar J. Dosman analyzes Canada's historic approach to multilateralism and its recent decision to engage in the inter-American system in a more sustained way. Dosman traces the evolution of Canada's foreign policies from policies based on national security interests toward policies less centered on the state and congenial to more cooperative approaches. Like the other contributors, Dosman notes the increasing number of new actors in the foreign policy-making arena, as well as the limits, opportunities, and dangers of current approaches to relations with Latin America.

In the following chapter, Sarah Anderson and John Cavanagh situate Latin America within the context of the global financial crisis of the late 1990s. The authors discuss the linkages between the growth of global capital and the rise of local inequalities. They find that the new global financial architecture ignores or undermines workers' interests, and that questions of national and hemispheric identity must be addressed in light of both the beneficial and detrimental dynamics of economic globalization. Their case studies of Brazil, Argentina, and Ecuador show that the greatest threats to peace in Latin America at the beginning of the twenty-first century are not security-related, but economic—namely, the volatility of global markets, and the continued gap between the rich and the poor. In response to such conditions, they document the consolidation of an active NGO sector in both the North and South and the evolution of a consensus on a North–South citizens' agenda for dealing with the global crisis.

In Part V, the final section of this book, a philosopher and a literary critic assume the difficult task of assessing the current state of inter-American relations with an eye toward the future. First, David A. Crocker's essay provides a framework for dealing with past violations of international and national codes of behavior. He provides profound insights into the relationship between democratic governance and human rights, and discusses the range of options open to newly democratic societies wishing to identify and clarify the ethical issues involved in dealing with past wrongs. Crocker provides a wealth of examples from around the globe and reinforces Crahan's argument that an international human rights regime has indeed taken hold. His chapter addresses the particular concerns of societies in a period of transition from dictatorial rule and repression to governments of newly elected civilians.[58]

Finally, Ana Patricia Rodríguez brings the volume full circle as she underscores the critical role of literature and the humanities in the debates over globalization. Schoultz begins this volume with the suggestion that Latin Americans must be allowed to engage in the hard work of creating democratic institutions to serve their needs; Rodríguez affirms that this work is well underway. Rodríguez argues that literature is playing an important role in the reconstruction of a region laid waste by war and ecological devastation. Her essay provides perspectives from a generation of Central American intellectuals whose voices demand inclusion in today's debates over globalization. Rodríguez underscores the ways in which the voices of Latin American literary critics and writers (who in the United States often are seen as outside the purview of U.S. policy formulation) have created their own intellectual space and are asserting cultural identities that are at once separate from and dramatically linked to policy decisions being made throughout the hemisphere. As the Uruguayan writer Eduardo Galeano has observed, "In Latin America a literature is taking shape and acquiring strength, a literature . . . that does not propose to bury our dead, but to immortalize them; that refuses to stir the ashes but rather attempts to light the fire . . . perhaps it may help to preserve for the generations to come . . . 'the true name of all things.'"[59]

Central American writers are defining "the true name of all things" as they invent new regional imaginaries that rupture national categories, propose new articulations of the North and South, disrupt official peacetime narratives, and interrogate the effects of neo-liberal policies in the region. As Rodríguez shows eloquently, Central American novels are registering the social contradictions of peace and official narratives of progress and development. Her chapter gives faces and personalities to those experiencing the economic effects of globalization and capital expansion described by Cavanagh and Anderson. Novels, she argues, provide "a defense against further cultural memory loss and [act] as a front against cultural homogenization induced by the expansion of global (cultural and economic) capital in the region." In the case of Central America, Rodríguez suggests, writers are seeking to establish a regional Central American (southern) identity that goes beyond the nation, falls short of a fully "Latin American" identity, and forms a contestatory response to the Pan-Americanism of earlier days.

The history of U.S.–Latin American relations is marked by deep historical memories and interpretations that are often at odds. Throughout the hemisphere, subconscious and conscious images of the North and the South are fraught simultaneously with admiration, fear, envy, disdain, and suspicion. These images are critical operatives in the shaping and executing of U.S. foreign policies toward Latin America. Yet all too often these images and the policies which they engender are woefully incomplete.

Contributors to this volume document the changes and the continuities of the past century in the United States, within Latin America, in the multiple relationships between the United States and Latin America, and within the greater international context in which these relationships have unfolded. As the authors question the goals and assumptions surrounding notions of democracy, intervention, human rights, and sovereignty, and place them within their particular historical and sociopolitical contexts, they help us to reclaim and restore meaning to these terms. They suggest that paradigms that are limited to bilateral governmental relations between nations are no longer adequate, and they bring into relief the often hidden traditions of progressive activism and the roles of women, international organizations, and nongovernmental organizations in the construction of hemispheric relations over the past century. In this era of globalization, such inclusive, interdisciplinary paradigms are needed to comprehend the past, present, and future directions of U.S.–Latin American relations.

NOTES

1. The conference, "Challenges to Peace in the Americas, 1898–1998: Lessons from the Past, Visions for the Future," was held at the U.S. Library of Congress in

October 1998. It was jointly sponsored by the Department of Spanish and Portuguese and the Latin American Studies Center at the University of Maryland, College Park (UMCP), and the Hispanic Division of the Library of Congress, with additional support from American University, Georgetown University, George Washington University, the Catholic University of America, Howard University, Johns Hopkins University, Trinity College, the Embassy of Spain, and the Consortium of Universities of the Washington Metropolitan Area.

2. The other conference papers, which focused specifically on the war of 1898 and its legacies, were published in an earlier volume, Virginia M. Bouvier, ed., *Whose America? The War of 1898 and the Battles to Define the Nation* (Westport, CT: Praeger, 2001).

3. Noam Chomsky and Heinz Dieterich, *Latin America: From Colonization to Globalization* (New York: Ocean Press, 1999).

4. See Heritage Foundation, *Issues 2000*, online at *http://www.heritage.org/issues/chap18part2.html*.

5. For background on the particulars of each of these regional configurations, see SELA, *Guide to Latin American and Caribbean Integration 1999*, online at *http://www.lanic.utexas.edu/project/sela/book/*.

6. "Guatemala Tries 5 in Bishop's Murder," *The Toronto Star*, 15 February 2001. All newspaper, periodical, and wire service reports, unless otherwise indicated, were found online at LEXIS–NEXIS Academic Universe.

7. Canute James, "Firmly on the Path," *Latin Finance*, December 2000, p. 62.

8. For a discussion of the Cold Warrior mentality, see Martha Cottam, *Images and Intervention: U.S. Policies in Latin America* (Pittsburgh: University of Pittsburgh Press, 1994).

9. Jonathan Hartlyn, Lars Schoultz, and Augusto Varas, *The United States and Latin America in the 1990s: Beyond the Cold War* (Chapel Hill: University of North Carolina Press, 1992), 1.

10. Steven Mufson, "Bush Urged to Champion Human Rights: Conservatives Call on President to Promote Democracy, Freedom in Foreign Policy," *Washington Post*, 26 January 2001, p. A5.

11. See Raymond Bonner and Christopher Marquis, "In Filling Latin Post, Bush May Reignite Feuds," *New York Times*, 9 March 2001, p. A6.

12. See Donald M. Fraser, "Freedom and Foreign Policy," *Foreign Policy* 26 (Spring 1977): 140–56; and John Salzburg, "A View from the Hill: US Legislation and Human Rights," in David D. Newsom, ed., *The Diplomacy of Human Rights* (Lanham, MD: University Press of America, 1986), 13–20.

13. See Richard E. Feinberg and Robin L. Rosenberg, eds., *Civil Society and the Summit of the Americas: The 1998 Santiago Summit* (Coral Gables, FL: North–South Center Press at the University of Miami, 1999).

14. Don Coerver and Linda Hall, *Tangled Destinies: Latin America and the United States* (Albuquerque: University of New Mexico Press, 1999), 242.

15. Economic statistics in this paragraph are from the Heritage Foundation, *Issues 2000*, online at *http://www.heritage.org/issues/chap18part2.html*.

16. Richard Chacón, "Sweet Talk, Tough Take on Island," *The Boston Globe*, 26 February 2001, p. A1; Manuel Ernesto Rivera, "Puerto Rican Governor Pleased with Suspension of Navy Exercises," *Associated Press*, 2 March 2001.

17. See Bernard Aronson, "A Good Time to 'Look South,'" *The Washington Post*,

6 February 2001; James Anderson, "South Americans Worried by U.S.-Backed Drug Plan for Colombia," *Associated Press*, 16 December 2000; Andrés Cala, "Coke and Gunpowder: Plan Colombia Might Export Wars to Neighbors," *The Gazette* [Montreal], 9 February 2001; Jane Perlez, "Mexico Warns of Colombia Drug War Spillover," *The New York Times*, 31 January 2001; Michael Shifter, "This Plan Isn't Working: U.S. Military Aid Alarms Colombia's Neighbors," *The Washington Post*, 10 December 2000.

18. Christopher Marquis, "Bush Expected to Toughen Stand on Venezuela," *International Herald Tribune*, 29 December 2000, p. 3.

19. Joseph Contreras, "The Year the Generals Came Back," *Newsweek*, 25 December 2000, p. 52.

20. See Victor Tokman and Emilio Klein, "La estratificación social bajo tensión en la era de la globalización," *Revista de la CEPAL*, n.72 (December 2000), online at *http://www.eclac.org/publicaciones/SecretariaEjecutiva/0/lcg2120/klein.pdf*. See Inter-American Dialogue, *The Americas at the Millennium: A Time of Testing* (Washington, DC: IAD, 1999) on the relationship between democratic politics and liberal economic policies and their call for developing collective responses.

21. Contreras, "The Year the Generals Came Back," 52.

22. "Containing Colombia's Troubles," *The New York Times*, 15 January 2001, p. A14; "Indigenous leaders call for dissolution of Congress," *CRE Satelital radio web site*, Guayaquil, 30 January 2001, transcript online at NEXIS–LEXIS Academic Universe; Fabio Castro, "Ecuadoran Indians, Military Face Off in Tense Protests," *Agence France Presse*, 29 January 2001.

23. The World Bank Group, *Poverty Trends and Voices of the Poor,* online at *www.worldbank.org/poverty/data/trends/index.htm*.

24. Ral Pierri, "Development-LATAM: Cooperation Key for Tackling Urban Challenges," *Inter Press Service,* 23 February 2001.

25. The World Bank Group, *World Development Report 2000/2001: Attacking Poverty,* online at *http://www.worldbank.org/poverty/wdrpoverty/report/index.htm*.

26. For land statistics, see Common Frontiers, "Alternatives for the Americas," *http://www.web.net/comfront/alts4americas/eng/00-foreword-e.html*. For income distribution by country, see World Bank, *World Development Indicators 2000*, cited in The World Bank Group, *Poverty Trends and Voices of the Poor,* online at *www.worldbank.org/poverty/data/trends/inequal.htm*.

27. World Bank, *World Development Indicators 2000*.

28. World Bank Group, *Poverty Trends and Voices of the Poor*.

29. Priscilla Hayner, talk at the United States Institute of Peace, 25 January 2001. See also Priscilla Hayner, *Unspeakable Truths: Confronting State Terror and Atrocity* (NewYork: Routledge, 2001).

30. Many of the reports of the Truth Commissions are available at the United States Institute of Peace Library website at *www.usip.org/library/truth.html*. On truth commissions, see also Priscilla B. Hayner, "Fifteen Truth Commissions—1974–1994: A Comparative Study," *Human Rights Quarterly* 16, no. 4 (November 1994): 597–655; and Esteban Cuya, *Las comisiones de la verdad en América Latina*, online at *http://www.derechos.org/koaga/iii/1/cuya.html*, 1 March 1999. See also Abraham Lama, "Human Rights-Peru: Truth Commission, A Pending Challenge," *Inter Press Service,* 4 January 2001.

31. See The United Nations, *De la locura a la esperanza, la guerra de 12 años en*

El Salvador: Informe de la Comisión de la Verdad para El Salvador (New York: United Nations, 1993).

32. See Human Rights Watch, "The Pinochet Case—A Wake-up Call to Tyrants and Victims Alike," *Human Rights Watch* (September 2000), 19.

33. "Pinochet's Lawyers Argue Charges Against Him 'Political,' 'Illegal,'" *Deutsche Presse-Agentur*, 14 February 2001.

34. "Events Leading Up to the Decision to Put Pinochet on Trial as Accessory," *Agence France Presse*, 8 March 2001; "Pinochet, Symbol of Latin America's Repressive Era, Divides Chileans," 29 January 2001. The importance of the work of Chilean human rights organizations and individuals in documenting the ongoing violations of human rights during the dictatorship cannot be understated. On the Caravan of Death, see the eloquent new translation of Patricia Verdugo's *Los Zarpazos del Puma* by Marcelo Montecino: *Chile, Pinochet, and the Caravan of Death*, intro. Paul E. Sigmund (Boulder, CO: Lynne Rienner, 2001).

35. Diego Cevallos, "Rights-Mexico: Former Argentine Officer to Fight Extradition," *Inter Press Service*, 5 February 2001.

36. Cevallos, "Rights-Mexico," n.p.

37. Human Rights Watch, "The Pinochet Case," 18.

38. Giancarlo Capaldo, "Proceedings in Italy against Latin American Dictators and Military Personnel of the 1970s and 1980s," remarks submitted for "The Pinochet Precedent: Individual Accountability for International Crimes," Washington, DC, American University's Washington College of Law, 26 March 2001.

39. "Judge Revokes Amnesty Laws Protecting Army in Argentina," *Deutsche Presse-Agentur*, 6 March 2001.

40. Mary A. Dempsey, "Booking on Justice," *Freedom Magazine International, Inc.*, March 2001.

41. "Urgent—Swiss Block 50 Million Dollars Linked to Montesinos," *Agence France Presse*, 3 November 2000; "Banks Unite in Global Battle Against Money Laundering: Set Guidelines," *Agence France Presse*, 24 October 2000.

42. "Dear Mr. Drug Lord: Your Money is No Good Here," *National Post* [Toronto], 4 November 2000.

43. For some of the best examples of the recent boom in literature on these international networks, see bibliographic essay at the end of this volume.

44. Arturo Fox, *Latinoamérica: Presente y Pasado* (Upper Saddle River, NJ: Prentice-Hall, Inc., 1998), 113.

45. See Philip S. Foner and Richard C. Winchester, eds., *The Anti-Imperialist Reader: A Documentary History of Anti-Imperialism in the United States* (New York: Holmes & Meier Publishers, Inc., 1984).

46. Such noble sentiments were clearly manipulated by those who had designs on Cuba. See Louis A. Pérez, Jr., *The War of 1898: The United States & Cuba in History & Historiography* (Chapel Hill: University of North Carolina Press, 1998).

47. On the Anti-Imperialist League, see E.B. Tompkins, *Anti-Imperialism in the United States: The Great Debate* (Philadelphia: University of Pennsylvania Press, 1970); Robert L. Beisner, *Twelve Against Empire: The Anti-Imperialists, 1898–1900* (New York: McGraw-Hill Book Company, 1968); and Fred Harvey Harrington, "The Anti-Imperialist Movement in the United States, 1898–1900," *Mississippi Valley Historical Review* 22 (1935): 211–30.

48. See Mark Falcoff and Frederick B.Pike, eds., *The Spanish Civil War, 1936–39:*

American Hemispheric Perspectives (Lincoln: University of Nebraska Press, 1982). Both the Mexican Revolution and the Spanish Civil War were popular causes among American socialists and anarchists, although this topic has been somewhat neglected. See Candace Falk, ed., *Emma Goldman: A Documentary History of the American Years (1890–1919)* (Berkeley: University of California Press, forthcoming 2003).

49. The Inter-American Foundation, *A Guide to NGO Directories: How to Find Over 20,000 Nongovernmental Organizations in Latin America and the Caribbean*, 2nd ed. (Arlington, VA: The Inter-American Foundation, 1995).

50. For documentation of the growth of NGOs in the United States and Latin America, see Kathryn A. Sikkink, "Nongovernmental Organizations, Democracy, and Human Rights in Latin America," in Tom Farer, ed., *Beyond Sovereignty: Collectively Defending Democracy in the Americas* (Baltimore: Johns Hopkins Press, 1996), 150–68. Also helpful are Schoultz, *Human Rights and U.S. Policy;* Keck and Sikkink, *Activists beyond Borders;* Lowell W. Livezey, *Non Governmental Organizations and the Idea of Human Rights* (Princeton: Princeton Center for International Studies, 1988); Jackie Smith and Ron Pagnucco (with George A. López), "Globalizing Human Rights: The Work of Transnational Human Rights NGOs in the 1990s," *Human Rights Quarterly* 20, no. 2 (May 1998): 379–412; Henry J. Steiner, *Diverse Partners: Non Governmental Organizations and the Human Rights Movement* (Cambridge, MA: Harvard Law College, 1991); and Peter Willets, ed., *"The Conscience of the World": The Influence of Non-Governmental Organizations in the UN System* (Washington, DC: Brookings, 1996).

51. Jim Lobe, "Rights-US: 2000 Another Mixed Year, Says State Department," *Inter Press Service*, 26 February 2001.

52. Keck and Sikkink, *Activists Beyond Borders.*

53. Patrick Moser, "Cancun Forum Discusses Poverty," *Agence France Presse*, 26 February 2001.

54. Roland Barthes, "Jeunes Chercheurs," cited in James Clifford, *Writing Culture, The Poetics and Politics of Ethnography* (Berkeley: University of California Press, 1986).

55. See Jim Zwick, "The Anti-Imperialist Movement, 1898–1921," in Virginia M. Bouvier, ed., *Whose America? The War of 1898 and the Battles to Define the Nation* (Westport, CT: Praeger, 2001), 171–92.

56. Carrie A. Foster, *The Women and the Warriors: The U.S. Section of the Women's International League for Peace and Freedom, 1915–1946* (Syracuse: Syracuse University Press, 1995).

57. For a discussion of nineteenth century standards for intervention, see Sylvia L. Hilton, "U.S. Intervention and Monroeism: Spanish Perspectives on the American Role in the Colonial Crisis of 1895–1898," in Bouvier, *Whose America?* 37–60.

58. Ruti G. Teitel, *Transitional Justice* (New York: Oxford University Press, 2000) provides a legal framework for a discussion of the scope of remedies available for such transitional societies.

59. Eduardo Galeano, "In Defense of the Word," (1978) in Eduardo Galeano, *Open Veins of Latin America* (New York: Monthly Review Press, 1997).

PART I

DEMOCRACY AND U.S. INTERVENTIONS IN LATIN AMERICA

1

Evolving Concepts of Intervention: Promoting Democracy

Lars Schoultz

Whenever the term "intervention" crops up in a discussion of inter-American relations, it is almost always employed to designate the invasion of Latin American territory by U.S. armed forces. Using that definition, there have been about forty instances of unilateral U.S. intervention in Latin America during the twentieth century. Although those interventions represent a significant historical legacy that conditions the thinking and behavior of today's foreign policy officials, particularly Latin Americans, they do not help us understand much about contemporary inter-American relations, because armed interventions have become fairly infrequent. Unlike the first part of the twentieth century, today invasions constitute an extreme form of behavior. What has happened over the course of the twentieth century is that the United States has gradually developed a panoply of more subtle mechanisms to encourage Latin Americans to behave as Washington wishes. In the process, the term "intervention" has been redefined.

Perhaps the best way to understand today's intervention is to begin with an example—the contemporary U.S. policy of promoting democracy in Latin America—and, to make the example specific: the effort of the U.S. Agency for International Development (AID) to promote democracy in Nicaragua, a tiny, poverty-stricken Central American country whose government has rarely been considered democratic. AID's 1998 budget request outlined the problems Nicaragua faced:

Civil society institutions must take hold and provide an outlet for people to express their interests. Local authorities must exercise more power relative to national government. The legislature must mature and demonstrate that it is a professional body capable of making legislative compromises that overcome partisan interests for the benefit of society as a whole. The judicial system must be modernized and reformed to achieve credibility in the eyes of the public as a fair arbiter of criminal and civil disputes. The military and police must scrupulously avoid appearances of partisanship, demonstrate a commitment to punish human rights abusers among their ranks, and take strides to modernize. The civil bureaucracy must slim further, and become more efficient and accountable to the public at large.[1]

To help Nicaraguans accomplish this, AID asked Congress for approximately $12 million in fiscal year 1998. As in the U.S. promotion of democracy generally, in this case no armed forces are involved; instead, AID is using money and expertise to encourage Nicaraguans to restructure the major institutions of their society.

WHY INTERVENE FOR DEMOCRACY?

During the 1980s, when today's U.S. policy of promoting democracy abroad was created, many U.S. officials thought of democracy primarily as a mechanism to stop the spread of communism. The goal was to protect U.S. national security. As President Reagan told the British Parliament in a 1982 speech, "What I am describing now is a plan and a hope for the long term—the march of freedom and democracy which will leave Marxism–Leninism on the ash-heap of history."[2]

As the Cold War faded into history, the United States converted the mechanism into a goal, and now spends tens of millions of dollars each year to help countries like Nicaragua become more democratic. This evolution in the rationale behind the U.S. effort has typically been explained as the product of two fundamental changes in contemporary international relations. One is the hegemony of liberal democratic ideals—a growing worldwide consensus on the desirability of increasing elite accountability through improved institutions operating under the rule of law. In Latin America, this consensus is driven by the opinion that democracy is more desirable than any of the various forms of left- or right-wing authoritarianism. This opinion is even more dominant in Washington, but the U.S. contribution to the consensus is driven by an additional factor: the "democratic peace" hypothesis that well-functioning democracies do not fight one another or foster the conditions that facilitate high levels of internal political turmoil and violence. None of the waves of Latin American refugees that have periodically washed up on U.S. shores has come from a democracy. Washington realists argue that democracy is not simply good for Latin America; it is also in the self-interest of the United States.

The second change is the erosion of the traditional boundary between domestic and international politics, making today's effort to strengthen democracy a transnational activity. This is especially evident at the nongovernmental level, where uncounted thousands of democracy-promoting NGOs representing an array of diverse interests (religious, human rights, gender, labor, environment) are increasingly linked in coordinated networks across national boundaries.[3] In this transnational context, AID is simply one more institution reaching across borders to strengthen democracy. That AID is a governmental institution is also unexceptional: the Swedes, the Canadians, the Dutch—virtually all of the world's bilateral aid agencies—are doing the same thing.

What stands out as unique about the U.S. effort to strengthen democracy in Latin America is its continuation of an historical attitude. Look once again at AID's statement about Nicaraguan democracy, this time recalling the history of U.S.–Nicaraguan relations. Note how AID's goals for Nicaragua today can be interpreted as the logical extension of an attitude U.S. officials have held about Nicaraguans since the mid-nineteenth century, when one of the first U.S. envoys reported that "were it not for the civilizing influence of the United States, this country would revert to the aboriginal state."[4] Also note the attitude communicated by AID's repeated use of the imperative verb "must," which seems reminiscent of the imperative attitude that has repeatedly accompanied U.S. policy toward Nicaragua since the presidency of William Howard Taft. Finally, note that AID communicates an attitude simply by writing about how the citizens of another country must behave if they are to strengthen their democracy. Nicaraguan government officials would never dream of writing a similar statement about the steps U.S. citizens must (or even might) take to improve their democracy.

Viewed from this perspective, AID's statement about Nicaraguan democracy reveals an attitude[5] that became a central part of U.S. policy toward Latin America long before the more recently established hegemony of liberal democratic ideals or the blurring of national boundaries. Attitudes affect policy. AID's statement is based upon the way U.S. officials have always looked at Latin America and conceived of Latin Americans. To be specific, for almost two centuries U.S. foreign policy officials have considered Latin Americans inferior—or, for the squeamish, "underdeveloped."

Today's policy of intervening to promote democracy is the product of a gradual evolution in the attitudes of U.S. officials about Latin American politics. Early in the nineteenth century when Latin Americans were struggling for independence, the consensus in Washington was captured by former President John Adams, who wrote that any attempt to establish democracy in the region—or in any Catholic country—would be "as absurd as similar plans would be to establish democracies among the birds, beasts, and fishes." He clearly passed this view to his son, John Quincy Adams, who as secretary of state (1817–1825) and then president (1825–1829) set the initial tone of U.S. policy toward Latin America. Just before initiating the process of diplomatic recognition, Adams told Henry Clay that Latin

Americans "have not the first elements of good or free government. Arbitrary power, military and ecclesiastical, was stamped upon their education, upon their habits, and upon all their institutions. Civil dissension was infused into all their seminal principles. War and mutual destruction was in every member of their organization, moral, political, and physical."[6]

This initial attitude toward Latin Americans' capacity for democracy represented little more than anti-Catholic prejudice, but it was soon confirmed by the first generation of U.S. envoys to the region. One wrote that Venezuela's "Ministers of State are inferior men"; another that the government of Nicaragua had been "left to incompetent men"; a third that Brazilians were a "degraded & corrupt people, who are ignorant of the first rudiments of either administrative or judicial justice"; and a fourth wrote more generally that "in these new countries all is intrigue, treachery and bribery."[7]

The problem was not that a few bad apples had managed to seize power. All Latin Americans were considered "*fac-similes* of the old Spaniards[:] proud, bigoted, narrow minded and oppressive." This made democracy impossible. "The Spanish Americans are incapable of calmly examining a subject of public interest or dispassionately discussing the acts of a Government," was a typical comment from Peru, as was that of the U.S. chargé in Caracas, who reported that Venezuelans were incapable of "acting upon any settled principle." A U.S. chargé in Buenos Aires depicted Argentines as edgy adolescents "who spend their whole lives in trifling with great subjects, and in exhausting their utmost powers in disputing about small ones."[8]

One outcome of these character traits was a disturbingly high level of violence, another roadblock to democracy. Advising Washington of the approach of war between Peru and Bolivia, an 1840 despatch from Lima observed that "there is really no cause for war; but [to] the military adventurers who rule these countries, being ever ready to shed blood, it is not material, whether there is cause or not." An envoy to Colombia wrote that "again, Venezuela, seems almost determined to pick a quarrel and Get up a war between the two Republics" although it had only "pretended Grievances, no one of which would justify a school boy fight." A despatch from Uruguay referred to "the restless spirit of a people, whose appetite for rapine, blood, and revolution, can never be satiated," and from Chile came the summary evaluation that "all these new countries appear to be dissatisfied in Peace and prosperity. They must fight within themselves or against one another. They cannot be content in tranquility and settled order."[9]

The composite picture sent to Washington by early nineteenth-century U.S. envoys, then, was of a politically unstable region where democracy could not set its roots because Latin Americans, heirs to Hispanic civilization, were immature and often uncontrollably violent. The U.S. response was to accept the inevitable, as Secretary of State James Buchanan advised in a reprimand of a U.S. consul who was attempting to promote democracy: "It is impossible that you can reform either the morals or the politics of

Peru, and . . . you ought to take Peru's institutions and its people just as you find them and endeavor to make the best of them for the benefit of your own country."[10]

This hands-off policy continued through most of the nineteenth century, but beginning in the 1880s U.S. officials slowly came to believe that they could "improve" Latin American politics. The first glimmerings of this policy shift were visible at the lower levels of government; an example is the 1886 report of a trade commission, which asserted that if U.S. envoys were to become proconsuls "they could avert many a revolution, suppress incipient wars, and foster the enactment and enforcement of wise legislation." Moreover, "the fact that our Government is taking a more particular interest in the domestic policy and progress of the Republics than is manifested by other foreign powers, would tend to tranquillity [sic] and inspire confidence in the stability of the constituted authority. In other words, we advise that our representatives to these Republics be charged to respond to that feeling that is so often expressed by them as that of a child to a mother."[11]

Although it first surfaced as the initiative of individual envoys, this urge to help Latin America reform was converted into policy in the 1890s, as Social Darwinists such as Theodore Roosevelt and Henry Cabot Lodge reached the pinnacle of political power. An assistant secretary of state captured their Social Darwinism perfectly: "Nature, in its rough method of uplift, gives sick nations strong neighbors."[12]

Nowhere has this effort at uplift been pursued with greater tenacity than in Nicaragua. Today's effort to help Nicaragua become democratic had its origin in the Taft administration (1909–1913), when U.S. officials helped overthrow the regime of Nicaraguan Liberal José Santos Zelaya, whose multiple sins included destabilizing the region around the new U.S. canal at Panama. With Zelaya out of the way and U.S. gunboats anchored on both Nicaraguan coasts, in late 1910 the Taft administration sent Thomas Dawson to Managua to negotiate four separate agreements with leaders of the victorious Conservative party. The first provided for the creation of an assembly to adopt a democratic constitution and to elect the rebellion's leader, Juan Estrada, as president and Adolfo Díaz as vice president for a two-year transitional term. The second agreement (the establishment of a claims commission) and the third (the negotiation of a private loan and the initiation of a customs receivership) were primarily economic—the Taft administration's first try at what came to be known as Dollar Diplomacy. The fourth called for a popular election of Estrada's successor but specified that "the one chosen must represent the revolution and the Conservative party."[13]

Interim President Juan Estrada, a Liberal, was thus converted into the lamest of lame ducks, and in mid-1911 he resigned, acting, according to the U.S. minister, "in a fit of drunken insanity."[14] The resignation catapulted Vice President Adolfo Díaz into the presidency. An accounting clerk in the La Luz & Los Angeles Mining Company, a firm created to develop the gold-mining concession granted to the Pittsburgh-based United States and Nicaragua Company, Díaz was also a figurehead assistant secretary–treasurer of the latter company since, as U.S. Consul Thomas Moffat explained, "one of the officials had to be a Nicaraguan."[15] Díaz, who had no political roots prior to the rebellion against Zelaya, had the good sense to declare himself a Conservative.

With the country led by a president lacking a constituency and with the Liberals angry at having been disenfranchised by the Dawson accords, the Conservative minister of war, Luis Mena, launched an armed rebellion and was soon joined by the Liberals. In response, President Díaz asked the United States for help, and President Taft sent an additional 2,700 U.S. Marines to Nicaragua. Illness soon obliged Mena to surrender, and he was taken as a prisoner to the Canal Zone, but the revolt ended only after marines seized the Liberal stronghold of León in October. The full U.S. force remained for a few weeks to implement the fourth Dawson accord—Adolfo Díaz's presidential election—following which all but about 130 marines left the country. This force, which subsequent administrations would refer to as a "legation guard," was kept in Managua from 1911 to 1926.

The marines stayed because, given the type of democracy they had imposed on Nicaragua, they expected instability. In 1916 it was time for another election, and the Wilson administration was worried because the hostile Liberals were united behind the candidacy of Julián Irías, while the favored Conservatives were split into three factions. Seeking to ensure that the Conservatives settled on a single candidate, U.S. Minister Benjamin Jefferson and Admiral William Caperton met with Díaz, then reported to Secretary of State Robert Lansing: "Have just had a most satisfactory conference with President Diaz [who] will gladly accept the name of any candidate for the presidency of Nicaragua that the secretary might indicate." But Díaz decided to seek reelection himself when it became obvious that his rival, Emiliano Chamorro (who had been Nicaragua's minister in Washington), would be Secretary Lansing's choice. The U.S. response was to send military reinforcements. Shortly after two additional warships dropped anchor in Corinto, Admiral Caperton reported that "with the advent of a squadron of American ships, political leaders are again giving the usual weight to the Minister's words. . . . The Commander-in-Chief [Caperton] and American Minister then had a conference with President Diaz, who agreed to use his utmost to reunite the three factions of the Conservative party in favor of General Chamorro."[16]

The State Department next turned its attention to the Liberals, whose constituency was reported to be "the ignorant masses of the people who either do not appreciate the intentions or policies of this Government or who are readily susceptible to political oratory." To solve this sticky problem of voters lacking sufficient wisdom to make an appropriate decision, Caperton and Jefferson notified the Liberals that anyone who had been associated with the Zelaya administration—Julián Irías, for one—would not be allowed to run for office.[17] With their candidate proscribed, the Liberals decided to abstain, assuring Chamorro of an uncontested victory.

Thereafter, the U.S. collector of customs and the legation guard appeared to have the situation well in hand. The only obvious problem was the absence of democracy, since three consecutive rigged elections had shredded the government's thin veil of popular legitimacy. The fraud was brazen, beginning with the first U.S.-supervised election in 1912. Marine Corps Major Smedley Butler, who helped to arrange the unopposed election of Adolfo Díaz, later bragged that by manipulating the electoral rolls "our candidates always win."[18] The U.S.-favored candidates were invariably Conservatives, with Conservative Emiliano Chamorro elected to succeed Conservative Adolfo Díaz in 1916; four years later another Conservative—uncle Diego Chamorro—was elected, and when he died in office, Conservative Vice President Bartolomé Martínez succeeded him.

It was after the 1920 sham that the increasingly angry voices of Nicaragua's Liberals began to be heard in Washington, and their accusations were supported by reports of fraud from U.S. observers. Reacting to these complaints, the State Department notified President-elect Diego Chamorro that it required a promise of free elections in 1924 prior to recognition of the 1920 results. Chamorro promptly made the required commitment and accepted the U.S. suggestion that he hire a U.S. expert to reform Nicaragua's electoral system.[19] The Department of State had in mind Harold Dodds, then secretary of the National Municipal League and soon to be the president of Princeton University. A public administration technocrat, Dodds easily could have written AID's 1998 list of needed improvements in Nicaraguan democracy.

Dodds prepared an allegedly fraud-proof electoral code, which the Nicaraguan Congress enacted into law in 1923. By that time, the Conservatives had split once again, with a portion of them joining with Liberals to offer a coalition slate in the 1924 elections: Conservative Carlos Solórzano for president and Liberal Juan Sacasa for vice president. Incumbent President Bartolomé Martínez also offered his candidacy, as did former President Emiliano Chamorro. Since the Nicaraguan constitution prohibited the president's immediate reelection, State Department officials eliminated Martínez by informing him that the United States "would be highly indisposed to recognize him as the constitutional President of Nicaragua after the expiration of his present term of office." Martínez promptly threw his support to Solórzano and spent his remaining months in office undermining the Dodds reforms and harassing Emiliano Chamorro. As a result, the October 1924 election was clearly unfair.[20]

Realizing that he possessed a weak mandate, President-elect Solórzano asked the Coolidge administration not to withdraw the marines, but from Washington's perspective nothing more remained to be done: Nicaragua's finances had been put in order and Dodds had done his best to set the government upon a democratic foundation. Solórzano was inaugurated on New Year's Day 1925, and by August the marines had left the country.

Within two months Emiliano Chamorro had launched a rebellion, and by early 1926 he was president. Dismayed by the backsliding, the United States refused to recognize Chamorro's government and, lacking what had become the imprimatur of legitimacy in Nicaragua, Chamorro soon found his position weakened by a counter-rebellion on the Caribbean coast, which was supported by the landing of U.S. Marines at Bluefields and Corinto. Seeing the handwriting on the wall, Chamorro promptly resigned, but his banner of rebellion was seized by the long-disenfranchised Liberals led by Vice President Sacasa. In response, the marines reoccupied the entire country and placed Washington's long-time favorite, Adolfo Díaz, back in the presidency.[21]

As in 1912, in 1926 Díaz could not have lasted a week without the continuing presence of U.S. troops, and so the Coolidge administration dispatched additional marines. It did so only reluctantly, however, for the U.S. public had clearly grown tired of intervening in Nicaragua. To ensure that the intervention would be brief, President Coolidge also sent former Secretary of War Henry Stimson as his personal mediator.

Arriving in Managua in mid-1927, Stimson began his negotiations with the ultimatum that Nicaraguans had better be democratic or else:

"I am authorized to say that the President of the United States intends to accept the request of the Nicaraguan Government to supervise the elections of 1928; that the retention of President Diaz during the remainder of this term is regarded as essential to that plan and will be insisted upon; that a general disarmament of the country is also regarded as necessary for the proper and successful conduct of such election; and that the forces of the United States will be authorized to accept the custody of the arms of those willing to lay them down including the government and to disarm forcibly those who will not do so."

Then Stimson presented the Liberal military leader, José María Moncada, with a plan designed to permit Liberal success at the polls. While reluctant to permit Adolfo Díaz to continue as president, the Liberals were given no choice; as Stimson wrote in his diary, "we know no other Nicaraguan whom we could trust to so cooperate." For the future, however, Stimson had identified a promising young member of Moncada's military staff: "Somoza is a very frank, friendly, likable young Liberal and his attitude impresses me more favorably than almost any other."[22]

Within days Stimson was able to report Moncada's acceptance: "while there will probably be resistance by small irreconcilable groups and scattered bandits, I believe that there will be no organized resistance to our action."[23] That proved almost accurate. Moncada was able to convince eleven of his twelve military lieutenants to accept Stimson's plan; only Augusto Sandino refused. Retreating into Nicaragua's rugged northwest, in mid-July Sandino's forces attacked a detachment of marines at Ocotal. The marines called in U.S. air support, which killed between 50 and 300 Nicaraguans—a strike that shattered President Coolidge's effort to limit the domestic controversy over his intervention in Nicaragua. "Afternoon papers here carry sensational reports concerning bombing operations," cabled Secretary Kellogg to Managua. "Extremely important to have at earliest possible moment fullest details concerning Sandino's attack."[24]

While deploying additional forces—the maximum troop strength quickly rose to 5,673—the Coolidge administration launched an effort to defuse the public's outrage over the bombing of innocent civilians by converting Sandino from a Liberal military leader into a bandit. "Sandino is reported to be an erratic Nicaraguan about thirty years of age with wild Communist ideas acquired largely in Mexico," read the first sentence of Minister Charles Eberhardt's reply to Kellogg's urgent request for details. Rejecting the Stimson plan, the reply continued, Sandino "returned to Northern Nicaragua where he has since roamed at will with a few followers committing every known depredation and acts of outlawry," and where he "preached Communism, Mexican brotherly love and cooperation and death to the Americans, until the rabble of the whole North country joined him in his plan to massacre Americans there."[25] This legend, which had no basis in fact, became the Coolidge administration's response to its critics.

As the war against Sandino expanded, the U.S. public's opposition increased, and this opposition clearly affected officials in Washington, including Secretary Kellogg, who cabled his envoy in Nicaragua: "There is a great deal of criticism in this country about the way in which these operations are being dragged out with constant sacrifice of American lives and without any concrete results. . . . People cannot understand why the job cannot be done, and frankly I do not understand myself."[26]

Once again, democracy was the answer, with the Coolidge administration seeking to oversee an occupation-ending election. It dispatched Harold Dodds to prepare yet another electoral law and General Frank McCoy to supervise the subsequent election. Nicaraguans dutifully marched to the polls once Dodds had corrected the glitches in his first law, and on New Year's Day 1929 José María Moncada was installed as Nicaragua's president.

This left one major problem. The 1927 Stimson ultimatum had disbanded Nicaragua's partisan armed forces, replacing them with the U.S. Marines. If the U.S. forces were now to be withdrawn, some new institution would have to maintain law and order. The United States therefore created the Nicaraguan National Guard, and over the next few years provided it with arms and training, while at the same time continuing the fight against Sandino's rebels.

Herbert Hoover's desire to remove the remaining U.S. troops from Nicaragua only increased after the October 1929 stock market crash signaled the onset of the Great Depression, but President Moncada requested that the United States supervise Nicaragua's 1930 non-presidential elections. Since U.S. Marines were still in the country fighting Sandino and training the National Guard, Hoover agreed. Congress consented, but the honeymoon (and Republican control over the House of Representatives) was over by late 1931, when President Hoover indicated that the United States would also supervise Nicaragua's 1932 presidential election. Sandino was still the problem. His forces had waxed and waned over the years, but his opposition was never to cease completely until the United States withdrew its troops, and by that time 135 marines had lost their lives. Eight marines had died in a Sandinista ambush on the last day of 1930, and in April 1931 nine more U.S. citizens had been killed by another antigovernment group. The congressional reaction was to prohibit the use of Navy funds to supervise Nicaragua's 1932 election.

President Hoover found sufficient money elsewhere to chair half the election boards, and Juan Sacasa won the 1932 election. At almost the same time, U.S. Minister Matthew Hanna tapped Anastasio Somoza to replace the marine commander of the *Guardia Nacional.* "I look on him as the best man in the country for the position," he reported to Washington. "I know no one who will labor as intelligently or conscientiously to maintain the nonpartisan character of the Guardia, or will be as efficient in all matters connected with the administration and command of the Force."[27] The United States turned the National Guard over to Somoza on the same day Sacasa was inaugurated—January 1, 1933—and within hours the last contingent of marines had left the country.

An uneasy jockeying for political power ensued. Sandino was assassinated by the *Guardia* in early 1934, and Sacasa watched helplessly as Somoza stripped him of his authority. By mid-1936 there was nothing for Sacasa to do but resign, and Anastasio Somoza assumed the presidency. As he observed this process unfolding, a new U.S. ambassador wrote that "the people who created the G[uardia] N[acional] had no adequate understanding of the psychology of the people here. Otherwise, they would not have bequeathed Nicaragua with an instrument to blast constitutional procedure off the map. Did it ever occur to the eminent statesmen who created the G.N. that personal ambition lurks in the human breast, *even* in Nicaragua? In my opinion it has been one of the sorriest examples on our part of our inability to understand that we should not meddle in other peoples' affairs."[28]

Somoza provided the United States with the stability it desired during the final years of the Depression and through World War II. But then, with the war over, for a brief interlude the United States began to withdraw support from Latin American dictators and to encourage a transition to democracy. A master at packaging his needs to serve U.S. interests, this time Anastasio Somoza misread U.S. policy, and in a personal note to FDR in late 1944 he argued that Nicaragua's *Guardia Nacional* needed arms because it was the only force capable of holding off Mexico's imperial ambition: "This purpose of Mexico, which does not hide its repugnance for the United States, has encountered and will continue to encounter my opposition and that of Nicaragua, [which has] become a stronghold for the closest collaboration and friendship with your nation on the worthy basis of Good Neighborship. Nicaragua is likewise a stronghold and breakwater against the communism which diligently seeks to infiltrate into Central America as an aspect of Mexican policy."[29]

What Somoza failed to recognize was that U.S.–Mexican relations were more cordial than at any time since 1910, and that communism was not yet a credible threat; indeed, when Somoza wrote his note the United States was actively involved in helping the Soviet Union to establish diplomatic ties with Latin American governments. Somoza quickly realized his misstep and agreed to a free election. Not long thereafter he sent his ambassador to warn the State Department that without Somoza's presence on the ballot, "leftist elements" might win the election. Assistant Secretary of State Spruille Braden replied "that we believe that the best way to practice democracy was to practice it and that sometimes the way was hard. If leftist or anti-American elements should become active, well, that was only a part of the difficult progress toward the democratic goal."[30] Somoza promptly withdrew his candidacy.

Then in March 1947, just days after Nicaragua's voters had selected Somoza's successor, President Truman paid a brief visit to Mexico, where he went out of his way to underscore the U.S. commitment to nonintervention, continuing a twenty-year effort to dispel Mexicans' fears of further U.S. imperial ambition. Somoza apparently interpreted Truman's reassurance to mean that he, too, had no reason to fear intervention; twenty-seven days after the inauguration of his successor, Somoza ordered his National Guard to overthrow the new government. Disgusted, the United States joined in the effort to exclude Nicaragua from the 1947 Rio conference, and it waited nearly a year before sending a new ambassador to Managua.

This was a discouraging setback for the fledgling U.S. policy of promoting democracy in Latin America, and as State Department officials licked their wounds over additional failures in Argentina and the Dominican Republic, they came to believe that the United States had been trying to accomplish the impossible. This belief was captured best by the foreign service officer who had helped to midwife democracy in Nicaragua from 1929 to 1933, and later served as a Cold War ambassador in Latin America: "I knew that Tacho [Somoza] was *mañoso*; that he was on the clever, even cunning, side. But let us be frank: in Nicaragua's society a degree of *maña* might be a requisite to survival. Nicaraguans were not Groton graduates."[31]

This type of thinking led to the abandonment of democracy as a policy goal. The formal end came in 1950, when a senior foreign policy official,

Louis Halle, published an article in *Foreign Affair*—-"On A Certain Impatience with Latin America." Halle argued that the U.S. effort had been doomed from the beginning, because the region had "a tradition of political behavior marked by intemperance, intransigeance [sic], flamboyance and the worship of strong men"—all undemocratic cultural characteristics that could be summarized in one word: immaturity. "Worship of the 'man on horseback' (through self-identification) is another manifestation of immaturity. It is characteristic of adolescence, this admiration for the ruthless hero who tramples down all opposition, makes himself superior to law, and is irresistible to passionate women who serve his pleasure in droves."[32]

This type of thinking also led directly to the Cold War policy of supporting Latin American dictators. At a 1955 meeting of the National Security Council, Treasury Secretary George Humphrey, one of the coldest of cold warriors, asserted that "wherever a dictator was replaced, communists gained," and therefore "the U.S. should back strong men in Latin American governments." When Nelson Rockefeller challenged Humphrey's point, he was immediately silenced by a lighthearted comment from President Eisenhower, who quoted Portuguese dictator Antonio Salazar: "free government cannot work among Latins."[33] So it was that U.S. policy in the 1950s came to focus on the support of Latin American dictators.

The principal problem with this policy was that Washington's favorite dictators kept getting shot. "President Carlos Castillo Armas, of Guatemala, has just died of an assassin's bullet, fired by a palace guard who stood revealed as an acknowledged Communist," announced Representative Gardner Withrow to his House colleagues in mid-1957. "Just previously, President Jose A. Remón, of Panama, was murdered, followed by President Anastasio Somozo [sic], of Nicaragua. These three were not only devoted friends and allies of the United States, but each was bitterly anticommunist. The pattern is too widespread to be purely localized political unrest." Withrow asked his House colleagues to extend McCarthyism to Latin America: "We owe it to Christian and anti-Communist governments to help search out and expose the Communists."[34]

Combined with Vice President Richard Nixon's hostile reception during his 1958 trip around South America, the overthrow of several friendly Latin American dictators led to a period of genuine intellectual uncertainty about Cold War policy toward Latin America. To some U.S. officials, assassinations, demonstrations, and other forms of instability were caused by Latin America's inferior political culture (i.e., hot-headed populist leaders provoking the region's ignorant masses), while to others they were caused by the legitimate but unheard grievances of impoverished Latin Americans, now caught up in the global revolution of rising expectations.

These two views about the cause of instability led the Eisenhower administration to develop the bifurcated approach that would characterize U.S. policy until the end of the Cold War. Where anticommunist authoritarian leaders (including the second generation of Somozas in Nicaragua) appeared able to maintain stability, U.S. support continued, particularly in the form of military assistance. But then there was something genuinely new: in a path-breaking concession to the revolution of rising expectations, the Eisenhower administration reversed its opposition to U.S.-sponsored economic development programs. By mid-1958 the administration had announced that it would no longer oppose the negotiation of commodity stabilization agreements, that it would no longer oppose the creation of the soft-loan International Development Association, that it would support a plan to double the World Bank's lending authority, that it would dramatically increase Eximbank loan authority, and that it would support the creation of a Latin American common market.

Then in January 1959 Fidel Castro used one of Fulgencio Batista's U.S.-supplied tanks for his victory parade into Havana. At first no one in Washington knew what to make of the new Cuban leader; in April, when he met with Richard Nixon, the vice president concluded that Castro was "either incredibly naive about Communism or under Communist discipline—my guess is the former."[35] As U.S. officials pondered their response, the Castro government accelerated the transformation of Cuban society, and much of that transformation damaged U.S. economic interests. This economic damage was accompanied by a rapidly developing security threat—a blossoming in Soviet–Cuban friendship. Within eighteen months of Castro's victory parade, Nikita Khrushchev warned that "Soviet artillerymen can support with rocket fire the Cuban people if aggressive forces in the Pentagon dare to start intervention against Cuba."

Two days after Khrushchev's warning, the Eisenhower administration threw fiscal caution to the wind and embraced Operation Pan America, an ambitious development proposal from Brazilian President Juscelino Kubitschek that would soon be puffed up and renamed the Alliance for Progress. "We need to consider with the other American Republics practicable ways in which developing countries can make faster progress," Eisenhower told reporters in mid-1960. "I have in mind the opening of new areas of arable land for settlement and productive use. I have in mind better land utilization, within a system which provides opportunities for free, self-reliant men to own land, without violating the rights of others. I have in mind housing with emphasis, where appropriate, on individual ownership of small homes. And I have in mind other essential minimums for decent living."

The Kennedy New Frontiersmen injected steroids into the bifurcated policy it inherited from the Eisenhower administration. Stability would be pursued with dramatically increased assistance to what had come to be known as Latin America's "modernizing military"; economic development would be pursued by enlarging the existing U.S. aid program. Guiding both pursuits was the traditional U.S. attitude that considered Latin American culture inhospitable to democracy. But unlike nineteenth-century officials who considered Latin Americans incorrigible, and unlike earlier twentieth-century officials who sent special envoys backed by the marines to impose democracy, the New Frontiersmen pulled out their checkbooks and began bribing Latin Americans to change their culture.

At its core, the Alliance for Progress was an ambitious effort to encourage Latin America's backward Hispanic people to adopt progressive Anglo values: "Many kinds of changes in attitudes and values are involved," explained President Kennedy's assistant secretary of state for inter-American affairs. He continued, "Among them is a view of the importance of precision in measurement, whether of time, or costs, or distances; a pragmatic rather than doctrinaire approach to the solution of differences and problems; an appreciation of the value of work with the hands and of scientific knowledge as compared to humanistic studies; a sense of public responsibility and public trust and through this of more respect for the contribution of good government to the public welfare; more team spirit and less individualism; an understanding of the importance of social and economic opportunity and mobility guided by performance rather than status." Assistant Secretary Edwin Martin acknowledged that "thousands of Latin Americans understand these matters and have made these changes, but it must become millions."[36]

Nicaragua was not the only country that failed to live up to this Camelot-era vision of an ideal human society, but it was perhaps the one that failed most thoroughly—the Somoza family held on until 1979, when the Frente Sandinista de Liberación Nacional (FSLN) ousted it from power in a bloody civil war.

Although the Carter administration (1977–1981) made an initial effort to befriend the Sandinistas, its time was soon up, and in early 1981 the successor administration of Ronald Reagan began the decade-long process of determining once again the nature of Nicaragua's government. President Reagan clearly believed the Sandinistas were communists and therefore a threat to U.S. security—he told a prime-time television audience that "the Soviets and the Cubans are operating from a base called Nicaragua"[37]—but he often expressed his administration's policy in terms of democracy, praising the U.S.-created *contra* guerrillas as "freedom fighters" and telling the public that Fidel Castro's deceit underlay the Nicaraguan revolution. According to President Reagan, Castro had called the Sandinistas to Havana, where "he told them to tell the world they were fighting for political democracy, not communism. But most important, he instructed them to form a broad alliance with the genuinely democratic opposition to the Somoza regime. Castro explained that this would deceive Western public opinion, confuse potential critics, and make it difficult for the Western democracies to oppose the Nicaraguan revolution without causing great discontent at home."[38]

For eight years the Reagan administration ratcheted up the cost of threatening the United States, eventually exhausting the Nicaraguan population.

Then the United States demanded that Nicaragua hold an election, and when the Sandinistas agreed, the United States used the National Endowment for Democracy to fund the opposition UNO coalition, which emerged as the victor in the 1990 election.

Since 1990, the U.S. government has continued to promote its vision of democracy in Nicaragua. The hope, of course, is that AID, the National Endowment for Democracy, and the host of cooperating U.S. government and quasi-governmental organizations will get it right this time. History suggests that this hope represents nothing more than a mixture of wishful thinking and shallow hubris. The documents we keep in the National Archives demonstrate beyond the slightest doubt that previous generations of bright, well-intentioned U.S. officials thought that they, too, were getting it right. Yet somehow exceptionally competent, well-intentioned officials such as Thomas Dawson got it wrong; so did Henry Stimson, Harold Dodds, Edwin Martin, and hundreds of other U.S. officials over nearly a century. They tried the marines with a Big Stick and the New York bankers with Dollar Diplomacy; they sent in the Peace Corps; they offered military and economic aid; they trained thousands of Nicaraguans in U.S. universities, including Anastasio Somoza Debayle at West Point. Every single one of these efforts failed to make Nicaragua democratic.

Now comes the current generation of U.S. officials, armed once again with the best of intentions and waving AID's list of steps that Nicaraguans must take in order to improve their fledgling democracy. Perhaps our era's officials will get it right this time, but anyone familiar with the history of U.S. intervention in Nicaragua would wager that it will not work out differently.

A safer wager would be that today's U.S. effort will *retard* democracy's development in Nicaragua. That is because democracy, at its core, is a perpetual process of negotiation. When a major power decides to intervene in this negotiating process by giving money or other forms of support to some Nicaraguans, it tips the political balance. Especially in small, poverty-stricken countries like Nicaragua, the side the United States government decides to support now has more power, and that affects its negotiating position within Nicaraguan society. As Anastasio Somoza demonstrated, it sometimes eliminates entirely their incentive to negotiate—their incentive to be democratic.

All this is clear beyond debate, but today's AID officials often respond with the assertion that it is a good thing to tip the balance of negotiating power in favor of the groups it currently supports—civil society organizations that battle for gender equality, human rights, environmental protection, and similar worthy causes. But Thomas Dawson thought that he, too, was weighing in on the side of the angels when he supported the Conservatives over the Liberals. So did U.S. Minister Matthew Hanna when he tapped Anastasio Somoza to lead the National Guard: "I know no one who will labor as intelligently or conscientiously to maintain the non-partisan character of the Guardia, or will be as efficient in all matters connected with the administration and command of the Force."[39]

After almost a century of experiencing what happens when the United States launches yet another effort to improve their country, Nicaraguans today are dutifully lined up for a share of AID's money. The "lining up" process is one in which groups of Nicaraguans adjust their behavior to fit U.S. views—by learning English (as Adolfo Díaz did) or by becoming virulently anticommunist (as the Somozas did). At the present time, the United States favors organizations that represent "civil society," and so nongovernmental organizations have sprung up like mushrooms in every corner of Nicaragua. The United States also wants to give money to local authorities instead of national-level government entities, and so Nicaraguans are spreading their administrative responsibilities from Managua ministries to local town councils, despite clear evidence that this neo-conservative experiment with subsidiarity weakens the voice of the poor. AID is also supporting Nicaraguans who agree with the need to modernize the judiciary, to reform the military and the police, and to slim the bureaucracy. As Thomas Dawson discovered in 1911, Nicaraguans will always be available to help the United States do whatever it wants to improve their country. The only difference between Dawson and today's U.S. officials is that the former brandished a stick, while the latter has first impoverished the country by instigating and funding a needless decade of civil war, and now dangles carrots before the destitute remains of a once-proud population.

Forgotten in all this carrot-dangling is the need for Nicaraguans to develop their own consensus on democratic policies and procedures—to negotiate continuously among themselves an appropriately sized bureaucracy, a military subordinate to civilian authorities, a police respectful of civil liberties, a judiciary impartial to rich and poor, and all the thousands of additional issues that arise out of human interaction. Thomas Jefferson knew this. In the Declaration of Independence he wrote that people need to throw off the fetters of foreign domination before they can negotiate their own forms of political power. With no foreign list of needed improvements to guide them, he advised U.S. citizens to institute their government in such forms as to them seem most likely to effect their safety and happiness.

NOTES

1. U.S., Agency for International Development, *Fiscal Year 1998 Congressional Presentation* (Washington, DC: AID, 1997).

2. "Address to Members of the British Parliament," 8 June 1982, *Public Papers of the Presidents of the United States* (hereafter PPP), *Ronald Reagan, 1982* (Washington, DC: Government Printing Office, 1984), 747.

3. Margaret E. Keck and Kathryn Sikkink, *Activists Beyond Borders: Advocacy Networks in International Politics* (Ithaca, NY: Cornell University Press, 1998).

4. Henry Savage to James Buchanan, 5 February 1848, about Nicaragua but filed with *Despatches from Guatemala*, National Archives (hereafter NA) Record Group (hereafter RG) 59, *General Records of the Department of State*, microform set M121, reel 4.

5. "Attitude" is defined here in the social scientific sense: a manner of thinking or behaving that indicates underlying beliefs, opinions, and dispositions.

6. John Adams to James Lloyd, 27 and 30 March 1815, *Works of John Adams*, Charles Francis Adams, ed., 10 vols. (Boston: Little Brown, 1850–1856), 10: 144–145, 150; John Quincy Adams Diary, 9 March 1821, *Memoirs of John Quincy Adams*, Charles Francis Adams, ed., 12 vols. (Philadelphia: J.B. Lippincott, 1874–1877), 5: 325.

7. Benjamin Shields to John Clayton, 15 August 1849, *Despatches from Venezuela*, RG 59, NA, microform set M79/R8; Ephraim George Squier to John Clayton, 23 June 1849, *Despatches from Guatemala*, RG 59, NA, microform set M219/R5; Henry Wise to James Buchanan, 9 December 1846, *Despatches from Brazil*, RG 59, NA, microform set M121/R18; Richard Pollard to John Forsyth, 27 December 1836, *Despatches from Chile*, RG 59, NA, microform set M10/R4.

8. Francis Baylies to Edward Livingston, 24 July 1832, *Despatches from Argentina*, RG 59, NA, microform set M69/R5; John Randolph Clay to Daniel Webster, 8 April 1852, *Despatches from Peru*, RG 59, NA, microform set T52/R9; John Williamson to John Forsyth, 13 February 1837, *Despatches from Venezuela*, RG 59, NA, microform set M79/R2; William Harris to James Buchanan, 17 October 1847, 14 July 1846, 15 January 1849, 16 May 1847, *Despatches from Argentina*, RG 59, NA, microform set M69/R7.

9. James Pickett to John Forsyth, 4 January 1840, *Despatches from Peru*, RG 59, NA, microform set T52/R5; James Bowlin to William Marcy, 3 January 1856, *Despatches from Colombia*, RG 59, NA, microform set T33/R13; William Harris to James Buchanan, 10 October 1846, *Despatches from Argentina*, RG 59, NA, microform set M69/R6; Richard Pollard to John Forsyth, 17 August 1836, *Despatches from Chile*, RG 59, NA, microform set M10/R4.

10. Buchanan to Jewett, 1 June 1846, *Instructions to Peru*, RG 59, NA, microform set M77/R130.

11. U.S. Congress, House, *Reports of the Commission Appointed Under an Act of Congress Approved July 7, 1884 . . .* , House Executive Document No. 50, 49th Cong., 1st sess., 1886, pp. 23–24.

12. Huntington Wilson, "The Relation of Government to Foreign Investment," *Annals of the American Academy of Political and Social Science* 68 (November 1916): 301.

13. The Dawson agreements are reprinted in U.S., Department of State, *Papers Relating to the Foreign Relations of the United States, 1911* (hereafter FRUS), Washington, DC: GPO, 1918, pp. 652–653.

14. Elliott Northcott to Knox, 11 May 1911, 817.00/1575, RG 59, NA, microform set M632/R10.

15. U.S. Congress, Senate, Committee on Foreign Relations, *Foreign Loans*, 69th Cong., 2d sess., 1927, p. 35.

16. Jefferson to Lansing, 10 August 1916, 817.00/2465; Admiral William Caperton, "Review of Conditions," 16 September 1916, 817.00/2510; the warning message is Lansing to Jefferson, 25 August 1916, 817.00/2475a; Report of Admiral

William Caperton, Commander in Chief, U.S. Pacific Fleet, 24 September 1916, enclosed with Josephus Daniels to Lansing, 14 October 1916, 817.00/2150, all in RG 59, NA, microform set M632/R16.

17. Memorandum from J. Butler Wright, Acting Chief, Division of Latin American Affairs, 28 February 1916, 817.00/2435 1/2, RG 59, NA, microform set M632/R15; Jefferson to Lansing, 21 September 1916, 817.00/2493, RG 59, NA, microform set M632/R16.

18. *Pittsburgh Post Gazette*, 6 December 1929, p. 11; *New York Herald Tribune*, 7 December 1929, p. 11.

19. Colby to Jefferson, 15 December 1920, 817.00/2745, RG 59, NA, microform set M632/R18.

20. Munro to Francis White, 19 November 1923, 817.00/2989; Hughes to Thurston, 29 May 1924, 817.00/3078a; Hughes to Thurston, 5 June 1924, 817.00/3079, all RG 59, NA, microform set M632/R20; for the reports of irregularities and intimidation, see Thurston to Hughes, 29 October 1924, 817.00/3199, and especially 5 November 1924, 817.00/3222, both RG 59, NA, microform set M632/R21.

21. Kellogg to secretary of the navy, 24 August 1926, "Memorandum: The Nicaraguan Situation," 1 December 1926, 817.00/4169, RG 59, NA, microform set M632/R29, p. 15. For the complex details of Díaz's restoration, see aforementioned memorandum.

22. Stimson to Coolidge, 4 May 1927, 817.00/4753, RG 59, NA, microform set M632/R32; *Stimson Diary*, 3 May 1927, Stimson Papers, Yale University.

23. Stimson to Coolidge, 4 May 1927, 817.00/4753, RG 59, NA, microform set M632/R32.

24. Kellogg to Eberhardt, 18 July 1927, 817.00/4936, RG 59, NA, microform set M632/R34.

25. Eberhardt to Kellogg, 20 July 1927, 817.00/4940, RG 59, NA, microform set M632/R34.

26. Kellogg to McCoy, 3 March 1928, 817.00/5444a, RG 59, NA, microform set M632/R38.

27. Hanna to White, 28 October 1932, 817.1051/701 1/2, RG 59, NA, microform set M1273/R23.

28. Arthur Bliss Lane to Willard Beaulac, 27 July 1935, Box 61, Folder 1102, Arthur B. Lane Papers, Yale University.

29. Somoza to Roosevelt, 23 December 1944, *FRUS* 1945, 9: 1194.

30. Memorandum of conversation with Sevilla-Sacasa, 17 December 1945, *FRUS* 1945, 9: 1230.

31. Willard L. Beaulac, *The Fractured Continent: Latin America Close-Up* (Stanford: Hoover Institution Press, 1980), 212.

32. "Y" [pseud. Louis Halle, Jr.], "On A Certain Impatience with Latin America," *Foreign Affairs* 28 (July 1950): 565–569.

33. "Memorandum of Discussion at the 237th Meeting of the National Security Council, Washington, February 17, 1955," *FRUS* 1955–1957, 6: 4–5.

34. *Congressional Record*, 8 August 1957, p. 14149.

35. Nixon's memorandum of his 19 April 1959 meeting with Castro is reprinted in *Diplomatic History* 4 (Fall 1980): 426–431.

36. Edwin M. Martin, "Cuba, Latin America, and Communism," Department of State *Bulletin* 49 (14 October 1963): 581.

37. *PPP, Ronald Reagan, 1983*, p.1044.

38. *Weekly Compilation of Presidential Documents* 20 (May 14, 1984): 667–678.

39. Hanna to White, 28 October 1932, 817.1051/701 1/2, RG 59, NA, microform set M1273/R23.

2

Hemispheric Domains: 1898 and the Origins of Latin-Americanism

Julio Ramos

—En Pan-Am mi pana fui y salí
Marvin Santiago

WORLDINGS

Today, many of the barracks and military commissaries that line Gailard Avenue are almost empty, cleared of the supplies and soldiers that once occupied them. A humid breeze brushes by, pregnant with resignation and abandonment. Until recently, Fort Clayton had been one of the centers of the North American military presence in the Panama Canal. Now neither the corps of military engineers nor the high officials of the Southern Command are accountable for the buildings and remnants of military supplies strewn along Gailard Avenue, archaeological pieces of another time.

The year 1999, the cutoff date for the U.S. Army to comply fully with the conditions stipulated by the Carter–Torrijos Treaty in 1977, has come and gone. These stipulations effectively transferred this property—not to mention the inter-oceanic administration of the Panama Canal—to the Panamanian government.[1] At the time of the treaty's conception, General Omar Torrijos feared that the very sovereignty of the national (Panamanian) state was at stake. Perhaps this is the reason he failed to consider certain details of the transfer: what his government would have to do, for example, with the useless weight of the trucks and military jeeps parked on the side streets of the old Clayton base. One needs to bear such details in mind to imagine why the Southern Command rendered $370 million to the Panamanian economy in repayment for the U.S. withdrawal, a whopping 8 percent of Panama's gross national product.[2] Even more uncertain (and less ascertainable) is the fate of the local and informal economies—the cottage garment industries, food production enterprises, domestic services, and prostitution, to cite a number of examples—that have proliferated around the military complex since 1900. It was then that Theodore Roosevelt identified the Panama Canal as the very heart of a new aperture for the United States into the Caribbean, South America, the Pacific, and a new planetary order.[3]

Times have changed; and the maps have changed colors. After the end of the Cold War, the military presence in the Canal no longer had the same meaning that it had throughout the first decades of the century, when it was in effect considered essential to both the "security" of North American hegemony in the central zone of the Caribbean, and to the expansion of finance capital and global trade. Hence the marked contrast between the utopian dreams elaborated around the techno-medico–military-financial apparatus of the Canal at the time of its inauguration in 1914, and the recent abandonment of Fort Clayton, where the grass grows to almost seven feet today. Perhaps the traveler who reported such a sight meant to suggest that after the North American withdrawal from the Isthmus of Panama, the same forest that had been contained for almost a century—dominated without respite by engineering and tropical medicine in a permanent war against mosquitoes, yellow fever, and malaria—has impetuously returned.[4]

It was in Panama that the new colonial science of tropical medicine was institutionalized, committed to proving to the world that "even the most remote tropical localities would soon be centers of white civilization, as powerful and cultured as every other that exists in the temperate zones."[5] Of course, the genealogy of this science brings us to the Spanish–American War, particularly in Cuba, where the insect bites and terror of contagion wreaked more havoc and caused more deaths among the North American soldiers than the weapons of the Spanish army. The taking of San Juan Hill in Santiago, Cuba may have brought into relief the symbolic dimension of military heroism, but it distracts us from that more minimalist (and certainly in the long run more decisive) scenario involving the war against the mosquitoes in the history of medico-military colonization inaugurated in the Spanish–American War. For this war was also a bio-war without precedent in the history of imperialism in that it placed hygiene and public health at the very heart of colonial discourse, deploying new forms of domination based on the administration of bodies.[6] It was this war that continued long after Roosevelt and the Rough Riders victoriously withdrew from Cuba. The medico–military complex founded new Departments of Health in Cuba, the Philippines, and Puerto Rico, and immediately extended its dominion to Panama. Here, the construction of the Canal was made possible (at least in part) by the intense and successful intervention of tropical medicine under the charge of Colonel W.C. Gorgas, an 1898 war veteran.[7] Colonel Gorgas is thus an emblematic figure of a complex colonial apparatus, a point of intersection among financial and technological interests, and military and medical knowledge. This leads us to place both the War of 1898 and the construction of the Panama Canal in the wider context of a new *worlding* of the world—a new planetary order, reconfigured by the modern turn-of-the-century *tecne*.[8]

As an inter-oceanic passage and point of articulation between the North and South, the Canal was as much an effect as a condition of possibility for such a worlding. In fact, it was constructed by nearly forty thousand migrant workers hailing from Jamaica, Martinique, Costa Rica, Guatemala, Trinidad, and Guadalupe, not to mention China, Scandinavia, and Galicia—a heterogeneous or *discrepant* cosmopolitan force (as anthropologist James Clifford would say) that inhabited and labored in a profoundly transnational zone of contact. That zone of contact was maintained under the strong-arm control of an elaborate police apparatus that monitored and partitioned the area in accordance with a strictly stratified order of castes. The violence of imperial racism can thus be found at the very base of the modern project of worlding, undermining any other libertarian or dialogical assertion of global(izing) "contact."[9] Henry Franck, a member of the police force during that time, candidly recalls the racial and linguistic hierarchies in the small world articulated and compacted by the project of constructing the Canal:

Here are the Basques in their Goinas, preferring their native "Euscarra" to Spanish; French "niggers," and English "niggers," whom it is to the interest of peace and order to keep as far apart as possible; occasionally a few sunburned blond men in a shovel gang, but they prove to be Teutons or Scandanavians [*sic*]; laborers of every color and degree—except American laborers, more than conspicuous by their absence. For the American Negro is an intractable creature in large numbers. . . . [10]

In the epoch of its construction, the Canal was called *The Cut* by its engineers. In accordance with its namesake, the Canal inscribed and coordinated the intersection of forces, tensions, and articulations in a codifying network of a new world. "The history of wars for humanity," Peter Sloterdijk writes, "are seen in a different light when certain wars or kinds of war are placed in relation to the crisis of changes in the larger forms of the world."[11] In the almost immediate aftermath of the 1898 war, the pronouncements of President William McKinley in 1899, and the drive to construct the canal after the Panama secession in 1904, the military-financial–medical–technological complex elaborated a large-scale program of *shrinking* the hemisphere by condensation and compression. Such a program would permanently disrupt those maps and routes traversed by the circulation of capital, and, in turn, the cartography of transcultural currents and the very conception and self-representation of America. In its wake, we saw both the utopic ebullience in the multiple celebrations of the canal, "the new [world] wonder" that would unite the North to the South, the East to the West and the fear of certain critics who remarked on its expansive power—a power that was intimately linked to the emergence of a new empire. These attitudes were best represented by Theodore Roosevelt, on the one hand, with his peculiar Pan-Americanist ideal, and on the other hand, by those *Latinoamericanistas*, Latin-Americanists, committed to keeping watch over the borders of "Our America." Hence, the marked contrast between the utopian mission to shrink the hemisphere at the turn of twentieth century and the reconfiguration of coordinates and maps—the form of the world—at the turn of our own. For now, let it suffice to say that the gradual withdrawal of North American troops from Fort Clayton and the handing over of the Canal to the Panamanian government in 1999 closed the history of an entire epoch, and with it a specific mode of colonial domination.

New problems have since emerged. For example, there is the question of what to do with the abandoned buildings strung across Gailard Avenue and where to relocate all of the seemingly useless military surplus. Some of the scrap metal, recycled or perhaps resemanticized, might travel north, where it could possibly serve to add height and thickness to the Tortilla Wall—a wall designed to contain the immigratory flux along the U.S.–Mexico border. At its terminal point in California, one finds tons of recycled scrap metal, refunctionalized remnants of the Gulf War, as if blown there by magic by the terrible wind of Desert Storm.

The solution proposed in 1994 by Panamanian president Ernesto Pérez Balladares and his administration would have been costly—$50 million at the outset alone. But at least it would initiate a new beginning to another stage in the life of a post-Cold War Panamanian society beset with, among other things, the challenge of recovering the now-missing 8 percent (by conservative estimates) of the gross national product. One profound believer in the Pan-Americanist network of power and intervention, minister Gabriel Lewis, proposed a new *Universidad Americana*, similar to that of Cairo or Beirut. "We hope to replace North American soldiers with an international army of students and professors," he said in an interview. "Where before troops were trained for battle, we hope to soon educate the best Latin-American academics and professionals. I can't imagine a better use for these operations."[12] The military barracks would be reoccupied and converted into student housing and the old club for military officials transformed into a comfortable faculty club for the distinguished professorate of a new university complex. Such a complex would easily accommodate more than 2,500 students from the North and the South; their future *alma mater* would be Fort Clayton, where throughout the terrifying decade of the 1970s the North American army trained South and Central American military officers. Yet without entirely abandoning the utopian resonance this central zone has held since the turn of the century, the university was to be called the *Ciudad del Saber* (City of Knowledge), a new point of conjuncture in the reconfiguration of inter-American hemispheric space. It would provide a new hinge that would affirm regional unity—but not as an effect of engineering, hygiene, or military intervention, as Theodore Roosevelt would have had it at the turn of the last century. Rather, its integrity would be based on what is perhaps a more solid foundation in the long run—academic exchange and the formation of Pan-Americanist subjects in the City of Knowledge.

Of course, the source of funds to finance the new Pan-American university remains unclear, which leads one to doubt the viability of such a project in this period marked by a profound crisis in higher education. In any case, the City of Knowledge situates us at once before the current discussion of the political roles of inter-American intellectual exchange in the context of the changing relations between the North and the South. Such a discussion seems imperative today, now that the system of domination inaugurated at the turn of the past century, in the emblematic moments of the War of 1898 and the invention of the state of Panama in 1904, seems to be drawing to a close.

GLOBALIZATION OF KNOWLEDGE AND THE PRESENT CRISIS OF *LATINOAMERICANISMO*

This exergue brings us to the contemporary discussion of the difficult place of knowledge and discourse of regional identity, as well as the dislocation of Latin-Americanist subjects confronted with the impact of gradual denationalization and the globalization of knowledge from or about Latin America. Inspired by the now classic genealogy of Orientalism proposed by Edward Said, the current discussion of Latin-Americanism reflects on its conditions of production and the possibility of articulating a specific set of discourses.[13] Such an investigation begins not only with the rhetorical texture of discourses on Latin American difference but also with its institutional and disciplinary foundations.[14] The crisis of Latin-Americanism marks a moment of self-reflection and self-critique in the history of a discursive and disciplinary field that questions the very territorialized categories and geopolitics that sustain it. As in the case of Said, the investigation of the Latin-Americanist archive in itself implies the critique of the inescapable relationship between, on the one hand, the discourse and knowledge of difference—including the identification of the Latin American "other"—and, on the other hand, the insertion of such heterologies into the specific formations of metropolitan power.

The analogy between Orientalism, as Said understands it, and Latin-Americanist discourses has generated many discussions and self-critiques of the field. Yet transplanting Said's thesis to the field of Latin American studies also obscures the multiplicity of subjects and discursive positions that intersect with the concept of *Latinoamericanismo*, Latin-Americanism. For

example, the critique of Latin-Americanism as a field of knowledge tied to
the history of international studies in European or North American universities neglects the problematic history of vernacular *Latinoamericanismo* as
an interpellative discourse produced by Latin American intellectuals.[15] Perhaps for strategic reasons, Said concerns himself primarily with delimiting
his object in the archive of knowledge and discourse that has constructed
and placed "the Orient" on the maps of European identity. He concerns
himself less with the interwoven network of intersections between the multiplicity of orientalisms produced in cultural institutions and the "occidental" European social imaginary, not to mention those in the Arab countries
themselves. To put it another way, the history of Nasser and a pan-Arabic
cultural nationalism constructs its own archive apart from the European
imaginary, as well as tropes and strategies of geopolitical differentiation
and identification. In the same way, the present concern with the nature of
Latin Americanist knowledge and power frequently obscures the key
distinction between metropolitan formations and those vernacular identifi-
catory discourses that—at least since José Martí and, even more important,
the Spanish-American War—have postulated either various defenses of the
local, of one's "own" specificity, or emancipatory programs of "Our America," at different conjunctures of globalization and the "worlding" of the
world. Such are the formations of vernacular Latin-Americanisms, criss-
crossed by multiple wills to power and framed by claims to authenticity that
seem problematic to us today.

And yet, by making the distinction between a metropolitan Latin-
Americanism and the vernacular defenses of regional specificity, in no way
do I attempt to dissolve the gray areas that relativize the borders separating
the "metropolitan" and the "vernacular"—borders that are at once porous,
well-traversed, and perforated by continuous migrations and the exile of
vernacular intellectuals. Historically, the exile has played a constitutive role
in metropolitan Latin-Americanism, contributing (from different angles and
diverse political positions) to the invention of Latin America as an object of
Latin American studies in the universities of North America. Such gray areas
destabilize any facile attempt to essentialize the differences between knowledge from or about Latin America and continue to problematize the very
category of "vernacular" discourse, even as they radically undermine the
homogeneity of the metropolitan territories that feel the impact of transnational flows of globalization and contemporary migrations.

Alert and lucid until his final days, Antonio Cornejo Polar was a friend
and colleague at Berkeley who faced the present disjuncture of Latin-
Americanism in a sustained reflection on the borders and frontiers of the
contemporary field. I refer particularly to "Mestizaje e hibridez. Los riesgos
de las metáforas. Apuntes" ("Race Mixture and Hybridity. Risks of the
Metaphors. Comments"), his final contribution to the Latin American Studies Association (LASA). The paper was read in absentia at the international

convention celebrated in Guadalajara in March 1997, just two months prior to Cornejo's death in Lima.[16] What follows is a brief examination of this text that, in more than one sense, concerns the tropes of "ending." As the last piece written by a crucial author whose influence was felt in both vernacular and metropolitan expressions of Latin-Americanism, it alerts us to the possibility of "the unhappy and undignified finale of *hispanoamericanismo*."

It is not by chance that the concerns raised in "Mestizaje e hibridez" connect with the wider historical background of 1898, particularly in the sense that Cornejo's essay can be read as one of the possible closures to a variety of discursive positions that have been posed in the field. In a sense, "Mestizaje e hibridez" broaches the closure of a concept of Latin-American culture and a way of conceiving the tasks of regional knowledge, including the defense of regional borders. One may recall that these tasks were laid out precisely a century ago, with the same set of strategies and responses to the shrinkage of hemispheric space brought to a head in the War of 1898 and the construction of the Panama Canal. It is in this respect that Cornejo's essay reflects doubly on closures: its autobiographical dimension appears to identify the last scene of writing for the author with the closure of an entire discursive field.

Such an association is not an exaggerated one. In various respects, Cornejo can be considered a humanist intellectual of a philological formation, placed in the context of Latin-Americanism, the legacy of the essayists, and the tradition that sustained the work of figures who narrativized the canon and the historical memory of the field that we inhabit today. These figures include Pedro Henríquez Ureña, Alfonso Reyes, and Angel Rama—"public intellectuals," to borrow a phrase, whose activities were not limited to the university, and whose wide field of intervention and political authority presupposed certain ties between culture and the public sphere that are perhaps no longer viable in contemporary neo-liberal societies. Cornejo's own reflection on "the end of Latin-Americanism" thus assumes and reiterates a history of intellectual and academic labor, yet places it in the context of the current crisis characterized by the liberal-republican state in the orbit of globalization. The mere suggestion of a closure to this legacy is one effect of the erosion in those models of cultural integration frequently posed by the humanities and the modern university. At least since Andrés Bello's time, the university has legitimized the production of humanistic knowledge and its pedagogical interventions by defining its function(s) in terms of constructing citizenship in the sphere of interpellations and education in literacy and culture. It would seem that the social formations of *our* turn of the century, marked by the globalization of perpetually "developing" societies, no longer require the legitimizing intervention of those narratives that were taught as tools for national integration. Perhaps the cultural models of national integration—or the notion of integration itself—are no longer necessary, inasmuch as the state has reneged on its "social contracts" to represent the common good. At the same time, systems of mass communication and consumption (to follow García Canclini's argument) continue to produce alternative parameters for defining one's citizenship—both by the exclusions they imply and the awareness of new and growing areas of abandonment.[17] As Beatriz Sarlo reminds us, in the field of cultural institutions (and their successive transformations) tied to the republican state, the very concept of the public intellectual has come under question.[18] The study of literature and culture, in turn, runs the risk of becoming the simple profession of experts, frequently based in the United States, who increasingly replace the evanescent figure of the public intellectual and the traditional Latin-Americanist humanist.

"Mestizaje e hibridez" questions the destiny of Latin-Americanism, "the unhappy and undignified finale of *Hispanoamericanismo.*" In the process, Cornejo Polar's essay summarizes various key positions in the debate on the transnational channels or "canals" of production and the circulation of knowledge from or about Latin America. Written in the shadow of the discourse whose end he explores, Cornejo's text paradoxically reinscribes various tropes of origin, the borders of territoriality, and the continual presence of a legacy—all of which, historically speaking, have been central aspects of Latin-Americanist rhetoric. The essay explores the changing frontiers of the field by considering the proper and improper ways in which the field borrows, translates, and incorporates concepts from other disciplines, even as it questions the legitimacy of exchanges and contacts between itself and other languages and traditions. Cornejo ends by proposing a defense of the borders; in addition, he expresses alarm at the risk to the field's identity or immanence before those forces currently at work that threaten the field's constitution from the "outside"—forces generated by the contact, commingling, and hybridization of discourse itself.

Not coincidentally, in Cornejo's essay, the Althusserian *problematic* of contact and the porosity of borders is first and foremost posed as a question of linguistic order. According to Cornejo, Latin-Americanism currently suffers from a condition of *diglossia*—a profound split that antagonistically separates those studies of Latin America produced in Latin American countries from Latin American studies produced in the United States. Creating a rupture between the interior and the exterior, between the proper and the improper, between the authentic and the inauthentic, diglossia manifests itself first and foremost in the growing prestige of English among Latin-Americanists in the United States, and the supposed crisis of Spanish teaching in North American pedagogy. The passage to English in and of itself would not be a problem, were it not accompanied by the increasing marginalization of vernacular Latin-Americanist knowledge produced in Spanish, in a cultural and ideological circuit entirely distinct and each day more precarious. Moreover, in the context of this linguistic divide, Cornejo reiterates the trajectory of an even more profound and dangerous fracture—the division of labor that converts Latin American cultural objects into raw material exported to the United States and Europe, while metropolitan academic institutions produce epistemological models for theoretical elaboration and the consumption of that cultural raw material.

One need not agree with Cornejo to recognize that "Mestizaje e hibridez: los riesgos de las metáforas" touches the very heart of the contemporary debate on the globalization of Latin American cultures, including the effects of the globalization of knowledge produced about these cultures. Cornejo identifies the crisis of cultural discourses and vernacular institutions in this neo-liberal era, and advises caution before the growing influence, even in Latin America, of metropolitan theoretical paradigms—cultural, postcolonial, and subaltern studies. Cornejo's essay thus sets off a chain of associations and oppositions that can be abbreviated to the antagonism between the local and the global—the interior field and the "outside" of culture—and the contradictions that render problematic the possibility of "regional" knowledge (or discourse of identity) in an increasingly homogenized world. One may add that even intellectual production becomes subordinated to the leveling demands of the market, penetrated by the velocity of transnational travel and impacted by the consequent rapid turnover of ideas. By reiterating the classic question regarding the specificity and originality of American knowledge, "Mestizaje e hibridez" projects itself into the very historical and discursive network of vernacular Latin-Americanism that had motivated Cornejo's essay from the beginning to announce an ending. How does one write at this liminal point of closure? How does a discourse assume the authority to reflect precisely on the crisis that calls all mechanisms of validation and authorization regarding its field into question? From what location and position does one write?

1898 ORIGINS OF LATIN-AMERICANISM AND THE QUESTION OF LOCAL KNOWLEDGE

Beginning with José Martí's foundational essay, "Nuestra América," and the series of texts on Pan-Americanism that prepare and anticipate the writing of that essay in 1891, vernacular Latin-Americanism has often been invoked as a defense of the local in diverse instances of globalization and worlding—hence the assertion that 1898 and the reconfiguration of the hemispheric domain at the turn of the last century marks a decisive moment in the history of Latin-Americanism.[19] Although Martí died in the early months of that same war (which began in 1895, not with the sinking of the U.S. ship *Maine* in 1898), his *Latinoamericanista* essays can indeed be read as an early response to the reconfiguration and displacement of those borders produced by North American expansion following the Civil War and the colonization of the West facilitated by the Mexican–American War in

1848. It is no coincidence that the points of departure for Martí's Latin-Americanist discourse in "Nuestra América," as well as his *Versos sencillos*, would be the intense debate over inter-American relations and specifically, the official pan-Americanism generated around the Pan-American Congress in Washington and its culmination in the 1891 International Monetary Conference.[20] Indeed, I do not believe that the relationship between Martí's texts on the dangers of pan-Americanism—the risks of hemispheric compression—and his own compaction of a "mestizo America," ("our America") has been sufficiently emphasized. It should suffice to recall that his speech entitled "Madre América," a direct antecedent of "Nuestra América," was dedicated as the welcome greeting on behalf of an exile (Martí) to the South American delegates participating in the inter-American conferences, some of whom he met during their stay in New York.[21]

As early as the late 1880s, the North American government, represented by Secretary of State James G. Blaine, proposed a series of inter-American commercial and industrial agreements that would spur the construction of railway and telegraphic networks, along with the relaxation of customhouse and border controls. These pan-American projects were motivated by the ideal of a common currency that would at long last unite the American nations. The new map was to erase once and for all the obstinate boundaries separating the North and South. Such an erasure would make possible the creation of an American power capable of undermining the hegemony of the European powers in the world order. Yet Martí was unmistakably critical of this vision. He identified the condition of modernity with the internationalization not only of capital but also cultural flows. His telluric Americanism thus set forth an alternative vision of modernity—one guided by the knowledge of the *earth*. According to Martí, such knowledge would "guide" and "unite" an alternative hemispheric dominion. Martí's Latin-Americanism operates as a reversal of hegemonic modernity and its "worldings." It emerges, however, from the same historical conjuncture; it becomes displaced in the same space under compression and the same networks of modernity—the market, the intensification of transnational contacts, and the inevitable cultural exchanges of a new cosmopolitan order—articulate it. Hence, Latin-Americanism in its turn would give way to the importance of journalism and the chronicle, texts of those traveler–mediators who traversed the new order, often serving as mediators between the metropolitan cultures and the Latin American reader.[22] It is thus no coincidence that the founders and inheritors of Latin-Americanism begin as travelers and/or exiles: such was the case for Martí, Pedro Henríquez Ureña, Rubén Darío, Alfonso Reyes, and Gabriela Mistral.

In this new, disputed, and unequal space—and in an epoch that historians generally identify with the gradual incorporation of Latin America into the world—the positions of intellectuals became redefined. Their new task was to ascertain the specificity and limits of a field dedicated to their "own, proper" identity; to propose models for cultural contact and translation; and to determine the possibilities and risks of transcultural exchange in a global, cosmopolitan order. Hence the defense of local knowledge and vernacular cultures in Martí may be considered both a critical response to and an effect of the compression of hemispheric space, produced by the intense re-worlding of the Americas. The seizures of Cuba, Puerto Rico, and the Phil-ippines in 1898, as well as the subsequent invention of the state of Panama and the construction of the canal, are events that emblematize that re-worlding. The construction of the canal in particular was at once a trope and a real effect of pan-Americanism, a strange and wondrous emblem that sprang from the new articulations between North and South.

Might it not be said, then, that Latin-Americanism—up until and includ-ing Cornejo and our turn of the century—is a field of investigation into the precarious balance among the cultural formations of international capital and vernacular cultures? Attentive to the varied conjunctures of worlding, the Latin-Americanist subject emerges and institutionalizes his topographic and territorializing imaginary on the frontiers of mediation, separating the zones of contact from the danger zones and deciding the norms for a "sanitary" cultural exchange. "The haughty villager believes that the entire world is his village," Martí once said.[23] Confronting this perspective, the Latin-Americanist subject deploys two interrelated gestures: first, looking "out-side" ("the tiger from the outside," as Martí would say) and then reflecting on the process of globalization; second, looking "within" ("the tiger within") and then reflecting on the internal contradictions that sought to prevent the consolidation of political and civil institutions that would pro-vide the democratic foundation of a virtual American order. Both positions call for mediation and translation. The authority of the emergent Latin-Americanist subject relies on the translation of foreign models, of course, but also on the translation of those obscured and subaltern voices—the "mute masses of *indios*," the "despised Negro," and the "peasant, creator." The gesture of incorporating and representing these other voices authorized and legitimized the aesthetic and intellectual project in the otherwise wide-open field of modern Latin American literature. One might argue that this is still true today. "Speak through my words and my blood," Pablo Neruda writes in "Alturas de Macchu Picchu" ("The Heights of Macchu Picchu").[24] Yet beyond Neruda, Martí, or, more recently, Miguel Barnet, the claim to representativity is one of the foundations of the literary institution and its testimonial vocation: literature endows the other with the "gift" of speech. The Latin-Americanist intellectual thus performs a dual task: he mediates between the world and the local on the one hand, and provides the internal translation necessary for the *construction* of the local, on the other. The latter task involves the invention of a vernacular tradition, along with its alternative legacies.

Yet this gesture of mediation defines only one ostensible pole of Latin-

Americanism. José Enrique Rodó's *Ariel* occupies the other. For Rodó, the War of 1898 and the compression of hemispheric space provided the incentive for a new point of departure. In its polemical and immediate insertion into the emergent field of Latin-Americanism, *Ariel* is a cultural-aesthetic critique of "[North-] Americanization," which Rodó placed in opposition to the alternative of a legacy and archive inspired by the invention of Euro-American Latinism.[25] Of course, Rodó largely avoided the term "cosmopolitan"; and when he did use the word, he used it in a pejorative sense. In *Ariel*, cosmopolitanism is synonymous with foreign influences and related to a popular and working-class immigration that threatened the very integrity of Latin-American "high culture."

Without attempting to minimize the differences, one can nevertheless see how in both Martí and Rodó—whose models are frequently opposed in the historiography of Latin-Americanism—the reflection on the border and the practice of mediation(s) also responds to globalization and the necessity of constructing a Latin American legacy, memory, and archive. Of course, the archives and notions of legacy proposed by Martí and Rodó were on the one hand radically distinct. While Rodó and his followers, at war with "Americanization" and modernity, proposed a Euro–Latin American legacy, Martí founded his identity–narrative on a fiction propelled by subaltern, "autochthonous," or vernacular "voices." Nevertheless, the practices of Latin-Americanist mediation in both cases are based on the varied inflections of a cultural–aesthetic authority that privileges the role of literature in the construction of citizenship, or what Schiller has called "the aesthetic education of man."[26] The intellectual subject in both is called into being and given authority as the one responsible for reflecting on the necessary conditions for a democracy in which cultural–aesthetic representation would satisfy a regulatory principle. Such a role would, for Martí, contribute to the representation of particularity under the stigma of subalternity; for Rodó, it would provide the "aesthetic of conduct" necessary for the self-administration of the soul and the constitution of disciplined subjects. [27]

Indeed, has not the reflection on democracy and the search for regulative principles extended all the way to our present? Wouldn't such a reflection include even the distinctive registers of cultural–aesthetic authority in Beatriz Sarlo and Nelly Richard, for example—both of whom take up, from different political positions, the defense of literature and the aesthetic? For both writers, the aesthetic retains the capacity to present alternative worlds to the instrumental logic of the market and the neo-liberal middle ground, both of which prefigure precisely in postdictatorial contexts and democracies in transition. John Beverley has recently gone so far as to refer to these and other reconfigurations of the aesthetic subject in terms of a "new Arielism."[28] Without a doubt, one must qualify the almost epic heroism ascribed by Sarlo to artists as defenders of an autonomous and critical space in the postmodern scenario, on the one hand, as well as the (political) radicalization of the aesthetic subject in the anarchist, avant-garde discourse of Nelly

Richard, on the other.[29] But there is no doubt that both Sarlo and Richard, who arise from theoretical and writing practices that are quite distinct, assign a certain privilege to aesthetic authority in the ongoing debate on democracy.

Without avoiding the obvious differences, in Martí and Rodó the question of delimiting boundaries of the "proper" in modernity is inescapably tied not only to North American expansionism, but also to the "internal" problem of democracy. Modernity brought about the emergence of new political agents—women and workers, as well as unforeseen social alliances—that pressured the public sphere and forced a rethinking of the intellectual's place, as well as the place of high culture, in societies on the road to modernization. In this respect, it is not coincidental that for many of the new social subjects identified with the relative aperture produced by modernization, the War of 1898 would not necessarily represent a trauma or disaster. As many of the more radical working-class intellectuals of the epoch thought (particularly in the case of Puerto Rico), North-Americanization would, paradoxically, make possible the democratization of the public sphere and the creation of certain conditions and guarantees for the constitution of an anticapitalist working-class movement. Such movements would certainly have held suspect many of the aesthetic–cultural discourses that privileged the mediating and representative role of the intellectual in the defense of nationalism and the Latin-Americanist registers that multiplied after 1898. I refer, for example, to Luisa Capetillo and the libertarian discourses tied to the emergence of the Puerto Rican workers' movement lucidly studied and anthologized by Angel Quintero Rivera.[30]

The working-class intellectuals at the beginning of the twentieth century, that ever-changing and voluble epoch, also intervened in the debate on globalization, producing local knowledge (albeit quite cosmopolitan in nature) and alternative libraries. Taking into consideration the Uruguayan and Argentine context of a nascent vigorous working-class movement at the time, one sees how in *Ariel,* Rodó places the proletarian immigrant subject at the unspoken and terrifying margins of the cultural–aesthetic subject in formation. Martí, on the other hand, became deeply involved with the most politically radical sectors of tobacco-workers and immigrants—many of them anarchists—who constituted the social and financial base of the Cuban Revolutionary Party (PRC) during the period of its establishment.[31] Without a doubt, the grounds of aesthetic authority were profoundly transformed in these arenas. As Martí headed for war (and his death), he cleared new paths for the aestheticization of politics.

The Year 1998

As we have seen, "Mestizaje e hibridez" reinscribes and recalls the tone, the subject-positions, and some of the rhetorical strategies of vernacular Latin-Americanism and its defense of local knowledge. It is organized around the binary of the global and the local; in addition, it traverses and retains the borders that distinguish its "own" territory, advising caution when faced with the borrowings of other disciplines (characteristic of cultural studies and its trans-disciplinary passion) and other languages (especially English). But, in contrast with its antecedents, a certain pessimism in this essay leads the author to suggest that the current impact of globalization may well be decisive in drawing the final curtain on Latin-Americanism. This is perhaps because for Cornejo, as for Sarlo, the current crisis within cultural institutions (and the republican pedagogical apparatus) tends to cancel both the intellectual's representative role and the privilege granted to the cultural–aesthetic project as two forms of authority central to the interpellation of subjects as citizens. Hence, the organizational and legitimizing bases of vernacular Latin-Americanism—the representation of subaltern voices, the construction of models for translation, and the appropriation of foreign materials for the nation's benefit—have definitively lost their viability. To reiterate, this loss comes by way of the crisis of the liberal notion of representativity, as well as the difficulties confronted by any and every reification of the local, of the *proper*, in this epoch of intense globalization.

The globalization of culture is not necessarily new. It may well be considered constitutive of the logic of capital. Yet what has certainly changed is the authority and the institutional basis of those discourses that once (at least until the 1970s and the beginning of the crises of the *Latinoamericanista* left) vigorously responded to the new worldings. As late as 1971, it was still possible for Roberto Fernández Retamar to believe that the cultural–aesthetic realm, the sphere of arts and literature, could satisfy a central, organic role in a territorial defense of culture insofar as it could generate the necessary mediations for the formation of a national popular culture.[32] In his late classic of Latin-Americanism, *Calibán*, this national popular culture represented no less than the crystallization of class warfare.

Still, the categorical oppositions of the metropolis and the periphery, the global and the local, the interior and the outside, the authentic and the inauthentic are radically impacted by the acceleration and intensification of globalization. The phenomenon of continual travel, for example, or the migration of intellectuals and ideas, or, the more recent critical interventions of Chicano, Puerto Rican, and Latino critics and students in the field of Latin-Americanism shake the foundations of territorial representation. These have produced subjects whose vital experiences and intellectual labor either introduce new tensors or at times cross paths with the old, cutting diagonally across those territorializing notions of roots, linguistic purity, fixed origins, or continuous legacies that still manifest themselves today as tropes of vernacular Latin-Americanism. If we believe that Latin-Americanism is, after all, a complex archive of discourses on territoriality and locality—discourses that attempt to define the specificity of their objects in terms of regional or geopolitical difference—we can today question the efficacy and viability of those modes whose task it once was to draw lines and boundaries over the field of identity. Such a project is particularly imperative in an epoch wherein the transnational flows of flexible capital have violently thrown open zones of contact and exchange, while the mass migrations of Caribbeans, Mexicans, and Central Americans have produced enclaves of speech and Spanish culture at the very heart of the key metropoles in the United States. Perhaps it is not entirely imprudent for us to ask, along with Tato Laviera, if Manhattan is not, after all, an island in the Antillean archipelago; or if Loaiza is a barrio of the Lower East Side. Perhaps it is not inappropriate to wonder where Latin America, a locality mapped and protected by discourses of territorial identity, is now.

Neither is it extraneous to recall that in Washington, DC one hundred years after the invasion of Cuba and Puerto Rico in 1898, the relative Caribbeanization and Latinization of the very urban area that situates today's discussion on North and South rearticulations challenges any facile, monolingual notion of juridical citizenship, as well as any attempt to perpetuate the maps and inflexible territorial categories institutionalized by the discourses of vernacular identity.

NOTES

The author wishes to acknowledge the able assistance of John D. Blanco in the translation of this chapter into English.

1. For the full text of the 1997 Panama Canal (Carter–Torrijos) Treaty, see Library of Congress, "Appendix B: Texts of the Panama Canal Treaties with United States Senate Modifications–Panama," at *http://lcweb2.loc.gov/frd/cs/panama/pa_appnb.html*, 1–22.

2. Colin Woodard, "In a Swap of Sword for Pen, Panama wants U.S. Base to Be Knowledge City," *Christian Science Monitor*, 10 June 1997.

3. For a history of the Canal's construction and its representations, see David McCullough, *The Path Between the Seas: The Creation of the Panama Canal 1870–1914* (New York: Simon and Schuster, 1977).

4. Calvin Sims, "Filling the Void and the Bases in Panama," *New York Times*, 30 October 1994, pt. IV, 5: 1. Stella H. Nida has an interesting series of historical anecdotes on the war against the mosquitoes in *Panama and Its 'Bridge of Water'* (Chicago: Rand McNally and Co., 1913).

5. Report of Colonel Dr. W.C. Gorgas, who was a member of the Isthmanian Canal Commission and later head of the Department of Health in Panama. Cited by Charles F. Adams, *The Panama Canal Zone: An Epochal Event in Sanitation* (Boston: Proceedings of the Massachusetts Historical Society, 1911), 27. For a suggestive exploration of the body–technology relationship, as well as technologized bodies, in the imperialist discourses at the turn of the twentieth century (particularly throughout the construction of the Canal and during the Panama–Pacific Exposition celebrated in San Francisco in 1915), see Bill Brown, "Science Fiction, the World's Fair, and the Prosthetics of Empire, 1910–1915" in Amy Kaplan and Donald Pease, eds.,

Cultures of United States Imperialism (Durham: Duke University Press, 1993), 129–163.

6. I refer to the concept of "noso-politics" and "bio-power" discussed in Michel Foucault, "The Politics of Health in the Eighteenth Century," in *Power/Knowledge: Selected Interviews and Other Writings 1972–1977*, ed. Colin Gordon (New York: Pantheon Books, 1980); and *The History of Sexuality. Volume I: An Introduction*, trans. Robert Hurley (New York: Vintage Books, 1990), 139–143. For an analysis of the politics of health as a series of devices for ordering society and the nation, see Julio Ramos, "A Citizen Body: Cholera in Havana (1832)," *Dispositio* 19:46 (1994), 179–195. Special issue on "Subaltern Studies in Latin America," ed. José Rabasa (published 1996).

7. Gorgas recounts his experiences in Cuba and Panama in William Crawford Gorgas, *Sanitation in Panama* (New York: Appleton, 1915).

8. On *tecne* as an operation of inscription and the creation of "worlds" as discursive constructs, see M. Heidegger, "The Question of Technology" and his critique of the category of the "conception" or "vision of the world" in "Comments on Karl Jaspers's Psychology of World-Views," *Pathmarks*, ed. W. McNeill (Cambridge: Cambridge University Press, 1998), 1–38.

9. See Michael Taussig's brief analysis of the construction of the Canal in *Mimesis and Alterity: A Particular History of the Senses* (New York: Routledge, 1993).

10. Harry Franck, *Things as They Are in Panama* (London: T. Fisher Unwin, 1913), 119.

11. Peter Sloterdijk, *En el mismo barco* (Madrid: Ediciones Siruela, 1994), 81.

12. Cited in Sims, "Filling the Void."

13. See Edward Said, *Orientalism* (New York: Vintage Books, 1979), 12. For Said, Orientalism involves:

a *distribution* of geopolitical awareness into aesthetic, scholarly, economic, sociological, historical, and philological texts; it is an *elaboration* not only of a basic geographical distinction (the world is made up of two unequal halves, Orient and Occident) but also of a whole series of 'interests' which . . . it not only creates but also maintains; it *is*, rather than expresses a certain *will* or *intention* to understand, in some cases to control, manipulate, even to incorporate what is a manifestly different . . . world; it is, above all, a discourse that is by no means in direct, corresponding relationship with political power in the raw, but rather is produced and exists in an uneven exchange with various kinds of power" (Italics in text).

14. Some recent studies of this field include Alberto Moreiras, "Fragmentos globales: latinoamericanismo de segundo orden" in *Teorías sin disciplina (latinoamericanismo, poscolonialidad, y globalización en debate)*, ed. Santiago Castro-Gómez y Eduardo Mendieta (México: Miguel Ángel Porrúa, 1998), also available online at *http://ensayo.rom.uga.edu/critica/teoria/castro/moreiras.html*); Román de la Campa, *Latin Americanism* (Minneapolis: University of Minnesota Press, 1999); and Julio Ramos, *Divergent Modernities: Culture and Politics in Nineteenth-Century Latin America*, trans. John D. Blanco (Durham, NC: Duke University Press, 2001).

15. Vicente Rafael explores the politics of knowledge in constructing geopolitical difference: see "The Cultures of Area Studies in the United States," *Social Text* 41 (Winter 1994), 91–111. See also Moreiras, "Fragmentos." For an analysis of vernacular Latin-Americanism as a discourse of identity, see Ramos, "Mass Culture and

Latin-Americanism" and "'Our America': the Art of Good Government" in *Divergent Modernities*.

16. This essay appeared in *Revista de crítica literaria latinoamericana* 24:47 (1998): 7–11. I examine this text more fully in "Genealogías de la moral latinoamericanista. El cuerpo y la deuda de Flora Tristán," in Mabel Moraña, ed., *Nuevas perspectivas desde/sobre América Latina: el desafío de los estudios culturales* (Santiago: Editorial Cuarto Propio, 2000).

17. Nestor García Canclini, *Consumidores y ciudadanos. Conflictos multiculturales de la globalización* (Mexico City: Grijalbo, 1995).

18. Beatriz Sarlo, *Escenas de la vida posmoderna: intelectuales, arte y videocultura en la Argentina* (Buenos Aires: Ariel, 1994), 181.

19. Arcadio Díaz Quiñones has shown how the crisis of Spanish imperialism that culminated in 1898 was also decisive for the formation of Hispanism and its literary histories. In fact, up to this day Hispanism maintains a certain acceptance in U.S. Hispanic studies, wherein Latin American literature frequently appears as one of many offshoots of a Spanish Castilian and imperial history inaugurated by *El Cid Campeador*. See Arcadio Díaz Quiñones, "1898: Hispanismo y guerra," in Walther L. Bernecker, ed., *1898: su significado para Centroamérica y el Caribe* (Berlin: Vervuert Verlag, 1998), 17–35.

20. I am referring here to the texts on the International and Monetary Conferences held in Washington, DC (1899), included in José Martí, *Nuestra América* (Caracas: Biblioteca Ayacucho, 1977), 35–132.

21. José Martí, "Madre América" in Martí, *Nuestra América*, 19–26.

22. On the role of the traveler–mediator and the import-journeys conducted by them, see Ramos, *Divergent Modernities*, esp. "Limits of Autonomy" (ch. 4).

23. Martí, "Nuestra América" in *Nuestra América*,, 26–33.

24. Pablo Neruda, *Alturas de Macchu Picchu* (Santiago: Ediciones de Librería Negra, 1947), pt. 12.

25. José Enrique Rodó, *Ariel* (Caracas: Biblioteca Ayacucho, 1976). First published in 1900.

26. Friedrich Schiller, *On the Aesthetic Education of Man in a Series of Letters*, trans. Reginald Snell (New York: Frederick Ungar Publishing Co., 1983). First published in 1795.

27. On the other hand, one must not reduce the complexities of the aesthetic subject. Rodó himself, for example, maintains a very ambiguous relationship with the aesthetic and the rhetorical "excesses" of literature, which he opposes at times to the priority of a desired "manhood" ["energía viril"] for the citizen–subject. See Rodó, *Ariel*, 51.

28. John Beverley, comment at the symposium, New Perspectives on/from Latin America: The Challenges of Cultural Studies, at the University of Pittsburgh from 29 to 31 March 1998.

29. Sarlo, *Escenas*; Nelly Richard, *Residuos y metáforas: ensayos de crítica cultural sobre el Chile de la transición* (Providencia, Santiago [Chile]: Editorial Cuarto Propio, 1998).

30. Angel Quintero Rivera, *Workers' Struggle in Puerto Rico: A Documentary History*, trans. Cedric Belfrage (New York: Monthly Review Press, 1976); Luisa Capetillo, *Amor y anarquía: los escritos de Luisa Capetillo*, ed. Julio Ramos (Río Piedras, Puerto Rico: Huracán, 1992).

31. See in particular Martí's two speeches delivered in Tampa (1891), popularly known under the titles "Con todos y para el bien de todos" and "Los pinos nuevos." José Martí, "Discursos" in *Sus mejores páginas*, ed. Raimundo Lazo (Mexico City: Editorial Porrúa, S.A., 1985), 54–64.

32. Roberto Fernández Retamar, *Calibán: apuntes sobre la cultura en nuestra América* (Mexico City: Editorial Diogenes, 1971).

3

Challenges to U.S. Economic Imperialism, 1915–1930: The Case of the Women's International League for Peace and Freedom

Carrie A. Foster

Founded in 1915 as the Woman's Peace Party (WPP) by social worker Jane Addams, the Women's International League for Peace and Freedom (WILPF) became an important part of an active peace movement both in the United States and overseas in the two decades between World Wars I and II. While not the only antiwar organization composed solely of women, the WILPF was firmly entrenched by 1925 as the only sizeable women's peace group that had a broadly based program of action for peace and justice and was intent on direct political action to achieve these goals. In this struggle, a determined coalition of pacifists and antiwar groups focused on three main objectives in the latter half of the 1920s: to eliminate government protection of private business investment abroad, to obtain global support for the idea of making war an international crime as the first step toward universal disarmament, and to ensure disarmament in the United States and overseas.

Although many historians have characterized the nation's peace movement in the interwar period as a part of a prevalent mood of isolationism, the facts of the matter do not warrant such a conclusion, particularly in the case of the WILPF. In pursuing its goals from the mid-1920s through the early 1930s, the WILPF was one of only two U.S. peace groups to be truly internationally organized, the other being the Fellowship of Reconciliation (FOR).

Despite efforts by the War Department to divide American women over the issue of national loyalty by the mid-1920s, the peace movement emerged stronger and more active than ever. Most numerous were the moderate and radical pacifist organizations, which included the women's groups—the WILPF, the Women's Peace Society (WPS), and the Women's Peace Union (WPU)—as well as the War Resisters League, which was founded in 1924 by Tracy Mygatt, Frances Witherspoon, and Jessie Wallace Hughan and included both men and women. Also important among pacifists were the American Friends Service Committee (AFSC); the American branch of the FOR, founded in 1915 by a group of Quakers, YMCA officials, and Social Gospel clergymen; and the Committee on Militarism in Education, created in 1924 by FOR leaders to combat military training in the schools. Liberal but generally non-pacifist reformers in the National Conference on the Cause and Cure of War (NCCCW) and the National Council for Prevention of War (NCPW) formed the second group, and the more conservative internationalists of the League of Nations Non-Partisan Association (1923), the Carnegie Endowment for the International Peace (1910), and the Foreign Policy Association (formerly the League of Free Nations Association of 1918 but renamed in 1921) composed the third.

Ideologically, all three wings were opposed to war as a method of settling international disputes; however, where the conservative internationalists emphasized collective security and thus the threat, if not the use, of coercion in the quest for peace, pacifists focused on the nonviolent creation of economic, political, and social justice to remove the causes of war. Liberal reformers tended to oscillate between the other two positions, depending on the issue and strategy involved. There was also a good deal of overlap between one wing and another, both organizationally and individually. The WILPF, FOR, and AFSC, for example, were all members of the NCPW, and individual members of the WILPF were also members of one or more of the women's organizations that composed the NCCCW.

The glue that held them all together in one very vocal and active peace movement in the 1920s was their belief, as peace historian Charles De-Benedetti has put it, that "peace was the necessary reform."[1] This confidence that peace was right, desirable, and necessary forged a positive, energetic drive to persuade the electorate and its governmental representatives to embark upon a systematic program of creating a climate internationally to give peace a chance. Such a program involved the interrelated issues of disarmament, outlawry of war, and mechanisms of a global nature to establish international communication and cooperation, such as the League of Nations and a World Court. And because economic instability within nations created political instability that could lead to war, a program for peace meant confronting the problem of economic inequity between and among nations, as well as the related issue of economic imperialism.

It was a formidable task that peace seekers set for themselves, and the immediate postwar period was not auspicious for ultimate success. Party politics played upon American anger, resentment, and frustration over the peace settlement to cause the rejection of the Treaty of Versailles and U.S.

membership in the League of Nations. The military's attack upon the peace movement and women's organizations had been part of the same phenomenon.[2] Yet there were hopeful signs as well. Coalition politics among peace advocates pushed the Harding administration into the Washington Naval conference. That resulted in some degree of naval arms reduction, as well as a moratorium on additional buildup. Not long thereafter, the president came out publicly in support of U.S. membership in the World Court (the League of Nations' Permanent Court of International Justice). Should the United States agree to participate in the Court, reasoned peace reformers, perhaps U.S. membership in the League would not be far behind.

Regardless of the issue involved, cooperation among the three wings of the peace movement was more prevalent in the pro-peace effort of the 1920s than during the antiwar struggle of the 1930s. The most significant example of such coalition politics in the postwar decade was the formation in 1927 of a group of more than thirty organizations to work for a peaceful resolution of the growing crisis between the United States and Central America. This crisis was the result of over two decades of smoldering resentment against "Yankee imperialism" in Mexico and Nicaragua, resentment that had been exacerbated by U.S. policymakers.

U.S. economic imperialism was at the heart of the problem, not only in regard to Latin America but also in terms of U.S. foreign policy as a whole in the interwar period. U.S. leaders envisioned an international order wherein each and every nation would keep an "open door" through which the capitalist businessman could come and go at will, whether in search of cheaper raw materials, new markets, or areas of investment. This "Open Door World" would be controlled by the industrial–creditor nations—Great Britain, France, the United States, Germany, Italy, and Japan—all of which, asserted diplomatic historian William Appleman Williams, shared a "community of ideals, interests, and purposes" under the domination of the strongest among them, the United States.[3]

Peace and stability throughout the world were absolutely essential to the success of this "Open Door" vision. Therefore, it would be necessary for these "great powers" to police the underdeveloped areas of the world to ensure that nationalistic revolutions did not occur; such upheavals interrupted the free flow of trade and, if allowed to succeed, might cause reform-minded governments in those Third World countries to embark upon policies detrimental to the economic and financial interests of the industrial–creditor nations. Ideally, as Williams pointed out, this "commercial conquest of the world" would not come as the result of military force, but rather by "political intervention of the subtle and behind-the-scenes variety that would not arouse the antagonism of the natives or the American public."[4]

The WILPF viewed economic imperialism of whatever variety as one of the most serious threats to world peace because the government of a creditor nation invariably used the indebtedness of weaker countries "to acquire control over those countries" and because private business interests of the creditor nation relied upon government support "to secure their ventures." For both reasons, the WILPF perceived that economic imperialism was "big with menace."[5] In the former case it was a matter of the weak being exploited by the strong, and this was morally unacceptable; in the latter instance, imperialistic policies could too easily result in military coercion—that is, war.

There was a philosophical issue at stake here as well, one that had to do with the quality of life rather than with the quantity of things. As WILPF leader Madeleine Z. Doty observed, "The competitive struggle to acquire possession of things has always been a cause of violence." Although she had enthusiastically supported it, she pointed to the Russian Revolution as an example of this struggle. "The thing that is so disastrous to life," she lamented, "is this willingness of workers and capitalists alike to bring all life down to an economic basis. All morality, all Christianity, all spiritual values are reduced in the last analysis to the economic standard. This spells death to beauty, death to truth, death to life. It seems to me," she concluded, "we women have to set up another standard, a standard that does not make 'economics' the end and all of existence." The implication was clear: The female value system stressed quality of life while the male value system destroyed that quality by a focus on material acquisitiveness.

If U.S. bankers or industrialists decided to invest in foreign countries, then, declared Doty, the WILPF could respond by pointing out to these businessmen that "friendship, understanding, and love are more important than any material possessions." It may be, she acknowledged, that a financier benefits the foreign country by helping to build a railroad. But he does not aid that country "if he brings in the army and navy to protect 'his interests' and kills hundreds of foreigners and Americans alike in the securing for himself the benefit of his investment. Killing men," she asserted emphatically, "is a moral issue. It has got to come right out of the realm of economics."[6]

With these concerns in mind, the WILPF persuaded Senator E.F. Ladd of North Dakota and Rep. Roy O. Woodruff of Michigan to introduce in Congress on 1 December 1924 a resolution on the subject of economic imperialism. Originally drafted by E.C. McGuire of the Institute of Economics—who was reputed to be highly knowledgeable about Latin American affairs—and subsequently modified by Senator Edward Costigan of Colorado at the request of the WILPF upon the suggestion of Senator Ladd, this concurrent resolution provided that, first, "the United States government shall be relieved of all necessity of using the United States army to protect the business man who invests in foreign countries," and second, that "the United States government shall not recognize any arrangement which will commit the country to military intervention in connection with claims against foreign debtors."[7]

The sentiment expressed here was a direct outgrowth of the 1915 Hague

Congress, where women peace activists from around the globe had gathered to protest World War I. Voicing their opinion that "the investments of capitalists of one country in the resources of another and the claims arising therefrom are a fertile source of international complications," they urged that all nations adhere to the principle that such investment be made at the risk of the investor alone, without claim to the protection of his government.[8] An even stronger statement of this policy was made at the WILPF's Board meeting in November 1923 when the women passed the following resolution:

Whereas, powerful business interests of the United States have loaned many millions of dollars in various parts of the world, and,

Whereas, these interests have often called upon our government to protect their investments, and

Whereas, such protection has often resulted in the limitation of the sovereignty of the borrowing nations,

Be it resolved, that we urge upon the Congress of the United States the passage of a bill forbidding the use of the army or navy in collecting private debts or in protecting the investments of private individuals in foreign countries.[9]

By 1924, the WILPF's concern over the issue of governmental support for private business ventures abroad was heightened; by the end of that year more than two decades of U.S. imperialism in Latin America was compounded in the women's minds by the question of "what commitments, on the part of the United States, the Dawes Plan may involve in case the bonds should be defaulted on."[10] Formally announced in early 1924, the Dawes Plan involved U.S. loans to Germany for reconstruction, as well as for German reparation payments to England and France.

During the 1920s, the plan was just one in a series of attempts by U.S. policymakers to promote a peaceful, stable world conducive to the economic well-being of U.S. business enterprise. The Dawes Plan was important from the U.S. point of view if for no other reason than it would get Germany back on her feet so that she might join the other industrial–creditor nations in a stable world order geared to the growth and prosperity of capitalism. In addition, the financial experts who designed the plan ensured that German economic stabilization would bring a tidy sum into the coffers of U.S. banking institutions such as J.P. Morgan and Company, which agreed to underwrite $110 million of the initial $200 million loan.

Not without validity did the WILPF, among others, see this plan as a blatant example of the most undesirable kind of economic imperialism.[11] The major concern of the women pacifists was whether the bankers would insist on U.S. military intervention to collect their millions in the event that German prosperity did not materialize to the degree anticipated. Given that such a pattern had developed over the years in Latin America, where U.S.

armed forces had intervened twenty-one times between 1898 and 1924, the WILPF had cause for alarm.[12] Certain members of Congress shared this concern, so the WILPF-sponsored bill, now Senate Resolution No. 22, forbidding the use of the U.S. military to secure the foreign investments of U.S. business, was introduced immediately upon the convening of the 68th Congress in December 1924.

As part of their campaign to get the resolution translated into legislation, WILPF leaders urged their members to write their senators and representatives, solicited the support of seventy-eight other organizations interested in the cause of peace, furnished a copy of the resolution to sixty leading journals, and sent a press release to a selected group of large daily newspapers. The next step was to push for a congressional hearing, no easy task even with the cooperation of William Borah (Rep., Idaho), chairman of the Senate Foreign Relations Committee. The WILPF had just about given up hope when Republican Senator Henrik Shipstead of Minnesota, now in charge of the bill, announced suddenly on 18 February 1925 that hearings would begin on 25 February.

With only a week to gather a delegation in support of the resolution, the WILPF worked feverishly, contacting as many influential people as possible. On the twenty-fifth, the committee room was filled to overflowing. Jeannette Rankin spoke for the WILPF, and statements supporting the resolution from Professor John Dewey and James Weldon Johnson, U.S. consul in Nicaragua from 1909 to 1913, were read into the record. Other speakers for the bill during the two-day hearings were writer Dr. Ernest Gruening and Lewis S. Gannett, assistant editor of *The Nation*.

Citing the examples of El Salvador, Costa Rica, and Panama, Gannett commented that the United States "has found at its doors unorganized governments, peon labor, great undeveloped resources. These offer the opportunity to the more highly developed country to secure from government officials, eager to mortgage the future for present personal profit, the rights to monopolize trade, to keep labor subservient, and to control [the] economic policies of these backward people." Gruening's observations about the U.S. military occupation of Haiti paralleled those of Gannett.

Gannett and Dewey stressed the undemocratic nature of U.S. economic imperialism. "We have unawares been committed to a policy of empire," Gannett commented. "The people of this country have never been consulted about it. Their elected Representatives in Congress have never been consulted about it." Dewey concurred. Passage of Resolution No. 22, he asserted, would "protect the country from the evils of secret diplomacy and from the making of arrangements which, while apparently made openly, nevertheless commit the people of the country to later actions which they never intended and about which they have never been consulted."[13]

Nothing concrete materialized from the hearings before Congress recessed, so in the summer of 1925 the WILPF concentrated its efforts on preparations for a new hearing in the fall. Rankin's suggestions for a plan of attack were fairly typical of the way in which the national office would continue to enlist its members' support for legislative programs. She advised all WILPF members to write their senators and representatives, requesting a copy of the resolution and suggesting that these officials familiarize themselves with it. Each WILPF member should then study it and publicize it as much as possible among local organizations. Finally, she should again write her senators and congressman asking their opinion on specific items in the bill. As 1925 passed into 1926, however, hopes for a new hearing dimmed. From the WILPF's standpoint, it was more important than ever that Congress address the issue, since by 1926 an already tense situation between the United States and Mexico was deteriorating rapidly.

The key to understanding U.S.–Mexican relations in the early years of this century was oil. The development of this vast natural resource fell largely to foreign investors, especially Americans, and in December 1925, the Mexican government passed two new laws detrimental to the interests of American oil companies. U.S. oil magnates naturally protested, resulting in negotiations between U.S. Secretary of State Frank B. Kellogg and the Mexican Minister of Foreign Affairs which continued throughout 1926 with no settlement in sight. For their part, U.S. oil investors refused to comply with the new laws and commenced injunction proceedings to prevent their implementation.

These alarming developments between the United States and Mexico prompted the WILPF to even greater efforts to spur congressional action on its resolution. By the end of February 1926, Dorothy Detzer, WILPF Executive Secretary, suggested that perhaps interest could be renewed with a new bill to supplement Resolution No. 22. It would require the War Department to submit a public report whenever it was called upon to serve any other department within the government, any organization, or any U.S. citizen either to preserve peace, collect debts, supervise elections, or in any other way to employ the military when not authorized by Congress. The women, however, took no action on this idea, and congressional interest was now focused on the World Court. Borah asked the WILPF not to urge him to reintroduce the bill, now Concurrent Resolution No. 15, because of the amount of work involved in this latest and, to his mind, more pressing issue.

Congress adjourned in the spring with the matter still unresolved, a situation that alarmed the WILPF, particularly in light of the opinion in some quarters that lack of Mexican cooperation might compel the United States to "carry prosperity and education" to her southern neighbor by force of arms. "A war," declared an April editorial in *Liberty* magazine, "may be necessary to remove this obstruction to [American] economic advancement."[14] The situation remained unchanged by fall. By then another problem arose: the persistent resentment of the Nicaraguans over U.S. imperialistic policies down through the years was coming to a head.

Relations between the United States and Nicaragua in the early years of the twentieth century were no less exploitative than those with Mexico. Uprisings directed against the U.S.-controlled Nicaraguan government in 1912, 1921, and 1922 were quickly suppressed with the aid of the U.S. military. By 1925 the situation was considered to be under control, and the U.S. Marines, stationed in Nicaragua for over a decade, departed for home in early August.

Fresh revolutionary activity against the U.S.-backed government erupted again in October of the following year, and as 1927 approached, Kellogg, under growing pressure to settle the Mexican problem, decided upon an indirect tactic that would tie his problems with both Central American countries together and, it was hoped, result in a demand for military intervention to settle the mess once and for all. As diplomatic historian L. Ethan Ellis put it, Kellogg "countenanced, if he did not engineer, an inflammatory news report" in mid-November 1926, charging that Mexican communists were deliberately fomenting unrest throughout Central America.[15] Kellogg warned the Mexicans that the United States would not tolerate such subversion, prompting Detzer to observe that it was the old tried-and-true "red-baiting" technique, always useful in obfuscating the real issue.[16]

The WILPF's response was swift. "The habitual interference of the United States in Central American affairs," noted Detzer in a letter to the Secretary of State, "would seem to have set a most unfortunate precedent for the alleged action now taken by Mexico with regard to Nicaragua. The President and other government officials are continually assuring the citizens of the United States that our military and naval forces exist solely for the defense of this country and not for aggressive warfare nor for the pursuit of empire." If this was true, she continued, then it seemed that there were a few questions that Kellogg should answer:

1. On what legal ground can the Department of State threaten to risk the lives of American soldiers because of reported or actual interference by one Latin American country in the affairs of another?

2. How can the "warning" to Mexico by the State Department, as reported in the press, be interpreted in terms of "national defense"?

3. If the United States Government holds a warship in Nicaraguan waters[,] what is the explanation for the State Department's refusal to countenance the alleged or actual military presence or activities of another nation there?

4. To what extent does the reported loan by American bankers to the present government of Nicaragua influence the "warnings" of the Department of State?[17]

The State Department declined to respond to the WILPF's "interrogatories," because it was contrary to department practice "to indulge in general or hypothetical discussions with private individuals or associations regarding its position with respect to current questions of foreign policy."[18]

The fact that the War Department had requested all state governors to ready their militias for mobilization increased the seriousness of the situation as far as the WILPF and NCPW were concerned. Both groups redoubled their efforts to obtain a congressional hearing on the WILPF's resolution dealing with economic imperialism, more crucial than ever in light of the current administration's attitude toward utilization of the military. By a tortured definition of the word "war," Calvin Coolidge was able to argue that, at least as far as Latin American countries were concerned, U.S. "interventions undertaken 'to discourage revolutions' were not war 'any more than a policeman on the street is making war on passers-by.'"[19]

Growing revolutionary activity in Nicaragua finally forced President Adolfo Díaz, now almost bankrupt, to request direct U.S. intervention on his behalf in December 1926. Unfortunately, the Nicaraguan problem was made all the more serious by the developing crisis in Mexico. All foreign investors on Mexican soil were required by the 1925 laws to obtain, prior to 1 January 1927, "confirmatory concessions of limited scope and duration" from the Mexican government.[20] With less than a month until that deadline, not one U.S. oil company had complied, nor did any intend to.

As far as the WILPF was concerned, the situation in Mexico involved "something deeper and thicker than oil." It concerned two differing concepts of private property. Writing to Doty just prior to Christmas 1926, Detzer, then international secretary of the organization in Geneva, noted that Mexico "is no more Bolshevik in the academic Marxian interpretation of the word than the United States, but if one interprets Bolshevism as meaning a change in a country's attitude toward property, the Central American countries are developing a very different conception from that of the United States. It is this new development which is apparently at the bottom of the difficulty now."[21]

In the "Latin tradition," as Jane Addams pointed out, property vested in land and in the natural resources beneath that land were perceived as belonging to the whole people, to be developed in the interest of all, a concept at variance with the operative premise of U.S. capitalism, which dictated that property vested in land and natural resources belonged to the private owner to be developed as he saw fit.[22] As for the communist issue, the WILPF noted that the "sinister reports" of Bolshevik influence and plots in "certain administration newspapers have been definitely traced to certain officials in the Department of State." The WILPF was very much aware, however, that Kellogg's revival of "the red menace" had precisely the effect on the American public he desired. The American Federation of Labor, for example, and "groups of that kind which might be friendly [to the Mexicans] are of course," reported Detzer, "panic-stricken at the very suggestion of 'red.' "[23]

On Christmas Eve 1926, Coolidge ordered the military to Managua. The U.S. Marines arrived in Nicaragua's capital on 6 January 1927, and, shortly thereafter, "Kellogg presented his semi-hysterical memorandum on 'Bolshevik Aims and Policies in Latin America' to the Senate Committee on Foreign Relations, and a small public furor ensued."[24] Behind this "furor" was the united strength of the country's peace organizations, appalled at the belligerency of their government and its use of scare tactics, and more determined than ever that war between the United States and Mexico, which now appeared imminent, would not erupt.

In late 1926 and early 1927, a "Peace With Mexico" committee was organized, and pressure on the secretary of state to submit the dispute to The Hague Court of Arbitration was stepped up when it was learned that Mexican President Plutarco Elías Calles was willing to do so. On the evening of 16 January, with only three days notice, approximately sixty representatives from thirty-three organizations, including those of the "Peace With Mexico" committee, held an emergency meeting in Washington to discuss the most effective strategy for the immediate future. Three WILPF members attended. Among the other organizations represented were the American Federation of Teachers, the National Women's Trade Union league, and the Socialist League for Industrial Democracy, as well as various other peace groups including the War Resisters League, the FOR, and the NCPW.

"Gravely concerned" over deteriorating relations between the United States and Central America, the assembled peace advocates, now calling themselves the "Peace With Latin America Committee," drew up a position statement on the issue for each delegate to take back to his or her membership for consideration. With respect to the growing tension between the United States and Mexico, they affirmed their belief that "the present differences with Mexico should be settled through peaceful channels, and [we] emphatically protest against any attitude toward the Mexican government savoring of coercion. . . . In coercion we include the movement of troops toward the Mexican border, the sending of war ships into Mexican waters, the lifting of the existing embargo on arms, or the severing of diplomatic relations." As for Nicaragua, the conference called for the removal of the marines as the first step toward an equitable solution to the "present difficulties" there. Planned pressure on the Coolidge administration included a massive press campaign, dissemination of the "factual information" regarding both disputes, and a telegram-and-letter campaign to both the president and Congress.[25]

Conference members reminded their national policymakers of "the oft-declared purpose of this and preceding administrations to adjust all international differences through the peaceful channels of arbitration." Nor did they stop there. The president's own words from a 1925 speech were thrown back at him. "Our country definitely has relinquished," Coolidge had said in Omaha, "the old standard of dealing with other countries by terror and force and is definitely committed to the new standard of dealing with them through friendship and understanding. . . . I shall resist," the president had concluded, "any attempt to resort to the old methods and the old standards." Very good, exclaimed the peace seekers. "No excuse," concluded the delegates flatly, "will exist for coercive measures" in the present situation until "all peaceful methods have been fully tried and entirely exhausted."[26]

Detzer sent a letter to every WILPF member, asking cooperation in a campaign to inundate the White House with 10,000 telegrams within two weeks. She contacted other organizations to that same end, and wired Will Hays, former postmaster general, Presbyterian elder, and now "moral arbiter of the motion picture industry,"[27] protesting the belligerent and jingoistic headings in the newsreels, which proclaimed that "if the call comes for Nicaragua or Mexico our boys are ready."[28] In addition, she urged all WILPF branches to follow up with telegrams of their own.

By the end of January 1927, the peace organizations were also actively supporting two bills in Congress. The first stipulated that no troops would be deployed without congressional action. The second called for the complete withdrawal of U.S. troops from Nicaragua. Mass meetings of peace activists were being held in any number of large urban areas, including New York, Baltimore, Milwaukee, and Chicago. A "small public furor" indeed.

So long as Congress remained in session, peace groups felt relatively confident "that there will be no suggestion of war." It was the subsequent "nine months of executive control" after Congress adjourned that worried the pacifists.[29]

The peace seekers' faith in the power of Congress to influence the decisions of the executive branch was not wholly warranted. The situation in Nicaragua quickly deteriorated as the revolutionary forces of Juan Sacasa fought their way inland from the east. The State Department was besieged with pleas from the Díaz government for immediate, full-scale U.S. military intervention. Despite a 25 January vote of seventy-nine to zero in the Senate to submit the matter to arbitration—for which the WILPF correctly attributed credit to the concerted action of a unified peace movement—"within a month 2,000 troops were on Nicaraguan soil."[30]

Naturally enough, Resolution No. 15 on the "evils of American imperialism" acquired a greater sense of urgency in the first few weeks of 1927, and, at long last, Senator Shipstead agreed to take up the matter again. Detzer quickly went to work to round up speakers for a new hearing before a subcommittee of the Foreign Relations Committee—finally held on 16 February 1927. Despite intensive preparation, the hearing was a rather "dismal" affair.[31] Two of the scheduled speakers failed to show up, and Shipstead refused to accept testimony from a Nicaraguan citizen whom Detzer had persuaded to appear. After two years of futile effort on the part of the

WILPF to have it written into law, for all intents and purposes Resolution No. 15 was dead. Although frustrated and disappointed, the WILPF and the Peace with Latin America Committee still had urgent work to do; of great concern to peace forces even as Resolution No. 15 died was the April expiration of a treaty with Nicaragua that contained an arms embargo clause.

By mid-March, rumor was rampant in Washington that the U.S. ambassador to Mexico, just recently back at his post from a conference with State Department officials, carried with him the message that Kellogg planned to use "coercive measures" on 1 April after the expiration of the arms embargo.[32] Thus, the Peace with Latin America Committee—including journalists from the *New Republic*, the *Nation*, the *World Tomorrow*, and the *Christian Century*—decided to call upon the secretary of state, to question him about the rumor and to renew the demand for arbitration.

According to Detzer, Kellogg told the committee's deputation on 16 March that as far as lifting the arms embargo after 1 April was concerned, "embargoes were such difficult things and so troublesome he didn't know whether they should bother with it any more." Calling the embargo a "nuisance" and refusing to commit himself on the issue, Kellogg's blasé attitude "frightened" the peace workers and only served to reinforce them in their determination to keep the embargo from being lifted. Moreover, his mental and physical condition—"so terrible that they could hardly look at him"—gave the pacifists added cause for concern, and reports that he had sent "secret instructions" to Nicaragua convinced some of the committee members that "the time had come for a nationwide demand" for the secretary's resignation. Although he denied the allegation that he had sent secret instructions to anyone about anything, "the opinion is here," wrote Detzer to WILPF leader Emily Greene Balch, "that his word cannot be trusted as he has already denied things and then affirmed them within a few days."[33]

Described by DeBenedetti as "the single most successful anti-war undertaking of the decade,"[34] the efforts of the peace movement to prevent open hostilities between the United States and Mexico and to guide Kellogg in the direction of arbitration, or at the very least negotiations, finally bore fruit. Disconcerted by the public uproar, at the end of March 1927, Kellogg sent for Henry L. Stimson, secretary of war in the Taft administration, and requested the former New York district attorney to depart as soon as possible for Nicaragua to "straighten the matter out."[35] On 9 April Stimson, accompanied by his wife, departed for the troubled Central American country.

Although the State Department hoped that U.S. supervision of the 1928 Nicaraguan election would not be required, Stimson believed that it would be "absolutely necessary" if any degree of peace was to be maintained.[36] Such indirect intervention, thought the diplomat, would be more likely than military coercion to persuade the Sacasa revolutionaries and the anti-Díaz liberals to settle the unrest on U.S. terms.

Gaining the agreement of the Díaz regime to accept U.S. supervision of the upcoming election was accomplished almost immediately. Getting the forces of Sacasa, particularly the army under the authority of Liberal General José María Moncada, to accept the continuation of President Díaz in office was another matter. Stimson's warning to the general—a not-too-veiled threat that the United States was adamant on this issue—plus his written statement "that forces of the United States were authorized to take custody of all arms and to disarm forcibly those who would not voluntarily give up their weapons" apparently convinced Moncada to acquiesce. On 2 May 1927, both the Sacasa–Moncada forces and the Díaz conservatives signed the Tipitapa Agreement. Among the provisions of this settlement were "an immediate grant of peace and amnesty, the opportunity for Liberals to participate in the existing government, the creation of a nonpartisan constabulary, trained by Americans, and the supervising of elections in 1928 and succeeding years by Americans."[37]

Stimson returned home satisfied that a potentially threatening situation had been resolved, yet Nicaragua's internal difficulties were far from over. Only eleven of Moncada's generals agreed to the Tipitapa terms; the twelfth, General Augusto C. Sandino, and his followers, saw the agreement as a continuation of U.S. imperialism, and they were determined to fight until the Yankees went home for good. For the next six years, the Sandino forces fought a popular guerrilla war against the Liberals and Conservatives.

The U.S. Marines remained in Nicaragua until 2 January 1933. In the intervening years, sporadic incidents between U.S. troops and Nicaraguan nationals persisted, costing the lives of some forty-two marines and over 3,000 Nicaraguans. Detzer sent a protest to the White House each time a death resulted from one of these clashes. With what must have been annoying regularity from the perspective of both Coolidge and his successor, Hebert Hoover, telegrams and letters arrived from the WILPF. That of 21 July 1927 was typical:

Today's press dispatches indicated Nicaraguan catastrophe more serious than first reports. Since the landing of troops December 24th the Women's International League has repeatedly urged you to use your power to prevent the resort to violence which are [sic] so often the inevitable results of military occupation in a foreign country. . . . We pray that you will recognize this present crisis as an opportunity to manifest American forbearance and to demonstrate a spirit of non-violence dictated in accordance with the judgment of the righteous by immediately withdrawing American troops from Nicaragua.[38]

In the meantime, while Stimson was working out the Tipitapa Agreement, Kellogg still faced an equally threatening situation in Mexico. In midsummer 1927, Dwight W. Morrow, former Amherst classmate of the president and an attorney with the House of Morgan, was appointed ambassador to Mexico, a move, according to historian L. Ethan Ellis, that marked "the overt transition from hostility to conciliation in Mexican–American relations."[39] Morrow's appointment, combined with Stimson's efforts in Nicaragua, brought a sigh of relief from the Peace with Latin America Committee, although it was aware that months could elapse before negotiations produced anything concrete.

Praised by historians of U.S. foreign policy as an astute diplomat in a touchy situation, Morrow succeeded in winning over the goodwill of the Calles government, thereby obtaining a compromise in the controversy over the 1925 Petroleum and Alien Land laws satisfactory to all but U.S. oil producers. The latter continued to protest well into 1928, but to no avail. Morrow's settlement, in which the Calles government recognized the "binding validity of property rights" from the former regime, and in which the United States recognized Mexican sovereignty over her own natural resources, was accepted by both governments.[40]

With the success of the Stimson and Morrow missions, the crisis in Central America was over, at least for the moment, and peace workers could congratulate themselves for having played a critical role in averting war. But the issue of economic imperialism was still a live one, as the WILPF understood now more clearly than ever. And so the women reaffirmed their unequivocal opposition to the economic exploitation of one nation by another:

The increasingly open and cynical advocacy of imperialism and the constant extension of American control, financial and political, over weaker countries call for our utmost exertions to try to strengthen the true American doctrine and practice of respect and neighborliness toward all, strong and weak alike. We are convinced that it is possible to help backward countries forward to the point where they can maintain orderly conditions, and in general to assist their progress in civilization, without occupation or overlordship. The W.I.L.P.F. stands for co-operation, without any imposition of our national will upon other peoples, and as occasions arise we propose to do all in our power in favor of this policy in every case.[41]

As for government protection of private investment abroad, Emily Greene Balch, acting in her new capacity as WILPF Director of Policies, addressed "the complicated and difficult problem of the rights and duties of a home government in the matter of the protection of its citizens abroad and especially of the foreign investments of its citizens." She proposed that the issue "needs to be made the subject of international study and . . . agreements . . . reached constituting a code of the most enlightened practice to replace the present legal confusion."[42] To this end, she suggested that the League of Nations might undertake such a task.

The Peace with Latin America committee, as an ad hoc group, dissolved once the crisis ended. Coalition politics to create peace did not terminate, however, for antiwar organizations were already gearing up to support a diplomatic effort to outlaw war forever throughout the civilized world. In this endeavor, the WILPF again played a major role.

As the peace movement of the 1920s became the desperate antiwar struggle of the 1930s, the WILPF continued to work closely with other peace groups, not only to prevent the outbreak of World War II, but to keep the United States from becoming embroiled once it had erupted. Failure to do so did not end the WILPF's endeavors, however, for the women, convinced that fascism would come to America when war did, found themselves up against a new enemy of equally formidable proportions.

While other peace groups disbanded or were the victim of World War II, the WILPF survived to continue its efforts globally on behalf of peace and justice. In its role as a nongovernmental organization (NGO) at the United Nations, the WILPF protested the nuclear arms race, the conflicts in both Korea and Vietnam, the low-intensity warfare of more recent years, and human rights violations—regardless of where they have occurred or who the perpetrator has been.

In 1995, the WILPF marked its 80th anniversary with an international congress in Helsinki in early August. A peace train with some 200 women departed Finland for St. Petersburg and continued on through Eastern Europe for its final destination at the international gathering of women in Beijing, China. Never known for its massive numbers—it peaked in 1936 with approximately 16,000 members—the WILPF has consistently experienced the loyal and dedicated commitment of those women who embraced its goals and its pacifist and democratic methodology. It is certainly noteworthy that the only two American women ever to receive the Nobel Peace Prize did so for their unstinting service as WILPF activists: Jane Addams in 1931 and Emily Greene Balch in 1946.

NOTES

1. Charles DeBenedetti, *The Peace Reform in American History* (Bloomington: University of Indiana Press, 1980), 109.

2. As part of the "Red Scare" mentality of the immediate postwar period as manifested in the Palmer Raids, the War Department charged pacifists with being the major obstacle to stronger national defense policies and targeted the WILPF as being the most likely of the women's peace groups to be under the influence of communists. See Chapter 4, "Pacifism and Patriotism," in my larger work on the interwar, *WILPF, The Women and the Warriors* (Syracuse: Syracuse University Press, 1995), 36–57.

3. William Appleman Williams, *The Tragedy of American Diplomacy* (1959; reprint, New York: Dell, 1962), 115.

4. Ibid., 126, 127.

5. "Woman Objects to U.S. as Bill Collector," *The San Francisco Call*[?], 27 July 1923, WILPF Papers, Swarthmore College Peace Collection, series C1, box 1, 32, Swarthmore, Pennsylvania (hereafter cited as WILPF–SCPC).

6. Madeleine Z. Doty, "Editorial," WILPF, Section for the United States, *Bulletin* No. 13, March 1925, WILPF–SCPC, series E2, box 1.

7. Hannah Clothier Hull to Members of the National Board and Chairmen (or Secretaries) of State and Local Branches, 1 December 1924, WILPF–SCPC, series E4, box 1. The exact wording of Senate Concurrent Resolution No. 22 (68th Congress,1st sess., 1924, WILPF–SCPC, series E4, box 1) is as follows:

Resolved by the Senate of the United States (the House of Representatives concurring), that the President be and he is hereby requested to direct the Department of State, Treasury, and Commerce, the Federal Reserve Board, and all other agencies of the Government which are or may be concerned thereunder, to refrain henceforth, without specific prior authorization of the Congress from

1. directly or indirectly engaging in the responsibility of the Government of the United States, or otherwise on its behalf, to supervise the fulfillment of financial arrangements between citizens of the United States and sovereign foreign governments or political subdivisions thereof, whether or not recognized *de jure* or *de facto* by the United States Government or

2. in any manner whatsoever giving official recognition to any arrangement which may commit the Government of the United States to any form of military intervention in order to compel the observance of alleged obligations of sovereign or subordinate authority, or of any corporation or individuals, or to deal with any such arrangement except to secure the settlement of claims of the United States or of United States citizens through the ordinary channels of law provided therefor in the respective foreign jurisdictions, or through duly authorized and accepted arbitration agencies.

8. "The Resolutions," 1915 International Congress of Women, WILPF Papers, series I, box 13, University of Colorado, Boulder (hereafter cited as WILPF–Univ. of Colorado).

9. Amy Woods to Zonia Baber, 13 November 1924, WILPF–SCPC, 3, series C1, box 2. For an expression of this same sentiment by the NCCCW, see "Findings of the Conference on the Cause and Cure of War," *The Jewish Woman*, March 1925, NCCCW Papers–SCPC, 14–16, box 1 (95a).

10. Press release from the Publicity Department of the WILPF, 1 December 1924, WILPF–SCPC, series E4, box 1.

11. As Scott Nearing and Joseph Freeman pointed out at the time, the fact that the Dawes Plan did not specify the number of years Germany would be expected to make reparation payments amounted to "the most complete modern system of exploitation ever devised and applied in the relations between great powers"; they concluded (not unreasonably in 1925), that "Germany will pay until the Reparations Commission decides that she has paid enough." Furthermore, the "outsiders" who were to control German financial policy were the seven members of a fourteen-member General Board that would exercise that control over a new bank established by the Dawes Plan "entirely free from Government control or interference." Thus, they noted, "the ultimate financial policy of Germany is directed by foreigners, and the central financial system of the German Empire is a private and alien institution." See Scott Nearing and Joseph Freeman, *Dollar Diplomacy: A Study in American Imperialism* (New York: B.W. Huebsch and Viking Press, 1925), 299–331.

12. Williams, *Tragedy of American Diplomacy*, 149.

13. Quoted in "Congressional Hearing on W.I.L. Resolution," WILPF, Section for the United States, *Bulletin* 13 (March 1925): 5; and WILPF, Section for the United States, "Should the Government Put Pressure on Foreign Countries on Be-

half of Financial Claims of Private Citizens[?]," *The Pax Special* 1, no. 3 (October–November 1925): 4, WILPF–SCPC, series E2, box 1.

14. Quoted in WILPF, "Economic Imperialism," News of the United States Section, *Pax International,* June 1926, WILPF–SCPC, series E2, box 1.

15. L. Ethan Ellis, *Republican Foreign Policy*, 1921–1933 (New Brunswick, N.J.: Rutgers University Press, 1968), 243.

16. WILPF, News of the United States Section, Pax International, December 1926, WILPF–SCPC, series E2, box 1.

17. Dorothy Detzer to Frank B. Kellogg, n.d., included in "Report of the Executive Secretary," Minutes, Exec. Comm. Mtg., 14 Dec. 1926, WILPF–Univ. of Colorado, 1, series III, box 31.

18. WILPF, News of the United States Section, *Pax International,* Vol. 2, No. 3 (January 1927), WILPF papers, SCPC, series E2, box 1.

19. Williams, *Tragedy of American Diplomacy*, 126.

20. Ellis, *Republican Foreign Policy*, 243.

21. Dorothy Detzer to Madeleine Z. Doty, 23 Dec. 1926, WILPF–Univ. of Colorado, 2, series III, box 31.

22. Jane Addams, "Impressions of Mexico," WILPF, U.S. Section, *Bulletin* no. 14, April–May 1925, WILPF–SCPC, series E2, box 1.

23. Dorothy Detzer to Madeleine Z. Doty, 23 December 1926, WILPF–Univ. of Colorado, 2, series III, box 31.

24. Ellis, *Republican Foreign Policy*, 256.

25. Untitled three-page report on "Peace With Latin America" conference, 16 January 1927, WILPF—Univ. of Colorado, 1, series III, box 31.

26. Ibid., 1–2.

27. Ferdinand Lundberg, *America's Sixty Families* (1937; reprint, New York: Halcyon House, 1939), 153.

28. Dorothy Detzer to Branches, 18 January 1927, WILPF–SCPC, series E4, box 1.

29. Dorothy Detzer, "Report of the Executive Secretary," January 1927, WILPF–SCPC, 2, series A2, box 1.

30. Ellis, *Republican Foreign Policy*, 244.

31. U.S. Section, WILPF, Minutes, National Board Meeting, 5–6 March 1927, WILPF–SCPC, 4, series A2, box 1.

32. Ibid.

33. Dorothy Detzer to Emily Greene Balch, 17 March 1927, WILPF–SCPC, series C1, box 1.

34. DeBenedetti, *Peace Reform*, 118.

35. Ellis, *Republican Foreign Policy*, 257.

36. Elting E. Morison, *Turmoil and Tradition: A Study of the Life and Times of Henry L. Stimson* (New York: Atheneum, 1966), 225.

37. Ibid.

38. Dorothy Detzer to Calvin Coolidge, 21 July 1927, WILPF–SCPC, series C7, box 8.

39. Ellis, *Republican Foreign Policy*, 245–46.

40. Ibid., 249–50.

41. Emily Greene Balch, "Proposal as to Policy, by the Director of Policies, Cleve-

land, 1927," Minutes, Annual Meeting, 29 April–2 May 1927, WILPF–SCPC, series A2, box 1.

42. Dorothy Detzer, "Report of the Executive Secretary," May 1927, WILPF–SCPC, 1, series A2, box 1.

PART II

HUMAN RIGHTS, INTERVENTION, AND CONFLICT RESOLUTION

4

The United States, the Organization of American States, and the Origins of the Inter-American System

Michael Shifter

INTRODUCTION

The role of the United States in the promotion of democracy through the inter-American system can best be understood by examining the evolution of U.S.–Latin American relations over the past century. The U.S. relationship with its neighbors in the hemisphere has always been influenced by the economic and power asymmetries that exist between the United States and the countries of Latin America and the Caribbean. During the Cold War, U.S. interference in the domestic affairs of countries throughout the region undermined efforts at multilateral cooperation and fueled Latin American resentment of the hemisphere's "hegemon." Though the United States cloaked its unilateral actions with noble ideals (such as the defense of democracy and freedom), Latin American nations viewed U.S. policy as guided by self-interest and a disregard for national sovereignty. In light of these conflicting perceptions and power asymmetries, it is not surprising that the United States and Latin America had different expectations of the Organization of American States from its inception. While the United States regarded the OAS as a vehicle for marshaling support of U.S. policies and actions, Latin Americans looked to the inter-American organization as a means of blocking unilateral intervention by the United States in their domestic and regional matters.

With the end of the Cold War, and growing regional consensus among the region's political and economic elite about the desirability of democratic governance and free markets, U.S. support for inter-American institutions and initiatives seemed more likely. The early 1990s offered unprecedented opportunities for greater cooperation and the basis for a different, more productive relationship. However, although the last ten years of the twentieth century yielded some important advances—and witnessed a decline in inter-American tensions—the United States still appears relatively uninterested in hemispheric affairs or in the OAS as an important mechanism to advance policy goals.

This chapter will examine the U.S. role in promoting democracy in the Western Hemisphere through the inter-American system. The first section will focus on U.S. policy toward Latin America and the Caribbean from the early 1900s until the onset of the Cold War, with a particular emphasis on efforts to foster inter-American cooperation. The second section will trace U.S. involvement in the region during the Cold War, and its implications for democratic and multilateral institutions in the hemisphere. The third section will look specifically at the U.S. role in the promotion of democracy through the OAS since the end of the Cold War and, most recently, the Summit of the Americas process. Finally, the conclusion will identify some of the challenges and opportunities confronting the United States and the region in the twenty-first century.

THE UNITED STATES AND THE ORIGINS OF THE INTER-AMERICAN SYSTEM (1889–1945)

U.S. participation in multilateral initiatives began in the late 1800s, when Washington, D.C. hosted the First International Conference of American States, held from November 1889 to April 1890. U.S. Secretary of State James Blaine convened the meeting with the intention of encouraging trade within the hemisphere. The conference resulted in the establishment of the International Union of American Republics, and its members designated the Commercial Bureau of the American Republics—later known as the Pan American Union—as its permanent secretariat. Committed to the idea of building a hemispheric free trade zone, the United States quickly created an office devoted to the Pan American Union under the direction of the secretary of state.

In the early 1900s, the United States sought not only to foster trade but also to promote democratic reform, particularly in Central America and the Caribbean. It did so in a variety of ways—from monitoring elections and withholding aid to invading sovereign countries. As an illustration of the latter, in 1906 President Theodore Roosevelt sent U.S. troops to Cuba, where civil unrest threatened stability and U.S. business interests. The United States maintained a military presence in Cuba for the next three years, negotiating peace between the warring parties, helping to draft and implement new electoral legislation, and supervising an election during that period of time. As Paul Drake notes, "After restoring order, the invaders could point to the election as the completion of their mission and thus depart. In many respects, a model had been set for future democracy promotions."[1]

U.S. intervention in Cuba generated criticism from Latin American governments, which viewed U.S. actions as imperialistic and a violation of sovereignty. In an effort to pursue a more multilateral approach to the promotion of democracy, the United States hosted the Washington Conference of 1907, which brought together officials from the United States and Central America. At that conference, the participating states issued the General Treaty of Peace and Friendship—a document that formalized Central America's commitment to the principle of democratic governance. The parties to the treaty agreed not to recognize any Central American government that secured power by rebellion rather than fair elections. In 1909, the United States used the General Treaty of Peace and Friendship as justification for its decision to end diplomatic relations with Nicaragua's government, led by José Santos Zelaya, whom the United States viewed as a dictator and a threat to stability in Central America. The U.S. government supported those fighting the regime and recognized the new government of Juan Estrada once the rebels succeeded in removing Zeyala from power.

In 1913, President Woodrow Wilson intensified U.S. efforts to foster democratic reform and unveiled the Wilson Doctrine, which stated that the United States would not recognize any unconstitutional government in Latin America. Invoking that doctrine, Wilson refused to recognize the Mexican regime of General Victoriano Huerta, who overthrew the constitutional government headed by Francisco Madero. As opposition to Huerta mounted within Mexico, the U.S. president lifted an arms embargo to ensure that Huerta's opponents received weapons. In 1914, Wilson ordered an invasion of Veracruz. The U.S. invasion bred resentment from both Huerta and the opposition, all of whom argued against U.S. meddling in Mexico's internal affairs. Over the course of the next few years, Wilson sought to win multilateral support for his doctrine of nonrecognition and proposed a Pan American treaty that would defend republican governments in the Western Hemisphere. Although he was able to pique the interest of several Latin American governments, Wilson encountered strong resistance from a number of states—led by Chile and Argentina—which viewed his plan as an attempt to create a justification for U.S. intervention in the region. The Pan American Pact never took off.

The active U.S. role in promoting democracy within the hemisphere came to an end with the Hoover administration. Hoover abandoned the Wilson Doctrine, and began what would become known as the "Good Neighbor" policy. The new president believed that U.S. intervention could not bring democratic change to other countries in the hemisphere; rather, such change had to come from within. In 1928, during a tour of South America, Hoover stated, "True democracy is not and cannot be imperial-

istic."[2] Meanwhile, the Great Depression drove U.S. attention inward toward domestic concerns, further diminishing the likelihood of U.S.
intervention—or leadership—in the Western Hemisphere.

Despite the U.S. decision to withdraw into its own domestic affairs, support for cooperation and democratic governance in the Americas remained
strong. At the Inter-American Conference on the Consolidation of Peace
hosted by Buenos Aires in 1936, hemispheric governments adopted the
Declaration of Principles on Inter-American Solidarity and Cooperation.
The declaration recognized the "existence of democracy as a common
cause" in the Americas. It also recognized the power and economic
asymmetries between the United States and the rest of the hemisphere, and
responded to Latin American concerns that greater inter-American cooperation might open the way for U.S. intervention in their affairs. To this
end, the declaration prohibited direct or indirect intervention in the internal
or external affairs of any country in the region.

Nine years later, Uruguay's foreign minister, Eduardo Rodríguez Larreta,
sent a letter to the other governments in the hemisphere proposing multilateral cooperation in defense of democratic processes and human rights.
U.S. Secretary of State John Byrnes offered strong support for the proposal,
which linked the protection of individual freedoms with regional peace and
security. The proposal did not recommend any action that would violate
state sovereignty or the principle of nonintervention. Although this proposal
was never approved, it revealed the region's growing concern for democratic
rule.

U.S. POLICY TOWARD THE WESTERN HEMISPHERE
DURING THE COLD WAR

The 1948 Conference of Bogotá, which marked the creation of the OAS,
reaffirmed the region's commitment to democracy and the principle of nonintervention. The OAS Charter represented an "implicit bargain" between
the United States and the rest of the hemisphere, whereby the United States
would not intervene in the internal affairs of its neighbors and, in return,
the Latin American countries would support the United States at the international level and assume collective responsibility for peace and security in
the Americas.[3]

During the late 1940s and 1950s, the OAS enjoyed some success. The
United States seemed committed to making multilateral cooperation work,
supporting initiatives like the creation of the Inter-American Development
Bank and OAS technical assistance programs. Despite these positive initiatives, however, unilateral U.S. intervention in the region persisted. With the
ideological struggle of the Cold War shaping its actions, the United States
played out the conflict between East and West within the Americas. In defense of U.S. national security interests and in response to Soviet threats,

the United States established alliances with governments throughout the hemisphere, cooperated with dictators who opposed communism, and assisted authoritarian regimes looking to eliminate leftist parties and organizations.

Guatemala

The 1950 election of leftist leader Colonel Jacobo Arbenz Guzmán in Guatemala represented what was regarded as the first real "communist threat" in the Americas. Arbenz, committed to significant social change, made agrarian reform a central objective of his administration. In the summer of 1952, he won approval for a bill that allowed the Guatemalan government to seize uncultivated tracts of land and distribute them to roughly 100,000 Guatemalan families. The initiative quickly encountered fierce resistance from the U.S. government and the U.S.-based United Fruit Company, which owned vast plantations in Guatemala for its banana production.[4]

Representatives of United Fruit—who happened to enjoy close personal ties with top U.S. officials—argued that the Arbenz administration represented a threat to U.S. national security because it had communist tendencies. Daniel James expressed the U.S. position when he wrote in *The New Leader*, "The battle of the Western Hemisphere has begun. We enter upon a new era in our history. We face, for the first time, the prospect of continuous struggle against Communism on a hemispheric scale. . . . Such is the ultimate meaning of Moscow's first attempt to conquer an American country, Guatemala."[5]

In March 1954, the U.S. government, concerned about the recent turn of events in Guatemala, actively pushed for the passage of the Declaration of Caracas at the 10th Inter-American Conference of the OAS in Venezuela. That declaration called for action in the event that the "international communist movement" extended into the Americas. It stirred strong reactions from the member states, producing sharp divisions between those that supported the measure (Cuba, the Dominican Republic, El Salvador, Nicaragua, Peru, Venezuela, and of course, the United States) and those that viewed the resolution as nothing more than a cover for U.S. unilateral intervention in Guatemala (Mexico, Argentina, and Guatemala). Ultimately, the declaration passed with abstentions from Argentina and Mexico, and a "no" vote from Guatemala.

When the OAS rejected U.S. requests for multilateral intervention in Guatemala under the Declaration of Caracas, President Dwight Eisenhower chose to pursue covert, unilateral action. The CIA worked to organize and arm a group of Guatemalan exiles, which it stationed across the Guatemalan border in Honduras, and provided fighter planes for an attack on Guatemala City. President Arbenz resigned in the face of an invasion, and the exile force (led by Carlos Castillo Armas) swept in to seize power. The U.S.

government celebrated its victory while massive anti-United States protests erupted in Argentina, Chile, Cuba, Honduras, Mexico, and Panama. The United States had backed a military overthrow of Guatemala's democratically elected president, and the OAS, strongly influenced by U.S. dominance within the organization, had allowed it to do so.

Cuba

Meanwhile, unrest was growing in Cuba, causing alarm within U.S. policy circles. In 1952, Fulgencio Batista took power by force, provoking Fidel Castro to organize a leftist guerrilla force that would attack the newly established dictatorship. Castro's movement acquired significant popular support, allowing him to topple the Batista regime and seize power on the first day of 1959. In the eyes of the U.S. government, Castro's rise to power represented the most serious communist threat it faced in the hemisphere. As Castro confiscated U.S.-held companies and implemented a land reform program similar to that of Arbenz in Guatemala, the U.S. government became increasingly worried and determined to act.

In the spring of 1960, President Eisenhower approved a CIA "Program of Covert Action Against the Castro Regime." Six months later, the CIA began training hundreds of Cuban exiles to oust Castro from power. In January 1961, Eisenhower cut U.S. diplomatic relations with Cuba. On 17 April of that year, under the direction of President Kennedy, a U.S.-backed rebel force tried to land at the Bay of Pigs, on the south side of Cuba. Castro's Air Force struck back and the invasion ended in disaster.

When its unilateral attempts at overthrowing Castro failed, the United States worked to foster OAS opposition to the regime. In the early 1960s, the U.S. government pressured the member states to expel Cuba from the inter-American system. In 1962, at a meeting in Punta del Este, Uruguay, a majority of OAS members voted to suspend Cuba from membership in the organization. They concluded that the "present Government of Cuba, which has officially identified itself as a Marxist–Leninist government, is incompatible with the inter-American system." To justify their decision, member states referred to the Declaration of Santiago, which stated that "the existence of anti-democratic regimes constitutes a violation of the principles on which the Organization of American States is founded, and a danger to united and peaceful relationships in the hemisphere." (Some scholars note that although a number of regimes throughout Latin America could have qualified as "anti-democratic," only Cuba was suspended from OAS membership).[6]

The United States also lobbied (successfully) for OAS support during the Cuban Missile Crisis. In the fall of 1962, the OAS called for the removal of all Soviet missiles from Cuba and urged individual states to ensure—if necessary by force—that the Cuban government complied with OAS demands.

Two years later, at a meeting in Washington, D.C., OAS members determined that Cuba had committed an act of aggression against Venezuela by supplying Venezuelan guerrillas with weapons. The hemisphere's governments agreed to impose sanctions on Cuba and sever diplomatic relations with Castro's government.

At that moment, most Latin American countries viewed the inter-American system as a success, believing that the region had worked together to punish and isolate a threat to hemispheric security. Moreover, as Jorge I. Domínguez observed, "Though the United States pressured and cajoled the other governments to support its views, by late 1962 and certainly by mid-1964 few had doubts that Cuba was at odds with the values that the hemisphere proclaimed—though often forgot to honor—and the interests its governments characteristically defended. There was no contradiction in the end between the U.S. and the Latin American governments in their response to the Cuban revolutionary regime."[7]

Alliance for Progress

Optimism about the possibilities for multilateral action during the 1960s was also fueled by President John F. Kennedy's interest in fostering inter-American cooperation. In response to Castro's revolution in Cuba—and in an attempt to address the underlying factors that had led to it—President Kennedy proposed an alliance of the hemisphere's countries to deal more effectively with the economic and social problems they faced. He emphasized the need to strengthen democratic institutions within Latin America and the Caribbean, especially in light of the resurgence of authoritarian governments that had taken hold in the region.

In the summer of 1961, the member states of the OAS responded to Kennedy's proposal by adopting the Charter of Punta del Este, which officially established the Alliance for Progress. In support of the initiative, the Kennedy administration pledged nearly $20 billion (mostly in public funds) to Latin America within a ten-year period. This type of commitment to the region was unprecedented. The interest of the United States in the Alliance for Progress was clear: by assisting in the economic development of its neighbors, the United States would help strengthen democratic institutions in the region, discourage the rise of leftist revolutionary movements, and support traditional, centrist parties. As promised, the Alliance for Progress resulted in a dramatic increase in aid for Latin American countries, jumping from 9 percent of total U.S. foreign aid during Eisenhower's presidency to nearly 18 percent under Kennedy and Johnson.[8]

Despite the Kennedy administration's effort to consolidate democracy in the region, the early 1960s witnessed a succession of military coups throughout Latin America. In 1962–1963, six coups took place—in Argentina (March 1962), Peru (July 1962), Guatemala (March 1963), Ecuador (July

1963), the Dominican Republic (September 1963), and Honduras (October 1963).[9]

Dominican Republic

In 1965, the United States once again intervened in the domestic affairs of a neighbor—trying to prevent what it feared might become "another Cuba."[10] Like Cuba, the Dominican Republic had suffered for years under the rule of a dictator, Rafael Leonidas Trujillo Molina. After watching Castro's victory over Batista, the U.S. government worried about the rise of a Castro-like leftist opposition movement and takeover in the Dominican Republic. Thus, when a Dominican assassinated Trujillo in May 1961, President Kennedy responded immediately by sending a naval force to Santo Domingo to prevent the opposition from filling the political vacuum. The United States supported the Council of State that ruled the Dominican Republic from 1962 to 1963, providing it with economic aid and assisting in the development of a counterinsurgency unit within the national armed forces. The Council of State supervised the 1962 presidential elections, which brought Juan Bosch to power. Bosch, an advocate of social reform, alienated the armed forces, the business sector, and key politicians, causing them to consider a military coup, which ultimately took place in September 1963.

The coup gave way to the establishment of a weak civilian regime that attempted to provide a sense of order and stability. In late 1963, Donald Reid Cabral, then foreign minister, assumed the presidency. During his presidency, political tensions began surfacing within the Dominican military, with one group calling for the reinstatement of the Bosch government and another, the "loyalists," demanding the reconstruction of a military-controlled regime. As the pro-Bosch contingent grew stronger, the United States backed the "loyalists," who established a junta led by Colonel Pedro Benoit.

On 28 April 1965, Benoit, under siege by pro-Bosch forces, requested that the United States dispatch 1,200 marines "to help restore peace" to the Dominican Republic. Fearing a communist takeover by pro-Bosch forces, President Lyndon Johnson authorized over 20,000 American troops to land on Dominican soil.[11]

President Johnson, concerned that the U.S. invasion would breed resentment and alienate the countries of Latin America, looked to the OAS for support of the U.S. military presence in the Dominican Republic. The member states feared the internal unrest they had observed in Cuba, and were willing to act to prevent it from spreading. Thus, on 6 May 1965, the OAS convened a meeting of the hemisphere's foreign ministers, who agreed to support a U.S. proposal for the creation of an Inter-American Peace Force. Several countries in the region sent a small number of troops to the Dominican Republic, but the operation remained under U.S. control. In early June, the OAS secretary general traveled to the Dominican Republic with an ad hoc committee, composed of representatives from Brazil, El Salvador, and the United States. The United States used its position on the committee to strengthen OAS support for its actions and interests.

OAS support for the U.S. intervention was revealed in a number of ways. It issued a report confirming allegations that communists were working in the Dominican Republic to stir revolution and it negotiated an Act of Reconciliation that included amnesty for loyalist soldiers who had executed leftist political prisoners. The OAS also oversaw the inauguration of Héctor García Godoy as president of the Dominican Republic. One year later, he was succeeded by Joaquín Balaguer, a conservative politician and ally of the deceased dictator, Trujillo. As the United States had hoped, Bosch, and the threat of a communist takeover, faded from Dominican political life.

The OAS decision to support U.S. policy toward the Dominican Republic during this era seriously damaged its credibility. OAS support for U.S. actions resulted not only from a shared fear of civil unrest, but also from a lack of consensus within the Latin American membership. Those countries that opposed the U.S. intervention (Venezuela, Chile, Uruguay, and Mexico) struggled against those that favored U.S. military action (Colombia, Haiti, and Paraguay). This lack of solidarity allowed the United States to wield its influence within the organization, and to shape the OAS position. As Jorge Domínguez notes, "The U.S. intervention in the Dominican Republic in 1965, later endorsed by the OAS, raised the question whether the original bargain on which the OAS was founded had been broken: Instead of restraining U.S. intervention, the institutionalized inter-American system had become a mechanism to legitimate U.S. intervention."[12]

As the climate of the Cold War spread throughout the Americas, the United States and Latin American governments would come to articulate sharply opposing views regarding what represented a threat to the region's security. The U.S. insistence on intervening to address what it viewed as grave security threats often alienated its Latin American neighbors.

In the 1970s, the situation grew worse. The election of President Richard Nixon meant greater U.S. accommodation of Latin American dictatorships and reduced U.S. interest in multilateral cooperation. The Alliance for Progress collapsed, and the inter-American system faltered. The Cold War's intensity and deepening mistrust impeded any discernible progress in the OAS.

U.S. Intervention in Central America and the Latin American Response

This impasse continued throughout the 1980s, as the leftist Farabundo Martí Liberation Front (FMLN) threatened El Salvador's military-backed regime. While President Jimmy Carter opted to suspend U.S. assistance to the Salvadoran regime because of that government's gross human rights violations, Reagan offered his unwavering support for the Salvadoran government in its struggle against the Marxist rebels. For the next eight years, President Ronald Reagan's administration focused on the crisis in Central America, believing that a communist victory there would have serious implications for its struggle with the East.

In Nicaragua, the Reagan administration sought to topple the leftist government of the Sandinista National Liberation Front (FSLN). In 1981, Reagan cut all economic assistance to Nicaragua and authorized the CIA to take covert action against the Nicaraguan government. The CIA organized an opposition force, which soon became known as the "contras." Just two years later, the contra forces consisted of nearly 15,000 troops. Under the direction of Lt. Col. Oliver North, the National Security Council broadened its activities in Nicaragua, coordinating a covert war against the Sandinista government.

As U.S. interference in Central America deepened, the countries of Latin America joined together with the intention of mediating an end to the crises in El Salvador and Nicaragua. When attempts at working together through the OAS failed because of U.S. opposition, the Latin American member states chose to act independently of OAS authority.

In 1983, the foreign ministers of Colombia, Mexico, Panama, and Venezuela met on Contadora Island, Panama, to work out a strategy for negotiating a peaceful settlement to the conflicts in Central America. In 1985, the "Contadora Group" received the support of Argentina, Brazil, Peru, and Uruguay. The Reagan administration opposed the involvement of the Contadora Group in Central American issues and established the Forum for Peace and Democracy as an alternative. When the Forum failed to take off (because of its inability to win support within the hemisphere), the United States looked to the OAS for backing, only to learn that the member states favored the efforts of the Contadora Group.

The United States was encouraged as the Contadora mediation initiative faltered one year later. The Contadora Group and its four supporters did not disband at this point but decided to become a permanent body for consultation, now known as the Rio Group.

A second multilateral effort at peace resulted in the creation of the Esquipulas Group, which came into being when the Central American presidents met to negotiate an end to the conflict in Nicaragua. The group is named for the location in Guatemala where the presidents finally reached agreement on a settlement in 1989. Like the Rio Group, the Esquipulas Group continues to function in some form and has since become a consultative body that holds summit meetings each year.

The emergence of both groups revealed how U.S. actions during the Cold War had impacted the OAS. The legacy of U.S. intervention and OAS acquiescence in such matters prohibited the OAS from serving as a vehicle for multilateral action, forcing member states to create new, alternative institutions for dealing with common concerns. Characteristically, U.S. unilateralism encouraged Latin American solidarity and collective action.

By the end of the 1980s, U.S. intervention in the Central American conflicts had generated resentment and disillusionment within Latin America and the Caribbean. Its unilateral invasion of Panama in December 1989 (following a failed OAS attempt at mediation with General Manuel Noriega) appeared to be the final straw, undermining the efficacy and viability of the OAS.

Revival of Inter-American Cooperation

In the early 1990s, the end of the Cold War and the reemergence of democratic governments throughout the Americas opened the way and prepared the ground for a renewal of inter-American cooperation and improved relations between the United States and Latin America. A number of positive events advanced the cause of inter-American collaboration. In Nicaragua, OAS monitoring of the 1990 general election and the subsequent demobilization of the Contras represented a breakthrough in multilateral support for democracy and instilled a new sense of confidence in the OAS. President George Bush also offered hope for a more productive U.S. approach toward hemispheric relations when, in June 1990, he proposed the Enterprise for the Americas Initiative (EAI) to encourage foreign private investment in Latin America and foster the creation of a "free trade zone from Alaska to Tierra del Fuego."[13]

With an increased sense of optimism about the hemisphere's ability to act collectively—and growing regional consensus around the desirability of democracy and free markets—the member states of the OAS approved an historic agreement on 4 June 1991 at their 21st General Assembly, held in Santiago, Chile. The Santiago Commitment to Democracy and the Renewal of the Inter-American System declared the member states' "firm political commitments to the promotion and protection of human rights and representative democracy, as indispensable conditions for the stability, peace and development of the region" and their resolve to enact "efficacious, timely and expeditious procedures to ensure the promotion and defense of democracy."[14]

In the aftermath of the Santiago Commitment, Latin American countries began to change their approach to the United States. They increasingly viewed the cooperation of the United States as critical to confronting the challenges they faced. The United States, on the other hand, began to perceive that the governments of Latin America and the Caribbean shared its desire to promote democratic development and free trade within the hemisphere.

THE UNITED STATES AND THE OAS: PROMOTING DEMOCRACY IN THE AMERICAS IN THE 1990s

Constructing the Legal Framework

Following up on the commitments made in Santiago, the United States has supported the adoption of a series of resolutions aimed at creating a legal framework for the defense of democratic institutions in the hemisphere. The United States played an instrumental role in mobilizing support for and drafting Resolution 1080, approved in Santiago in 1991. The resolution calls for a meeting of the hemisphere's foreign ministers within ten days of a "sudden or irregular interruption of the democratic political institutional process or of the legitimate exercise of power by the democratically elected government in any of the Organization's member states." It instructs the foreign ministers to "look into the events collectively and adopt any decisions deemed appropriate."[15] By allowing an internal circumstance to serve as grounds for intervention, Resolution 1080 represents a departure from traditional OAS doctrine and provides an opportunity for reexamining and expanding the parameters of the principle of sovereignty. This resolution served as the basis for OAS intervention in Haiti (1991), Peru (1992), Guatemala (1993), and Paraguay (1996).

The United States also enthusiastically supported and actively campaigned for the adoption of the "Protocol of Washington," approved in December 1992 at the 16th Special Session of the General Assembly. The protocol amended the OAS Charter by inserting a new article (Article 9), which authorizes the General Assembly to suspend by a two-thirds vote the membership of any government that comes to power by overthrowing a democratic regime.

In addition, the United States backed the Declaration of Managua, approved in June 1993 by the 23rd General Assembly of the OAS. This document describes the region's commitment to democracy in terms of the objectives that member states are obligated to pursue. For instance, member states must work to strengthen their domestic political institutions, defend minorities, promote a "democratic culture," protect human rights, and ensure civilian authority over the military. The declaration also emphasizes that the OAS should not only seek to defend democracy when it is threatened, but should also strive to "prevent and anticipate the very causes of the problems that work against democratic rule."[16]

Responding to Crises under Resolution 1080

It is instructive in this context to examine in greater detail the U.S. role in responding to four crises that came into play under Resolution 1080. Although the four cases yielded mixed results, in all of them the U.S. government acted in a less unilateral fashion than had historically been the case, choosing instead to work in concert with multilateral institutions (the OAS and the UN) to defend democratic processes.

The first of these cases presented itself in Haiti in September 1991, when a military coup led by General Raúl Cedras removed Haiti's democratically elected president, Jean-Bertrand Aristide, from office.[17] Invoking Resolution 1080 for the first time in its short history, the hemisphere's foreign ministers issued a collective statement denouncing the coup, demanding the reinstatement of the elected government, and recommending an embargo against the unconstitutional regime in Haiti. Despite these efforts by the OAS, the military regime in Haiti remained, forcing thousands of Haitians to seek refuge in the United States. By the spring of 1992, the U.S. government had received from Haitian citizens more than 30,000 requests for asylum. President George Bush responded to the crisis by ordering the Coast Guard to search for Haitians sailing toward the United States and send them back to their country.

The refugee problem became a key issue in the 1992 elections, with Bill Clinton promising to reverse Bush's policy if elected. Nevertheless, when nearly 200,000 Haitians began preparations to travel to the United States following Clinton's election, the newly elected president explained that he would leave Bush's policy of repatriation in place after all. As Peter Smith notes, "The refugee problem confronted U.S. authorities with a serious dilemma. In order to justify forcible repatriation, they would have to deny political asylum on the ground that Haitians were taking to the seas for economic reasons; that is, they would have to maintain that applicants had no 'well-grounded fear of persecution' from the Cédras regime."[18]

As the situation in Haiti worsened and the refugee flow continued, the United States turned to the United Nations, encouraging its involvement in resolving the crisis. In December 1992, UN Secretary-General Boutros Boutros-Ghali and OAS Secretary-General João Baena Soares agreed to a joint OAS/UN mediation effort. In early 1993, the joint mission, known as the International Civilian Mission (MICIVIH), began work in Haiti. The United States clearly placed its support behind the OAS–UN mediation effort rather than exerting its own power unilaterally. Perhaps it had learned, as Viron Vaky notes, that "the efficacy of pressure and actions by nations individually can be amplified by being channeled, focused, and coordinated through the OAS or the UN."[19]

In June 1993, the United Nations Security Council, under pressure from the U.S. government, placed an embargo on petroleum shipments to Haiti. One month later, Jean-Bertrand Aristide and the commander in chief of the Haitian military, Raoul Cédras, agreed to a UN-brokered deal: (1) Aristide would return to power by the end of October; (2) he would grant general amnesty for those involved in the 1991 coup; and (3) the United States would provide training for the Haitian military and police.

In support of this agreement, the USS *Harlan County* carried U.S. and Canadian troops to Port-au-Prince on 11 October 1993 with the intent of maintaining order. There the soldiers found armed demonstrators protesting their arrival. The Clinton administration wished to avoid confrontation and ordered the *Harlan County* to retreat, undermining the UN deal and convincing Cédras that he had nothing to fear.

Soon after, African-American activists began lobbying hard for a change in the U.S. refugee policy and strong action in support of democracy in Haiti. In the spring of 1994, Randall Robinson, president of TransAfrica, a nongovernmental organization dedicated to policy issues affecting Africa and the Caribbean, started a hunger strike protesting the U.S. response to the plight of Haitian refugees. As Robinson's health deteriorated, Clinton designated William Gray, a former member of the Black Congressional Caucus, as the U.S. special envoy to Haiti, and announced that the U.S. government would provide asylum to those fleeing political repression. The policy change helped to spur a new wave of immigrants from Haiti.

It finally became clear to the Clinton administration that it would have to remove Cédras from power—by force if necessary—to put an end to Haiti's political crisis and to stem the flow of Haitian refugees to the United States. The U.S. government requested, and received, UN authorization to intervene militarily in Haiti in September 1994. As Peter Smith concludes, "Ultimately, it was the prospect of 300,000 refugees that determined U.S. policy."[20]

Aristide was able to return to Haiti, where, in December 1995, free elections were held. MICIVIH continued to monitor the human rights situation and to promote the strengthening of Haiti's democratic institutions in the late 1990s, while U.S. troops remained to provide a sense of order and security during the transition.

The bleak situation in Haiti today, however, suggests that the actions taken by the United States and MICIVIH did not result in unadulterated success. In early 1999, Haitian President René Preval dissolved the Congress and local governments, generating tremendous political instability. Moreover, the United States displayed increasing ambivalence about playing a long-term, supportive role in Haiti. As Peter Hakim observes, "There's increasing pressure from the US military and Congress to pull out troops, reversing the US commitment to nurture Haitian democracy, however unpromising its short-term prospects."[21]

On 5 April 1992, Peru's President Alberto Fujimori staged an *autogolpe*, closing the Congress, suspending the courts, and detaining his political opponents. Acting once again under the authority of Resolution 1080, the secretary-general responded to Fujimori's actions by convening a meeting of the Permanent Council, followed by a meeting of the hemisphere's foreign ministers. The foreign ministers issued a formal denunciation of Fujimori's actions and called for the restoration of democratic order in Peru.

The United States went beyond the position taken by the OAS, withholding economic and military assistance to Peru and convincing key officials in the international financial institutions to cut aid as well. The Inter-American Development Bank, for example, suspended a $420 million loan to Peru. According to David Scott Palmer, "the U.S. government took a strong and decisive stance. This was at least in part because various executive branch agencies as well as the Congress had paid remarkable attention to Peru's travails under democracy for a country that at no point represented a primary U.S. policy concern." He observed that "many U.S. officials felt betrayed, perhaps none more so than Assistant Secretary for Inter-American Affairs Bernard Aronson, who was in Lima for meetings, including one scheduled with President Fujimori, at the very time of the *autogolpe*."[22] In addition, Palmer recognized the role of human rights organizations in the United States—such as The Washington Office on Latin America, Americas Watch, and Amnesty International—that lobbied Congress in an effort to encourage U.S. action against Fujimori's "self-coup."

President Fujimori did respond to U.S. and OAS demands at the Nassau General Assembly in May 1992, where he stated his commitment to restore gradually democratic processes in Peru. He scheduled elections for a new Congress and a Constituent Assembly, which were held in November 1992; agreed to OAS monitoring of the elections; and accepted an investigation of the human rights situation in Peru by the Inter-American Commission on Human Rights. By early 1993, the OAS had come to accept Fujimori's efforts to restore democracy, according legitimacy to the Fujimori government and leaving the author of the "self-coup" in power.

When Guatemala's President Jorge Serrano Elias attempted to follow President Fujimori's example by suspending constitutional government in Guatemala in May 1993, the OAS invoked Resolution 1080 for a third time.[23] It also sent a fact-finding mission to Guatemala, warning Serrano that the international community would not tolerate his actions. Once again, the U.S. government imposed additional pressure, threatening to cancel the tariff concessions that it had extended to Guatemala. The loss of these concessions would have done serious harm to the important and influential nontraditional export industry that had emerged in the country. Less than a month later, Serrano was out of office and constitutional democracy was reinstated. In this case, regional and international pressure, combined with the objections of the Guatemalan private sector, whose interests would have been seriously damaged by the loss of U.S. tariff concessions, produced a reversal of anti-democratic action and a continuation of constitutional government.

The OAS invoked Resolution 1080 for the fourth time in 1996, when General Lino Oviedo led a coup attempt that threatened to disrupt the constitutional government in Paraguay headed by President Juan Carlos Wasmosy. The OAS responded under Resolution 1080 by calling for a meeting of the hemisphere's foreign ministers. In addition, the member states of Mercosur quickly exerted pressure in support of Paraguay's democratically elected president as foreign ministers from Brazil, Argentina, and Uruguay arrived to meet with Wasmosy. Mercosur's ability to influence the outcome in Paraguay suggests once again that, in addition to Resolution 1080, "complementary pressures at neuralgic points by individual nations with particular leverage can be effective."[24]

Critics have argued that Resolution 1080 should be strengthened to ensure greater effectiveness since it currently lacks mechanisms for rapid force mobilization in the event of a regime-threatening crisis. According to this perspective, the U.S. (and in Haiti, the UN) role in managing the crises was critical because it provided the threat of force that Resolution 1080 lacks. In fact, the OAS member states have little appetite for the use of force or "armed peacemaking to assist in the restoration of democracy."[25] Decades of U.S. unilateral intervention have contributed to such apprehensions about an inter-American force. As Tom Farer notes, the attitudes of member states have been shaped by "a not entirely happy historical experience with the policing activities of the hemisphere's hegemonic power."[26]

Indeed, though there may be a good case for seeking ways to strengthen Resolution 1080, it is important to note that the outcome of constitutional crises in Haiti, Peru, Guatemala, and Paraguay might have been worse if it were not for the hemisphere's swift response to the breakdown of democratic government in these countries. Even with its limitations, the new mechanism adopted by the OAS in 1991 has proven to be effective.

Strengthening Institutions

In addition to democratic defense, the OAS has also played a key role over the past decade in promoting democracy and strengthening institutions. The notion and rationale of this function are to avoid precisely the kinds of democratic breakdowns that triggered Resolution 1080. The organization's work in this area is consistent with and builds on the 1993 Declaration of Managua.

In this area, the United States has supported the creation of new organs within the OAS designed to improve the organization's capacity to promote and defend democracy in the hemisphere. It backed, along with Canada and others, the establishment of the Unit for the Promotion of Democracy (UPD) at the OAS Twentieth General Assembly in 1990. The UPD's responsibilities include providing research, training, and information as well as direct assistance (election monitoring and technical aid) to those member states that request its help. The UPD is most recognized for its electoral observation missions in the Dominican Republic, El Salvador, Guatemala, Haiti, Honduras, Nicaragua, Panama, Peru, and Suriname.

Although the United States has amply supported the UPD's work in specific instances, the U.S. government could do more to strengthen the institutional capacity of the UPD, and, more generally, the OAS. Electoral monitoring, peacekeeping, and other projects related to the promotion of democracy require enormous resources, as well as the support of an expert, capable staff. The failure of the United States to follow through on its financial commitments to the OAS has contributed to the organization's inability to fulfill its mandates effectively. In the late 1980s, the United States not only failed to pay its quota on time, but it also unilaterally reduced its share of the organization's total income. In 1990, the OAS approved a reduced quota for the United States. The U.S. quota now stands at 59.47 percent of the organization's total budget. The United States has since paid its full share on time but is still in arrears of US $24,563,210.

The Summit Process

From Mexico City in December 1993, Vice President Al Gore announced President Clinton's intention to invite the leaders of democracies throughout the Americas to meet and discuss issues of common concern. As host of this Summit of the Americas, set to take place in Miami the following year, the United States would play the lead role in shaping the agenda.

In Miami, the United States used its role as host to place the issues of democracy and human rights on the hemisphere's agenda. After receiving proposals from and consulting with almost 100 civil society organizations (including human rights groups) throughout the Americas, the United States issued a report, "The Unfinished Agenda for Human Rights and Economic Justice in the Americas," which called for participants in the upcoming Miami summit to consider ways to strengthen the hemisphere's democracies. This theme made its way into the Summit of the Americas' final *Plan of Action*, which included numerous and varied action items on democratic governance and human rights. In response to concerns that the limited resources and personnel available to work toward their implementation would not be sufficient, in February 1995 the United States recommended the creation of a Summit Implementation Review Group (SIRG) to monitor implementation of the Plan of Action adopted at the summit. The SIRG would bring together representatives of the hemisphere's subregional organizations, including the Rio Group, Caricom and Central America—in addition to Canada and the United States. Some governments criticized the U.S. initiative as an attempt to track the efforts of member states. In response, the United States recommended that other governments participate in the monitoring of post-summit activities. Subsequently, Canada and Brazil agreed to coordinate initiatives on democracy and human rights.

Since the summit in Miami, progress on these issues has been slow and sporadic, despite the work of the SIRG. Furthermore, inter-American cooperation has been affected by U.S. disengagement from the region, reflected most clearly in President Clinton's inability to secure fast-track authority for the negotiation of free-trade agreements in the Americas, which had been the cornerstone of the 1994 summit and U.S. policy toward Latin America in the post-Cold War period.

There is considerable ambivalence among member governments, including the United States, about the extent to which the OAS should assume a central, coordinating function in directing the summit process. Since the first Summit of the Americas in 1994, the OAS has been accorded an increasingly prominent role in several key areas, although many governments are still not prepared to yield control of the process. The role of the OAS in the next Summit of the Americas—which took place in Quebec City in 2001—posed a critical test and challenge for the organization in this sense.

CONCLUSION

Despite U.S. efforts in Haiti, Peru, Paraguay, and Guatemala, and its role in drawing attention to the issue of democracy through the summit process, the United States remains unwilling to devote the resources and the sustained attention required to consolidate democratic governance in all countries of the Western Hemisphere. As Luigi R. Einaudi, former U.S. ambassador to the OAS (and elected assistant secretary-general in 2000), has noted: "The region's oldest democracy and most prosperous country, the United States, has its attention focused mainly on domestic problems. Whatever attention is left for foreign issues tends to be intolerant and directed outside the hemisphere. . . . [D]espite our sporadic efforts to prove otherwise, our neighbors have the impression that we are generally indifferent to what happens to them and to their struggle for democratic progress."[27]

The hemisphere today faces serious challenges to democracy. In Venezuela, the plans of President Hugo Chávez to dissolve the Congress and establish a constituent assembly have raised fears about the state of Venezuela's democracy. In Colombia, the violent conflict between powerful guerrilla groups and paramilitary forces threatens to destabilize that country's democratic institutions. In addition, transnational criminal organizations represent a powerful threat to stability in the region. The promotion of democracy in the face of these challenges will require greater and more sustained U.S. engagement in the region.

A core, underlying problem that still needs to be addressed and overcome is the asymmetry in power between the United States and Latin America, as well as the suspicions and distrust that may have diminished but have hardly disappeared. To illustrate the continuing problem, it is useful to consider what took place at the OAS General Assembly in Guatemala City in June 1999. In response to the crisis that unfolded in Paraguay following the assassination of Vice President Luis María Argaña on 23 March 1999, the U.S. government proposed a more proactive approach to the defense of democracy.[28] According to the U.S. plan, the OAS would send a "group of friends" to help member states resolve potential threats to constitutional government before they evolve into full-blown crises. Although the United States received the support of several Latin American countries, the proposal stirred strong opposition, with many governments viewing it as a new form of interventionism.

Despite impressive advances, as the OAS faces the twenty-first century it must continue to deal with some of the same fundamental challenges that have always characterized its history.

NOTES

I would like to extend special thanks to Inter-American Dialogue intern Christine Lawson for her invaluable help in preparing this chapter.

1. Paul A. Drake, "From Good Men to Good Neighbors," in *Exporting Democracy*, ed. Abraham F. Lowenthal (Baltimore: Johns Hopkins University Press, 1991), 11.

2. Address delivered during the Visit of Herbert Hoover to Central and South America, November–December 1928 (Washington, DC: Pan American Union Press, 1929), cited in Drake, "From Good Men to Good Neighbors," 29.

3. Viron P. Vaky, "The Organization of American States and Multilateralism in the Americas," in Viron P. Vaky and Heraldo Muñoz, eds., *The Future of the Organization of American States* (New York: The Twentieth Century Fund Press, 1993), 9–10.

4. Peter H. Smith., *Talons of the Eagle: Dynamics of U.S.–Latin American Relations* (New York: Oxford University Press, 1996), 135.

5. Ibid., 136.

6. Heraldo Muñoz, "A New OAS for the New Times," in *The Future of the Organization of American States*, 78.

7. Jorge I. Domínguez, "The U.S., Revolutionary Regimes, and Inter-American Security," in *Alternative to Intervention*, ed. Richard Bloomfield and Gregory Treverton (Boulder: Lynne Rienner Publishers, 1990), 47.

8. Smith, *Talons of the Eagle*, 151.

9. Ibid., 154.

10. Ibid., 168.

11. Ibid., 169.

12. Jorge I. Domínguez, "Political Relations in the Western Hemisphere," in *Governance in the Western Hemisphere*, ed. Viron P. Vaky (New York: Praeger, 1983), 143.

13. Quoted in Smith, *Talons of the Eagle*, 249.

14. OAS "The Santiago Commitment to Democracy and the Renewal of the Inter-American System," adopted at the third plenary session, 4 June 1991.

15. OAS, "Resolution 1080," adopted at the fifth plenary session, 5 June 1991.

16. OAS, "Declaration of Managua for the Promotion of Democracy and Development," adopted at the fourth plenary session, 8 June 1993.

17. For a thoughtful account of the Haiti case, see Anthony Maingot, "Sovereign

Consent vs. State-Centric Sovereignty: The Haitian Case," in Tom Farer, ed., *Beyond Sovereignty: Collectively Defending Democracy in the Americas* (Baltimore: Johns Hopkins University Press, 1996).

18. Smith, *Talons of the Eagle*, 285.

19. Vaky, "The Organization of American States," 29.

20. Smith, *Talons of the Eagle*, 289.

21. Peter Hakim, "US–Latin America Policy Running on Empty," *Christian Science Monitor*, 24 June 1999.

22. David Scott Palmer, "Collectively Defending Democracy in the Western Hemisphere," in Farer, *Beyond Sovereignty*, 273.

23. See Rachel McCleary, "The Constitutional Crisis in Guatemala: The Responses of the International Community and Guatemalan Society," A report of an international conference (Washington, DC: United States Institute of Peace, January 1994).

24. Inter-American Dialogue, *Inter-American Agenda and Multilateral Governance: The Organization of American States* (Washington, DC: Inter-American Dialogue, 1997).

25. Muñoz, "A New OAS for the New Times," 84.

26. Tom Farer, "Collectively Defending Democracy in a World of Sovereign States: The Western Hemisphere's Prospect," *Human Rights Quarterly* 15 (1993): 738.

27. Luigi R. Einaudi. *The Common Defense of Democracy in the Americas* (Washington, DC: Inter-American Dialogue, June 1999). This policy brief was based on testimony Ambassador Einaudi prepared for a hearing on "Democracy and the Rule of Law" before the Subcommittee on the Western Hemisphere, Peace Corps, Narcotics and Terrorism of the U.S. Senate Foreign Relations Committee, held on 12 May 1999.

28. On 23 March 1999, four gunmen assassinated Paraguay's vice president, Luis María Argaña. Many accused former coup leader Lino Oviedo and then-president Raúl Cubas of orchestrating the crime. In the days following the assassination, thousands of protesters flooded the plaza in front of the National Congress to demand Cubas's resignation and the jailing of Oviedo, his mentor. Violence broke out on 26 March when pro-Oviedo snipers surrounded the protesters and began firing, killing six people and injuring 200. Two days later, Cubas, who had already been impeached by the lower house of the congress, resigned and left the country for Brazil. Meanwhile, Oviedo fled to Argentina, where he was granted political asylum by President Carlos Menem. In accordance with procedures laid out in Paraguay's Constitution, the president of the Senate, Luis González Macchi, was sworn in as Paraguay's president.

5

The Evolution of International Human Rights Standards and Organizations: Their Impact on Conflict Resolution

Margaret E. Crahan

INTRODUCTION

The progressive internationalization of human rights concepts, law and organizations, particularly since the 1940s, demonstrates increasing consensus on core human rights standards and a growing realization that respect for civil/political rights is directly related to the fulfillment of economic, social, and cultural rights. This process was stimulated by the post–World War II desire to reach agreement on a normative basis for peace without ignoring the real differences that exist among cultures and political and economic systems, which underlie the Universal Declaration of Human Rights (1948). The subsequent approval of implementing covenants, treaties, and conventions affirmed the principles expressed in this document. The eruption of human rights crises since the 1960s has served to reinforce the conclusion that gross violations are root causes of threats to both national and international peace and security. Improved levels of observance and fulfillment of the full spectrum of human rights are therefore linked to the resolution of long–standing intra- and extra-national conflicts, as seen, for example, in the recent peace processes in El Salvador and Guatemala.

The existence of an international human rights regime that reflects a consensus on basic standards of behavior by governments and societies has made peaceful conflict resolution more likely to be attempted via such mechanisms as preventive diplomacy, mediation, and humanitarian intervention. Nevertheless, the complexity of post-Cold War conditions in many nations and regions clearly suggests the necessity of refining and making more effective human rights strategies and related mechanisms for conflict resolution.

This essay will explore the above topics via a brief analysis of the emergence of an international human rights regime, its limitations, the development of humanitarian intervention, international mediation, and preventive diplomacy, as well as the involvement of the human rights movement in these processes. Special emphasis will be placed on Latin American phenomena. Because of limitations of space, this chapter will be highly schematic.

EMERGENCE OF AN INTERNATIONAL HUMAN RIGHTS REGIME

During the course of the twentieth century, there has emerged an international human rights regime, by which is meant an international system constituted by treaties, conventions, constitutions, laws, and other documents, together with customary law and practices, which set standards and norms for human rights observance. Also included are the international and national organizations and nongovernmental actors that monitor the implementation of such norms and standards. Obviously, the existence of such a regime has not guaranteed an end to widespread gross violations of human rights, but its growth over the course of this century has resulted in increasing commitments on the part of governments, and, more recently, some non–state actors, to the principles and standards set out.

The roots of the international human rights regime have been traced back to the beginnings of recorded history by some analysts.[1] Modern conceptualizations are linked to the emergence of nation-states in the seventeenth and eighteenth centuries and, more especially, to increasing attempts in the twentieth century by governmental and nongovernmental actors to respond more adequately to the causes of world wars, genocide, and other developments contributing to massive death and destruction. Such preoccupations resulted in the creation of the League of Nations and the United Nations, as well as a variety of other international and national organizations including the Organization of American States (OAS) and the Organization of African Unity (OAU).

Beginning with the League of Nations' concern for the rights of labor and the protection of the rights of minorities, there has been a gradual expansion of certain basic precepts of human rights, particularly the inviolability of life and physical integrity, as well as equality before the law. Promoting the very slow process of internationalizing and codifying human rights standards in the early twentieth century were a bevy of individuals and groups including the Chilean Alejandro Alvarez, cofounder of the American Institute of International Law (1917); the Russian exiles A. N. Mandelstam and Boris Mirkine Ouetzervitch, who promoted the inclusion of human rights in national constitutions; and the Greek jurist Antoine Frangulis, who championed the drafting of an international covenant of human rights. Such a covenant was published with the support of the International Law Institute in late 1929 as the Declaration of the International Rights of Man. By the early 1930s, there was an international movement aimed at focusing greater attention on human rights and an increasing number of related nongovernmental organizations.[2]

The emergence of Nazi Germany resulted in an upsurge of activity particularly related to the rights of minorities. While there were some efforts to use the League of Nations to counteract the threat of fascism, the withdrawal of Germany from the organization in 1933 stymied efforts to resolve the emerging conflict. The outbreak of war in the late 1930s galvanized the human rights community and stimulated an international educational campaign spearheaded by England's H.G. Wells in favor of a universal declaration of human rights. Wells maintained contacts in twenty–nine countries including the United States, where he lobbied President Franklin D. Roosevelt, influencing the latter's 6 January 1941 State of the Union message containing the first expression of FDR's four freedoms—freedom of speech and expression, freedom of worship, freedom from want, as well as freedom from fear. Subsequently, the defense of these human rights was included in the Allied war aims.[3]

The experience of the Holocaust and World War II stimulated a growing consensus that international peace and security were inextricably linked to that level of human rights enjoyment that was conducive to societal concord. During the course of the war, work began on an international bill of rights, as well as on the creation of a series of organizations aimed at dealing primarily with economic and political factors that had contributed to the rise of fascism and the outbreak of the war.

At the 1945 San Francisco conference that gave birth to the United Nations, the Latin American countries, as well as nongovernmental organizations, were active in lobbying for the inclusion of human rights in the charter. While the very first article stated that the promotion of human rights was one of the principal purposes of the UN, no mechanisms for implementation were specified. Rather, somewhat vague responsibility was accorded the General Assembly and the Economic and Social Council (ECOSOC) to promote rights through the drafting of recommendations and conventions. Chapter VII of the Charter did provide for multilateral intervention if there arose a serious threat to international peace and stability, a provision that was to be used later as a prime instrument for the defense of human rights. A Commission on Human Rights was also created during the first session of the UN General Assembly, but it had no power to take any action.[4] The conviction that a general declaration of human rights principles was essential prompted the drafting of the Universal Declaration of Human Rights, which was approved in 1948.

The debate over the Universal Declaration reflected Cold War tensions, particularly with respect to the Soviet Union's emphasis on social and economic rights versus the U.S. focus on civil/political rights. The Latin American countries, among others, supported the inclusion of specific social and economic guarantees, hence, they adopted articles 22–26, aimed at guaranteeing that level of socioeconomic security necessary for life with dignity. While the Universal Declaration was not legally binding, it did represent an important consensus statement on the rights and obligations of states, as well as the critical role of rights in the preservation of international peace and security. Today virtually every country in the world accepts these principles, even if they sometimes violate them, and these premises have entered into customary law. Several dozen states have incorporated the Universal Declaration in its entirety into their national constitutions.

The problem of implementation was tackled with the drafting of the Covenant on Civil and Political Rights and the Covenant on Economic, Social and Cultural Rights, which came into force in 1976. By that time the UN had added to the mechanisms available for the defense of human rights via treaties against genocide, racial discrimination, apartheid, and in favor of the rights of women and refugees. In addition, machinery was developed within the UN to better protect rights and to provide humanitarian assistance to those whose basic rights were being denied. Pressures from member states, in part prodded by a growing number of NGOs, moved human rights onto center stage, not only within the UN but also in the broader international community.

In 1976, Jimmy Carter declared that human rights would be the cornerstone of U.S. foreign policy if he were elected president. Prior to this, the U.S. Congress had passed a series of laws that restricted U.S. aid to countries that committed gross violations of human rights and thus was born the State Department's annual survey of human rights worldwide. The specific objectives of each subsequent administration, together with varying congressional agendas tended, however, to undercut human rights as a priority in U.S. foreign policy.

Human rights crises in Africa, Asia, Latin America, and Eastern Europe stimulated the growth of national and international human rights organizations, which tended to further the development of human rights law, strategies, networks, and consensus, thereby contributing to the fortifying of an international human rights regime. Its existence is reflected by the creation of regional human rights courts and related institutions in Europe, Latin America, and Africa, and in efforts to do so in Asia. The June 1998 approval of the creation of an International Criminal Court with jurisdiction over suits brought against individual violators of human rights again demonstrates the existence of international consensus, although some countries, including the United States, had reservations about particular aspects of the court's jurisdiction.

While the existence of an international consensus on human rights is clear, there are debates over a variety of issues, including cultural relativism, prioritizing rights and the relationship between civil/political and socioeconomic rights.[5] There is also increasing discussion of group or collective rights, including rights to self–determination and to development. The debate that has been the most constant, however, is the degree to which the requirements of human rights guarantees can impinge on state sovereignty.

When the UN was created in 1945, there was a consensus that human rights were an intrastate matter and the Charter strongly supported nonintervention, except in unusual cases. Since the late 1980s, the proliferation of humanitarian interventions has suggested that state assent to limitations on sovereignty is increasing and there is more inclination toward proactive human rights policies.

It is important to remember that the concept of state sovereignty developed out of the particular needs of emerging territorial states in Europe in the sixteenth and seventeenth centuries. Intent on subordinating heterogeneous social groupings within defined geographical areas, the emerging absolute monarchies of that era promoted the concept of national sovereignty. As nation-states were consolidated in the eighteenth and nineteenth centuries, it became increasingly apparent that there was also a need to regulate the interactions of sovereign states and, as a consequence, there developed supranational organizations and mechanisms. This was especially true in the aftermath of the extraordinary destruction and destabilization of the first and second world wars, when governments sought more effective means to ensure that local conflicts within and between states did not jeopardize international peace and security. States used their sovereign authority to impose limitations on their own sovereignty in order to better ensure peace and security. Nevertheless, the principle of nonintervention continues to take precedence. How, then, are the demands of nonintervention and the international guaranteeing of human rights resolved?

While the charters of the UN, as well as those of regional organizations such as the Organization of American States (OAS), strongly defend nonintervention and state sovereignty, they do admit exceptions. As early as 1923, at the Sixth International Conference of American States, the dangers of making absolute the principle of nonintervention were noted by the Cuban delegate who asserted that it would result in "sanctioning all the inhuman acts committed within determined frontiers."[6] Indeed, under the United Nations Charter, a member state that "in any way violates the dictates of humanity and shocks the conscience of mankind to such an extent that the breach of human rights constitutes a threat to international peace" cannot claim immunity from collective intervention by the organization.[7]

The adoption of the Universal Declaration and the related covenants and treaties by many countries in the world demonstrates the willingness of states to limit their sovereignty in order to guarantee human rights. This does not mean that there is agreement either on the precise limits of state sovereignty or the extent to which supranational authorities can intervene in defense of human rights. This issue underlies current debates over the legitimacy and efficacy in conflict resolution of humanitarian interventions.

HUMANITARIAN INTERVENTION

With the increase of complex emergencies in the 1980s and 1990s, together with the end of the Cold War and the emergence of a human rights regime, humanitarian intervention became a prime strategy for the defense of human rights. Despite the UN Charter's prohibition against interference in the internal affairs of member states, Security Council resolution 688 grants the UN the right to intervene, including with military force, to protect basic human rights. To be legitimate, such intervention, it is generally thought, should meet the following criteria:

1. There must be an immediate and extensive threat to fundamental human rights.
2. All other remedies for the protection of those rights must have been exhausted within the time constraints imposed by the threat.
3. An attempt must have been made to secure the approval of appropriate authorities in the target state.
4. There must be minimal effect on the extant structure of authority (i.e., the intervention must not be to impose or preserve a preferred regime).
5. Only the minimal requisite force must be employed, and the intervention must not be likely to cause more injury to innocent persons and their property than would result from the actual violations.
6. The intervention must be of limited duration.
7. The intervention must be collective.
8. The situation prompting the intervention must clearly threaten international peace and security.
9. All non–UN humanitarian interventions must be reported to the Security Council.
10. World Court jurisdiction must be accepted in the face of any challenges.[8]

These criteria, together with the concept of humanitarian intervention, have evolved in the light of actual interventions in such countries as Angola, Cambodia, Mozambique, Liberia, South Africa, the former Yugoslavia, Rwanda, El Salvador, Haiti, and Guatemala.

The increase in humanitarian interventions on behalf of human rights is obviously an outgrowth of the maturation of the original consensus expressed in the UN Charter that gross violations of human rights were a clear threat to international peace and security. Initially, the UN restricted its conflict resolution to peacekeeping. As a human rights consensus grew within the UN and the international human rights community was able to bring more pressure to bear, peacekeeping expanded into humanitarian intervention, peacemaking, and peacebuilding. The difficulties encountered by such mechanisms for conflict resolution have made clear the challenges of complex emergencies, particularly given the limited resources of the UN and the waxing and waning of the member states' enthusiasm for humanitarian interventions. As experience has deepened, there has come a new appreciation of the prerequisites for successful humanitarian interventions—including the existence of a functioning state, a strong desire on the part of the internal actors to resolve the conflict and engage in substantive negotiations, a degree of accountability on the part of the parties, a cease-fire, influential non–party actors facilitating the process, effective disarmament and demobilization, and local security forces increasingly operating within the rule of law. Even when these conditions are met, however, there are no guarantees that humanitarian interventions will be effective.

While the international community has accepted the legitimacy of humanitarian intervention, particularly when led by the UN, there has been increasing debate over its utility. Scholars Tom Farer and John Stedman have evaluated the humanitarian interventions of the late 1980s and early 1990s and reached somewhat contrary conclusions. Farer argues that humanitarian interventions are necessary, but that they could be improved to make for more effective conflict resolution. This would involve ensuring that UN actions cannot be interpreted as partisan, that efforts to rebuild failed states be recognized as impractical, that there should be no mixing of coercion with mediation, and that the UN should resist acting to affect the balance of power within a country but should not be unwilling to use coercion to prompt a resumption of good-faith bargaining. Finally, Farer recommends that the UN member states provide more financial resources and trained personnel to the organization for humanitarian interventions.[9] Stedman, on the other hand, argues for selective intervention under specific conditions. He holds that it is impossible to maintain a consistent policy of humanitarian intervention because the international community cannot intervene in every conflict; the resources to do so do not exist. Hence, intervention should occur only when the interveners have a clear-cut strategy and full capacity to carry it out. Stedman also feels that the timing of an intervention is critical; it should occur when the parties have exhausted themselves and recognize that they cannot achieve their aims through warfare. Hence, he feels that cease-fires may only prolong a conflict since they reduce the pressure to negotiate. He also believes that humanitarian assistance may possibly prolong a war or violent conflict. Stedman is, consequently, more enthusiastic about straightforward UN peacekeeping than humanitarian interventions that might involve peacemaking and peacebuilding.[10]

Other analysts recommend interventions that involve coalitions of private voluntary organizations (PVOs), humanitarian assistance agencies, and human rights and local groups. Such coalitions have proven somewhat effective in highly conflictive situations, including in Ethiopia and Eritrea where a cross-border operation in the 1980s spearheaded by PVOs, together with humanitarian assistance and relief agencies, appears to have aided local populations and reduced deaths and refugees. This effort focused on the participation of local communities in determining aid priorities and distribution mechanisms. In addition, it diminished the degree to which the contending forces could manipulate aid to their own advantage, since they had less control over the aid. Finally, it helped to maintain local self–government that was able to reassert itself once the conflict receded.[11] Such experiences demonstrate the variation in humanitarian interventions and the need to be flexible in determining the most appropriate responses to complex emergencies.

UN-led humanitarian interventions have, at times, been relatively effective, as indicated by the resolution of the civil wars in El Salvador and Guatemala in the 1990s. In both cases, human rights served as a fulcrum for broader international involvement in the peace processes, as well as for the participation of civil society stimulated by local human rights organizations and leaders.

HUMAN RIGHTS, CONFLICT RESOLUTION, AND PEACE PROCESSES

Conflict in El Salvador and Guatemala—rooted in extreme socioeconomic disparities, ongoing intra-elite conflict, exclusion and marginalization of the bulk of the population from political and economic decision making, and, in the 1970s and 1980s, Cold War politics—has been a constant in this century. Guerrilla movements emerged in Guatemala in the 1960s and in El Salvador in the 1970s, and by the 1980s war and repression had become widespread throughout Central America. The upsurge of repression resulted in the creation of human rights organizations, most notably Tutela Legal sponsored by the Archbishopric of San Salvador and the Office of Human Rights of the Archdiocese of Guatemala. The latter was not founded until the late 1980s, largely because the Catholic Church feared that its existence would jeopardize not only those who worked there but church personnel as well. This was not an unwarranted preoccupation; in 1980–1981 alone six priests and a dozen lay activists were assassinated in Guatemala. Repression there was so intense that the Catholic Church pulled all its personnel out of the diocese of El Quiché in 1980. Relatives of the disappeared, however, did establish the Mutual Support Group [Grupo de Apoyo Mutuo (GAM)], and there were a number of other human rights groups that operated out of neighboring countries. In addition, the Washington Office on Latin America, Amnesty International, Human Rights Watch, and the Lawyers Committee for Human Rights all monitored both El Salvador and Guatemala, closely documenting disappearances, assassinations, and massacres there in the 1970s and 1980s. Such work helped create a network of groups and individuals that played an important role in pressuring the UN, OAS, guerrillas, and governments (including that of the United States) to support a negotiated solution to the conflicts.

Such efforts encouraged the Contadora Initiative in 1983, sponsored by Mexico, Panama, Venezuela, and Colombia, which produced a draft peace agreement by September 1984. The agreement called for cease-fires, disarmament and demilitarization, national reconciliation, elimination of outside interference, and commitment to democratization and regional integration. Cold War politics blocked progress until Oscar Arias, president of Costa Rica from 1986 to 1990, convened the Central American presidents to sign the Esquipulas Agreement in August 1987. Its provisions allowed for roles for organized civil society, of which human rights organizations were principal actors. In addition, the agreement mandated international human rights monitoring, which was initiated by the UN in both El Salvador and Guatemala prior to the actual signing of the definitive peace accords in 1992 in the former and 1996 in the latter. Human rights monitoring helped stabilize conditions in both countries, providing a greater sense of security—particularly for the rural population—as well as contributing to the pressures for serious peace negotiations.

Human rights activists in both Central American countries also helped create a national dialogue that incorporated representatives of a broad cross section of society, including private enterprise, labor, cooperatives, political parties, professional associations, educational institutions and research centers, the press, nongovernmental organizations, and religious institutions. In El Salvador, the National Debate, championed by the Jesuits' Central American University and the Archdiocese of San Salvador, mobilized civil society based on what public opinion polls were indicating, namely, that there was overwhelming support for a negotiated solution to the conflict. It also pressed for a settlement that would end the warfare and address the causes of the conflict through increased respect for human rights, cultivation of political pluralism, the return and resettlement of refugees, and the ending of outside interference, particularly from the United States, Nicaragua, and Cuba.[12]

In Guatemala, the National Dialogue included representatives of religious, professional, labor, business, and other groups. Between September 1989 and March 1990, it convened close to 800 meetings to discuss human rights, socioeconomic justice, the role of the military, and indigenous rights, as well as to thrash out common positions that would influence the conceptualization and content of the peace accords. The National Dialogue helped sectors of civil society gain experience in building trust, coalitions, and consensus positions. This was critical as organized civil society was incorporated early on into the peace process via the Oslo Process, a series of meetings begun in 1990 with political parties, the private sector, religious representatives, labor and popular organizations, as well as with cooperatives, academics, and professional and small business associations. Funded largely by the Lutheran World Federation (LWF), it brought together government and guerrilla representatives, as well as organized civil society, to build a consensus for peace. Together with the National Dialogue, it helped prepare civil society to undertake a more formal role in the peace process when in 1994 an Assembly of Civil Sectors [Asamblea de Sectores Civiles (ASC)] began to generate specific consensus positions on the issues under discussion in the UN-moderated peace talks and to make recommendations for the accords signed by the parties. Representatives of the Mayan peoples were specifically included. While the recommendations of the ASC were not binding, they did help civil society—in which the human rights community played a considerable role—to mold the content of the final accords. Hence, the latter included an Agreement on Social and Economic Aspects and the Agrarian Situation that was far more substantial than the comparable accord in the Salvadoran peace agreements.[13]

In both cases, national and international human rights organizations played major roles in the drafting of the accords and in calling attention to new threats to peace and security, including the rise in common criminality and consequent decline in personal security. In addition, they pressured for greater accountability and transparency in government, constitutional, judicial, and other reforms, as well as for the institutionalization of mechanisms to ensure greater observance of human rights, such as national ombudspersons. Perhaps the greatest contribution of the human rights communities in El Salvador and Guatemala has been the stimulus they provided for the general population to become involved in local government and commissions and to testify before the truth commissions created in each country. This occurred despite continued attacks on human rights activists, most notably the Guatemalan Catholic bishop Juan José Gerardi Conedera, who coordinated the activities of the Interdiocesan Project on the Recuperation of Historical Memory [Proyecto Interdiocesano para la Recuperación de la Memoria Histórica (REMHI)] and who was assassinated in April 1994. Aimed at documenting past gross violations of human rights and encouraging responsibility for such violations in order to facilitate reconciliation, such truth commissions have a critical role in long-term conflict resolution.[14]

CONCLUSION

To date, the major focus of conflict resolution via human rights has been the mobilization of civil society within countries and within the international human rights community to bring pressure to bear for the non-violent resolution of crises, together with humanitarian intervention, principally under the aegis of the United Nations. All obviously have demonstrable limitations. Indeed, some analysts have called for the separation of human rights agendas and peace negotiations, arguing that:

The quest for justice for yesterday's victims of atrocities should not be pursued in such manner that it makes today's living the dead of tomorrow. That, for the human rights community, is one of the lessons from the former Yugoslavia. Thousands of people are dead who should have been alive—because moralists were in quest of a perfect peace. Unfortunately, a perfect peace can rarely be attained in the aftermath of a bloody conflict. The pursuit of criminals is one thing. Making peace is another.[15]

In response to this critique, Felice Gaer, director of the New York-based Jacob Blaustein Institute for the Advancement of Human Rights, held that:

In contrast to the pathetically weak response by nation-states and international organizations to ethnic cleansing and the war in Bosnia, the human rights community stands out for having focused world attention on atrocious abuses in flagrant disregard of all civilized behavior, and on the need to uphold international principles and premises. The human rights movement pursued the truth in a timely and principled manner, creatively championed emergency sessions and new international war crimes bodies to press international officials to look into rights abuses, and called urgently for the protection of those suffering. Its influence in making human rights issues a mainstream concern in the conflict was impressive.[16]

In addition, Gaer argues that it was the unwillingness of governments, the UN, and the European Union to act in defense of principles embodied in international law and treaties that encouraged the war and human rights violations in the former Yugoslavia. Furthermore, lack of leadership and shifts in policies and personalities also contributed to the conflict.[17]

As this exchange indicates, there does exist considerable debate about the role of human rights in conflict resolution. Several alternatives have been offered, most of which are refinements of the strategies tried to date. Growing attention is being paid to early warning and preventive diplomacy. The latter involves "the use of coercive or non–coercive means to avoid, deter, deflect, or reduce conflict" via conflict prevention—that is, avoiding disputes between states and other parties; conflict containment, namely, de-escalating hostilities; and post-conflict conciliation to avoid the restart of conflicts.[18] Essential to the success of preventive diplomacy is the elimination of the reasons for violence between contending forces, the use of military or observer forces to defuse situations and resolve outbreaks, and the preemptive resolution of disputes.[19] The latter depends on early warning, a task that in the past has frequently been undertaken by human rights and humanitarian organizations and personnel. Such involvement can sometimes interfere with the work of these organizations or place their personnel at risk. Nevertheless, there is increasing attention being paid to the role of human rights and humanitarian assistance groups in preventive diplomacy, in cooperation with international organizations such as the UN.[20]

The generation of such alternatives is rooted in the strength and efficacy of the human rights community worldwide. A recent survey of approximately 150 transnational human rights NGOs found that both their numbers and effectiveness appear to be growing. Moreover, there is increased networking and cooperation between international and national organizations. Current emphases are "(1) education; (2) standard setting; (3) monitoring compliance with international standards; and (4) enforcement."[21]

The survey found that NGOs from the south were more likely to work for social, economic, and cultural rights, as well as the right to development, than NGOs in the north. With the end of the Cold War, a large number of the survey respondents indicated that they have increased their focus on ethnic/sectarian conflicts, albeit they found such work enormously difficult given their limited resources. The survey also indicated that there has been substantial growth in terms of expertise and capacity building, and that human rights organizations are eminently better equipped today than just fifteen years ago.[22] Nevertheless, the complexity of the problems human rights NGOs face today is breathtaking. This has led to increased cooperation not only within the human rights community, but also sometimes within civil society, as well as with governments and international organizations. Hence, the international human rights regime today has more horizontal and vertical linkages to facilitate the promotion of human rights than ever before. While this can contribute to more effective conflict resolution, there is a fear that the deepening of existing crises is proceeding more rapidly than the capacity of human rights defenders to respond. Hence, the future success of the human rights community in conflict resolution is unclear, in spite of the considerable progress that has been made over the course of the twentieth century.

NOTES

1. The bibliography on the historical, philosophical, and religious origins of human rights is enormous. For general explorations of the concept of human rights, see the works of Maurice Cranston, Donald Dworkin, John Rawls, and Richard Rorty. A good summary of their work, and that of others, is Jerome J. Shestack, "The Philosophic Foundations of Human Rights," *Human Rights Quarterly* (hereafter *HRQ*) 20, no. 2 (May 1998): 201–34. See also Richard P. Claude, "Introduction" and "The Classical Model of Human Rights' Development," in Richard P. Claude, ed., *Comparative Human Rights* (Baltimore: The Johns Hopkins University Press, 1976), 3–50; Margaret E. Crahan, "The State and the Individual in Latin America: An Historical Overview," in Margaret E. Crahan, ed., *Human Rights and Basic Needs in the Americas* (Washington: Georgetown University Press, 1982), 23–45; Jack Donnelly, *The Concept of Human Rights* (New York: St. Martin's Press, 1985); Jack Donnelly, *International Human Rights*, 2nd ed. (Boulder, CO: Westview Press, 1998); Michael Freeman, "The Philosophical Foundations of Human Rights," *HRQ* 16, no. 3 (August 1994): 491–414; Micheline R. Ishay, *The Human Rights Reader: Major Political Writings, Essays, Speeches, and Documents from the Bible to the Present* (New York: Routledge, 1997); Johannes Morsink, "The Philosophy of the Universal Declaration," *HRQ* 6, no. 3 (August 1994): 309–334; James W. Nickel, *Making Sense of Human Rights: Philosophical Reflections on the Universal Declaration of Human Rights* (Berkeley: University of California Press, 1987); John O'Manrique, "Universal and Inalienable Rights: A Search for Foundations," *HRQ* 12, no. 4 (November 1990): 465–485; Michael Palumbo, *Human Rights: Meaning and History* (Malabar, FL: Robert E. Krieger Publishing Company, 1982); Henry J. Steiner and Phillip Alston, eds., *International Human Rights in*

Context: Law, Politics, Morals (New York: Clarendon Press, 1996). On religion and human rights, see John Kelsay and Sumner B. Twiss, eds., *Religion and Human Rights* (New York: The Project on Religion and Human Rights, 1994); and Robert Traer, *Faith in Human Rights: Support in Religious Traditions for a Global Struggle* (Washington: Georgetown University Press, 1991). On issues of cultural relativism and human rights, see Rhoda Howard, *Human Rights and the Search for Community* (Boulder, CO: Westview Press, 1995) and Michael J. Perry, "Are Human Rights Universal? The Relativist Challenge and Related Matters," *HRQ* 19 (1997): 461–509.

2. Margaret E. Keck and Kathryn Sikkink, *Activists Beyond Borders: Advocacy Networks in International Politics* (Ithaca, NY: Cornell University Press, 1998). For a detailed history of the development of an international human rights regime in the twentieth century, see Jan Herman Burgers, "The Road to San Francisco: The Revival of the Human Rights Idea in the Twentieth Century," *HRQ* 14, no. 4 (November 1992): 447–477.

3. Ibid., 469–70.

4. For an analysis of the evolution of human rights activities within the UN, see Tom J. Farer and Felice Gaer, "The UN and Human Rights: At the End of the Beginning," in Adam Roberts and Benedict Kingsbury, eds., *United Nations, Divided World: The UN's Role in International Relations* (New York: Oxford University Press. 1993), 240–296.

5. On the content of the Universal Declaration of Human Rights and the evolution of the UN human rights machinery, see Morsink, "The Philosophy of the Universal Declaration." On the debate over universality and cultural relativism, see Perry, "Are Human Rights Universal?" On the relation of civil/political and socioeconomic rights, see Human Rights Watch, *Indivisible Human Rights: The Relation of Political and Civil Rights to Survival, Subsistence, and Poverty* (New York: Human Rights Watch, 1992); and Amartya Sen, "Individual Freedom as a Social Commitment," *The New York Review of Books*, 14 June 1990, pp. 49–54.

6. C. Neale Ronning, ed., *Intervention in Latin America* (New York: Alfred A. Knopf, 1970), 13.

7. Ann Van Wynen Thomas and A. J. Thomas, Jr., *Non-Intervention: The Law and Its Impact on the Americas*, Foreword by Julio Cueto-Rua (Dallas: Southern Methodist University Press, 1956), 376–377.

8. Criteria for legitimate humanitarian interventions have developed over time based on international law and evolving interpretations of the UN Charter, as well as other international treaties and documents. See Tom J. Farer, "Intervention in Unnatural Humanitarian Emergencies: Lessons from the First Phase," *HRQ* 18, no. 1 (February 1996): 1–22; Tom J. Farer, "A Paradigm of Legitimate Intervention," in Lori Fisler Damrosch, ed., *Enforcing Restraint: Collective Intervention in Internal Conflicts* (New York: Council on Foreign Relations Press, 1993), 316–347; Louis Henkin, "Human Rights and 'Domestic Jurisdiction,'" in Thomas Buergenthal, ed., *Human Rights, International Law and the Helsinki Accord* (Montclair, NJ: Allanheld, Osmun and Co., 1977): 21–40; Louis Henkin, et al., *Right v. Might: International Law and the Use of Force*, Foreword and Afterword by John Temple Swing, 2nd ed. (New York: Council on Foreign Relations Press, 1991); Richard B. Lillich, ed., *Humanitarian Intervention and the United Nations* (Charlottesville, VA: University Press of Virginia, 1979); Thomas J. Weiss and Cindy Collins, *Humanitarian Challenges and Intervention: World Politics and the Dilemmas of Help* (Boulder, CO: Westview Press, 1996).

9. Farer, "Intervention in Unnatural Humanitarian Emergencies," passim.

10. Stephen John Stedman, "The New Interventionists," *Foreign Affairs* 72, no. 1 (1992/1993): 1–16.

11. Mark Duffield and John Prendergast, *Without Troops & Tanks: The Emergency Relief Desk and the Cross Border Operations into Eritrea and Tigray* (Lawrenceville, NJ: The Red Sea Press, 1992). See also David J. Scheffer, Richard N. Gardner, and Gerald B. Helman, *Three Views on the Issue of Humanitarian Intervention: Post–Gulf War Challenges to the UN Collective Security System* (Washington, DC: United States Institute of Peace, 1992).

12. "El Salvador: The 1988 National Debate," *LADOC* 19, no. 4 (March/April 1989): 12.

13. On the Salvadoran peace process, see United Nations, *The United Nations and El Salvador, 1990–1995* (New York: United Nations, 1995); Lawyers Committee for Human Rights, *Improvising History: A Critical Evaluation of the United Nations Observer Mission in El Salvador* (New York: Lawyers Committee for Human Rights, 1995); Human Rights Watch, *The Lost Agenda: Human Rights and UN Field Operations* (New York: Human Rights Watch, 1993); The Aspen Institute, *Honoring Human Rights and Keeping the Peace: Lessons from El Salvador, Cambodia and Haiti* (Washington, DC: The Aspen Institute, 1995). For the Guatemalan peace process, see Edelberto Torres–Rivas and Gabriel Aguilera Peralta, *Desde el Autoritarismo a la Paz* (Guatemala: FLACSO, 1998); Tania Palencia Prado, *Peace in the Making: Civil Groups in Guatemala* (London: Catholic Institute for International Relations, 1996); Bruce J. Calder, "The Role of the Catholic Church and Other Religious Institutions in the Guatemala Peace Process, 1980–1995," Paper presented at the XXI International Congress of the Latin American Studies Association, Chicago, Illinois, 17–24 September 1998; Denise Cook, "The Role of Civil Society in the Guatemalan Peace Process," ms., 1998. For comparisons of the Salvadoran and Guatemalan peace processes, see Cynthia J. Arnson, ed., *Comparative Peace Processes in Latin America* (Washington, DC and Stanford, CA: Woodrow Wilson Center Press and Stanford University Press, 1999); Pedro Nikken, "Los derechos humanos en la guerra y en la paz de Centroamérica," *Revista IIDH*, 25 (enero–junio 1997): 45–62.

14. Priscilla B. Hayner, "In Pursuit of Justice and Reconciliation: Contributions of Truth Telling," in Arnson, *Comparative Peace Processes*, 363–383.

15. Anonymous, "Human Rights in Peace Negotiations," *HRQ* 18 (1996): 258.

16. Felice D. Gaer, "UN–Anonymous: Reflections on Human Rights in Peace Negotiations," *HRQ* 19 (1997): 1

17. Ibid., 1–8.

18. Emily MacFarquar, Robert I. Rotberg, and Martha A. Chen, *Nongovernmental Organizations, Early Warning, and Preventive Diplomacy* (Cambridge, MA: World Peace Foundation, 1995), 5.

19. Ibid., 5ff.

20. Kevin M. Cahill, ed., *Preventive Diplomacy: Stopping Wars Before They Start* (New York: Basic Books, 1996).

21. Jackie Smith, Ron Pagnucco, with George A. Lopez, "Globalizing Human Rights: The Work of Transnational Human Rights NGOs in the 1990s," *HRQ* 20, no. 2 (May 1998): 387. The survey, sent to approximately 300 international human rights organizations, inquired about their activities, relations with international organizations and NGOs, structures and resources, and goals. Some of the questions in the survey were based on surveys used for studies of U.S. social change agencies.

22. Ibid., 379–412.

PART III

THE U.S. MILITARY IN LATIN AMERICA

6

Raising the National Conscience: Grassroots Organizing and the Debates over the U.S. Army School of the Americas

Molly Todd

"Good morning class! Today we are going to study *advanced interrogation techniques!* Can *you* say cattle prod?" So begins a 1995 episode of Tom Tomorrow's cartoon "This Modern World," which takes as its subject the United States Army School of the Americas, a U.S. military institution dedicated to training Latin American military personnel. In the episode, Tomorrow tackles issues central to the ongoing controversy surrounding the school: U.S. complicity in human rights violations committed in Latin America and the subsequent official damage control within the United States.

In the cartoon, Tomorrow presents unflattering portraits of several infamous graduates of the School of the Americas, evinces the sanctimonious behavior of members of the U.S. government bureaucracy who declare any unfortunate affair to be an aberration, and chastises the media for cooperating in government-initiated "ritual[s] of absolution." The cartoon ends with Sparky the Penguin's rhetorical question to his readers: "Isn't it sad that you had to learn about [the School of the Americas] from a *talking penguin in a comic strip?*"[1]

Sparky's question lays bare the difficulty of delving into the history of the School of the Americas. Such a task is rendered impracticable because information about the school is hard to come by, whether it be academic, journalistic, or otherwise. The sources available tend to be strictly divided between those that support the school and those that oppose it, and each side embraces an apposite rhetoric to support its position. Furthermore, a wealth of primary source material about the school remains classified, hidden away from public view in U.S. government and military archives.

Despite the limitations of the sources, there is much to be garnered from their collection and close examination. Drawing from the available government and nongovernment materials, this article will serve as an introduction to the School of the Americas and the highly charged debates surrounding it. The first section outlines the School of the Americas as an historical and present-day instrument of U.S. foreign policy in Latin America. The following section discusses the role of the School of the Americas Watch, a non-profit, grassroots organization, in bringing the unsavory aspects of the school to the fore of the national conscience. Finally, this chapter brings these two opposing sides into dialogue with each other, and concludes by offering a prediction on the eventual outcome of the debate.

In 1946, the U.S. Army first established what is today known as the U.S. Army School of the Americas (SOA).[2] When the school began in the Panama Canal Zone as the Latin America Center–Ground Division, its purpose was to provide instruction for U.S. Army personnel in garrison technical skills such as food preparation, maintenance, and other support functions. In 1949, the Army renamed the institution the U.S. Army Caribbean School–Spanish Instruction, and identified a secondary mission of instructing Latin American military personnel. The school eliminated English language instruction altogether in 1956 and focused its training efforts on Spanish speakers from Latin America. In 1963, the institution adopted the official name of the U.S. Army School of the Americas. In October 1984, the school suspended operations in Panama in accordance with the 1977 Panama Canal Treaty. Three months later, the School of the Americas reopened its doors at Fort Benning, Georgia, where it remains in operation today, authorized by Title 10 of the U.S. Code, section 4415, which defined the school's purpose as "providing military education and training to military personnel of Central and South American countries and Caribbean countries."[3]

In 1995, Russell Ramsey, an instructor at the SOA, wrote that the school began as "nothing more ambitious than a friendly gesture in 1946 to help [Latin America] train some soldiers in vehicular and electronic maintenance."[4] According to former Under Secretary of the U.S. Army, Joe Reeder, the school's first mandate was "to teach those skills we would refer to today as nation-building skills—bridge building, well digging, and other engineer skills."[5] Such a focus on mundane technical skills evinces a belief in the school's benign foundation, further supporting Ramsey's conclusion that "there was no sophisticated geostrategic scheme behind the school's existence, and no conscious awareness at that time that military instruction . . . would yield benefits."[6]

An alternative perspective comes to light, however, when the school is placed within its historical context. U. S. interests in Latin America, of course, antedate the SOA. Since the turn of the twentieth century, the United States has shown a steadily growing interest in the region. Early economic enterprises—such as the United Fruit Company, which began operations in Central America in 1898 and the Panama Canal agreements formalized in 1901—illustrate the initiation of a pattern of involvement based primarily on economic opportunism. The United States continued to expand its economic bases in Latin America throughout the first half of the century. This is exemplified by the growth in importance of coffee, a principal export crop of many Central American countries: whereas prior to 1934 the United States purchased a maximum of 25 percent of Central America's coffee harvest, by 1944 the United States accounted for 87 percent of the region's coffee exports.[7]

Although U.S. military training enterprises in Latin America can be traced back to at least 1902, when U.S. officers began training Cuban soldiers in the wake of Cuba's independence from Spain, such training did not become truly institutionalized until the 1930s and 1940s. During this period, in response to the fear of Japanese and German expansion into the Western Hemisphere, the U.S. Congress enacted a series of laws that broadened the mandate of the Department of Defense with respect to the training of Latin American forces. The Good Will Act of 1938, for example, legalized the training of Latin American soldiers at government institutions in the United States. As World War II flared and the United States sought to defend its "sphere of influence" against possible attack, the U.S. military expanded its installations; by the end of the war, U.S. military missions existed in all but three Latin American countries. Thus, the United States became the principle military tutor in the region.[8]

Also in light of World War II, Congress lifted a variety of restrictions on the sale to Latin America of U.S. surplus weapons and war materiel. The revised Neutrality Act of 1939 exempted Latin America from arms import restrictions, allowing the United States to openly trade military equipment with the region. The Lend–Lease Act of 1941 and the 1946 Inter-American Military Cooperation Act further facilitated the process. The transfers of military habiliments to Latin America presented an additional incentive for U.S. officers to instruct Latin American soldiers, as the newly acquired equipment required proper maintenance and use. By the 1970s, this vinculum between military sales and training had been conventionalized through a variety of U.S. government programs, such as the Foreign Military Sales (FMS) program. Even at the turn of the twenty-first century, the purchase of U.S. weaponry through FMS often guaranteed U.S. training and service.[9]

In general terms, then, during the first half of the twentieth century, U.S. economic and military interests in Latin America occupied parallel trajectories; financial investments increased on par with military training and sales. As seasoned scholars of U.S. foreign policy have shown, the U.S. military often defended the interests of U.S. business elites, and responded to real or perceived threats in the order they preferred.[10] This was the context into which the School of the Americas was born in 1946. Thus, while the school's original charges and duties may indeed have been benign, as Ramsey and Reeder indicated, one cannot dismiss the fact that, as the school opened its doors, it became part of a broader schema: a long-standing tradition of the U.S. military serving as a tool of U.S. foreign policy. When viewed from this perspective, then, the SOA was not exactly altruistic; but neither was it an aberration.[11]

U.S. military officials acknowledge, to differing degrees, the symbiosis between U.S. foreign policy (i.e., economic objectives and political issues) and the role of the military, and the SOA in particular. The United States Southern Command (SOUTHCOM), which oversees the School of the Americas, clearly identifies the economic functions of the U.S. military. According to SOUTHCOM, U.S. policy toward Latin America and the Caribbean "seeks to develop stable free market democracies throughout the region."[12] As part of that policy, SOUTHCOM pursues its "basic mission" of "defend[ing] U.S. interests within its assigned area of responsibility."[13] As a component of both U.S. policy and SOUTHCOM, the School of the Americas has an explicit objective of "promot[ing] and protect[ing] U.S. interests in the region by . . . Defend[ing] the Panama Canal and Canal Area . . . [and] Protecting [the] supply of strategic natural resources and access to markets."[14] In sum, according to SOUTHCOM, the School of the Americas, as an "Instrument of U.S. Policy," plays a "vital role in enhancing" the "stability" of Latin American nations.[15]

Military officials stationed at the School of the Americas, however, have rarely acknowledged in explicit terms the economic function of the military in general, or the school in particular. Yet, a 1999 SOA Command Brief indicated that within the school's "theater of operation," past decades have brought nothing but "economic good news": Latin American trade worldwide grew by 8.5 percent annually between 1985 and 1999; direct investments in Latin America more than doubled between 1990 and 1999; and, by late 1999, U.S. exports to Latin America were double those to Europe.[16] While these statistics do not explicitly address the role of the SOA in furthering U.S. business interests, it is significant that they were utilized as an indication of successful training efforts at the School of the Americas.

Nonetheless, rather than citing economic interests as the driving force behind the school's mission, SOA officials have highlighted how military training, as part of U.S. foreign policy in Latin America, "has tended to react to . . . threats to U.S. primacy in the region."[17] Following World War II, for example, as the fear of Soviet expansion replaced the threat of an attack by Japan or Germany, the United States became increasingly concerned with "containing Communism" and defending its "southern flank." During this period, the training mission of the school shifted from technical support to more complex soldier skills and combat operations in support of "hemispheric defense."

During the 1960s, in light of the Cuban Revolution, escalating violence in Vietnam, and the aftermath of McCarthyism on the home front, the threat of external attack gave way to an intense fear of communist infiltration from within the hemisphere. The SOA's assignment changed accordingly; in 1961, the Kennedy administration officially introduced the new mission of extricating insurgent forces within the Americas by "providing CI [Counter-Insurgency] training to Latin America militaries in support of U.S. policy in region."[18] Thereafter, instruction in counterinsurgency methods all but replaced training for protection against external armed attack. The training regimen during this period emphasized "population control," with new courses offered in psychological operations, intelligence, counter-guerrilla operations, riot control, and public information.[19]

Counterinsurgency training continued unabated throughout the 1970s and reached new heights in the 1980s during the presidential administration of Ronald Reagan. Determined to combat what it perceived as Soviet/Communist encroachment in Latin America—the "soft underbelly of the United States"[20]—the Reagan administration authorized massive increases in aid to the governments and armed forces of Central America in particular. Believing that the security forces of the region had been "forgotten" during the previous presidencies of Richard Nixon and Jimmy Carter, Reagan "actively sought military to military relationships to rebuild and professionalize" the militaries in Central America.[21] This led to an influx of Central American students at the School of the Americas. During this period, the majority of the students trained at the SOA hailed from Central America (particularly from Honduras and El Salvador). The extent of U.S. training efforts is visible, for example, in the rapid growth of the Salvadoran armed forces, which expanded fourfold during the 1980s, from approximately 14,000 personnel in 1979, to a peak of about 55,000 personnel in 1989.[22] Whereas between 1950 and 1980, International Military Education and Training (IMET) programs funded approximately 2,300 Salvadorans (an average of 76 students per year), between 1980 and 1995 some 4,200 Salvadorans (an average of 280 students per year) received training through IMET programs.[23]

With the 1989 fall of the Berlin Wall, the subsequent dismantling of the Soviet empire during the early 1990s, and the progress made toward peace in, for example, El Salvador and Guatemala, the SOA's CI mission lost the imperative it had held for three decades. Because the school had existed within the confines of the Cold War since its establishment, however, identifying a new mission and, hence, a new threat against which to rally, proved difficult. Ultimately, the "war on drugs" filled the void.

Prior to taking office, President-Elect George Bush proclaimed drugs to be the "gravest threat" to the security of the United States, a conviction that echoed throughout his administration's tenure. Building on a presidential directive issued by Reagan in 1986, which empowered the Department of Defense to become directly involved in anti-narcotics operations (a position previously deemed illegal), the Bush administration chartered the Andean Initiative. The initiative, revealed by President Bush in December 1989, was a five-year, $2.2 billion plan to stop cocaine "at its source."[24] The newly personified Latin American enemy—the *narco-guerrilla*—also extended Reagan's legacy by associating the illegal drug trafficking with revolutionary movements of the 1980s in Central America and "leftist guerrillas" throughout Latin America. This guerrilla–trafficker link, which "facilitated the shift from a Cold-War to a drug-war military posture [and brought] many old foes into the ranks of the new enemy," also eased the transition to narcotics-oriented training programs at the School of the Americas.[25]

Although at the start of the year 2000, the school had not been officially assigned an anti-narcotics mission, such a focus continued to be evident in SOA literature and statements, as well as in the origins of attendees. In a 1996 essay, Joseph Leuer, professor of Latin American Studies at the SOA, underscored the utility of anti-drug missions led by SOA graduates, the "successes" of which were measured by the number of coca plantations and clandestine airstrips destroyed.[26] A 1998 Army report on the School of the Americas also highlighted the importance of anti-narcotics training, concluding that such training helped "improve the ability and cooperation of host nation police and military forces to attack narcotics production and trafficking centers."[27]

Also during the late 1990s, as the number of Central American attendees fell drastically, the number of students from "key drug-producing countries" rose. Between 1996 and 1998, for example, approximately 75 percent of SOA graduates came from Mexico and the Andean countries of Colombia, Peru, Chile, and Bolivia. In 1997 alone, while 27 percent of SOA students were from Colombia and Chile and 33.6 percent were from Mexico, Salvadoran students accounted for just 1.5 percent.[28]

New training introduced at the School of the Americas during the 1990s illustrates the School's focus on counter-drug missions. An eleven-week Counter-drug Operations Course, for example, provides "specialized training . . . in the areas of planning, leading, and executing counter-drug operations." The course includes instruction on, among other things, close-quarters battle, surveillance and targeting techniques, development of intelligence networks, explosive entry techniques, and special infiltration techniques. Other courses, such as an eight-week Sapper Course, also include counter-drug components.[29]

Although fighting the drug war continued to be a principal justification for training at the SOA throughout the Bush and Clinton administrations, it is important to note the impact of President William Clinton's Security Strategy for the Americas. Revealed in 1994, this strategy delineated a variety of objectives considered paramount to U.S. national security, such as support for counter-drug efforts, promotion of anti-terrorism measures, and expansion of defense cooperation.[30] Unlike the Nixon and Reagan doctrines, Clinton's strategy identified a myriad of potential threats. The strategy, then, broadened both the concept of security and the potential causes of a breakdown in that security. According to Colonel William Spracher, former SOA commander and U.S. defense attaché to Colombia, "[W]e are now faced with a world that is somewhat gray and blurred, in which fear of communists has been replaced by fear of international terrorism, drug corruption, organized crime, contraband arms trafficking, and even industrial espionage."[31] With so many shadows lurking on the horizon, the School of the Americas does not lack possibilities for official missions in the foreseeable future.

Citizen-based, grassroots initiatives, however, call into question both the utility and morality of U.S. military involvement—including the training of soldiers—in Latin America. According to a variety of studies published in the past decades, the U.S. experience in Vietnam had an especially significant impact on the U.S. citizenry.[32] The high cost of the debacle, both in dollars and lives, led many to withdraw their support for direct U.S. involvement in distant armed conflicts. A palpable outgrowth of the "Vietnam Syndrome," as this disinclination has since come to be known, was the 1973 War Powers Act, which banned the extended deployment of U.S. troops abroad without congressional approval. Subsequently, many U.S. presidential administrations have felt the need to develop strategies to circumvent this restriction. The skirting of legal limitations paved the way to a distinct level of U.S. intervention in Latin America—that of covert action, defined in Executive Order 12333 as "special activities conducted in support of national foreign policy objectives abroad which are planned and executed so that the role of the United States government is not apparent or acknowledged publicly."[33]

Although many details of particular U.S. covert actions in Latin America continue to be hidden from public view, the immediate results of these operations have often been clearly visible. From the 1970s on, many organizations collected data and distributed reports on the violence, devastation, and abuses occurring throughout Central America as well as in Southern Cone countries such as Argentina and Chile, enveloped in so-called "dirty wars." These organizations encompassed faith-based groups such as parishes, dioceses, and church-sponsored commissions, and international human rights organizations including Human Rights Watch, Amnesty International, and the Inter-American Commission on Human Rights. In addition, a multitude of citizen "interest groups" (e.g., survivors of torture, former political prisoners, and mothers, grandmothers, and family members of the detained and disappeared) organized and drew attention to causes relating to human rights. Moreover, in some cases, international teams of forensic anthropologists released reports based on detailed investigations of mass graves and other alleged crime scenes.

The evidence provided by such organizations indicated that during the 1970s and 1980s rates of human rights abuses soared in many Latin American nations. The reported abuses most often occurred in the wake of coups d'etat which brought a country's armed forces to power, such as occurred in Chile in 1973 and El Salvador in 1979. In some countries, military governments were persistently repressive and often carried out indiscriminate anti-subversion campaigns (e.g., Bolivia under General Hugo Banzer, Chile under General Augusto Pinochet, Argentina under Generals Jorge Rafael Videla and Leopoldo Galtieri, Guatemala under Colonel Carlos Arana Osorio and Generals Romeo Lucas García and Efraín Ríos Montt, and Nicaragua under the Somoza dynasty). In light of the violence with which these and other military leaders consolidated their rule and sought to maintain power, human rights workers rarely lacked cases to investigate and chronicle.

In the United States, opposition to executive policies toward these countries and their governments came to a head in the 1980s, as the Reagan administration reacted with increasing aggressiveness to civil unrest and armed conflict abroad. Heightened U.S. military aid to Central America exacerbated already dour conditions, prompting many civilians to flee the violence at home and escape to other countries, including the United States. By 1982, more than one million Central Americans had left their homes. At times during the early 1980s, Guatemalans streamed into Mexico at the rate of 2,000–3,500 per week. And, between 1980 and 1982, the Salvadoran refugee population in the United States grew from 94,000 to somewhere between 300,000 and 500,000.[34]

Responding to the influx of immigrants and acting in opposition to Reagan's foreign policies, church-based groups in the southwestern United States began assisting the refugees to cross the U.S.–Mexico border undetected, search for shelter and employment in the United States, and frustrate deportation proceedings initiated by the U.S. Immigration and Naturalization Service (INS). In March 1982, after more than a year working clandestinely, those involved in such efforts went public with their protest activities by declaring Southside Presbyterian Church in Tucson, Arizona, a sanctuary for Central Americans fleeing political violence in their home countries. Other churches and organizations across the United States followed suit, and sanctuary soon became "the largest grassroots civil disobedience movement in North America since the 1960s."[35]

Citizen-initiated protest activities also extended beyond the sanctuary movement to ecumenical and nonfaith-based solidarity organizations such as the Committee in Solidarity with the People of El Salvador (CISPES) and Medical Aid to Central America (MACA). Such organizations pressured the U.S. Congress to formulate alternative policy options and provided material aid and moral support to battered communities of the war-torn countries. And, by the mid-1980s, the Pledge of Resistance had mobilized more than 80,000 individual U.S. citizens to threaten mass civil disobedience if the United States government continued to escalate the wars in Central America.[36]

Out of this political atmosphere emerged Roy Bourgeois, a decorated Vietnam veteran and Maryknoll priest who ultimately turned his attention to U.S. military involvements abroad and focused his energies on raising consciousness about the role of the School of the Americas in those interventions. Although Bourgeois' official campaign to close the SOA began with the founding of SOA Watch in 1990, his path toward the school began in Vietnam. Bourgeois recalls that, during his tour of duty with the U.S. Navy in Vietnam "[t]he violence, losing friends, and getting wounded forced me to look at my faith and ask questions I hadn't asked before."[37] Some answers came to Bourgeois through his volunteer work at an orphanage near his base. He found inspiration in the Canadian priest and his small, under-resourced staff who cared for hundreds of local children. He saw them as healers and peacemakers, and thought, "What a wonderful way to spend life," being a healer and peacemaker amid so much suffering and darkness.

Upon leaving the Navy, Bourgeois entered the Maryknoll order and studied in seminaries in Illinois, Massachusetts, and New York. Following his ordination in 1972, he moved to a poverty-stricken neighborhood on the outskirts of La Paz, Bolivia. There he spent the next five years, saying Mass in a vacant lot and working with the community to establish a health clinic, a daycare center, and a literacy program. He came to see the poor around him as his teachers; from them he learned about religion, poverty and oppression, and his own country's foreign policy. Furthermore, in Bolivia, Bourgeois learned about life and survival under a military dictatorship. He witnessed the violence imposed by General Banzer's soldiers, and personally felt the insecurity and fear it inspired. When Bourgeois began working with political prisoners, the soldiers came for him. Under the cover of darkness, they took him to a cemetery and roughed him up—a not-so-subtle warning that his safety could no longer be guaranteed in Bolivia. He returned to the United States and dedicated himself to educating people about what he had seen and heard abroad.

Roy Bourgeois became deeply involved in the Salvadoran conflict in 1980, following two momentous events. In March, El Salvador's Archbishop Oscar Romero was assassinated while saying Mass. Days before his death, Romero had made a special public appeal to the men of the Salvadoran armed forces to end the repression and violence that engulfed the country. Also shortly before his death, Romero pleaded to then President of the United States Jimmy Carter for a prohibition of U.S. military aid and training. He argued that "instead of favoring greater peace and justice in El Salvador, [continued aid] will undoubtedly aggravate the repression and injustice."[38] Despite Romero's best efforts, U.S. military aid to El Salvador not only continued, but dramatically increased to $5.7 million—eleven times the average annual aid to that country since World War II.[39] In December 1980, four U.S. churchwomen were raped and murdered by Salvadoran soldiers. Two of the women, Maryknoll Sisters Maura Clarke and Ita Ford, were friends of Bourgeois and, he says, "Their death forced me to confront what was happening."[40] So, he went to El Salvador, where he traveled the country, met and spoke with victims and witnesses of state-sponsored violence, and spent time in the mountains with the armed opposition forces. Bourgeois eventually returned to the United States, loudly denouncing U.S. support of the military regime in El Salvador.

Two years after the deaths of the churchwomen, the situation in El Salvador had worsened and U.S. military aid continued virtually unabated.[41] In May 1983, upon learning that 500 Salvadoran soldiers were training with U.S. advisers at Fort Benning in Columbus, Georgia, Bourgeois changed tactics. Speaking out was not enough. He planned and carried out an action of nonviolent civil disobedience, designed to call attention to the U.S. military's role in prolonging the war in El Salvador. One evening, he donned drab green (purchased at a military surplus store) and walked onto the Fort Benning military base. He located the barracks of the Salvadorans, climbed a nearby tree, and waited for dark. When the last light finally went out, Bourgeois pushed the "play" button of the boom-box he had brought with him; Oscar Romero's voice thundered through the night, calling on the military to stop the killing and lay down their arms. Military police quickly arrested Bourgeois and charged and convicted him of trespassing and impersonating an officer. For this action, Bourgeois served eighteen months in a Minnesota federal prison.

In 1990, Bourgeois was prompted to focus his attention specifically on the School of the Americas. This decision came after the November 1989 murder of six Jesuit priests, their female employee, and her teenage daughter at a university in San Salvador. The unprovoked massacre spurred a serious U.S. investigation which culminated in the April 1990 release of the report of a congressional task force headed by Representative Joseph Moakley (D-MA). The report revealed that the soldiers responsible for the Jesuit murders had been trained at the U.S. Army School of the Americas at Fort Benning.[42]

Four months after the release of the Moakley task force report, Bourgeois rented a small apartment just outside the gates of Fort Benning and, along with three others, established the School of the Americas Watch (SOA Watch). There, they spent the final decade of the twentieth century researching the School of the Americas, tracking hundreds of its graduates, and building a massive grassroots movement to close the school.

SOA Watch started small; the first organizational meeting included just three people and the first public protest action involved ten people.[43] The latter took place in September 1990 when, in an effort to draw more widespread attention to the school, Bourgeois and nine others (members of the clergy, a teacher, and a group of Salvadorans and Vietnam veterans), held a thirty-seven-day, water-only fast at the entrance to Fort Benning. A few weeks later, Bourgeois and two brothers, Patrick and Charles Liteky,[44] observed the first anniversary of the Jesuit massacre with another protest action: After placing a white cross with photos of the murdered eight on the lawn outside the school, they entered the main building and, in "a room like a museum," scattered blood-covered photos of SOA graduates and instructors. They left behind a letter to the school's commandant, asking him to close the school. Says Bourgeois, "We wanted to impress upon our country that we cannot wash our hands of the blood shed in El Salvador by soldiers trained in the United States." All three were arrested, charged, and convicted of damaging government property. Bourgeois received a jail sentence of fourteen months; the Liteky brothers, six months each.[45]

Bourgeois recalls that during this early period of SOA Watch, very little was known about the School of the Americas—only the basics revealed by the congressional task force, such as when the school opened and the names of two notorious graduates: General Manuel Noriega, former leader of Panama, now serving a forty-year sentence in a Miami prison for drug-trafficking; and Roberto D'Aubuisson, prime mover behind El Salvador's dreaded death squads and founder of ARENA, the country's dominant, right-wing political party. The little information that was available, however, prompted many organizations to pledge support for SOA Watch, and several nationally recognized groups officially and publicly called for the closing of the school. Among the early groups to join the campaign were Veterans for Peace, Presbyterian Church USA, the Evangelical Church of America, Leadership Conference of Women Religious, United Methodist Bishops, and the Methodist Board of Church and Society.

The year 1993 brought several discoveries crucial for the organizational growth of SOA Watch. First, in response to a Freedom of Information Act request, Bourgeois and his associate Vicky Imerman[46] received a list of graduates of the School of the Americas. Then, in March, the United Nations Commission on the Truth for El Salvador issued its report, *From Madness to Hope*, which indicated U.S. complicity in large-scale human rights violations and civilian deaths during the Salvadoran civil war.[47] By comparing the UN report with the list of graduates, SOA Watch calculated that 73 percent of the soldiers cited for human rights violations by the UN Truth Commission were alumni of the School of the Americas, including two of three officers cited for the March 1980 assassination of Archbishop Oscar Romero, three of five officers cited for the December 1980 rape and murder of the four U.S. churchwomen, ten of twelve officers cited for the 1981 massacre of approximately 1,000 civilians in the rural hamlet of El Mozote, and eleven of the sixteen officers cited for the massacres at El Junquillo, Las Hojas, and San Sebastian that resulted in the deaths of some 140 civilians.[48]

These revelations spurred the first national mainstream media coverage critical of the school; on 9 August 1993, *Newsweek* ran an article entitled "Running a 'School for Dictators.' "[49] Media attention prompted congressional discomfort and, eventually, legislative action. Armed with a copy of the *Newsweek* article, Representative Martin Meehan (D-MA) took the House floor on 6 August, demanding congressional action on the issue. Meehan questioned the utility of spending $5.8 million a year to operate the school if it continuously graduated "some of the most unsavory thugs in the Western hemisphere."[50] In September, Joseph Kennedy (D-MA) introduced the first anti-SOA legislation in the House of Representatives. Although Kennedy's effort failed by a 174–256 vote, the school had, at last, broken into the national consciousness.[51]

In 1996, the school was again linked to several major scandals, resulting in much criticism in the national media, the public eye, and Congress. First, in June, an Intelligence Oversight Board (IOB) report verified allegations that a paid agent of the U.S. Central Intelligence Agency (CIA), Guatemalan Colonel Julio Alberto Alpírez, had been directly involved in the murder of a U.S. citizen in Guatemala.[52] Alpírez attended the U.S. Army School of the Americas on at least two occasions: once in 1970 for a brief cadet orientation course and again in 1989 for a forty-eight-week Command and General Staff officer's course. Barely six months after he returned to Guatemala from his second SOA stint—and while still on the CIA payroll— Colonel Alpírez participated in the murder of Michael DeVine, a former Peace Corps volunteer who managed a tourist ranch in northern Guatemala. Alpírez also directed the 1992 kidnapping, interrogation, torture, and murder of Efraín Bámaca, a leader of the Guatemalan armed opposition married to U.S. lawyer Jennifer Harbury. In September 1996, the Pentagon declassified and made available to the public seven U.S. Army training manuals that advocated tactics such as "executing guerrillas, blackmail, false imprisonment, physical abuse, using truth serum to obtain information, and paying bounties for enemy dead." Prepared in 1982 by U.S. military personnel at the School of the Americas, the manuals—with titles like *Interrogation*, *Handling of Sources*, and *Revolutionary War and Communist Ideology*— were used throughout the 1980s by U.S. trainers in Latin America, and distributed to intelligence schools in Colombia, Ecuador, El Salvador, and Peru. The manuals were also used in SOA courses attended by soldiers from Bolivia, Colombia, Costa Rica, the Dominican Republic, Ecuador, Guatemala, Honduras, Mexico, Peru, and Venezuela.[53]

The release of the IOB report and the "torture manuals" led to a veritable media feeding frenzy throughout the year.[54] Such sustained media attention, the first of its kind for the School of the Americas, was instrumental in drawing attention to, and support for, the SOA Watch campaign. This is made evident by the leap in numbers of people protesting at the school. In

August 1996, a delegation of some 400 members of the Leadership Conference of Women Religious gathered at the School of the Americas, calling for its closure. In November 1996, more than 500 people gathered to observe the seventh anniversary of the Jesuit murders. Following a peaceful vigil and march, sixty protesters participated in a civil disobedience action by "crossing the line" onto the military base. All sixty were arrested.[55]

Since 1996, support for SOA Watch and its mission to close the school has continued to grow at an unprecedented rate—most apparent in the number of persons attending the yearly November protests. Whereas in 1990 seven individuals crossed the line and were arrested by Fort Benning police, in 1997 2,000 people attended the protest and more than 600 crossed the line and were arrested. The following November, more than 2,300 of the 7,000 persons in attendance crossed the line onto the base. The military police at Fort Benning were clearly overwhelmed by the numbers; rather than arrest anyone, they herded protesters onto waiting school buses, drove them to a park several miles from the base, and released them. In 1999, to commemorate the tenth anniversary of the Jesuit murders, more than 12,000 gathered to protest the school. Despite warnings from SOA officials that the previous year's strategy would not be repeated, the majority of the 4,500 people who marched onto the military base were again bused to the nearby park and released. Only those protesters who made up the "high-risk" category were detained and charged with trespassing and destruction of government property.

The creation of a high-risk category occurred as the mass of protesters grew and SOA Watch developed new strategies to draw attention to its cause. The "high-riskers" were volunteers who participated in an action of civil disobedience that could carry a felony conviction (e.g., digging "graves" on the military base or tossing blood or red paint on military property). Such actions were preplanned and kept secret until the day of the general protest. The volunteers—many of whom had prior convictions for similar acts of civil disobedience—expected arrest and even anticipated imprisonment, but considered it a sacrifice that was necessary for the continued education of the U.S. public and the progress of the movement. As Roy Bourgeois explained, "Every movement for justice needs people in jail to inspire people."[56]

During the late 1990s, anti-SOA energy also spread beyond Fort Benning, Georgia. Washington, D.C. became the site of a second SOA Watch office, directed by Carol Richardson, a long-time peace activist who in 1994 staffed the Georgia SOA Watch office for six months while Bourgeois served another SOA-related prison sentence. The second office, which opened in January 1997, had two full-time staff members and a steady flow of volunteers by 1999. Washington, D.C. also became the site of another yearly mass demonstration, held in the spring and devoted to lobbying on Capitol Hill and protest actions at the Pentagon. Furthermore, each year, at the time of the major spring and fall protests, solidarity vigils occur in cities across the Americas.

By the year 2000, the SOA Watch mailing list topped 18,000. In addition, some 200 community-based and national organizations, including peace and justice organizations (e.g., the NAACP); labor unions (e.g., AFL–CIO); government parties (e.g., the state assemblies of New York and New Jersey); and many religious groups, churches, and congressional representatives, have pledged their support. SOA Watch also receives support from many international groups such as Canada's New Democratic Party, the Guatemala Human Rights Commission, Amnesty and Pax Christi International, as well as other organizations in Mexico, El Salvador, Venezuela, Colombia, and Brazil.[57]

Popular figures have also contributed to the visibility of the anti-SOA movement. In 1995, a documentary film about the school's controversial history, narrated by actress Susan Sarandon, was nominated for an Academy Award.[58] Since 1998, actor Martin Sheen has become a regular among the thousands of protesters risking arrest during the November demonstrations at Fort Benning. Many musicians—including Iris Dement, Tish Hinojosa, the Indigo Girls, and Odetta—have lent their talents on behalf of SOA Watch. Pete Seeger and his grandson also have become regular performers at both the spring and fall protests, and in 1998 they celebrated Pete's eightieth birthday by playing a concert to benefit SOA Watch.

While these celebrities have certainly introduced the controversial issues surrounding the School of the Americas to a broader audience, the foundation of support for the SOA Watch mission must be attributed to the new allegations and evidence that each year link graduates of the School of the Americas to criminal acts, such as coups and countercoups, drug-trafficking, corruption, police brutality, bombings, kidnappings and disappearances, torture, rape, and murder. Such crimes, many of which may be defined and punished under international law as war crimes, crimes against humanity and even genocide, were condemned during the early 1990s. As previously discussed, the UN Commission on the Truth for El Salvador released its conclusions in 1993. Also in 1993, an international human rights tribunal cited 246 Colombian officers, more than 100 of them SOA graduates, for war crimes. Likewise, many of the central figures of the infamous Honduran Battalion 316 are graduates of the School of the Americas—including the founder, General Luis Alonso Discua, four of the five organizers, and at least nineteen of the ranking officers.[59]

Acknowledging the massive amount of evidence compiled and presented by SOA Watch, high-ranking officers associated with the School of the Americas have recognized that the forced closure of the school is possible, even probable. Former SOA Commandant Colonel Roy R. Trumble recalls how, when he was notified in 1994 of his transfer to the School of the

Americas, his superiors tried to dissuade him from accepting the assignment. Trumble's supervisor, for example, warned him that the "opponents of the school were going to bury it and would bury me along with it." Trumble made the transfer anyway, and in July 1998 he gingerly noted, "[H]ere we are . . . still above ground."[60]

Pressure to close the SOA continues to mount, however, and, in light of recent legislative gains, the school's days appear to be numbered. In July 1997, the U.S. Senate passed legislation requiring an annual review of the school to ensure that its training programs were consistent with respect for human rights and civil control over the military. In July 1999, the House of Representatives voted 230 to 197 to cut funding to the SOA. Although the amendment to cut SOA funding ultimately lost in a House–Senate conference committee by a vote of 7 to 8, it is clear that to keep the school operating has become a much more laborious and time-consuming task.

Increased public awareness of, and congressional action on, the controversial school has resulted in a shifting of the burden of proof from the school's opponents to the SOA itself. At the same time, SOA officials have more frequently responded to criticism with knee-jerk defenses. Some officials altogether deny SOA connections to human rights violations. Russell Ramsey, for example, attributed the high level of human rights abuses in the 1980s in Central America to "the massive Soviet–Cuban tutelage apparatus [which] advocated a deliberate policy of abuse against the non-Communist and anti-Communist populace."[61] While other officials do not categorically deny SOA graduates' links to violations, they do not acknowledge any explicit connection between training at the SOA and the alleged crimes. Officials contend, in fact, that the SOA bears no responsibility for the actions of its graduates. In the words of Colonel William Spracher, "[T]here are bad apples in any barrel [and] just because an ex-SOA student of twenty years ago commits a crime, his behavior cannot be blamed on his experience at [the] SOA."[62] Thus, those alumni who have been cited for human rights violations are simply "a few bad apples" whose actions constitute "aberrations from the norm." Of the school's more than 60,000 graduates, less than one percent, officials claim, have been charged with violating human rights or international law.

The school's opponents note the misleading character of this statistic. First, few of the reported human rights abuses committed in Latin America ever become the subjects of thorough investigations. Many—if not most—reports receive scant attention or are simply ignored. In other cases, officials scoff at the claims and instead hold the victim responsible, as in the case of U.S. citizen Diana Ortiz. When Ortiz pressed the U.S. and Guatemalan governments for information relating to her abduction, rape, and torture by soldiers from the Guatemalan military, General Héctor Gramajo publicly asserted that the hundreds of scars found on Ortiz's body were from a lesbian love affair gone awry.[63] In yet other cases, officials seem to do everything possible to drive any investigation off course. Months after the brutal assassination of Guatemalan Bishop Juan Gerardi, for example, credible investigations stalled while accusations were leveled against a dog.[64]

Given these patterns, SOA Watch argues that rather than comparing the number of cited SOA graduates with the total number of SOA graduates, as the school's defendants do, focus should instead be placed on the percentage of SOA graduates implicated in atrocities that have been officially investigated by reputable organizations. When viewed from this perspective, the percentage of cited SOA graduates soars. (Recall that 73 percent of those cited in the Salvadoran Truth Commission's report were SOA alumni.) SOA Watch is also careful to point out how very few of the cited soldiers and officers are ever tried in a court of law or imprisoned for their crimes.

Another method of defense used by SOA representatives is placing any "mistake" made by the school (such as the use of controversial training materials) in the distant past, and averring that the school has since reformed. During the July 1999 House of Representative debates on an amendment to cut SOA funding, for example, Representative Callahan (R–AL) acknowledged that although atrocities have indeed been committed by SOA graduates, "we cannot condemn the School of the Americas forever for something that happened 15 or 20 years ago." Callahan further asserted that continued debates on the subject were pointless because the SOA had "cleaned up its act."[65]

SOA Watch, on the other hand, points to the evidence which continues to surface, linking graduates to both old and new crimes. For example, the 1999 U.S. State Department Report on Human Rights in Colombia cited various SOA graduates for their involvement in human rights abuses, including Army Major David Hernández Rojas. According to the report, in March of 1999 Hernández and five others of the Fourth Counterguerrilla Battalion (Fourth Brigade) murdered the Antioquia Peace Commissioner, Alex Lopera,[66] and two others. Aware that Lopera and his companions carried a large amount of money as they traveled toward Sonson, Antioquia, Hernández and his subordinates "set up a military roadblock, detained them, killed them, stole the ransom money, and then pushed the victims and the vehicle into a deep crevice."[67] At the end of the year, as a civilian judiciary launched proceedings against the six members of the Fourth Brigade, Hernández "escaped from military detention and remained a fugitive from justice."[68] A Human Rights Watch report issued in February 2000 corroborated the State Department findings on Hernández, and noted that Hernández had attended the School of the Americas on two separate occasions: first in 1985 for a six-week cadet orientation in combat weapons, and then in 1991 for a two-and-a-half-month course in Psychological Operations.[69] The Human Rights Watch report cited at least six other SOA graduates, including Brigadier General Jaime Ernesto Canal Albán and General Carlos Ospina Ovalle, for violations of human rights and connections to Colombian paramilitary groups during 1999.[70]

Also in 1999, the Guatemalan Historical Clarification Commission (*Comisión para el Esclarecimiento Histórico–CEH*) explicitly linked the high number of atrocities committed during the Guatemalan civil war to military training provided by U.S. forces. Although the CEH report was not allowed to identify individual perpetrators, a report from the Archdiocese of Guatemala, released several months earlier, included many of the same cases and provided the names of those responsible. Not surprisingly, many of those alluded to or directly cited as responsible for massive violations of human rights are graduates of the School of the Americas. For example, three top directors and various leaders and members of the notorious and fearsome D-2 (G-2) intelligence agency attended the SOA. In addition, three servicemen cited for the murder of internationally known anthropologist Myrna Mack, three officers cited for the cover-up of the murder of U.S. citizen Michael Devine, and the creator of the vigilante groups known as the civil patrols (PACs were responsible for some of the most brutal war-time violations) were all School of the Americas graduates.[71]

Another extremely high profile case with direct links to the School of the Americas is that of the Chilean General Augusto Pinochet who, in October 1998, was arrested and detained in the United Kingdom on charges of "crimes of genocide and terrorism."[72] Although Pinochet himself did not attend the School of the Americas, he does have extensive ties to the school. The Spanish lawyer who presented the charges that resulted in Pinochet's arrest in London also presented charges against thirty other high-ranking officials of the Pinochet dictatorship, ten of whom are graduates of the School of the Americas. Among those cited were General Manuel Contreras Sepúlveda, former chief officer of the *Dirección de Inteligencia Nacional* (DINA), the feared Chilean secret police which operated from June 1974 through late 1977,[73] and General Odlanier Mena, former director of the *Central Nacional de Informaciones* (CNI), the secret police agency which supplanted DINA in 1977 and operated throughout the 1980s.[74] Other SOA graduates cited in the Spanish case were two officers—Colonel Jaime Lepe Orellana and Colonel Pablo Belmar[75]—who tortured and murdered Spanish citizen and United Nations official Carmelo Soria. Other SOA graduates have been cited for their participation in the operation of the infamous torture centers of Villa Grimaldi, Tres Alamos, and Cuatro Alamos.[76] Despite these and other indecorous facts, in 1991 the School of the Americas' Commandant prominently displayed on his office wall a note and a ceremonial gold sword—personal gifts from Pinochet.

Both the detention of Pinochet and the exhumation of Guatemala's wartime truths can be considered historic turning points with direct implications for the future of the School of the Americas. Pinochet's detention has pushed the School of the Americas further into the spotlight of international justice, as demonstrated by Roy Bourgeois' December 1998 testimony before the prosecution about "Operation Condor" and the School of the Americas.[77] Prominent international lawyers maintain that "the foundations of [Operation] Condor were laid at the School of the Americas in Panama"—a conclusion which has been supported by official documentation recovered from a once-secret Paraguayan archive.[78] In Guatemala, the release of the CEH report prompted an unprecedented U.S. executive-level public acknowledgement of the negative impact of U.S. military training and aid. As President William Clinton stood before an audience in Guatemala City on 10 March 1999, he admitted that U.S. "support for military forces or intelligence units which engaged in violent and widespread repression of the kind described in the [CEH] report was wrong, and the United States must not repeat that mistake."[79]

Nonetheless, officials of the School of the Americas continue to emphasize that SOA training professionalizes Latin American soldiers. Despite repeated references to this professionalization imperative, however, the term has yet to be adequately defined or explicated. Speaking at the Fiftieth Anniversary Ceremony of the School of the Americas in September 1996, former undersecretary of the U.S. Army, Joe Reeder, presented a rather indistinct definition when he referred to the SOA mission of "enhancing military professionalism" as teaching "soldier skills." This "bottom line challenge" for the School of the Americas, Reeder continued, meant "train[ing] soldiers how to react smartly where it is hard to tell the difference between good guys and bad guys."[80] U. S. Army Colonel Glenn Weidner provides a somewhat more direct definition of professionalism in a 1998 paper presented to Harvard University's Weatherhead Center for International Affairs. In the paper, Weidner indicated that Latin American forces underwent "significant modernization and professionalization" during the 1950s and 1960s, as they became better "equipped with modern U.S. surplus weapons and equipment," and "consolidat[ed] their dominant position of organizational discipline and effectiveness" in society.[81]

Along with such references to soldier professionalism, SOA supporters maintain that training at the school promotes democracy and democratic values. A 1998 SOA publication announced, for example, that the School of the Americas was "widely recognized as a significant positive contributing force for the emergence of democracy throughout the Americas."[82] Likewise, a May 1999 Command Briefing from the school concluded that, by virtue of U.S. training assistance, "Democracy is prospering" in the Latin American region.[83]

In response to criticism and claims of human rights abuses by SOA graduates, the school's supporters maintain that "misconduct among graduates is the *atypical* behavior" and, therefore, "let us not throw out the whole barrel of apples because of a few bad apples."[84] They argue that the School has learned from its past mistakes and has reformed. The SOA curriculum, and the human rights component in particular are considered proof of positive change. As a 1995 briefing stated, "Since 1990, [the SOA] has become the only U.S. Army academic institution where human rights instruction is incorporated into every course."[85] According to a 1998 Army report on the School of the Americas, students receive one four-hour block of human rights instruction per course—twice the amount received by most students at other Army schools.[86]

The School's opponents, however, question the adequacy of the SOA curriculum with relation to democracy and human rights issues. Retired Army Major Joseph Blair, a Latin American specialist and former instructor at the School of the Americas, became a critic of the school when the U.S. Army repeatedly denied knowledge about atrocities committed by SOA graduates and, at the same time, began its public relations campaigns emphasizing training in human rights and democratic values. In a 1998 documentary video, Blair described his experiences at the SOA and concluded that the school "has no curriculum which would change the values or the political views of anyone in Latin America." According to Blair, the SOA does not even offer a human rights course; the one course carrying "human rights" in the title consists of the "same four hours of instruction they've had for 20 years. Nothing's changed." Furthermore, Blair revealed that during his tenure at the SOA, "we routinely had Latin American students who were known human rights abusers and it didn't make any difference to us."[87]

With respect to the purported role of the SOA in the democratization of Latin American nations, Blair scoffed that "It's a joke."[88] He raised the question that if all nations in the hemisphere, except one, are democracies, why does the School of the Americas need to continue "teaching" it? Furthermore, he asked, how can the U.S. Army be entrusted with the task of "teaching" the subject of democracy, considering that "there is nothing democratic about the Army to begin with?" "The fact is," he continued, "the only course offered at the School of the Americas dealing with anything having to do with democracy has had less than 30 students since its inception. If the United States government wants to teach democracy they'd be better off shutting down the SOA and sending the Latin American students to our United States universities." Blair emphasized that training at the School of the Americas sends the "wrong message [because] it actually teaches a non-democratic response."[89]

Major Blair, SOA Watch, and opponents of the SOA also call into question the claims by SOA officials that the school has reformed. They note that graduates cited for criminal offenses continue to be recognized as heroes by the SOA. In 1991, for instance, a U.S. federal judge found Guatemalan General Héctor Gramajo guilty of numerous war crimes, and awarded Diana Ortiz and eight Guatemalans a total of $47.5 million. Six weeks after this ruling, Gramajo was welcomed at the School of the Americas, where he had been invited to speak at a commencement ceremony.[90] Similarly, Chilean Colonel Pablo Belmar was a guest instructor at the SOA despite having been directly implicated in the 1976 torture and murder of United Nations official Carmelo Soria.[91] If the school does not take definitive action against such acknowledged criminals, opponents query, how can citizens be assured that the school will comply with its vows to respect human rights, U.S. law, and international law?

Countering criticism and questions such as these, SOA supporters maintain that "the School of the Americas is a School for good." In the words of General Wilhelm, the SOA is a "priest in his pulpit" who, every Sunday, tells his congregation to "go out during the coming week and do good things and sin no more."[92] The school's opponents, however, want the SOA closed. They argue that it is a stain on the United States of America; its sordid history alone should merit its immediate closure, and the fact that graduates continue to be linked to criminal acts further strengthens their demands. Yet, school officials continue the struggle to keep the SOA open, and many state that if it is forced to close they will resuscitate it. Says General Wilhelm, "[I]f this School would cancel today, tomorrow I will assemble my staff and simply recreate it."[93]

The continued expansion of the opposition movement initiated by SOA Watch in 1990 indicates that it, too, will continue the struggle. As Roy Bourgeois states, "[W]e will shut down the 'School of Assassins'—whatever they call it."[94] The increased attention paid to the School of the Americas within the U.S. Congress, combined with unprecedented events such as President Clinton's expression of regret to the Guatemalan people, provide every indication that SOA Watch and its followers now have the upper hand in this lengthy debate. To its credit, SOA Watch recognizes that the ultimate closure of the SOA will be a symbolic gesture which does not attack the root of problems with U.S. foreign policy. SOA Watch maintains, however, that the eventual closure of the School of the Americas will mark one step in the right direction, toward a more just and more humane future.

NOTES

The author is particularly indebted to Thad Crouch for research aid, and Daniel Gregor and Virginia M. Bouvier for editing assistance. The following people provided valuable information and insights through personal interviews and communications: Joseph Blair, Roy Bourgeois, Nicholas Britto, Heather Dean, Ray Laport, and Carol Richardson.

1. Tom Tomorrow, "This Modern World," *Des Moines Sunday Register*, 14 May 1995.

2. The official U.S. Army acronym for the school is USARSA.

3. U.S.Code § 4415 (1998).

4. Russell W. Ramsey, "Forty Years of Human Rights Training," *Journal of Low*

Intensity Conflict and Law Enforcement 4 (Autumn, 1995): 10. Ramsey is Resident Civilian Professor of Latin American Studies at the School of the Americas. Despite his civilian title, he is a career Army officer who notes that he has been part of U.S. Army training of Latin American forces since 1960. This and other essays and speeches are available from the U.S. Army School of the Americas' official website at http://www.benning.army.mil/usarsa.

5. Joe R. Reeder, Speech given at the 50th Anniversary Ceremony of the United States School of the Americas, Fort Benning, Georgia, 25 September 1996.

6. Ramsey, "Forty Years," 7.

7. Jenny Pearce, *Under the Eagle: U.S. Intervention in Central America and the Caribbean* (London: Latin American Bureau, 1982), 25. The two percentages are derived from data for the years 1930–1934 and 1940–1944. There are a myriad of other sources which address U.S. business and economic interests in Latin America, only a few of which will be mentioned here. Directly relating to the School of the Americas, see Jack Nelson-Pallmeyer, *School of Assassins* (Maryknoll, NY: Orbis Books, 1997). For a broad historical perspective, consult Noam Chomsky, *Year 501: The Conquest Continues* (Boston: South End Press, 1993); Walter LaFeber, *Inevitable Revolutions: The United States in Central America*, 2nd ed. (New York: W.W. Norton and Company, 1993); Walter LaFeber, *The New Empire: An Interpretation of American Expansion, 1860–1898* (Ithaca: Cornell University, 1963); and Emily S. Rosenberg, *Spreading the American Dream: American Economic and Cultural Expansion, 1890–1945* (New York: Hill and Wang, 1982).

8. El Salvador, Uruguay, and Nicaragua began receiving assistance in 1947, 1951, and 1952, respectively.

9. For a comprehensive overview of the FMS and other military assistance programs, consult Latin American Working Group (LAWG), *Just the Facts: A Civilian's Guide to U.S. Defense and Security Assistance to Latin America and the Caribbean* (Washington, DC: Latin American Working Group and Center for International Policy, 1999). Full text also available from the Center for International Policy website at http://www.ciponline.org/facts.htm.

10. For excellent overviews of two distinct historical periods, consult Walter LaFeber, *The New Empire*; and Thomas McCormick, *America's Half-Century: United States Foreign Policy in the Cold War and After*, 2nd ed. (Baltimore: Johns Hopkins University Press, 1995).

11. In fact, the SOA was not the only institution used by the U.S. military to train Latin American troops. Panama was the major site of programs for Latin America, particularly following the passage of the National Security Act in 1947, and then with the development and expansion of the International Military Education and Training (IMET) program during the 1950s. In the Canal Zone alone, the United States operated four schools dedicated to the training of Latin American militaries, one of which was the School of the Americas. Worldwide, the United States military provided training at approximately forty-five institutions.

12. U.S. Department of the Army (DOA), "US SOUTHCOM and U.S. Army School of the Americas: Partners in Regional Engagement," Congressional Briefing (1995), slide 2.

13. Information on SOUTHCOM taken from the official SOUTHCOM website at www.ussouthcom.com.

14. DOA, SOUTHCOM and USARSA, slide 11.

15. DOA, "SOUTHCOM and USARSA, slide 14.

16. DOA, 1999 USARSA Command Brief (Ft. Benning, GA: School of the Americas, 1999), slide 3.

17. Colonel Glenn Weidner, "Overcoming the Power Gap: Reorienting the Inter-American System for Hemispheric Security" (Paper prepared for the Weatherhead Center for International Affairs, Harvard University, June 1998), 2.

18. DOA, "U.S. Army School of the Americas: Certifications and Report to Congress," Washington, DC, January 1998, p. 4.

19. Lars Schoultz, *Human Rights and United States Policy toward Latin America* (Princeton: Princeton University Press, 1981), 232.

20. The Committee of Santa Fe, "A New Inter-American Policy for the Eighties" (Washington, DC: Council for Inter-American Security, 1980), ii. Quoted in Nelson-Pallmeyer, *School of Assassins*, 62.

21. Joseph C. Leuer, "Information Paper: School of the Americas and U.S. Foreign Policy Attainment in Latin America" (Unpublished essay, 1996), 3.

22. Michael T. Childress, "Effectiveness of U.S. Training Efforts in Internal Defense and Development: The Cases of El Salvador and Honduras" (Santa Monica, CA: Rand, 1995): 24, n.22. Childress also notes that the number of maneuver battalions increased from eight in 1980 to forty-four in 1990.

23. Childress, "Effectiveness of U.S. Training Efforts," 21, n.15. As a point of comparison, only ten Salvadorans graduated from SOA courses in 1998. See DOA, *1999 Command Brief*, slide 34.

24. By the end of Bush's presidency, more than $65 billion had been spent in support of counter-drug strategies. See Peter Zirnite, "Washington's Addiction to the War on Drugs," *NACLA Report on the Americas* 32, no. 3 (November/December 1998): 28; and Ricardo Vargas Meza, "A Military–Paramilitary Alliance Besieges Colombia," *NACLA Report on the Americas* 32, no. 3 (November/December 1998): 26.

25. Zirnite, "Washington's Addiction," 28.

26. Leuer, "Information Paper," 8, 10.

27. DOA, "SOA Certification," 12. It is also relevant to note the creation of the International Narcotics Law Enforcement Affairs (INLEA) program, which provides an additional source of funding for the School of the Americas.

28. See LAWG, *Just the Facts*. In 1997, the SOA trained 99, 145, 305, and 14 students from Colombia, Chile, Mexico, and El Salvador, respectively.

29. See U.S. Army School of the Americas (SOA), *Course Catalog 1998–1999* (Fort Benning, GA: SOA, 1998).

30. See Leuer, "Information Paper," 6.

31. Colonel William Spracher, Speech given at the Military Intelligence Officer Graduation Ceremony, Fort Benning, Georgia, 17 June 1997.

32. An excellent discussion about the legacy of Vietnam with respect to Central America is Cynthia J. Arnson's "Central America and the Post-Vietnam Congress," in *Crossroads: Congress, The Reagan Administration, and Central America* (New York: Pantheon, 1989), 3–23. See also George C. Herring, "Vietnam, El Salvador, and the Uses of History," in *El Salvador: Central America in the New Cold War*, ed. Marvin E. Gettleman et al. (New York: Grove Weidenfeld, 1986), 369–379; William Leogrande, *Our Own Backyard: The United States in Central America, 1977–1992* (Chapel Hill: University of North Carolina Press, 1998), 5–8, 94–103;

Kenneth E. Sharpe, "U.S. Policy Toward Central America: The Post-Vietnam Formula Under Siege," in *Crisis in Central America: Regional Dynamics and U.S. Policy in the 1980s*, ed. Nora Hamilton et al. (Boulder, CO: Westview Press, 1988), 15–34; and Christian Smith, *Resisting Reagan: The U.S. Central America Peace Movement* (Chicago: University of Chicago Press, 1996), 93–97.

33. Allan Goodman and Bruce Berkowitz provide a thorough background on covert action in "Covert Action and American Democracy," Tms [photocopy], National Security Archive, Washington, DC, 1989.

34. Ann Crittendon, *Sanctuary: A Story of American Conscience and the Law in Collision* (New York: Weidenfeld and Nicolson, 1988), xvi, 19.

35. Robin Lorentzen, *Women in the Sanctuary Movement* (Philadelphia: Temple University Press, 1991), 14. See also Renny Golden and Michael McConnell, *Sanctuary: The New Underground Railroad* (New York: Orbis Books, 1986).

36. Smith, *Resisting Reagan*, 60.

37. Information for the following paragraphs about Roy Bourgeois was culled by the author from personal communications with Bourgeois between 1996 and 2000; a telephone interview with Bourgeois, 23 September 1999; Roy Bourgeois, "Going to Jail for Justice: A Priest Writes from Prison," *Catholic Digest*, 7 April 1997; Roy Bourgeois, "Bringing Salvador Home: Training for Terror vs. Faith in Action, *Christianity and Crisis*, 11 May 1992; and Peter Carlson, "The Priest Who Waged a War," *Washington Post*, 29 November 1998.

38. Romero's 17 March 1980 letter to President Carter is reprinted in *The Central American Crisis Reader*, ed. Robert Leiken and Barry Rubin (New York: Summit Books, 1987), 503–504. For additional information about Archbishop Romero and his work, consult Catholic Institute for International Relations (CIIR), *Romero, Martyr for Liberation* (London: CIIR, 1982). For declassified U.S. government documents on the case, consult the National Security Archive, *El Salvador: The Making of U.S. Policy, 1977–1984*, 2 vols. (Washington, DC and Alexandria, VA: The National Security Archive and Chadwyck-Healey Inc., 1989).

39. Tommy Sue Montgomery, *Revolution in El Salvador: From Civil Strife to Civil Peace*, 2nd ed. (Boulder: Westview Press, 1995), 131.

40. Also killed were lay missionary Jean Donovan and Ursuline Sister Dorothy Kazel.

41. Responding to public uproar about the murder of the U.S. churchwomen, as well as pressure from Congressmen Joseph Moakley (D–MA) and James P. McGovern (D–MA), the Carter administration did place a temporary hold on aid shipments. The hold remained in effect for just two weeks, however. Furthermore, after the full resumption of aid shipments, Carter authorized an "emergency delivery" of a bonus $5 million worth of U.S. military material and advisers. See Michael McClintock, *The American Connection: State Terror and Popular Resistance in El Salvador* (London: Zed Books, 1985), 275–285. For an in-depth discussion on policy debates during this period, see Arnson, *Crossroads*.

42. A report issued in 1993 by a United Nations commission corroborated these findings. See also note 47.

43. Information about the early years of SOA Watch was culled by the author from telephone interviews with Roy Bourgeois (23 September 1999), Carol Richardson (23 September 1999), and Ray Laport (29 September 1999).

44. Charles Liteky, a Medal of Honor winner in Vietnam, is a former U.S. Army chaplain. Patrick Liteky trained at Fort Benning's Infantry School.

45. Bourgeois interview, 23 September 1999.

46. Vicky Imerman, a U.S. Army veteran officer once stationed at Ft. Benning, directed SOA Watch while Bourgeois served a fourteen-month prison term for his November 1990 civil disobedience action.

47. See United Nations, *De la locura a la esperanza, la guerra de 12 años en El Salvador: Informe de la Comisión de la Verdad para El Salvador* (New York: United Nations, 1993).

48. These killings occurred in December 1981, February 1983, and September 1988, respectively. See Nelson-Pallmeyer, *School of Assassins*, 6–7; United Nations, *De la locura a la esperanza*; and Ecumenical Program on Central America and the Caribbean (EPICA), *Condoning the Killing: Ten Years of Massacres in El Salvador* (Washington, DC: EPICA, 1990). A comprehensive list of SOA graduates is available from the School of the Americas Watch website at http://www.soaw.org/grads.

49. Douglas Waller with D. Richard De Silva, "Running a 'School for Dictators,'" *Newsweek* (9 August 1993).

50. Representative Meehan of Massachusetts responding to *Newsweek* article "Running a School for Dictators," *Congressional Record* (6 August 1993): H6296.

51. Amendment 333 (to amend H.R. 3116) received a vote on the day of its introduction by Rep. Kennedy (30 September 1993). The amendment would have cut $2.9 million from the SOA budget.

52. U.S. Intelligence Oversight Board, *Report on the Guatemala Review* (Washington, DC: Government Printing Office, 1996). For critical responses to the report, consult the Center for International Policy (CIP), "Some Initial Thoughts on the Intelligence Oversight Board Report on Guatemala" (Washington, DC: CIP, 1996). See also the National Security Archive (NSA), *Guatemala Update* (Washington, DC: NSA, June 1996); and the Washington Office on Latin America (WOLA), *Military Intelligence and Human Rights in Guatemala: The Archivo and the Case for Intelligence Reform* (Washington, DC: WOLA, March 1995).

53. Lisa Haugaard, "Textbook Repression: U.S. Training Manuals Declassified," *Covert Action Quarterly* 61 (Summer 1997): 33. See also Lisa Haugaard, "Torture 101," *In These Times* (14 October 1996): 14–16. The manuals, as well as critical responses to their release, are available through the SOA Watch website at http://www.soaw.org/manuals.html.

54. One study found that sixteen stories about the School of the Americas appeared in four mainstream news sources during 1996, compared to an average of just one story per year for the previous seventeen years. See Molly Todd, "(De)Constructing El Salvador: U.S. Foreign Policy and the Press, 1979–1998" (M.A. Thesis, University of Texas, Austin, 1998). For further information on U.S. press coverage during this period, consult Edward Herman and Noam Chomsky, *Manufacturing Consent: The Political Economy of the Mass Media* (New York: Pantheon Books, 1988).

55. Compare this number to the November 1995 protest, when just thirteen people were arrested for nonviolently reenacting the murder of the Jesuits. These thirteen were still incarcerated at the time of the 1996 protest, which amplified the energy of protesters at the rally. It is also relevant to note that in 1996 the SOA Watch launched a site on the World Wide Web. The creation of the website was an impor-

tant step in the SOA Watch's development as an organization *cum* movement; the Internet has since proven to be a crucial tool in organizing and education efforts.

56. Quoted in Carlson, "The Priest Who Waged a War."

57. A complete list of organizations that have passed resolutions and made statements of support for closing the School of the Americas is available from the SOA Watch website at http://www.soaw.org/Articles/statemen.htm.

58. *School of Assassins*, 18 minutes., Maryknoll World Productions, 1995, videocassette.

59. For an excellent study on the 316 Battalion, see Gary Cohn and Ginger Thompson, "Unearthed: Fatal Secrets," four-part series, *The Baltimore Sun*, 11–19 June 1995. For further details, consult Leo Valladares Lanza, *Los hechos hablan por si mismos: Informe preliminar sobre los desaparecidos en Honduras, 1980–1993* (Tegucigalpa: Editorial Guaymuras, 1994) [published in English as *Honduras: The Facts Speak for Themselves*, trans. Human Rights Watch/Americas and the Center for Justice and International Law (New York: Human Rights Watch, 1994)]; and Leo Valladares Lanza and Susan C. Peacock, *In Search of Hidden Truths* (Tegucigalpa: Comisionado Nacional de los Derechos Humanos en Honduras, 1998).

60. Col. Roy R. Trumble, Remarks at U.S. Army School of the Americas Change of Command, Fort Benning, Georgia, 17 July 1998.

61. Ramsey, "Forty Years," 5.

62. Spracher, Speech, 2.

63. A compelling overview of Diana Ortiz's case history can be found in Julia Lieblich's "Pieces of Bone," *Agni* 47 (1998): 1–20.

64. In January 2000, SOA alumnus Colonel Byron Disrael Lima Estrada was arrested, along with his son, for the murder of Bishop Gerardi. For excellent overviews of the Gerardi case, consult Francisco Goldman, "Murder Comes for the Bishop," *The New Yorker* (15 March 1999); and Keith Slack and Margaret Popkin, "The Investigation into the Murder of Guatemalan Bishop Juan Gerardi, A One-Year Update" (Washington, DC: Robert F. Kennedy Memorial Center for Human Rights, 1999).

65. Rep. Callahan of Alabama addressing the House in response to Amendment No. 1 offered by Rep. Moakley, *Congressional Record* (29 July 1999): H6701.

66. Lopera was also the former Vice Minister for Youth.

67. Lopera and his companions were stopped as they attempted to deliver a 150 million peso (approximately $75,000) ransom for a kidnapping victim.

68. The State Department's report is available online at www.state.gov/www/ global/human rights/1999 hrp report/colombia.html.

69. SOA Watch also notes that, in August 1996, troops under Hernández's command fired into and used tear gas against a group of protesting peasants, wounding four of them. The troops also stole money from the protesters and burned their tents. For more information on the Human Rights Watch report and the SOA, see "Human Rights Watch Report Cites 7 SOA Graduates," at www.soaw.org/Articles/ current%20info/country%20information/hrwcolombia.htm.

70. Canal, Commander of the 3rd Brigade, has been accused of the July 1998 murder of five civilians in Colombia's Navino Department. He trained at the SOA in 1980. Ospina, now head of Colombia's Fourth Division, attended the SOA at least once, in 1967. For more details, consult Human Rights Watch/Americas, *The Ties that Bind: Colombia and Military–Paramilitary Links* (New York: Human

Rights Watch, 2000). Also available online at www.hrw.org/reports/2000/colombia.

71. Consult Proyecto Interdiocesano de Recuperación de la Memoria Histórica (REMHI), *Guatemala: Nunca Más* (Guatemala City: Oficina de Derechos Humanos del Arzobispado de Guatemala, 1998); and Comisión para el Esclarecimiento Histórico (CEH), *Guatemala: Memoria del Silencio* (Guatemala City: CEH, 1999). REMHI report available from http://www.odhagua/infremhi/default.htm. For a concise summary of the REMHI report as it relates to the School of the Americas, see "Nunca Más–Never Again: School of the Americas Graduates Involved in Guatemala's Worst Violence," SOA Watch pamphlet, 1999. Full Spanish text of CEH report obtained from http://www.hrdata.aaas.org/ceh/mds/spanish. Conclusion and recommendations in English are available from http://www.hrdata.aaas.org/ceh/report/english.

72. As of fall 2001, Great Britain had suspended Pinochet's possible extradition to Spain and authorized his return to Chile, due to his "old and infirm" condition. Pinochet now awaits possible criminal trial in his home country, following a Chilean court's decision to strip him of his self-declared immunity from prosecution. For background on the Pinochet case, consult Peter Kornbluh, "Prisoner Pinochet: The Dictator and the Quest for Justice," *The Nation* (21 December 1998): 11–12, 15–19, 22, 24. On the international legal ramifications of the case, see Anne-Marie Slaughter, "The Long Arm of the Law," *Foreign Policy* (Spring 1999): 34–35. A contrasting view can be found in Ricardo Lagos and Heraldo Muñoz, "The Pinochet Dilemma," *Foreign Policy* (Spring 1999): 26–33, 36–39.

73. In 1997, a U.S. court charged and convicted Contreras for the 1976 car-bombing in Washington, DC, which killed former Chilean Ambassador to the United States Orlando Letelier and his assistant Ronni Moffitt, a U.S. citizen. For a comprehensive account of the Letelier–Moffitt assassination, which also provides an illustration of Pinochet's commission of international terrorism, see John Dinges and Saul Landau, *Assassination on Embassy Row* (New York: Pantheon Books, 1980).

74. For a compelling overview of the DINA and the CNI, consult Pamela Constable and Arturo Valenzuela, *A Nation of Enemies: Chile Under Pinochet* (New York: W. W. Norton and Company, 1993): especially chapter four, entitled "Army of the Shadows," 90–114. For additional details regarding the DINA in particular, see Samuel Blixen, "Pinochet's Mad Scientist," *IF Magazine* 3, no. 1 (January–February 1999): 11–13; Peter Kornbluh, "Declassifying U.S. Intervention in Chile," *NACLA Report on the Americas* 32, no. 6 (May/June 1999): 36–42; and Alvaro Tizon, "The Judge and the Dictator," *IF Magazine* 3, no. 1 (January-February 1999): 13–15. A list of Chilean graduates of the School of the Americas can be obtained through www.soaw.org/graduates.html.

75. Lepe Orellana attended the SOA at least once, in 1968. In 1976, he allegedly participated in the murder of Soria. When legal proceedings against him reopened in 1991, Lepe was Pinochet's personal secretary. Belmar also received training at the SOA in 1968 and allegedly participated in Soria's murder. Despite the allegations and supporting evidence, the School of the Americas hired Belmar as a guest instructor in 1987.

76. For example, Lieutenant Colonels Manuel Rolando Mosqueira Jarp and Alfonso Faundez Norambuena, and Colonels Manuel Provis Carrasco and Marco Antonio Saez Saavedra have all been cited for their roles at Villa Grimaldi.

77. Operation Condor was an illicit network of the security services of Chile, Argentina, Bolivia, Brazil, Paraguay, and Uruguay, which was established during the 1970s to track and eliminate political foes across national boundaries.

78. "Pinochet Witness Links CIA to Coordinated Latin American Repression," BBC Summary of World Broadcasts (7 December 1998), obtained on the Internet through Lexis–Nexis. Information attributed to El Pais (4 December 1998); quote attributed to Paraguayan lawyer Martín Almada. See also "SOAW Testifies in Pinochet Case," SOA Watch Update (Winter/Spring 1999): back cover; and Stella Calloni, "The Horror Archives of Operation Condor," CovertAction 50 (Fall 1994): 713, 57–61.

79. William J. Clinton, "Remarks in Roundtable Discussion on [Guatemalan] Peace Efforts," (Guatemala City: White House Office of the Press Secretary, 10 March 1999): 1. Despite his expression of regret and his declaration that the United States not repeat such mistakes, on 13 July 2000, President Clinton signed into law a bill that will provide $1.32 billion in counter-drug aid to the Andean region. Of this total Colombia will receive $860 million, about three-quarters of which is earmarked for training and equipment for the military and police forces. U.S. funding and training of Colombian counternarcotics battalions shows remarkable parallels to U.S. assistance to Central American counterinsurgency battalions during the 1980s. Evidence demonstrates that U.S. aid to Central American entities (Salvadoran and Guatemalan governments and militaries, the Nicaraguan "contras") did much to exacerbate and prolong the pre-existing civil conflicts in each of these countries. There is mounting evidence that U.S. counter-drug aid to Colombia is having the same negative impact on the nearly four-decade civil war there. On the Colombia aid package, tracking its evolution from the original proposal through its passage into law and providing the text of congressional responses and analyses from varying perspectives, see the Center for International Policy website at www.ciponline.org/colombia/aid/.

80. Reeder, Speech.

81. Weidner, "Overcoming the Power Gap," 6.

82. DOA, 1998 Command Brief (Ft. Benning, GA: School of the Americas, 1998): 41. It must be noted that the publication did not indicate by whom the school was so recognized; nor did it provide sources or references in support of its arguments.

83. DOA, 1999 Command Brief, slide 3.

84. DOA, "SOUTHCOM and USARSA," slide 16; and Rep. Callahan, CR, H6702.

85. DOA, "SOUTHCOM and USARSA," slide 16.

86. For more information on SOA human rights training, see DOA, "SOA Certification," 16–18 and Appendix.

87. SOA: An Insider Speaks Out! 16 minutes, Maryknoll World Productions, 1998, videocassette. Blair's own list of former students includes several of the Salvadoran soldiers involved in the 1989 Jesuit murders.

88. Joseph Blair, personal interview, Columbus, Georgia, 21 November 1999.

89. SOA: An Insider Speaks Out! For additional critical views on issues related to the SOA curriculum, see Haugaard's "Textbook Repression" and "Torture 101"; Waller and De Silva, "Running a 'School for Dictators' "; and Latin America Working

Group (LAWG), "Memo Regarding the School of the Americas Certification Report" (Washington, DC: LAWG, 1998).

90. See Lieblich, "Pieces of Bone," 14; and Vicky Imerman, "Notorious Guatemalan School of the Americas Graduates" (Columbus, GA: SOA Watch, 1998).

91. Vicky Imerman and Heather Dean, "Notorious Chilean School of the Americas Graduates" (Columbus, GA: SOA Watch, 1998).

92. General Charles Wilhelm, "Speech to the 1998 graduates of the Command and General Staff Officer Course," Fort Benning, Georgia, 17 December 1998.

93. Ibid. On 18 May 2000, Congress approved a proposal to close the School of the Americas and open the Defense Institute for Hemispheric Security Cooperation. The Defense Institute will utilize the School of the Americas campus at Fort Benning and continue the SOA tradition of training Latin American soldiers. Opponents of the school argue that the Defense Institute is a simple clone of the SOA, and that despite the "new name" the Institute is tarnished with the "same shame." A long-time critic of the school, Representative Moakley stated, "It still smells. As long as the school is there–even with a new name–we're going to have problems." (Tom Bowman, "School of Assassins: Democratic Congressman Says that Clinton's Reforms 'Smell,' " *Baltimore Sun*, 2 May 2000.)

94. SOA Watch, "Human Rights Advocates Vow to Shut Down 'School of Assassins,' " press release, 18 May 2000.

7

U.S. Military Engagement in Latin America

Douglas Farah

During the decades of the Cold War, the justification for a strong U.S. military presence in Latin America was the ongoing threat of Soviet bloc expansion into an area of vital national interest, both because of Latin America's proximity to the United States and because the United States desired access to natural resources such as tin and oil found in that region. U.S. policy was premised on the concept of competition with the Soviet bloc for the region, a policy framework that gained wider currency when Cuba staged a successful Marxist revolution, leftist military and civilian regimes came and went in Peru and Chile, the Sandinistas triumphed in Nicaragua in 1979, and a civil war exploded in El Salvador. During those years, U.S. military aid focused on counterinsurgency training for armies around the region coupled with, toward the end of the 1980s, human rights programs that tried to stem the continual reports of torture and summary executions by American military allies.

What is surprising is that since the fall of the Berlin wall and the end of the Soviet threat, the U.S. military presence in Latin America has not diminished, a fact I discovered while researching a three-part *Washington Post* series on U.S. military involvement in the drug war, published in July 1998. Details of the program and the work of the U.S. Special Forces were gathered during the course of trips to the new U.S.-funded counter-drug center in Iquitos, Peru; trips to observe U.S. training exercises in Lago Agrio and Tarapoa, Ecuador; several trips to Colombia, and a series of special briefings by the U.S. Southern Command (SOUTHCOM) in Panama in late 1997 and early 1998. During the course of the reporting trips for the newspaper,

I interviewed dozens of U.S. officials involved in the programs, including senior military officials, U.S. troops on the ground, and civilian officials involved in the program.

I reported on and witnessed the training provided by U.S. Special Forces in El Salvador in the 1980s, and it is clear that the U.S. military has simply assumed slightly modified roles and changed the names for much of what it does, while continuing to carry out the same basic functions as in earlier conflicts. In a successful attempt to remain relevant in the region as the Marxist insurgencies faded away or negotiated their way into the existing political structure, the military, especially the U.S. Special Forces Seventh Group, which operates throughout Latin America, began defining drug traffickers as the principal enemy, replacing the Marxist guerrillas of the Cold War. Not only did the rapid shift in emphasis help ensure that the budgets of the Special Forces units would not be decimated as Pentagon funding was cut, but counter-drug activities also provided a reason to retain a U.S. military presence in the region. Ten years after the end of the Cold War, the Pentagon had a counter-drug budget of $444 million in fiscal 1997, four times the State Department's counter-drug budget of $161 million.[1] This difference exists even though the State Department is supposed to be the lead agency in implementing and funding U.S. counter-drug programs abroad, and the funding advantage gives the Pentagon the ability to dispense training courses and resources that are vital to shaping U.S. policy. Furthermore, instead of working only with selected allies around the region, by 1997 virtually every country in Latin America was carrying out joint training programs with U.S. Special Forces. In fiscal year 1998 the United States deployed 2,700 Special Forces troops to nineteen countries in Latin America and nine Caribbean nations. On any given day 250 special forces trainers are operating in fifteen countries. The number of deployments ranged from a high of thirty-five in Venezuela to thirty in Bolivia, and twenty-four in Colombia to one each in Suriname and Belize. The number of special operations deployments in Latin America increased from 147 in 1995 to 198 in 1998. The special operations missions are only the most dynamic part of a larger U.S. military involvement with Latin America. In all, roughly 56,000 U.S. troops rotated through Central and Latin America in fiscal year 1997, according to a study by the Washington-based Latin American Working Group.[2] About 40 percent of those troops were from Reserve and National Guard units, along with high-profile humanitarian, peacekeeping, and road-building brigades.[3]

Most of the programs currently offered by U.S. trainers, especially those in the special forces, remain virtually unchanged from Cold War days. They include small unit training, weapons handling, rural patrols, urban commando operations, map reading, and basic intelligence gathering and analysis.[4] The difference is that now the training is purported to equip the students to confront drug traffickers rather than Marxist guerrillas and to destroy cocaine and heroin laboratories rather than guerrilla camps. How-ever, the mock-ups for the battles carried out on training trips with U.S. forces were identical to those used in the 1980s to train special forces in El Salvador to combat insurgents and those used to train Contra rebels seeking to overthrow the Sandinista government in Nicaragua. U.S. Special Forces troops on the ground argue that there is little difference in the skills needed to take out a guerrilla camp or a cocaine laboratory protected by heavily armed drug traffickers. And, they argue, there is little difference in intelligence-gathering methods or small unit deployments whether the tar-get is a Marxist rebel group or a heroin trafficking organization.

However, not all of the Special Forces deployments are related to direct military training, although the percentage of deployments classified as having a counter-drug mission has risen from 48 percent in 1995 to 62 percent in 1998. Among the other skills taught and practiced are de-mining techniques, especially useful along the heavily mined Nicaragua–Honduras border and in El Salvador, where both the military and the guerrillas left thousands of land mines scattered across the country. The Special Forces also concentrate heavily on disaster relief and medical training, and carried out extensive relief responsibilities following Hurricane Mitch and other nat-ural disasters in Central America in recent years.[5]

But the heart of the Special Forces training is tied to counter-narcotics, and much of the training of Latin American militaries is being done under the auspices of the Pentagon's Joint Combined Exchange Training (JCET) program. According to Law 2011 of Title X of the 1991 Defense Author-ization Act, such special operations exercises are allowed only if the primary purpose is to train U.S. troops. However, many of the deployments in Latin America appear to go well beyond the intent of the law and clearly seek to provide training to the host country with few visible benefits to U.S. troops. U.S. training is loosely defined at best, and training other military forces is certainly not discouraged. U.S. forces often leave behind their weapons and communications gear for the host army as well, providing a small but un-supervised pipeline of new technologies to the militaries in the region.[6] And because they are funded under an obscure line item in the Pentagon budget, the JCET program receives almost no congressional oversight, not because it is classified as secret but because few people know it exists. Following a series on the JCET program worldwide in the *Washington Post*, the Penta-gon, bowing to congressional pressure spearheaded by Sen. Patrick Leahy (D–VT), agreed to tighter controls and reporting requirements in the JCET program and also attempted to define the program more precisely.[7]

Just how loosely defined the JCET program has been was shown in the discrepancy in numbers provided to me on how many JCETs were carried out in Colombia in 1996 and 1997. While the numbers provided to the *Washington Post* by the Pentagon showed no JCET programs in Colombia for 1996 and 1997, SOUTHCOM in Miami, in charge of Latin American programs, listed thirty-two JCET deployments to Colombia in 1996 and thirty-eight in 1997. Despite heated discussions between generals, the difference could not be bridged.[8] If the military itself cannot agree on the number or definitions of JCETs, it is almost impossible for Congress to understand the program, much less monitor it. This raises serious concerns among human rights organizations and among some in Congress because several of the armies that benefit most from the JCET program—including those in Colombia, Peru, and Mexico—have the worst human rights records in the hemisphere, according to Human Rights Watch and the State Department's own annual human rights reports.

While the JCET program is also nominally subject to the control of the U.S. ambassador in each country, in practice the civilians in most embassies know little and care even less, according to political and military officials at embassies across the region. As diplomatic staffs shrink and aid programs are cut back, often it is the military—the most visible and most impressive presence—that sets its own policy and, to a growing degree, U.S. policy. There have been several battles between U.S. commanders and U.S. ambassadors over who has ultimate control of the U.S. troops and what they do. In 1994, Gen. Barry R. McCaffrey, then commander of SOUTHCOM, circulated a letter asserting his authority over the troops, infuriating the region's ambassadors. Ambassador Charles Bowers in Bolivia was so angry he threatened to expel U.S. troops from Bolivia.[9]

Despite severe human rights and corruption problems in Mexico, Peru, and Colombia, the U.S. military is going a step beyond basic training there. In conjunction with the Central Intelligence Agency (CIA), the Special Forces are providing extensive intelligence training to selected, vetted units of the militaries of those countries. In each case, the primary focus of the training is purportedly counter-drug operations. Over time it is hoped that a regional group of uncorrupted officers could share information with each other and greatly reduce the drug corruption and security leaks that have plagued counter-drug operations. But, in fact, the units are routinely assigned to other jobs. In both Peru and Colombia, with insurgencies still active, the special units are often sent on counterinsurgency missions. In Peru, the center of the training is a new riverine training base just outside of Iquitos. It will be used for U.S. Navy Seals not only to train Peruvian soldiers and police in riverine interdiction but also for training troops from Bolivia, Colombia, and possibly, Ecuador. In no country are troops trained by U.S. special forces under any obligation to stay in counter-drug units for a specified period of time, so in practice many are trained and then simply rotated out to counterinsurgency units, which are often given a higher priority and greater prestige.[10]

Thus far the results of working with vetted units have been mixed. In Mexico, the program was begun in 1996 when groups of elite Mexican army troops were given special forces combat training at Ft. Bragg together with special intelligence training, then equipped with helicopters to give them the mobility necessary to pursue drug traffickers. The plan was to create an elite unit in each state of the country that could help fill the law enforcement vacuum until the police and judicial authorities could be trained and begin to work. According to the plan, the military then would be phased out of the drug war. But by September 1998, the program suffered a devastating blow, when eighty members were found to be trafficking in cocaine and illegal migrants at the Mexico City airport—taking payoffs of hundreds of thousands of dollars to allow the drugs and illegal aliens to pass through. This came shortly after an army general who had been placed in charge of the nation's counter-drug efforts was found to be on the payroll of some of the nation's most notorious drug traffickers.[11]

In 1991, the U.S. military and the CIA sent special teams to Colombia to help assess and reorganize the Colombian army's intelligence structure, leading to the creation of new military intelligence units that reported to the newly formed Twentieth Brigade. By 1993, many of the new units, set up in accordance with a plan developed by U.S. military advisers and led by a paid CIA informant had become closely allied with right-wing paramilitary groups. In the petroleum-producing region around Barrancabermeja, one unit was responsible for at least fifty-seven documented assassinations. The head of the Twentieth Brigade, with overall responsibility for all of the new groups, was Ivan Ramirez, who was a salaried CIA asset during his bloody tenure as intelligence chief. Finally, in 1995 the CIA severed its relationship with Ramirez because of his alleged ties to paramilitary death squads. In 1998, when Ramirez had risen to the rank of general and was the army's third in command, the United States took the unusual step of revoking his U.S. visa because of human rights concerns. The current Colombian high command, led by General Fernando Tapias, has, with strong U.S. support, removed two other generals because of alleged ties to human rights violations.

In contrast to the army's grim experiences, however, vetted units in the Colombian National Police, who received Special Forces and CIA training, have proved effective in tackling some of the strongest and most complex drug empires in the world, successfully bringing down the Medellín and Cali cartels.[12]

The U.S. military sees no contradiction in the apparent dichotomy between counterinsurgency and counter-drug training. According to a Special Forces internal doctrine, while counter-drug activities are a "sustained focus" of the post-Cold War era, the "primary focus" continues to be training for Foreign Internal Defense (FID), which is, in essence, training regional forces to deal with internal threats. The FID doctrine was also the cornerstone of the Special Forces operations and training programs during the Cold War.[13] Brigadier General Robert W. Wagner, commander of Special Operations Command South under SOUTHCOM, said in an interview that

FIDs were "at the heart" of special operations forces and that the term "internal defense," once applied to counterinsurgency, now applies to drug trafficking as well. He said the concept was broadened to include other roles for the military, such as disaster relief and participation in multinational peacekeeping forces.[14]

Under the FID rubric, the U.S. forces carry out another primary goal, namely, engaging in "military to military contacts." Essentially, this means that the Special Forces officers, who tend to specialize and remain in one region of the world for most of their careers, maintain contact with their counterparts in militaries across the regions for years at a time. Because of the personal relationships and language abilities of the Special Forces troops, officers argue that they play a valuable role in averting civilian–military conflicts in the region. In 1997 and 1998 Special Forces officers were dispatched to Colombia to warn military officers there of a coup d'etat planned to overthrow president Ernesto Samper and were dispatched to Paraguay with the same message for the military there. U.S. Special Forces also were the first international troops on the ground when Peru and Ecuador had a brief shooting war in 1996. Officers involved in the missions were convinced that their ability to reach out quickly, with a degree of trust, to a fellow officer in another military averted major disasters in those and other cases. "We are a catalyst for regional changes," Wagner said. "We can gain access. We can get in there."[15]

Complicating the role of the U.S. military in important countries like Mexico, Peru, and Colombia, is that lingering insurgencies continue to compete for the military's attention, resources, and training needs. Nowhere is the line between counter-narcotics and counterinsurgency so blurred as in Colombia, and nowhere is the role of U.S. forces under greater scrutiny. Like Mexico, the United States has decided that the only way to combat drug trafficking successfully is to get the military more deeply involved. The belief stems from the growing sophistication of the Marxist-led guerrillas of the Revolutionary Armed Forces of Colombia (FARC), who derive hundreds of millions of dollars a year from protecting cocaine and heroin laboratories, clandestine airstrips, and trafficking routes of the Colombian cocaine and heroin cartels. The FARC has also presided over regions where the growth of coca, the raw material for making cocaine, has exploded, allowing Colombian drug traffickers to be less dependent on Peruvian and Bolivian coca to make their drugs. The influx of cash, largely from taxing every phase of the cocaine business in the areas it controls, has allowed the FARC to grow from about 7,000 combatants in 1995 to an estimated 17,000 today, enticing recruits in part by paying higher salaries than those offered by the government's army. The infusion of capital has also allowed the FARC to upgrade its weapons and communications equipment, purchase a fleet of small airplanes and helicopters, and deal the Colombian army a string of humiliating defeats. As the defeats have mounted, the FARC has slowly spread its effective political and military control over more than half the country—an area which does not, however, include any major cities. Despite the Colombian National Police's success in dismantling the Medellín and Cali drug syndicates, the police do not have the firepower to enter FARC-controlled areas to carry out effective eradication or interdiction efforts there.

Already the United States has some 200 troops deployed at any one time in Colombia, engaged in activities ranging from training police and army troops to guarding three radar sites deep in the Amazon jungles. Furthermore, Colombia is already the third-largest recipient, after Israel and Egypt, of U.S. security assistance, which totaled $289 million in fiscal year 1999. Now, a deeper, longer involvement is underway. In the first months of 2000, senior Clinton administration officials requested an emergency supplemental disbursement of about $1.2 billion, to be disbursed in fiscal years 2000 and 2001.[16] In June 2000, the U.S. Congress approved a $1.3 billion disbursement of aid to Colombia.[17] The heart of the new U.S. push in Colombia is to train an elite, fully vetted counter-narcotics battalion in the army. This 980-man unit with 18 helicopters was trained in 1999 by some 70 U.S. Special Forces troops. The battalion was formally inaugurated in mid-December.[18] If congressional funding is forthcoming, two more battalions, trained by U.S. Special Forces on the ground, will be fielded by the end of the year 2000. In addition, the Clinton administration is preparing to help the Colombian air force greatly increase its air interdiction capabilities by refurbishing its fleet of A-37 jets. The decision to help the air force came after Colombian president Andrés Pastrana agreed to begin a policy of shooting down suspected drug flights when the pilot refused to respond to orders to land the craft. Peru already has such a policy, which is widely credited with helping to disrupt the air bridge between Peru—where the coca leaf is grown and processed into a raw form of cocaine—and Colombia, where the paste arrives and is turned into the cocaine that is sold on the streets of the United States and Europe. The U.S. aid, expected to be approved by Congress, will help build and equip a joint intelligence center in the jungle area of Tres Esquinas, where a classified number of U.S. Special Forces troops with CIA support will help man and operate an electronic listening post.[19]

The wisdom of the policy of expanding military aid and the role of U.S. Special Forces in implementing that policy through more extensive training is being sharply questioned by activists and human rights groups such as the Washington Office on Latin America (WOLA), Human Rights Watch, and Amnesty International, in part because the Colombian military has an abysmal human rights record and has suffered for years from drug corruption at the highest level.[20] But there is a more fundamental problem. While the strategy addresses the threat posed by the FARC, it does not touch in any significant way on the problematic activities of vicious paramilitary groups, who have long maintained alliances with the military while carrying out a host of massacres in recent years. Human rights groups in Colombia and the United States estimate that over the past three years paramilitary squads have been responsible for about 70 percent of the human rights abuses in Colombia, including thousands of extrajudicial executions.[21]

Like the FARC, the paramilitary groups have become increasingly dependent on drug trafficking to fund their activities, and have grown at a rapid rate, from an estimated 3,000 in 1995 to about 8,000 today. But while the FARC primarily engages at the lower end of the drug production scale—for example, guarding cocaine laboratories and protecting and taxing those who grow the coca leaf—the paramilitary groups, especially those led by Carlos Castano, own and operate cocaine and heroin laboratories and directly control drug trafficking routes to the United States. The U.S. Drug Enforcement Administration lists Castano as a "major drug trafficker," something it has not done with any FARC leader. The ties between Castano and the Colombia state are deep and complex, which in part explains why journalists can interview Castano on a regular basis but the police and military cannot seem to capture him. In the early 1990s, Castano, once an ally of Medellín cartel leader Pablo Escobar, switched sides and began working for the rival Cali organizations. Castano provided intelligence on Escobar, who at the time was the most wanted man in the world, to the Cali drug trafficking organizations, which in turn passed the information on to the police and military. Castano also carried out a series of attacks against Escobar's military infrastructure, which eventually helped lead to Escobar's death in a shoot-out. As payment for his assistance, the Cali cartel gave Castano control of drug trafficking routes that ran through a large swath of Cordoba province, and the police and army granted him a hands-off policy that is now proving costly, not just for the Colombian state but for U.S. efforts to help the Colombian military. "The objective fact is that the army has not gone after the paramilitaries," a U.S. official said, adding that the military usually commits "sins of omission, not commission, where they lie low if something is happening and often what is happening is a massacre."[22]

U.S. troops in Colombia and around the region argue that human rights violations are no reason to refuse to engage with another military. In fact, U.S. Special Forces in the region said that the presence of U.S. troops was even more necessary in areas where violations were likely to occur because the U.S. presence often kept the abuses from happening at all. A key touchstone for Special Forces troops is El Salvador, where the conventional wisdom now is that thanks to U.S. involvement in general and the involvement of Special Forces troops in particular the Salvadoran military was able to hold off a Marxist insurgency and negotiate an honorable peace. Across Latin America, Special Forces troops stated their belief that it was their presence on the ground and in the barracks with Salvadoran troops that brought an end to the most egregious human rights violations by the Salvadoran military and allowed the army to gain at least a measure of popular support.[23]

What role the U.S. military, and especially the Special Forces, played in bringing down human rights violations there and elsewhere is open to debate. Even if one accepts that the U.S. military presence helped reduce the number of human rights violations in El Salvador, the jury is still out on whether Special Forces deployments and other forms of military training and assistance actually help fragile democracies to become more stable on a continent where the military has traditionally been and continues to be an autonomous power. The effectiveness of the Special Forces deployments is especially debatable given the absence of a broader Clinton administration policy toward Latin America coupled with congressional reticence to fund other types of diplomatic engagement there. Defining the role of the U.S. military, including the objectives and oversight of its missions, is crucial as Latin America has seen a spate of movements toward authoritarianism and away from open democratic processes. Paraguay has barely survived as a democracy; Venezuela has a president who makes no bones about his desire to move the military into many new facets of national life; the military in Peru remains virtually beyond civilian control; and Colombia has made little progress in holding the military accountable for egregious human rights violations, or exerting effective civilian control or oversight. There is no question that the U.S. military has a role to play, both for its own training and the training of armed forces around the region. What is lacking, however, is a clear articulation of U.S. policy goals and objectives which would provide a context for the acceleration of military engagement and training currently being undertaken. As it now stands, the rapidly accelerating engagement is taking place without regard for who is being trained or how that training is being conducted, or how the accompanying prestige is accruing to its beneficiaries. Until that is defined, the United States risks strengthening militaries that are repudiated by their own people, such as that in Colombia, or becoming part of the drug trafficking problem they are supposed to be solving, as in Suriname. At a time of historic change in Latin America, it behooves the United States to help the continent move from its legacy of military dictatorships and brutality by supporting efforts there to build more solid democratic institutions that can guarantee civilian authority and basic freedoms.

NOTES

1. Unpublished budget documents provided to *Washington Post* by U.S. Department of Defense and U.S. Department of State, June 1998.

2. Adam Isacson and Joy Olson, *Just the Facts: A Civilians' Guide to U.S. Defense and Security Assistance to Latin America and the Caribbean* (Washington, DC: Latin American Working Group, 1998), 1.

3. U.S. SOUTHCOM, "Briefing Paper for the *Washington Post*," Panama, April 1998.

4. Trips by author with U.S. Special Forces to Iquitos, Peru and Lago Agrio, Ecuador, 1998.

5. U.S. SOUTHCOM, "Briefing Paper for the *Washington Post*: Panama."

6. Author interviews with U.S. Special Forces in Iquitos, Peru and Lago Agrio, Ecuador, 1998.

7. Douglas Farah, "A Tutor For Every Army in Latin America," *Washington Post*, 13 July 1998.

8. SOUTHCOM briefing paper for the *Washington Post*; Pentagon briefing paper for the *Washington Post*; author interviews in Washington and Miami, 1998.

9. Douglas Farah, "Tutor."

10. Author interviews with senior military officers in the United States, Peru, and Colombia, 1998.

11. Douglas Farah and Molly Moore, "Mexico Probing Anti-Drug Troops," *Washington Post*, 9 September 1998.

12. Douglas Farah and Laura Brooks, "Colombian Army's Third in Command Allegedly Led Two Lives," *Washington Post*, 11 August 1998.

13. Author interviews with senior U.S. Special Forces officers in Panama, Colombia, and Ecuador, 1998.

14. Farah, "Tutor."

15. Ibid.

16. Author interviews, October 1999.

17. See Steven Dudley, "U.S. Aid Plan Heats Up Colombia War; Leftist Rebels Describe Anti-Drug Program as Offensive Against Them," *Washington Post*, 4 August 2000.

18. Author interviews, December 1999.

19. Douglas Farah, "U.S. Ready to Boost Aid to Troubled Colombia," *Washington Post*, 23 August 1999.

20. Douglas Farah, "U.S. Widens Colombia Counter-Drug Efforts," *Washington Post*, 10 July 1999.

21. Human Rights Watch, "Colombia," in *Human Rights Watch World Report 2000* (New York: Human Rights Watch, December 1999), 116–124.

22. Douglas Farah, "Massacres Imperil U.S. Aid to Colombia," *Washington Post*, 31 January 1999.

23. Author interviews in Peru, Ecuador, Colombia, Bolivia, and Panama with Special Forces, 1998.

PART IV

GLOBAL PARADIGMS

8

Beyond the Cold War Paradigm: Canadian Perspectives on Security in the Western Hemisphere

Edgar J. Dosman

INTRODUCTION

Latin America was not a priority in Canadian foreign policy during the first four decades after the Second World War. Notwithstanding long commercial and missionary relationships and growing civil society interaction with Latin America after 1945, Canada did not identify itself as a "country of the Americas" until 1989, when a new "Latin American Strategy" was adopted by the government of Prime Minister Brian Mulroney. This represented a significant change in direction in Canada's overall foreign policy. Until then the United States had long been Canada's overwhelming preoccupation, followed by Europe, and the Asia-Pacific region after the latter's economic success in the 1960s. But before 1989, Latin America was at the margins, and regional multilateralism in the Americas was virtually nonexistent as an official priority.

In no area was this limited Canadian engagement more apparent than security policy. Canada was neither a member of the inter-American security system before the end of the Cold War in 1989, nor had it developed a distinctive security policy toward the Americas before it joined the Organization of American States (OAS) as a full member in 1990. There were no Canadian peacekeeping missions or military attachés posted to the region, for example, and there was no comparable intensity in Ottawa's conflict resolution role in southern Africa, the Mideast, or Asia. Canada's Department of National Defence avoided the Inter-American Defense Board (IADB) and College like the plague. Such Canadian security interests as there were related to its obligations as a member of the North Atlantic Treaty Organization (NATO): ensuring allied control of Caribbean sea lanes, maintaining access to strategic resources such as Venezuelan oil, overseeing the security of the Panama Canal, and so forth. Even Canada's policy of normal diplomatic relations with Cuba after its revolution in 1959 and its support during the 1980s for the Contadora/Esquipulas peace processes in Central America were driven more by containing the danger posed by these conflicts to intra-NATO relations through direct U.S. intervention than by any thought of a permanent role in the region.

The result for Canadian–Latin American security relations was a blank slate, and Ottawa's new Latin America strategy of 1989 sought a new approach towards the region. On one thing Canada was firm: it rejected the established U.S.–Latin American security paradigm inherited from the Cold War, and even conditioned OAS membership on remaining outside the terms and obligations of the Rio Treaty of 1947. The inherited dynamic of U.S.–Latin American relations was not very well understood or admired in Ottawa; neither the quixotic U.S. preoccupation with communism and counterinsurgency in the region nor the Latin American military governments which had emerged in earlier decades were particularly appealing. Conversely, these dictatorships did not exactly rush northwards seeking closer relations with Canada. Indeed, few countries were as disliked as Canada by General Augusto Pinochet for accepting Chilean refugees after his 1973 military coup. To a remarkable extent, therefore, Canada could develop a new security policy toward the Americas without much historical deadweight and in the happy context of trade liberalization and widespread democratization in Latin America.

The big surprise, therefore, has been the dramatic change that has occurred in Canadian policy toward the region since the 1989 formulation of a Latin American strategy. Not only has Canada emerged as an active and visible participant in inter-American governance, but security policy has also become a core regional interest. In 1999, the Canadian Department of Foreign Affairs and International Trade noted in its official publication that "Piece by piece . . . Canada and its hemispheric neighbours have been bolting together a system of regional security."[1] Ottawa's decision to mark the first decade of its OAS membership by hosting a wide variety of events and new initiatives—including the OAS General Assembly in 2000, the Heads of Government Summit in 2001, and the first round of the Free Trade of the Americas (FTAA) negotiations—underlines its long-term commitment to promoting peace and democracy in the Americas. The foundations were laid in the first year after joining the OAS with its first trademark initiative to create a special secretariat within the OAS called the Unit for the Promotion of Democracy (UPD) with the mandate of assisting member states to strengthen the post-Cold War democratic opening in the Americas. Similarly, Canada worked closely in 1991 with Chile, the United States, and other governments in achieving unanimous support for OAS Resolution 1080, the so-called Santiago Commitment, which called for joint and immediate action against extra-constitutional challenges to democratically elected governments. In addition, Ottawa mounted a formidable diplomatic campaign to strengthen regional multilateralism in the security field that has promoted inter-American conventions on issues such as Confidence and Security Building Measures (CSBMs), anti-terrorism and arms control, the elimination of land mines, the drive against corruption, the reform of Latin American judicial systems, and the strengthening of democracy. Peacekeeping missions in Nicaragua (the United Nations Observer Group for Central America, ONUCA), El Salvador (the United Nations Observer Mission in El Salvador, ONUSAL), and Haiti (the UN/OAS Observer Mission in Haiti, MICIVIH)—where Canada fielded the largest force after the U.S. Army left in 1995—provided an unprecedented military presence in the region.[2] The more recent sponsorship of a Foreign Minister's Dialogue on Drugs and the creation of the new Multilateral Evaluation Mechanism (MEM) to strengthen the role of the Inter-American Drug Abuse Control Commission (CICAD) confirms Canada's continuing security engagement in the Western Hemisphere within the OAS as well as outside the OAS through, for example, the Nicaragua Support Group.[3]

But what, in fact, has been the balance of accomplishments and setbacks— and the new challenges facing Canada—in its inter-American security policy since the Latin American strategy was formulated a decade ago? Such an evaluation is complex, requiring an assessment of Canada's own foreign policy requirements as well as the broader issue of building a new inter-American security system to replace the discredited Cold War paradigm.

FROM "COOPERATIVE" TO "HUMAN" SECURITY

Canada was anxious to strike a fresh approach based on partnership and to locate "like-minded" friends in Latin America to strengthen its own options in the post-Cold War period, as well as to compensate in part for the inevitable downgrading of the historic ties to Europe. Both Canada and Latin America faced the common problem of managing the U.S. relationship. In both cases, middle powers were adjusting to the challenges of globalization; therefore, the logic of strengthening cooperation along a broad spectrum to locate common policy interests and bargaining frameworks seemed obvious. Given Canada's relatively small economic size (about the same as Brazil's), and its location next to the United States and far from other continents and neighbors, the Americas loomed as the only region in which community-building appeared as a viable long-term option. After the Cold War, it seemed that similar converging interests in Latin America and the Caribbean opened the prospect for a Western Hemisphere community of nations in which Canada would be a full member. Trade access was obviously important, but the notion of community-building implied a broader political involvement in the region in defense of democracy and human rights. Indeed, the trade and democracy objectives of Canadian foreign policy were linked: while the opening of Latin America to the international economic system offered the prospect of enhanced trade and reciprocal commercial benefits, the Canadian public would lose interest in Latin America should the region relapse into dictatorship. Since democracy and growth depended on the peaceful resolution of external and internal disputes, the timing of Canada's entrance into the inter-American system brought with it an attractive agenda based on the triad of security, democracy, and prosperity.

Canada's preferred instrument for promoting its new hemispheric policy was multilateralism rather than bilateralism, as, at the global level, its so-called "multilateral vocation" was a product of necessity as well as idealism. As a small country but large trader, with international trade comprising over 40 percent of its gross domestic product (GDP), Canada has long been in the forefront of international regime-building to strengthen the trading system with effective and predictable rules and procedures applicable to all countries regardless of size or power. Moreover, since the bulk of Canada's trade (80 percent) was in North America, in a highly integrated economy with an overpowering U.S. cultural projection, a vigorous multilateralism remained an essential foreign policy orientation in maintaining an autonomous foreign policy. Finally, although its military capabilities were modest, with a small and over-extended defense establishment, Canada's membership in key northern clubs such as the Group of Seven (G–7) and NATO could bring significant diplomatic assets to the inter-American system in certain functional areas. The challenge was to locate a new security doctrine for inter-American relations that could revive regional multilateralism, transform the inherited dynamic of U.S.-Latin American security relations from antagonism to collaboration, and underpin Latin America's return to prosperity after the dead years of the 1980s. Coincidentally, such changes would also benefit Canadian business and civil society.

Cooperative Security

Canada's approach to inter-American security policy after 1989 fell clearly into two periods. From its entrance into the OAS in 1990 until the Miami Heads of Government Summit of the Americas in December 1994, Canada promoted a concept of "cooperative security," articulated by Foreign Minister Joe Clark in his 1990 address to the United Nations General Assembly. "Cooperative security" provided an initial declaratory break with the national security doctrine of the Cold War years, and in effect endorsed the conclusions of the Brandt Commission's *Report on International Development* that threats were multifaceted and inter-dependent, that security required justice and equity among states and, therefore, that the traditional security agenda was narrow and outmoded.[4] But while the new concept recognized the essential link between security and development, it retained the state-centric approach which had characterized regional multilateral initiatives such as the North Pacific security dialogue and the earlier Council on Security and Cooperation in Europe (CSCE). Canada was closely involved in both of these regional initiatives and it was no great surprise that it proposed a similar dialogue in the Western Hemisphere to fill the post-Cold War void.

In fact, cooperative security offered a good fit with Canada's emerging interests in Latin America and the Caribbean. By defining security more broadly than defense policy, cooperative security provided a bridge to Latin American governments searching for new approaches. Washington at the end of the Cold War was also interested in rebuilding U.S.–Latin American relations. The result was an unusual inter-American opportunity, grasped by a coalition of inter-American governments including Canada, to revive regional multilateralism around an agenda that linked the three themes of security, democracy, and prosperity within a strengthened system of regional governance headed by the OAS. The concept of cooperative security was consequently endorsed and adopted by all thirty-four governments at the Twenty-First General Assembly of the OAS in 1991 when that body formed a new Standing Committee on Hemispheric Security in the Permanent Council to re-design regional security doctrine in light of post-Cold War realities.[5]

The first years after 1990 marked the most successful efforts at regional multilateralism in decades in the inter-American security field, both at the hemispheric level and in the subregions. Canadian, U.S, Latin American, and Caribbean initiatives were surprisingly robust in the three primary areas affecting Western Hemisphere security: the reshaping of the principal institutions such as the OAS and the Inter-American Defense Board (IADB); subregional détente on the pattern of Mercosur; and the pursuit of security regimes and confidence- and security-building measures to promote the peaceful resolution of disputes and transform civil–military relations.[6] By the Miami Summit in December 1994, Canada had good reason to believe that a revised inter-American agenda was taking shape behind a new post-Cold War leadership in Washington. President Aristide had just been restored to power in Haiti with the threat of U.S. military intervention. The Clinton Administration had gained congressional approval for the North American Free Trade Agreement (NAFTA) and supported its expansion to include Chile, the U.S. delegation to the OAS since 1990 had been strong and constructive and now had taken the initiative in calling the first Summit of the American Heads of Government since 1969. For its part, Canada had emerged as a visible and permanent actor in the inter-American system.

From the narrower perspective of Canadian–Latin American relations, the

Canadian government had reason to be pleased with its record between 1990 and the Miami Summit, and took considerable credit for the adoption of the Miami Action Plan. Bilateral military linkages and exchanges with Latin America had also developed a pattern consistent with regional partnership, terminating the previous absence of service contacts in the region beyond the United States. Canadian and Latin American forces found themselves cooperating in the expanding UN peacekeeping missions abroad, with the Argentine Peacekeeping Center, in regional military exercises, and, of course, within the regular regional military conferences and inter-American forums from which Canadians were absent before 1990. The assignment of Canadian military attachés in the region and participation in courses of the Inter-American Defense College were symbolic of a new era. This quantum leap forward was officially recognized in Canada's *Defence White Paper* (1994). The Royal Canadian Mounted Police (RCMP) also began to interact regularly with its Latin American counterparts in joint inter-American anti-crime operations and surveillance. The Miami Summit and its Action Plan seemed to confirm the validity of the policy triad of security, democracy, and prosperity: NAFTA seemed to be the model for free-trade negotiations, and Chile was invited to become its fourth member; the triumphant return of President Aristide in Haiti seemed to confirm a deepening commitment in the Western Hemisphere to defend democracy. After five years, the Canadian commitment to security in the Americas had become a permanent fact.[7]

Cooperative security did not satisfy everyone. It was argued that it promised too much, that it was more process than doctrine, and that norm- and confidence-building measures represented only one step forward in the central task of redefining U.S.–Latin American security relations based on a mutually acceptable post-Cold War doctrine.[8] Other critics complained that cooperative security was too narrow a concept—and that the new security agenda included a far broader range of environmental, socioeconomic, indigenous, and other threats.[9] Both criticisms missed the positive contribution of "cooperative security" in laying the foundation for post-Cold War security cooperation in the Americas. Essentially, it recognized the inherent obstacles to redefining inter-American security doctrine as long as the United States retained its global superpower role, while recognizing the need for immediate cooperation in resolving urgent post-Cold War security challenges in Latin America and the Caribbean on the basis of mutual respect. The goal was to create a habit of cooperation which could replace the inherited legacy of U.S. unilateralism and Latin resentment.

Human Security

By 1995, however, the Canadian government had again refocused its foreign policy, shifting its approach from one of cooperative security to "human security." Whereas cooperative security had already identified threats facing the international community beyond traditional military and defense categories, the new approach marked a significant evolution and was much more comprehensive. Accepting a definition proposed by the United Nations Development Program (UNDP) in 1994, Canada rejected a solely state-centric approach altogether and agreed instead that security involved the provision of safety and basic needs at the human level across boundaries. The proper scope of security was therefore the impact of global, regional, and national policies on societies, communities, and, finally, the individual.[10] "Our basic unit in security matters," explained Canada's Foreign Minister Lloyd Axworthy, "has shrunk from the state to the community and even the individual . . . international issues that strike home to the individual: the threats posed by illicit drugs, terrorism, environmental problems, human rights abuses and weapons proliferation."[11] The challenge facing the global community was to move from a state- to a people-centered approach to security—one which could link development and security within states as well as between them. "These problems largely ignore state boundaries," Axworthy continued, "This is no longer simply a matter for nation-states. New players on the international scene, including corporations, nongovernmental bodies and regional organisations, have a growing role to play." In effect, human security challenged the international community to redefine and expand its thinking on security and development, and specifically called for governments to abandon their monopoly in defining security interests facing their countries. In regional terms, the Canadian foreign minister challenged his counterparts in the Americas to accept a definition of democracy that recognized civil society and other sub-state actors as legitimate stakeholders, and to recognize that for some individuals and communities the state itself might be the most important source of insecurity.[12]

Translated from diplomatic jargon, human security proclaimed a "new" multilateralism to challenge the root causes of conflict more aggressively and to pursue a just order within and between states. Unlike the old multilateralism, which was top-down and state-to-state, the newer approach featured partnerships between governments, civil society, and activist international organizations. The international campaign to ban anti-personnel mines (spearheaded by Axworthy himself), which culminated in the Ottawa Convention in December 1997, quickly became the model for success in Canadian foreign policy. In this highly contested case of arms control, an ad hoc alliance of nongovernmental actors from around the world with a coalition of middle powers had been successful against the opposition of the great military powers including the United States, China, and Russia. It was a heady experience. Here was a bottoms-up, assertive multilateralism that had appealed to human values across borders and gathered enormous international public support.

Although foreign policy makers in Ottawa viewed human security in a global framework, the Americas constituted a key testing ground for their international agenda comprising land mines, small arms, terrorism, narcotics, sustainable development, and so forth. Canadian officials claimed a good fit with hemispheric needs and deemed human security to be a logical extension of cooperative security. They also claimed widespread Latin American support for the new concept, pointing, for example, to the Central American peace processes in the early 1990s that had linked armed conflict with economic, political, and social deprivation and had elaborated a series of confidence- and security-building measures to limit violence. Latin American governments had also long viewed development as a national security objective. The "Plan of Action"[13] adopted in Santiago at the Second Heads of Government Summit of the Americas in 1998 further identified a broad range of nonmilitary threats to regional security, and recommended four areas of commitment (education, democracy, integration, and poverty reduction) consistent with a human security perspective. Canadian officials at the OAS could report Latin American support for arms control measures such as the land mine convention, which facilitated global norm-building and constituted a regional caucusing on behalf of human security.

Indeed, at the theoretical level, human security was a potentially powerful and attractive concept because it both personalized threats and linked them specifically to their social, economic, cultural, and environmental roots. It evoked, for example, the social crisis throughout Latin America and the Caribbean, in which personal safety had markedly deteriorated almost everywhere during the 1990s. At first glance, the term was rhetorically irresistible, calling for the reconstruction of state–society relations by discarding outmoded concepts, calling for the empowerment of civil society and marginalized non-state actors, and demanding attention to the impact of globalization on developing countries. Canada, for its part, strengthened its promotion of civil society involvement in trade negotiations and regional institutions as a core element of community-building. Far from diminishing Canadian attention to the Western Hemisphere, the adoption of human security deepened its commitment and engagement in the region.

HUMAN SECURITY AS VISION AND REALITY

Despite its attractiveness in principle, the concept of human security has not provided a coherent framework for promoting security, development, and democracy in the Americas. The first major problem lies in the dilemma of priorities. Cooperative security in the Americas was already a broad concept, going beyond the established security-related issues which remained after the Cold War. To some experts, it was already too broad.[14] But because virtually every conceivable threat can be included in human security, the term is as inclusive and conceptually amorphous as "sustainable development."[15] Canada has even lumped hemispheric free trade into the human security agenda. For a middle power with narrow resources, hyperactive Canada seems all over the global map—an active partner in the NATO bombing of Yugoslavia during the Kosovo crisis, invoking human security to intervene militarily with its allies on human rights grounds (with the endorsement of the United Nations Security Council and the strong support of Canadian civil society); vocally supporting an effective International Criminal Court (much to the dislike of Washington); lecturing Mexican President Ernesto Zedillo over his government's handling of the Chiapas crisis; leading a Commonwealth initiative to restore democracy in Pakistan; participating in East Timor peacekeeping; and so forth. While there is some overlap between the agendas of Latin American countries and Canada's peacekeeping, peace-building, and disarmament agenda (for example, land mines, narcotics, small arms control, and measures such as the International Nuclear Test Ban Convention and the International Criminal Court), many Latin American countries face the more immediate challenges of boundary disputes, guerrilla insurgencies and political cohesion, and armed inter-American criminal organizations, which require military capabilities. Arms sales from the United States and other suppliers have not promoted stability in the region; civil–military relations remain fragile in some countries, and the rise of domestic crime and violence has coincided with regional recession, increasing poverty, and an increasing democratic malaise most evident in the Andean countries, Paraguay, and the Caribbean. Crises in Colombia, Venezuela, and Ecuador preoccupy neighbors; small Caribbean countries require U.S. assistance in containing the narcotics trade; and the old Cuban–U.S. standoff continues. Traditional security threats have not disappeared after the Cold War. Despite earlier and important successes in regional conflict reduction—most recently the Peru–Ecuador border conflict which flared up suddenly in February 1995 but which was mediated by the four-power guarantors group established in 1942 (United States, Brazil, Argentina, and Chile) after the first round of undeclared war—the stability of Latin America cannot be taken for granted. Thus, while human security offers an interesting diagnostic or academic tool, the fragility and complexity of the region hinder its application and leave Canada open to the charge of "opportunistic multilateralism"—trying to muster regional support for its own international causes in newsworthy global issues such as Kosovo or East Timor, which have only secondary interest in Latin America and the Caribbean.

The second related problem with the human security approach concerns its implementation, particularly given the current crisis of transition in Latin America and the Caribbean. It is in fact strongly interventionist, endorsing a new multilateralism potentially at odds with the norms of traditional state-to-state multilateralism in which Canada has excelled (and for which it achieved respect in Latin America after 1990 as an honest broker). While cooperative security rested on a notion of consensus, human security appeared more strident and ideological. While Latin American countries adopted Santiago Resolution 1080 in 1991 and had moved some distance away from their earlier strict interpretation of nonintervention, they overwhelmingly opposed the NATO bombing campaign in Kosovo. In the case of Haiti, another example of CNN-driven humanitarian intervention, skeptical Latin Americans have witnessed the successful return to power of President Aristide and the exile of the previous military leaders in 1984, but since then they have observed the failure of the new regime and the inability of the West and international civil society to restore sustainable human development. Haiti remains Latin America's poorest country, a failed state that could not be revived by good intentions. Human security raises far-reaching expectations, but it is not clear that its architects have a strategy which can help the region to promote development. The promotion of civil society is a case in point. Some Latin governments are skeptical about Canadian and U.S. motives for supporting civil society representation in trade negotiations where powerful nongovernmental organizations (NGOs) demand human rights or environmental conditionalities; from a southern perspective such demands often seem to promote protectionist interests in North America at their expense. Canada and the United States already have strong states, unlike most countries in Latin America, and their civil societies expand the realm of public debate across borders without compromising governmental cohesion.

In practice, human security demands nothing less than a full-scale overhaul of state–society relations—long overdue in the region, as Latin Americans well know. But this fundamental transition to democracy cannot be promoted by empowering civil society and non-state actors unless the state's capacity to maintain basic order and channel globalization is assured; otherwise, such activism might weaken the state and undermine civil–military relations or empower organized crime across uncontrolled borders. Definitions of security and development differ throughout the region because circumstances differ; there is no magic inter-American recipe or solution for security. Instead, countries confront their own internal challenges and share vulnerability in important areas such as trade, migration, narcotics, and other inter-American criminal behaviors that require multilateral solutions, and therefore more effective regional governance. The specific contribution of the interventionist side of human security remains unclear.

The third obstacle to a human security agenda in the Americas is the prevailing turbulence since the Miami Summit. After the first post-1990 period of optimism, the promotion of regional multilateralism in the security field has stalled. While U.S. Secretary of Defense William Perry provided an initial boost by inviting his counterparts to a "Defence Ministerial" in Williamsburg (with follow-ups in Argentina and Colombia), overall U.S. interest in Latin America has evidently flagged, marked by the failure of the Clinton Administration to obtain fast-track authority for hemispheric free trade negotiations (FTAA)—a devastating blow to regional multilateralism. Similarly, the OAS strengthening process waned after Miami; instead, the summit process took on a life of its own, with Chile hosting the second meeting in 1998 and with Canada selected to host the third summit in April 2001. Economic and social woes in the region, combined with the depth of the crisis affecting "Gran Colombia," have contributed to a growing Latin and Caribbean fatigue with inherited democratic institutions. Crime and poverty have eroded public safety to an alarming degree, while the falling urban crime rate in the United States and Canada appears to accentuate the North–South divide.

The OAS, which seemed reinvigorated after Resolution 1080, has remained silent on the major issues affecting Latin America, including multiple challenges to democracy across the hemisphere, the financial crises in Brazil and Ecuador, the collapse of constitutional government in Haiti, the internal war in Colombia and its potential spill-over to neighboring countries, and the future of Cuba. The OAS again faces a financial crisis as governments fall behind in their annual commitments. Quite apart from the U.S. Congress, neither Mexico nor Brazil, the two largest Latin American economies, supports the FTAA. With its clarion call for human security and tireless promotion of the FTAA, Canada at the end of the decade had become a curiously lonely champion of regional multilateralism among an unhappy family of American states.

Canada's fourth problem in promoting human security lies in Canada's limited capabilities and very limited bilateral leverage in the Americas. Beyond its role in NAFTA and the peculiar cases of Cuba, Haiti, and the Commonwealth Caribbean, Canada is a small economic player in the Americas. Only 1.8 percent of its exports go to Latin America compared with 87 percent destined for the United States. Canadian investment in mining, banking, and telecommunications in Latin America has grown more rapidly, however. Canadian Official Development Assistance (ODA) in the region is not insignificant, but $100 million can make only a small contribution to sustainable development. Together with NAFTA, the Canadian free-trade agreement with Chile and the more recent framework agreements with the Mercosur and Andean Group have encouraged Ottawa's long-term strategy for trade promotion in the region, and the FTAA is promoted with conviction by the Ministry of Foreign Affairs and International Trade. But Canada has little leverage and few resources to promote regional trade agreements. In the military and security fields, Canada's increasing global commitments in the name of human security in the Balkans, East Timor, and other locations have strained its capabilities to the point where it could not undertake another major peacekeeping mission in the Americas. Such commitments also represent a diversion of scarce resources from long-term international development needs.

Finally, U.S. power conditions Canada's practical options in the Americas.

U.S. capabilities are pervasive and particularly overwhelming in the Caribbean Basin. Without U.S. leadership and assets, major security operations in support of regional multilateralism cannot be envisaged. Although Latin and Caribbean governments may share Canada's concerns with Washington's tendency to militarize the drug war, the fact remains that many of them require U.S. capabilities for their defense against international criminal organizations. Nor is it coincidental that the eventual resolution of the Peru–Ecuador boundary dispute was brokered by U.S. Ambassador Luigi Einaudi as the de facto leader among the four guarantors. Although U.S.–Latin American asymmetry places limits on such cooperation, this important success in conflict resolution demonstrates the continuing necessity for such collaboration. But Washington's unique superpower role in both the Americas and in global management affects Canada very differently than it does the Latin American middle powers. For the latter, asymmetry effectively rules out the forging of a new cooperative security paradigm, notwithstanding the continuing efforts on both sides to recast hemispheric relations. Canadian–U.S. military relations, on the other hand, have become increasingly close during the 1990s and particularly after the war in Kosovo, with Canada's defense forces now fully interoperative with those of its much larger partner. In the end, Canada and the United States enjoy a security community; Latin America and the Caribbean are not members of this North Atlantic reality. The core U.S. alliance remains NATO, and this remains true for Canada as well. If pressed, no Canadian government would consider endangering its relationship with the United States for its secondary interests in Latin America. Human security or not, the prospect of major Canadian peacekeeping missions opposed by Washington can be safely set aside.

THE FUTURE CHALLENGE: OPERATIONALIZING HUMAN SECURITY

The timing of Canada's entrance into the inter-American system proved fortunate, enabling it to help transform an exhausted Cold War paradigm that had long soured U.S.–Latin American relations. Cooperative security offered an avenue for the thirty-four governments in the Americas to open a new dialogue and deepen regional partnerships outside Cold War memories, at least with the exception of U.S.–Cuban relations. Meanwhile, the OAS revived after 1990 and was able to debate and adopt a host of new resolutions on security ranging from anti-terrorism to confidence-building measures in which member states formally adopted new commitments, standards of behavior, and a new regional vision. Whether or not these grand OAS resolutions would ever be applied, few observers would deny that cooperative security in the pre-Miami Summit period between 1990 and 1994 yielded important steps forward in inter-American security relations. In addition, some progress had been made in opening issues previously consid-ered taboo—such as the willingness of the Mexican military to open a dialogue with the Pentagon, or even U.S.–Cuban relations.

Canada's promotion of human security after the Miami Summit can be seen as an even bolder attempt to address the broad range of traditional and nontraditional threats in the region, and, in the absence of leadership from Washington since 1995, Canada should be applauded for its efforts to strengthen regional multilateralism. Indeed, it is hard to imagine a more vigorous diplomatic campaign or the hosting of more initiatives to inau-gurate the new millennium. However, if wrongly applied, human security risks the danger of being ineffectual at best or further aggravating difficulties in inter-American relations. The most successful Canadian security initiatives in the Americas since 1990, including garnering support for the Santiago Resolution 1080 or more recently the OAS Multilateral Evaluation Mech-anism (MEM), have been loyal to its traditional role of consensus-building associated with state-to-state multilateralism. This diplomatic style remains Canada's most appropriate role with regional partners. Ottawa has a strong civil society engagement in its foreign policy as well as its traditional com-mitment to multilateral institutions such as the OAS, but the crusading and interventionist thrust of human security evident in Kosovo is a counterpro-ductive and unacceptable approach for the Americas. In short, its successful implementation in this region—its neighborhood—requires much greater theoretical and conceptual work that links security and development, iden-tifies the range of traditional and non-traditional threats to be addressed, recognizes the evolution of differing subregional security identities, and se-lects priorities in cooperation with its Latin and Caribbean partners within the geopolitical limits of U.S.—Latin American relations. Comparative ap-plied research for cases including Southeast Asia and southern Africa would also assist this work.

Canada's own security priorities in the Americas include the impact of the looming crises in Cuba, Haiti, and the Caribbean; the control of inter-American crime; and the sorting out of key long-term relations with sub-regions such as Mercosur. The first priority, however, lies in North America and the complex trilateral relations with the United States and Mexico.[16] Canadian–U.S. relations benefit from deep civil society underpinnings, and the human security approach builds to a certain extent on shared values and perceived threats, such as the war in Kosovo. But at the official level, Canada and Washington find themselves in increasing disagreement on numerous security issues such as Cuban policy, migration, the latest version of Star Wars, land mine policy, the International Criminal Court, and ratification of the Comprehensive Test Ban Treaty, to name only a few. The U.S. Con-gress appears increasingly strident and inward-looking, with a strong mi-nority fundamentally opposed to multilateralism itself while Canada is increasingly committed to that concept. Meanwhile Canadian–U.S. economic and defense integration is deepening. Poised unsteadily between North and South America, Mexico is reinventing its foreign policy in a charged political climate and problematic border relations with its northern neighbors, and Canadian–Mexican relations are not supported by the civil society foundation that cements relations with the United States and supports bilateral ties through crises over particular issues. The operationalization of Canada's human security policy should therefore begin with NAFTA, where the common challenge of globalization is readily apparent. There the need for greater cross-border coordination at every level has been identified by Foreign Minister Axworthy, who recently noted: "We need to update our shared instruments and institutions to deal with challenges across a broad spectrum: everything from our shared natural environment to movement of goods and people, and to education and human resources."[17]

In conclusion, Canada brought a new and useful multilateral perspective to governance in the Americas after 1990 and the Cold War, and its overall policy triad of security, democracy, and prosperity remains sound. Whether or not the concept of human security eventually provides a viable basis for a new inter-American security system, its implied commitment to strengthening regionalism will remain a priority for Canada. If Ottawa no longer has illusions about the difficulties of building a Western Hemisphere community of nations, the Far North will remain a willing partner in the search for sustainable development in the Americas.

NOTES

The author expresses his appreciation for the assistance of Mr. Paul Durand and Dr. Peter M. Boehm in Canada's Department of Foreign Affairs and International Trade in the preparation of this paper. For current official Canadian policy, see Government of Canada, Department of Foreign Affairs and International Trade (DFAIT), *Latin America and Caribbean Regional Strategy*, Ottawa, November 1997.

1. Hal Klepak, "The Inter-American Dimension of Canadian Security Policy," *Canadian Foreign Policy* 5, no. 2 (Winter 1998): 107–28. See also Government of Canada, DFAIT, "Una Gran Familia," *World View*, Ottawa, no. 4 (entire), 1999.

2. Klepak, "Inter-American Dimensions," 111.

3. Paul D. Durand, "Preventive Diplomacy—The Support Group for Nicaragua: An Assessment," DFAIT, Ottawa, Canada, July 1996.

4. David B. Dewitt, "Cooperative Security: Canadian Approaches to the Promotion of Peace and Security in the Post-Cold War Era," *Canadian Defence Quarterly* (March 1994): 11–18; Jean Daudelin (with the assistance of Fen Osler Hampson), "Human Security and Development Policy," Background Paper prepared for the Canadian International Development Agency, Ottawa, December 1998, 18–24.

5. Inter-American Dialogue, "The Inter-American Agenda and Multilateral Gov-

ernance: The Organization of American States" (Washington, DC: OAS, April 1997), 22–25.

6. Richard Downes, "Emerging Patterns of Security Cooperation in the Western Hemisphere," *North South Issues* 5, no. 1 (1996): 1–8; "Multilateral Approaches to Peacemaking and Democratization in the Hemisphere," North–South Centre, Miami, April 1996.

7. Government of Canada, *Defence White Paper 1994* (Ottawa: The Queen's Printer, 1994).

8. Organization of American States, *Confidence- and Security-Building Measures In the Americas*, AG/RES. 1409 (XXVI-0/96) (Washington, DC: OAS, 1996); John A. Cope, "Hemispheric Security Relations: Remodelling the US Framework for the Americas," National Defence University (INSS), *Strategic Forum*, no. 147 (September 1998); also Downes, "Emerging Patterns," 6.

9. James Rochlin, "Redefining Mexican 'National Security' During an Era of Postsovereignty," *Alternatives* 20, no. 3 (July-September 1995): 369–402.

10. *Human Development Report* (New York: United Nations Development Programme, 1994).

11. Lloyd Axworthy, "Notes for an Address to a Meeting of the Mid-America Committee," DFAIT, Ottawa, 10 September 1998.

12. Ibid.

13. See Peter M. Boehm and Christopher Hernandez-Roy, "Multilateralism in the Americas," *Canadian Foreign Policy* 7, no. 2 (Winter 2000).

14. Downes, "Emerging Patterns," 6–8; also Jorge I. Domínguez, "International Peace and Security in the Americas" (Washington, DC: Inter-American Dialogue, October 1996).

15. Daudelin, "Human Security," 15–18. See also Graham Fraser, "Canada Urges New Approach to Drug War," *Toronto Globe and Mail*, 1 September 1999; Stephen Baranyi, "Drugs and Human Security in the Americas," DFAIT, Ottawa, December 1998.

16. On NAFTA and human security, see Axworthy, "Notes for an Address"; also (within an expanding literature) Raúl Benítez-Manaut, "Mexican National Security at the End of the Century," Woodrow Wilson Center for International Scholars, Latin American Program, Washington, DC, 23 April 1998.

17. Axworthy, "Notes for an Address."

9

Latin America and the World Economic Crisis

Sarah Anderson and John Cavanagh

In the aftermath of the global financial crisis that exploded in July 1997, tens of millions of workers lost their jobs around the world. Hundreds of millions watched their real wages fall. Millions of immigrant workers were sent home. Workers felt the ripple effects in every country. Meanwhile, those most responsible for causing the crisis suffered little of the pain. As former World Bank Chief Economist Joseph Stiglitz put it,

[I]n East Asia, it was reckless lending by international banks and other financial institutions combined with reckless borrowing by domestic financial institutions— combined with fickle investor expectations—which may have precipitated the crises; but the costs—in terms of soaring unemployment and plummeting wages—were borne by workers. Workers were asked to listen to sermons about "bearing pain" just a short while after hearing, from the same preachers, sermons about how globalization and opening up capital markets would bring them unprecedented growth.[1]

By the end of 1999, most of the crisis countries were showing signs of recovery in terms of their economic growth rates. But while international investors celebrated, working families in these countries saw little improvement in their own lives. A World Bank study released in January 2000 reveals that incomes of the low and middle class in East Asia have not been restored. Urban poverty has risen as laid-off industrial workers struggle to survive with little or no social safety nets. In many countries displaced workers have returned to rural villages, where they try to eke out a living on small family plots.[2]

Perhaps even more disturbing than the lingering effects of the financial crises of the last half decade is that little has been done to prevent such tragedies in the future. Although the crisis did provoke a vigorous debate around a "new global financial architecture," no clear and comprehensive vision has emerged from official policymakers. Moreover, even though workers bore the brunt of the last crises, their representatives are not among those at most tables where the new financial architecture is being debated and drawn. Hence, it should come as little surprise that official proposals for change either ignore workers' interests or undermine them.

This said, there are well-developed proposals for new rules and institutions that would serve workers' interests.[3] In addition, it is widely recognized that the massive demonstrations against the World Trade Organization by the international labor movement and others in Seattle in December 1999 and those against the World Bank and International Monetary Fund (IMF) in Washington, DC in April 2000 have opened up new opportunities for promoting a labor and social agenda within all the international financial institutions. There remains, however, a major challenge to educate and mobilize more people on this issue in order to raise the profile of workers' concerns in both the public and the official debates.

This chapter attempts to bring alive the impact of the financial crisis on working people. It outlines the mechanisms by which the crisis has hurt workers, then offers an analysis of the impact of the crisis on workers in three countries of Latin America—Brazil, Argentina, and Ecuador. A final section outlines the official debate on resolving the crisis, as well as components of an emerging North—South citizens' agenda on the global financial crisis that advances the interests of workers.

THE CRISIS

Today international financial markets resemble a global casino where traders gamble in split-second trades on market fluctuations. In 1980 the daily average of foreign exchange trading was $80 billion; today more than $1.5 trillion flows daily across international borders. More than nine-tenths of capital flows are speculative rather than productive in nature.

The global financial casino is the conscious creation of public policy. Over the past decade, the World Bank, the IMF, and the U.S. Treasury expanded their focus on free trade to press governments around the globe to open their stock markets and financial markets to short-term international investments. The resulting quick injections of capital from mutual funds, pension funds, and other sources propelled short-term growth in the 1990s; however, they also encouraged bad lending and bad investing. According to the World Bank, the amount of private financial flows entering poorer nations skyrocketed from $44 billion in 1990 to $256 billion in 1997. Roughly half of this was long-term direct investment, but most of the rest—as recipient countries were soon to discover—was footloose, moving from country to country at the tap of a computer keyboard.

When international investors got spooked in Thailand, Indonesia, and several other countries in mid-1997, the "hot money" panicked and left much faster than it had arrived. Big-time currency speculators like George Soros deepened the crisis by betting against the currencies of the crisis nations. IMF policy advice seemed only to quicken the exodus. Currencies and stock markets from Korea to Brazil nose-dived, and as these nations slashed purchases of everything from oil to wheat, prices of these products likewise plummeted. As the financial crises have spread to the productive economies of Indonesia, Russia, and several other countries, there have been widespread pain, dislocation, death, and environmental ruin. According to U.S. President Bill Clinton, "the world faces perhaps its most serious financial crisis in half a century."

THE IMPACT ON WORKERS IN CRISIS COUNTRIES

The impact of the financial crisis on workers is often swift and direct. In crisis countries, the chain reaction of economic events typically has started with a plunge in the currency and stock market as investors flee. Desperate to regain investor confidence and obtain emergency funds, countries turn to the IMF or the World Bank or both to get a "seal of approval" and a quick loan. Before new funds are disbursed, the World Bank and IMF demand certain "structural adjustment" reforms. These invariably hurt workers through any of seven effects: rising interest rates, massive public sector layoffs, spending cuts in basic social services, crippling wage freezes and labor suppression, devaluation of local currencies, promotion of export-oriented production, and the abolition of price controls on basic necessities.[4]

Countries are encouraged to raise interest rates to strengthen the currency and to attract back the foreign investment. Yet higher interest rates cripple domestic business, which must repay debts at higher rates, as well as workers who have borrowed funds. In Mexico, Brazil, and elsewhere, thousands of small enterprises have gone bankrupt, adding millions to the ranks of the unemployed. Furthermore, sky-high interest rates discourage new borrowing, which reduces investment and makes an economic downturn even more severe.

Massive public sector layoffs are also encouraged. World Bank and IMF policies in poor countries can be summed up in four words: "Spend less, export more." As governments cut expenditures, civil service downsizing is often one of the first targets. In addition to public sector layoffs, governments have been pressed by adjustment loans to cut basic social services. As education, health care, and other social program budgets are cut, not only are jobs lost directly but the future health and productivity of the workforce are undermined.

The World Bank and IMF also press countries to slow or stop the rise in wages, both to attract foreign investment and to repress demand. In some countries, the lending programs have also undercut workers by promoting so-called "labor market flexibility" measures. These can include making it easier for firms to fire workers and weakening the capacity of unions to negotiate on behalf of their members. Meanwhile, the IMF and World Bank refuse to promote actively the enforcement of international core labor standards. In a letter to American University Professor Jerome Levinson, Joanne Salop (World Bank Vice President for Operations Policy and Strategy) explained that "with respect to freedom of association and the right to collective bargaining, the Bank is in the process of analyzing the economic effects in order to form an informed opinion."[5]

One of the prominent reasons why workers face rising prices in adjusting countries is the common policy prescription that countries should devalue their currency. Devaluations have the effect of making a country's exports cheaper and its imports more expensive. Workers' wages, in local currency, buy fewer imported goods. In addition, more of their tax money is required to meet interest payments on foreign debt that is denominated in foreign currency.

The World Bank and IMF pursue a series of policies in addition to devaluation to encourage countries to shift more land from basic food crops to export-oriented production of shrimp, broccoli, cut flowers, coffee, and dozens of other products. In addition to hastening ecological decline (shrimp farmers can ruin the water table, the cash crops often rely on more chemical inputs, and so on), this shift has often been accompanied by increased malnutrition as basic food prices rise and millions of peasants and indigenous people are displaced from their land. The World Bank has also been a big promoter of "free-trade zones" where young women often work in exploitative conditions to produce light manufactured goods for export to Wal-Mart, Sears, K-Mart and other outlets. While a small elite gains from these new export ventures, the rising inequalities between the winners and the workers create new tensions and instabilities.

A favorite target of IMF and World Bank policies is the low prices on basic necessities, often government-subsidized in urban areas. The elimination of these subsidies can be devastating and in several countries has led to riots and bloodshed.

In sum, in their zeal to correct macroeconomic imbalances and speed the generation of foreign exchange to repay creditors in the rich countries, the IMF and World Bank have visited enormous suffering on the workers of the poorer two-thirds of the world.

BOOMERANG EFFECTS ON U.S. WORKERS

As workers in the global South suffer, the same World Bank and IMF policies have boomerang effects on U.S. workers. In pressing southern countries to export their way out of crisis with depressed wages, the World Bank and the IMF also increased low-cost exports to the United States. Likewise, World Bank and IMF policy-based lending has a negative impact on U.S. exports, and hence on U.S. jobs. First, many of the loans prescribe currency devaluations that have the effect of making imports of U.S. and other products more expensive. Second, the loans prescribe cuts in government spending that eliminate government jobs and hence cut purchasing power. Third, many of the loans push for the elimination of government subsidies on the prices of locally produced basic necessities, which decreases the income people have to spend on U.S. goods. Finally, many of the loans prescribe a privatization agenda that in most developing countries has cost jobs, which again cuts the purchasing power of people to buy U.S. goods. The World Bank and IMF structural adjustment programs also destroy U.S. jobs by promoting policies that encourage U.S. firms to shift production offshore. Many of the loans are conditioned on the creation of export processing zones, which provide cheap labor and a liberal regulatory environment to attract foreign investors.

IMPACTS ON WORKERS BY COUNTRY

The global financial crisis began in Asia in 1997, spread to Russia in 1998, and engulfed much of Latin America by 1999. In a world of financial deregulation, crisis in one country can spread like wildfire across borders and even oceans. The Asian crisis that erupted in mid-1997 spread to other countries through three main channels: trade relations, commodity prices, and investor panic. Faced with negative economic growth and weak currencies, the crisis countries are importing less, affecting the exports of countries around the world. For the United States, reduced exports to Asia contributed to record trade deficits in 1998 and 1999. For Latin America, which does not rely heavily on Asian markets, the primary concern has been a drop in exports to Brazil. A less direct, but equally serious effect is the impact of a global financial crisis in depressing world commodity prices. This is particularly devastating for developing countries that remain dependent on the export of raw materials. Between June 1997 and August 1998, oil prices dropped about 30 percent (affecting Ecuador, Mexico, Russia, and Venezuela, among others), coffee prices fell 43 percent (affecting Brazil and Colombia), and gold prices sank 17 percent (affecting Russia and South Africa).[6]

The Asian crisis prompted investors, nervous about emerging markets in general, to shift their capital to developed economies that they considered safer. Investors were particularly spooked by countries such as Brazil that bore resemblance to the Asian crisis countries in terms of high budget deficits. In response, governments of developing countries have been forced to jack up interest rates as they attempt to put the brakes on capital flight. High interest rates in turn hurt locally owned businesses.

In the following section, we describe three Latin American countries that have been affected, to varying degrees, by these channels of contagion.

THE CRISIS IN LATIN AMERICA

In the aftermath of the Asian financial crisis and even more after Russia defaulted in August 1998, Latin America suffered from an overall drop in investor confidence in emerging markets. Private lending to the region declined from $119 billion in 1997 to $77 billion in 1998, and many countries suffered from depressed prices for their leading export commodities.[7] Overall, Latin America GDP growth was a mere 0.3 percent in 1999, and many countries experienced severe recession. By contrast, the region's GDP growth rate in 1997 was 5.3 percent. Faced with extreme instability, many countries took emergency loans from multilateral banks. As a result, their external debt increased by $10 billion to a total of $750 billion.[8]

Brazil: Origin of the "Samba Effect"

The most dramatic impact of contagion occurred in Brazil, which began struggling in 1997 to prevent crisis through spending cuts, tax increases, and high interest rates. According to Peruvian economist Humberto Campodonico, Brazil was particularly vulnerable because it had pursued economic policies similar to East Asia's, maintaining high interest rates to attract capital in order to defend a fixed exchange rate tied to the dollar. The result was a massive inflow of volatile capital, increasing Brazil's risk of rapid capital flight in the event of external financial problems.

In January 1999, the country gave up efforts to shore up its currency, the *real*, allowing it to fluctuate against the dollar, leading to a drop in value of almost 36 percent. This set off a dramatic plunge in the country's stock market and created fears that Latin America could be in for an Asia-style crisis. Brazil is the eighth biggest economy in the world and the largest in Latin America, producing about half of the region's industrial output. Many countries in the region depend on exports to Brazil.[9]

A month after the crash, the Brazilian government agreed on the framework of an austerity program as required by a $41.5 billion rescue package from the IMF, the United States, and other world lenders.[10] By the end of 1999, Brazil showed better than expected economic growth (slightly positive average growth, compared to the decline of 3.5 to 4 percent projected in March 1999). Nevertheless, the official unemployment rate persisted at 7.7 percent in the period from April–September 1999, only slightly lower than the 7.9 percent rate in the same period of 1998.[11] Independent groups claim that the true unemployment rate is closer to 20 percent. By contrast, Brazil's official unemployment rate was only around 3 percent in the late 1980s and early 1990s.[12]

Workers in the automobile sector suffered the hardest immediate impact in the aftermath of the Asian crisis. General Motors cut 1,800 workers in 1998 in a first round of layoffs, and in January 1999 dismissed another 1,000, out of a total of 8,900 employees. Ford laid off 2,800 workers at its São Bernardo plant the day before Christmas in 1998. According to Kjeld Jakobsen of Brazil's Central Unica dos Trabalhadores (CUT) labor federation, workers occupied the plant for twenty days and in the end managed to negotiate a dismissal program that provided the workers with higher compensation. In early 1999, Ford threatened to lay off a third of its 1,800 workers at a lorry factory in Ipiranga.

In the midst of rising unemployment, Brazilians also faced rising costs for basic necessities. The number of *reals* needed to purchase a typical basket of goods rose 3.5 percent in January 1999.[13] Soon after the crisis, the Brazilian government also cut back on spending for programs such as agrarian reform, social protection, food aid, and welfare for the poor. In addition, according to Friends of the Earth, Brazil's spending on environmental enforcement was cut by 50 percent.

Brazilian labor unions worked to oppose IMF-imposed austerity measures and criticized the undemocratic nature of the bailout negotiations, while at the same time working to ease the immediate burden of the crisis on workers. For example, two major trade union federations, the CUT and the Força Sindical, reached an agreement with car manufacturers in the São Paulo region designed to prevent mass layoffs. The plan proposed that the government lower the industrial production tax in exchange for the employers guaranteeing jobs and reducing the price of cars to "pre-devaluation" levels. The union estimated that the proposal would result in increased car sales that would make up for the government's loss in tax revenue.[14] Similarly, at the railway company Ferroban, workers threatened with a 50 percent cut in jobs negotiated with the firm, offering reduced working time and wages in order to preserve as many jobs as possible.

In early 2000, as the country began to show signs of recovery, the Brazilian government announced a plan to spend more than $22 billion over 10 years to fight poverty. Despite the IMF's recently proclaimed commitment to eradicating poverty, Fund officials were sharply critical of the plan. The *New York Times* quoted the IMF representative in Brazil as saying that "the government plan established a precedent that could become dangerous. . . . this money has to be used more effectively."[15] Although this official later retracted his statement, then-IMF Managing Director Michel Camdessus later reacted to the Brazilian plan by commenting that countries should pay off debts and achieve economic growth before handing out charity.

Argentina: Hurt by Dependence on Exports to Brazil

The Brazilian crisis spread quickly to other Latin American countries in what was called the "Samba Effect." Particularly hard hit was Argentina, for which Brazil is the main export market. Prior to the crisis, as much as 40 percent of Argentine exports went to Brazil. With the depreciated *real* making Argentine products more expensive for Brazilian consumers, Argentine exports to Brazil dropped by about 30 percent in 1999.[16] The auto sector, which typically exports 60 percent of its products to Brazil, has been wracked by layoffs. For example, Fiat and Renault announced layoffs of 5,200 workers in late January 1999. Ford initiated a voluntary retirement program, aiming to reduce its workforce by 1,430 workers. Other Argentine sectors that rely heavily on the Brazilian market are textiles, pork, poultry, footwear, and rice.[17]

In the immediate aftermath of the Brazilian crisis, Argentina also saw significant losses in construction jobs, as well as the first-ever drop in service sector jobs. An Argentine official attributed the strain in these sectors to high interest rates driven up by the Brazilian crisis.[18] Immediately after Brazil's devaluation, prime rates in Argentina rose from 10.62 to 15 percent, while rates for small- and medium-sized firms were near 20 percent.[19]

Throughout 1999, Brazil's troubles continued to contribute to Argentina's economic problems. Argentina's GDP declined by about 3 percent, down from an increase of 8.1 percent in 1997. The rate of unemployment increased to 14.3 percent in 1999.[20] Argentines were dismayed to see their unemployment rate rise once again after having made progress in driving down the high jobless rate caused by the "tequila effect" of the 1994 Mexican financial crisis. From 18 percent in 1995, the rate had dropped to 12.4 percent in 1998. As recently as 1991, Argentina's unemployment rate had been only 6.3 percent.[21]

Backed by the IMF, the Argentine government delivered another blow to Argentine workers in the spring of 2000. In the face of a general strike by tens of thousands, Argentine legislators passed a labor law reform that workers criticized for undermining the power of unions by giving precedence to company agreements with workers over sector-wide collective bargaining agreements. Although the legislature had considered a less harsh reform proposal, this version was pushed through after IMF officials spoke out strongly in support of it.

Ecuador: Victim of Low Commodity Prices and Other Contagion Effects

The contagion effects of the global financial crisis have contributed to extreme political and economic turmoil in Ecuador. The country suffered particularly severely from the drop in prices for oil, its main export, as well as capital flight related to the international financial crisis. El Niño storms also socked the country with billions of dollars worth of damage during this period.

Between January and March 1999, the real exchange rate of the *sucre* dropped by 29 percent. In March, Ecuador's then-President Jamil Mahuad announced a package of harsh austerity measures and plans to privatize state-run enterprises. The austerity measures included an increase in gas prices of 170 percent and in the sales tax from 10 to 15 percent, as well as restrictions on bank withdrawals.

Labor unions, indigenous groups, and others responded to the plan with hostility, arguing that it would exact the most economic pain on the poor. (Some two-thirds of the Ecuadoran population lives in poverty.) When unions called for a two-day general strike, President Mahuad countered by declaring a 60-day state of emergency and deploying troops to keep the peace.

Two days into the state of emergency, the president of the Ecuadoran Confederation of Free Trade Unions (CEOSL) reported that the head-quarters of the federation was surrounded by police and that some labor leaders were being followed constantly. He also said that the police were breaking up groups of protesters through indiscriminate tear-gassing.[22] Nevertheless, strikers persevered. For several days, taxi and bus drivers blockaded roads in the capital city with cars and burning tires. On 15 March, IMF head Michel Camdessus lamented that the lack of unity behind an emergency program for Ecuador was the only factor preventing approval of an IMF bailout.

Tensions have continued to escalate as economic conditions have worsened, despite a recent rise in oil prices. In 1999, Ecuador's output fell by 7.5 percent, inflation was more than 60 percent, and living standards plummeted. Unemployment stands at about 16 percent and average wages are about $48 per month.[23] The rate of under-employment in urban areas has also markedly increased, from 45.8 percent in 1998 to 56.9 percent in 1999. According to the United Nations, the deterioration in the labor market has contributed to a rise in the poverty rate from 46 percent to 69 percent overall, with rates as high as 88 percent in rural areas.[24]

In September of 1999, the Mahuad government defaulted on about half of Ecuador's $13 billion in foreign debt. In January 2000, Mahuad began a controversial process of "dollarizing" the economy (substituting U.S. dollars for local currency) in an attempt to regain economic stability. Unions joined with other groups to stage massive protests against the extreme measure, which they feared would make their savings worthless and force further austerity policies. On 15 January 2000, police arrested the president of CEOSL and other opponents on charges of subversion (they were released two days later). Then on 21 January 2000, indigenous groups allied with the military in a coup that ousted Mahuad. However, the military backed out shortly after assuming power, allowing Mahuad's Vice President Gustavo Noboa to become president. Noboa soon announced that he would continue to pursue the process of dollarization. As of August 2000, unions and others were continuing to protest the policy.

ALTERNATIVE AGENDAS

For the first time since the end of World War II, there is now a genuine debate over the institutions and rules of the global financial system. The AFL–CIO has stated well a central goal for workers engaged in the debate: "We need a global New Deal that establishes new rules to temper the excesses of the market; promote sustainable egalitarian growth; and assure the rights of working people everywhere are respected."[25] But first, workers must fight their way to the table where the new "architecture" is being planned. As the International Confederation of Free Trade Unions has pointed out: "The debate over financial market reform has been held behind closed doors by bankers and financial ministry officials. There must now be full public participation."[26]

The context for workers' organizations demanding a place at the table is that for the first time in decades there is significant elite discord over how best to govern our international financial system. The views of these dissidents have appeared in the op-ed pages of all the major mainstream newspapers. For example, former Secretary of Defense Robert McNamara was quoted in the *Wall St. Journal* as likening the crisis to the Vietnam War: in both situations, the managers lost control.

As early as 1997, two sets of elite actors began to emerge. A first set of elite critics supports free markets for trade in goods and services but not for short-term capital. This set was well represented in a task force sponsored by the Council on Foreign Relations, which issued a proposal in September 1999 for the future international financial architecture. Task force–members—including well-known free-trade supporters such as former U.S. Trade Representative Carla Hills, former Federal Reserve Chairman Paul Volcker, and MIT economist Paul Krugman, among others—endorsed the report, which called for strong IMF support of capital controls. Specifically, the report stated that "the IMF should not merely permit holding-period taxes of the Chilean type on short-term capital inflows but should advise all emerging economies with fragile domestic finance sectors and weak prudential frameworks to implement such measures."[27]

There is also some support for this point of view in governments. The Canadian and Finnish parliaments endorsed the idea of an international tax on foreign currency transactions to discourage speculative transactions. A resolution modeled after the Canadian one is being sponsored in the U.S. Congress by Representative Peter DeFazio (D–OR) and Senator Paul Wellstone (D–MN). Most Western European governments also support at least limited versions of capital controls, and the government of France was instrumental in pulling the plug on the proposed Multilateral Agreement on Investment, which would have further lifted barriers to investment.

A second set of Washington Consensus dissidents includes harsh critics of the IMF, who root their critique in a profound defense of free markets.

They charge that IMF rescue packages bail out investors, thus eliminating the discipline of risk in private markets (a phenomenon they refer to as "moral hazard"). They also criticize the IMF's long-term lending as an unnecessary use of public funds in an age when private financial institutions have dramatically increased their lending to the developing world. The proposed solutions of this camp range from abolishing the IMF altogether to drastically reducing the IMF's role in providing assistance.

The views of this camp were reflected in a report issued in March 2000 by the International Financial Institutions Advisory Commission, a congressionally appointed bipartisan group chaired by Carnegie Mellon University Professor Allan Meltzer. The Majority Report of the Commission (signed by eight of eleven members) provides a severe and wide-ranging critique of the IMF, including its undue interference in countries' economic policies, its advocacy of financial bailouts that reward reckless international creditors, and interventions of no clear gain to recipient countries. The report charges that the IMF's long-term policy lending goes far beyond the Fund's original mandate of ensuring stability in the international exchange rate system. It recommends that the IMF be scaled back to serve only as a lender of last resort to solvent member governments facing liquidity crises. Long-term IMF assistance tied to conditions would be terminated under this proposal.

These aspects of the report were welcomed by IMF critics across the political spectrum. However, the details of the Meltzer Report's recommendations on the IMF's future role offer those on the progressive end of the spectrum little reason for enthusiasm. This is mainly because although the commission would abolish the IMF's power to impose conditions on developing countries in return for long-term assistance, it would still require that countries meet a list of rigid "pre-conditions" in order to be eligible for short-term (120 days maximum) crisis assistance. These "pre-conditions" include freedom of entry and operation for foreign financial institutions, adequate capitalization of commercial banks, and assurances that IMF resources would not be used to sustain "irresponsible budget policies." The first requirement would disqualify from emergency assistance countries such as Brazil, which announced in early 2000 its intention to place controls on foreign banks. Indeed, in many countries, the growing influence of foreign banks is a volatile political issue, stemming from the fear that these global banks are not as committed as domestic financial institutions to meeting local credit needs or maintaining the country's financial stability. In the case of Brazil, for example, a former central bank president charges that in the midst of the country's economic crisis, foreign banks advised their clients not to purchase Brazilian government bonds and other securities.[28]

The second pre-condition for the IMF stamp of approval is that commercial banks must be adequately capitalized. This, the report says, should be consistent with recommendations from the Basel Committee on Banking

Supervision, an organization based at the Bank for International Settlements formed by the G-10 central bank governors to set voluntary standards for the international banking industry. The Basel Committee promotes a ratio between a bank's investments and outstanding loans that is far higher than that in most countries in the world. In fact, most developing countries currently have no standards at all on capitalization. If they could not meet this standard, they would be hung out to dry in the event of a liquidity crisis. Moreover, even if countries were to adopt such a standard, it is unclear whether this would have the desired stabilizing effect. According to Jane D'Arista of the Financial Markets Center, such a standard could worsen the impact of recession in developing countries since banks during these periods face difficulty in attracting investments and thus would need to call in loans to maintain the required capitalization ratio.

The third pre-condition would require fiscalization to ensure that IMF resources not be used to sustain "irresponsible budget policies." The problem with this requirement is that the IMF would be the body to define "irresponsible." In the past, its knee-jerk approach has been to urge governments to slash spending on social programs. The IMF even chastised Sweden, a country with low inflation, tremendous productivity growth, and falling unemployment, for providing overly generous unemployment insurance.[29] There is nothing in the commission's report that would require a different approach in the future.

The report also calls for IMF loans to be given a "clear priority claim on the borrower's assets." The method deemed "perhaps most promising" would involve requiring that other multilateral agencies and member countries refuse to provide loans or grants to any country that defaulted on its IMF loan.

These pre-conditions would allow the IMF to maintain tremendous influence over member country governments, even while terminating their long-term policy-based lending. Professor Jerome Levinson, a member of the commission who dissented from the Majority Report, argues that the pre-conditions are so strict that the countries probably most in need of IMF assistance would be cut off.[30] One needs only to consider how investors are likely to react when the IMF announces that a certain country has failed to pre-qualify for emergency assistance. The jitters this would likely provoke in the international financial markets would undermine the overall goal of stability.

Another aspect of the Meltzer Report that received favorable attention was a recommendation that the World Bank and IMF cancel all debts to the heavily indebted poorest countries. These debts, they concluded, are not repayable. However, the report conditions debt cancellation upon World Bank approval of the country's economic development strategy. This would likely perpetuate the same type of pressure to implement structural adjustment programs that has been the target of criticism in the past. Furthermore, as Commissioner Levinson points out, placing conditions on debt deemed not repayable is illogical. He advocates an alternative plan whereby debt would be canceled unconditionally, but future assistance for these countries would depend on whether they effectively handled the funds freed up through debt relief.

While the Meltzer Report's recommendations do not represent a model agenda for progressive activists, the commission has clearly served to widen the crack in the elite consensus on these issues. Hoping to prevent the Meltzer Report's recommendations from gathering support in the U.S. Congress, U.S. Treasury Secretary Lawrence Summers released his own IMF reform proposal in March 2000, which calls for a more modest reduction in the IMF's role in long-term policy lending. Summers proposed ending the IMF's long-term development loans to poor countries but not its long-term loans dealing with poverty reduction.[31] He argued that the Meltzer Report's more radical recommendations could put U.S. security at risk by preventing the lender from helping a wide range of countries that would not meet the pre-conditions laid out by the commission.

In a number of instances, elite actors have broken from the consensus policies in practice. In Hong Kong, long heralded by free market adherents as a supreme example of free-market trade and finance policies, the government intervened in the stock market and acted to prevent currency speculation. And, after riots greeted the removal of price subsidies on key items in Indonesia in 1998, the IMF implicitly acknowledged that there were occasions when the costs of free-market policies were unacceptably high. The IMF's post-Suharto agreement allowed for greater social spending and the maintenance of food, fuel, and other subsidies. At the World Bank, president James Wolfensohn has taken small steps to distance himself and his institution from the IMF and its policies. In 1997, he and several hundred NGOs agreed to carry out a multi-country review of the World Bank's structural adjustment policies. More recently, Wolfensohn's speeches and World Bank publications have included attacks on the social and environmental costs of free market policies. In February 2000, Wolfensohn even warned that there could be a backlash against globalization in Latin America if solutions could not be found to reduce the region's increasing inequality.[32]

With the ruptures in the elite consensus and widespread popular discontent, there is a battle over an alternative framework. The challenge for progressive citizens' organizations is to take advantage of this crack in the consensus to push forward an alternative set of goals and policies that promote the interests of workers and communities.

Unions, environmental groups, farmer organizations, and others in both northern and southern forums have already reached a certain level of consensus around a better alternative. They are suggesting that a broadening of development goals requires a reorientation of financial flows from speculation to long-term investment in the real economy at the local and national level. The International Confederation of Free Trade Unions (ICFTU) put it succinctly: "The aim must be to re-harness financial markets to facilitate long-term productive investment."[33] They are also suggesting that a premium be put on creating maximum space for local and national governments to set exchange rate policies, regulate capital flows, and eliminate speculative activity. They argue further that mechanisms should be put in place to keep private losses private.

Such goals require new action at the international, national, and local levels. Many of these proposals came together in December 1998 when Friends of the Earth, the International Forum on Globalization, and the Third World Network convened seventy representatives of the labor, environmental, faith-based, academic, and other northern and southern networks to address whether there was yet a North–South citizens–labor agenda on the global financial crisis.

At that meeting, groups drafted a "Call to Action: A Citizens' Agenda for Reform of the Global Economic System."[34] The call lays out an agenda that unites labor and other citizens' concerns in both North and South. It begins by asserting five goals of a new financial architecture. First, the rules and institutions of global finance should discourage all speculation and encourage long-term investment in the real economy in a form that supports local economic activity, sustainability, and equity, and also reduces poverty. Second, the rules and institutions of global finance should seek to reduce instability in global financial markets. Third, the rules and institutions of global finance should allow maximum space for national governments to set exchange rate policy, regulate capital movements, and eliminate speculative activity. Fourth, governments should not absorb the losses caused by private actors' bad decisions. Finally, the rules and institutions of the global economy should seek to decrease private speculative flows while increasing those public flows that support sustainable and equitable development activities. These institutions should recognize that development needs cannot be met by private capital flows alone.

POLICY PROPOSALS

In the following sections, we expand on these goals and the debate surrounding them, drawing heavily from the recommendations put forward in the Call to Action. We have organized the policy proposals according to whether governments should take these actions at the international, regional, national, or local level.

At the international level, the citizens' agenda calls for governments to establish an international bankruptcy mechanism, such as an international debt arbitration panel, to ensure that financial crises and sovereign debt obligations do not place undue burdens on countries and to prevent a liquidity crisis from becoming a solvency crisis. When sovereign debt service threatens the welfare of a country's people, the panel would restructure and/or cancel debts to ensure that important social services are not compromised in an effort to meet debt obligations. In a financial crisis, the panel would prevent a liquidity crisis from becoming a solvency crisis by arbitrating an agreement that meets the needs of sovereign debtor and creditor, thereby helping reduce the need for bailouts by the international community.

There are, by one recent count, at least ten proposals on the table to attempt a move in this direction,[35] all of them drawing from U.S. bankruptcy laws as a model. Under U.S. law, Chapter 9 proceedings deal with the insolvency of municipalities, and Chapter 11 deals with insolvent firms. The most interesting of the proposals is to remove the IMF or World Bank as the key arbiters in crisis situations. Instead, the key institution is an international court composed of nominees put forward by the debtor and creditors.

One of the more developed proposals, an international Chapter 9 for sovereign borrowers proposed by Kunibert Raffer of the University of Vienna, would allow those people affected by the solution to be represented by trade unions (as in U.S. Chapter 9), UN agencies, or nongovernmental organizations. Raffer argues for symmetrical treatment for all creditors, including the World Bank and IMF, so that multilateral agencies cannot insist on priority repayment. He suggests holding the multilateral institutions to account for the damaging effects of adjustment. Hence, in Africa, where much of the debt has built up as a part of adjustment, governments would be entitled to claim compensation for failed projects and reduce the debt burden further.

The major criticism of these types of proposals is that they are impractical in today's global system, since the legal framework to force creditors to accept a Chapter 11 or Chapter 9 type workout does not exist on a global scale. Currently, there is no single jurisdiction internationally that covers all of the creditors involved.

Groups are calling for the reform or replacement of the IMF. With the establishment of the bankruptcy mechanism above, the IMF would ideally retain minimal capability as a lender of last resort and as a gatherer and publisher of international economic data. However, this will not be accomplished overnight. In the meantime, citizens' groups continue to press for IMF reforms. Their primary demands are that the international financial institutions such as the IMF and World Bank reorient the goals of lending; terminate pressure to liberalize capital accounts; and achieve a higher level of transparency, accountability, and public participation in decision making.

The goal of both IMF and World Bank lending must be to reduce poverty and support sustainable development. Although both the World Bank and the IMF have made recent gestures indicating a new-found interest in alleviating poverty, critics rightly question the commitment and expertise of these institutions in carrying out this stated goal. The ICFTU has called on the IMF and World Bank to support national policies geared toward social protection, primary education and health care, job training, labor rights, and sound industrial relations. Such measures are prerequisites if the IMF and World Bank are to be perceived as showing a serious commitment to poverty reduction.[36]

The ICFTU is calling on the IMF and World Bank to encourage member governments to introduce programs aimed at developing a comprehensive system of social safety nets—including retirement pensions, unemployment benefits, child support, and sickness and injury benefits. The financial institutions should support programs aimed at maintaining and enhancing school participation, especially for girls; increase the availability of health care for all; and request that countries develop or improve their strategies for eliminating child labor. Finally, the institutions should encourage labor market reforms based on respect for core labor standards as defined in the ILO Declaration on Fundamental Principles and Rights at Work. The World Bank and IMF should also support the enhancement of programs to increase vocational training, establish and improve job search systems, implement labor-intensive public works programs, and counteract discrimination. According to the ICFTU, "In the emerging global economy, competitive advantage will lie with those countries that have strong social cohesion built on investment in education and training, health care and a sound industrial relations system founded on strong trade unions."[37]

The U.S. executive director is required by law to use his or her voice and vote on the IMF's Board of Directors to support IMF programs that maintain and improve core labor standards. Unfortunately, it is currently impossible to monitor the extent to which the executive directors adhere to this obligation. A March 1999 report by the U.S. Treasury lists seven countries about which the U.S. executive director to the IMF had raised labor concerns.[38] However, an AFL–CIO analysis reveals that these interventions were virtually unmentioned in public IMF documents and appear not to have had any policy impact.[39] A better system for monitoring the U.S. executive directors' actions with regard to this legal obligation is clearly necessary. Jerome Levinson, a member of the International Financial Institutions Advisory Commission, goes further to argue that the U.S. government should condition its support for the World Bank and IMF upon the U.S. executive directors voting against financing proposals for countries that are egregious abusers of core worker rights.[40]

A second arena of reforms advocated by progressive citizens' organizations relates to the pressures exerted by the IMF and the World Bank to liberalize capital accounts. Critics charge that the IMF paved the way for the financial crises of the late 1990s by insisting in the early part of the decade that more "protectionist" nations of Asia eliminate restrictions on the inflow of foreign capital. While the resulting explosion of private money into Asia made many people rich, it enhanced the country's vulnerability when economic conditions deteriorated and investors got spooked. Thus, the IMF should terminate its support for capital account liberalization and instead stick to the mandate of its charter, which authorizes member nations to "exercise such controls as are necessary to regulate international capital movements."

While the World Bank has taken some steps to release more information to the public about its operations and to consult with nongovernmental organizations, the IMF remains largely closed to outsiders. In response to public pressure for more transparency, the IMF launched a pilot project in 1999 to make public full copies of reports on their "Article IV consultations." These reports form the basis of IMF advice and assistance to these countries. Unfortunately, the pilot program is voluntary, and only a small, unrepresentative fraction of IMF member countries have agreed to release the reports. Nevertheless, a review of the twenty-one reports that had been made public as of January 2000 provides some insights into the Article IV process. For example, IMF staff consulted with business representatives in nineteen cases, whereas labor unions had participated in only nine of the discussions and other nongovernmental actors were involved in only seven of them. The Article IV consultations are just one area in which the IMF needs to improve its process to introduce a higher level of public participation and transparency. The institution must go much further in releasing as much information as possible to the public about its operations.

The last major area of reform demanded by citizens' groups is that the IMF and the World Bank ensure that creditors bear their fair share of the burden. Large private banks deserve a good share of the blame for the financial crises because they lent a great deal of money to developing nations without rigorous checks. But while millions of workers suffered greatly as a result of the crisis, the IMF bailouts protected the banks and their executives from the pain. One indication of this protection is that the CEOs of the six U.S. banks that had the greatest loan exposure to the Asian crisis countries in 1997 gave their top executives average salary raises of 18 percent that year.[41] The IMF should have a stated policy that creditors and investors must make a substantial contribution before public monies are disbursed in any future bailout.

At this juncture, workers and their representatives should exert pressure on the IMF to reorient the institution to serve the needs of the world's people rather than international investors. This is being pursued through a variety of means, including direct engagement with IMF officials, lobbying of IMF funding appropriations (in countries where this is possible), demonstrations, public education, and written critiques. However, the IMF may prove unreformable. For this reason, groups are also developing proposals for what type or types of institutions, if any, should replace the IMF. Some scholars, such as Walden Bello, argue that developing countries would be better off with no international financial institution rather than the current IMF because this would allow local and national governments and citizens' groups more autonomy in pursuing alternative development strategies.[42] However, in an era of global capital, we would ideally have international financial institutions that could help reduce volatility and contagion in ways that cannot be accomplished through nation-states.

An international bankruptcy mechanism has already been discussed. In addition, a number of scholars have proposed the creation of a new Global Financial Authority or Global Central Bank. The most detailed proposals for such an authority come from economists John Eatwell and Lance Taylor.[43] They propose an institution that would: set global regulatory standards, such as capital requirements for financial firms, that national authorities would follow; consult with countries on their own capital market regime; and develop innovative means to direct capital flows toward long-term needs. (This proposal assumes that the IMF would continue to play the role of international lender of last resort.) Citizens' groups have emphasized that any plan for a new global financial institution would need to begin with the establishment of sound procedures for transparency and democracy.

At the international level, progressive groups are also calling for mechanisms to provide substantial debt reduction detached from IMF and World Bank conditions. Currently, debt payments cripple the ability of many developing countries to invest in development. Thanks to pressure from Jubilee 2000 and other groups, there is currently a great deal of momentum around the world for debt reduction. Several European governments have unilaterally canceled bilateral debts owed by poor nations. The G-7 richest countries also announced in June 1999 an initiative to cancel the debts of the thirty-three most impoverished countries. Specifically, the countries agreed to cancel $20 billion in debts owed to national governments and to add an additional $27 billion to a joint World Bank/IMF debt initiative known as HIPC (highly indebted poor countries).

In the U.S. Congress, there were six bills introduced in 1999 in the U.S. House of Representatives and two in the U.S. Senate that involved debt relief. Some required that debt relief be linked to World Bank and IMF conditionality, while others, such as the "HOPE for Africa" bill by Representative Jesse Jackson, Jr. (D–IL), did not. Others stipulated that the U.S. Congress should not give the IMF further funding until the institution canceled its loans to the poorest countries. As of this writing, these initiatives are pending.

We believe that any resolution of the debt crisis must include an expansion of the resources available and the countries eligible for bilateral and multilateral debt relief. This relief should not be conditioned on IMF and World Bank structural adjustment programs, and it should allow countries to dedicate sufficient resources to health care, education, social services, and environmental protection.

On another front, groups are calling for the establishment of a tax to discourage speculation. The lifting of barriers to private capital flows has led to an explosion of speculative "hot money" investments. Currency traders zip billions of dollars back and forth across borders every day, profiting from slight changes in currency values. The dependence on short-term investments does little to foster productive economic development and leaves countries vulnerable to the types of devastating economic crises that we have seen in Latin America and other regions of the world in recent years. A speculation tax would reduce the incentive to engage in this type of nonproductive investment activity. In the late 1970s, Nobel Prize–winning economist James Tobin of Yale offered a proposal to reduce short-term movements of capital by placing a small tax on foreign exchange transactions.[44] A tax as low as 0.2 percent would, in the words of economist Robert Kuttner, "be a trivial burden on genuine investments but a useful deterrent to transactions that were mainly speculative."[45] The United Nations Conference on Trade and Development (UNCTAD) predicts that a phased-in 0.25 percent transaction tax would reduce global foreign-exchange transactions by up to 30 percent, while generating tax revenues globally of around $300 billion.[46]

Since Tobin's proposal, there has been a flurry of proposals to tax short-term speculative flows. Some of the proposals posit the creation of a global development fund from the proceeds of the tax; a portion of the funds could be steered to environmental clean-up or other social goals. One of the most successful U.S. investors, Warren Buffet, has proposed a 100 percent tax on short-term (securities held less than a year) capital gains from stock trading, a measure that would encourage long-term productive investment. Former President François Mitterand of France attempted to get the Group of 7 industrial governments to consider a variant on the Tobin tax, but the United States and the United Kingdom opposed the idea. Critics claim that the Tobin tax would be hard to enforce and, unless all countries adopted it, trading would shift to tax-free havens. On the other hand, more than 80 percent of foreign-currency transactions take place on the exchanges of Europe, the United States, and Japan, so a tax adopted by these countries alone would have a significant impact. Moreover, if the political will exists, it would be possible to develop a mechanism for penalizing transactions with tax havens, and it is encouraging to see efforts in some governments to support the establishment of such a tax.

At a regional level, citizens' groups have looked toward regional models for crisis management. When Japan proposed an Asian Regional Fund during the fall of 1997 to swiftly inject capital into Asian nations as financial crises emerged, the U.S. Treasury Department moved quickly to kill the proposal. Likewise, it has opposed similar proposals in different incarnations that were tabled in 1998 and 1999. It seems that opposition to these proposals has more to do with the Treasury Department's desire to maintain control over the global financial system than with any legitimate criticisms of such funds. We believe that countries should be encouraged to form such regional funds if the funds are designed to respond quickly to crises while maintaining regional sensibilities and interests.

At a national level, we believe that governments should retain the right to apply speed bumps and capital controls. The rules and institutions of the global economy should allow maximum space for national government policy-making to regulate the amount, pace, and direction of capital movements. A financial crisis in one country often spreads panic quickly to a number of other countries with equally open and deregulated markets—the so-called "tequila effect." However, countries with some form of capital controls have weathered the storm far better. This has opened up a debate over the wisdom of capital controls, a topic which previously the IMF and other international institutions placed off limits.

In fact, a January 2000 report by the IMF marked a rather dramatic departure from the Fund's usual orthodoxy of encouraging openness to all forms of international capital. Authored by six IMF analysts, the study examined the experiences of Chile, Brazil, Colombia, Malaysia, Thailand, China, and India, all of which have used some form of capital controls for some period of time. While stopping short of giving an enthusiastic endorsement of all capital controls, the report concedes that these measures have been effective in certain situations. For example, with regard to the emergency capital outflow controls put in place by Malaysia in late 1997, the report states, "the controls gave Malaysian authorities some breathing space to address the macroeconomic imbalances and implement banking system reforms."[47] The report further concedes that the experiences of China and India with long-standing and extensive controls on capital flows "may have had some role in reducing the vulnerability of these countries to the effects of the recent regional crisis. In particular, they helped shift the composition of capital inflows toward longer-term flows."[48]

The IMF report supports the findings of an earlier study, conducted at the time of the 1994–1995 Mexican crisis by economists Barry Eichengreen and Charles Wyplosz. They examined the effects of the crisis on the interest rates of countries with some type of control on capital outflows (Brazil, Chile, Colombia, Indonesia, Malaysia, and the Philippines) versus those with none (Argentina, Mexico, Venezuela, Thailand, Singapore, and Hong Kong). In the first quarter of 1995, countries with controls maintained stable interest rates, while those without controls experienced significant increases in interest rates as they struggled to prevent rapid capital flight.[49] A poll of senior bank executives by BankBoston released in March 1999 revealed that capital controls may face a bright future. Two-thirds of all bankers surveyed expect that capital control use will be increased in the future.[50]

While supporting the right to impose capital controls, workers should nevertheless be aware that these measures are insufficient by themselves to defend living standards from global financial crisis. Economist Fernando Leiva points out that capital controls in place in Chile before and in the aftermath of the Asian financial crisis did make the contagion effect of the crisis less severe, but were not enough to prevent the country from entering a deep recession and experiencing a rise in unemployment. According to Leiva, "What is needed are more effective forms of social protection (unemployment insurance, job creation, training and re-training programs) that can temper negative social impacts from the increasing turbulence of the world economy. Ultimately, such protection requires transformation of the export-oriented models based on super-exploited labor and destruction of natural resources."[51]

Other proposals at the national level are designed to encourage long-term, productive investment by eliminating short-term manipulative instruments and placing performance requirements on investment.[52] A Tobin-style tax would discourage speculative capital flows at the international level. At the national level, governments should also set regulations and incentives on cross-border transactions to eliminate capital flows that are entirely speculative (i.e., gambling on market fluctuations as differentiated from hedging risk) and that can undermine the real economy. Governments should retain the power to impose requirements on foreign corporations to ensure that their investments benefit the local community. These can include requirements that the company use a certain percentage of local or national content in production, hire local personnel, achieve the transfer of technology, and repatriate only a certain amount of assets in a given year. Similarly, governments should place performance requirements on corporations that receive government subsidies or tax breaks.

Another goal advocated by citizens' groups is that national governments maintain stable exchange rate regimes. National governments should strive to reduce the volatility that has characterized exchange rates since the collapse of the Bretton Woods arrangements in the early 1970s. This problem could be solved in part through the implementation of taxes on foreign exchange transactions, such as a Tobin Tax, and through controls on short-term capital flows, since these measures would reduce the speculative financial activity that contributes to exchange rate volatility. However, according to economist Robert Blecker, even if these measures were in place countries would still need to choose carefully a foreign exchange rate regime that would maximize stability. The new global financial architecture should allow national governments the power to make decisions about their own exchange rate policy rather than mandating any one particular option.

In the wake of the financial crises of the 1990s, however, the orthodoxy on exchange rates holds that countries should go to one extreme or the other, by pursuing either rigidly fixed or freely floating rates. This is in response to the failure of pegged exchange rate regimes pursued by crisis countries in East Asia and Latin America. In an effort to prevent devaluation, many countries spent billions of dollars and raised domestic interest rates to sky-high levels—all to no avail.

Nevertheless, Blecker points out that neither firmly fixed nor fluctuating rates are without drawbacks. For example, fixed rates, such as the extreme proposal to "dollarize" the currency of Ecuador, impose severe constraints on a country's economy and could drastically depress domestic demand, employment, and growth.[53] Some have cautioned that the United States might even be able to use the dollar as a weapon, withholding currency from an intractable government to bend it to Washington's will. In fact, the Bush administration took just that step against Panama as part of its effort to overthrow General Manuel Antonio Noriega.

Fluctuating rates, on the other hand, theoretically allow countries more autonomy. In troubled economic times, countries can allow their currency to depreciate in the hope that a devalued currency will spur export growth. However, this approach is unlikely to pay off in situations where many countries are simultaneously trying to export their way to prosperity, since the glut of goods on the world market will result in lower prices. Moreover, depreciation increases the cost of servicing debts denominated in foreign currency.

Blecker offers two alternative approaches that, while not without risks, may be preferable to rigidly fixed or floating rates. He argues that governments should establish either fixed rates with real targets or target zones. By focusing on real (adjusted for inflation) rather than nominal exchange rates, the first approach avoids the risk of currencies becoming misaligned in real terms if inflation rates differ between countries. A proposal by Paul Davidson would create a new international institution to manage such a regime that also includes additional mechanisms that shift the burden of adjustment from debtor countries to creditor countries to foster higher average employment growth worldwide. Establishing target zones, on the other hand, would allow considerable but limited fluctuations in exchange rates. To compensate for international inflation differentials, the nominal targets would need to be revised periodically, allowing for "crawling bands." One advantage of this system is that it would not require the creation of a new international institution.

Finally, on a local level, the progressive agenda calls for governments to encourage local investment. As conventional wisdom begins to shift away from the free flow of capital across borders as the great panacea, there is a growing literature about the need to root capital locally. The AFL–CIO has created a Center for Working Capital to seek innovative ways to redirect workers' pension funds to meet the long-term investment needs of local communities. The Institute for Local Self-Reliance has been an incubator of such ideas and many of the current success stories can be found in a book by Michael Shuman entitled *Going Local.*[54] To support these initiatives, local and national regulations, taxes, and subsidies should be structured in a way that encourages local investment in enterprises that support living wage jobs and environmental sustainability. The Washington, DC-based organization Good Jobs First provides support for a booming number of local initiatives to ensure that taxpayer dollars are used to support investment that results in well-paying, stable employment and combats sprawl. Local education initiatives should also inform citizens about the power of using their assets.

Nearly three years after the onset of the international financial crisis that began in Asia, workers in many countries of the world are still suffering the consequences and the world still has no comprehensive system in place to prevent such crises from occurring in the future. However, proposals now exist that would advance workers' interests through a new global financial architecture. The success of these proposals in years to come depends on education, mobilization, and concerted political action.

NOTES

This chapter is a revised excerpt from the authors' *Bearing the Burden: The Impact of Global Financial Crisis on Workers and Alternative Agendas for the IMF and Other Institutions* (Washington, DC: Institute for Policy Studies, 2000), which was written for the Workers in the Global Economy Project, a collaborative effort involving the Institute for Policy Studies, International Labor Rights Fund, Economic Policy Institute, and Cornell University, and funded by the Ford Foundation. The original paper included case studies of Korea, Indonesia, Thailand, the Philippines, Russia, Brazil, Argentina, Ecuador, and the United States. The authors are grateful to the international labor experts—including Fernando Leiva, Kjeld Jakobsen, Lisa McGowan, Young-mo Yoon, and others—who provided useful comments on a first draft at a conference at the AFL–CIO's George Meaney Center in October 1999. Special thanks as well to IPS intern Katrin Jordan for research support.

1. Joseph Stiglitz, "Democratic Development as the Fruits of Labor," Keynote Address, Industrial Relations Research Association, Boston, January 2000.

2. World Bank, *Quarterly Regional Review, Southeast Asia,* 31 January 2000.

3. The best overall presentation of a reform agenda in the interests of workers is Robert Blecker's *Taming Global Finance* (Washington, DC: Economic Policy Institute, 1999). There are also strong statements by the AFL–CIO: "U.S. Workers Addressing the Global Crisis," Executive Council Statement, 14 October 1998, and the International Confederation of Free Trade Unions (ICFTU), December 1998 and April 2000. A December 1998 "Call to Action" by Friends of the Earth, the International Forum on Globalization, and the Third World Network weaves together a workers' agenda with those of other social sectors.

4. See Sarah Anderson, John Cavanagh, and Jill Pike, "World Bank and IMF

Policies Hurt Workers At Home and Abroad," Institute for Policy Studies, 2 September 1994.

5. Letter dated 30 December 1999.

6. Robert J. Samuelson, "Global Capitalism, RIP?" *Newsweek*, 14 September 1998.

7. World Bank, "Regional Overview: Latin America and the Caribbean," 27 September 1999.

8. Humberto Campodonico and Manuel Chiriboga, "The Financial Crisis of Latin America and the New International Financial Architecture: A Proposal by ALOP and Oxfam America," July 2000.

9. Daniela Hart, "Brazil Unveils Austerity Plan to Reassure Investors, Bolster Currency," *Washington Post*, 11 November 1997.

10. Anthony Faiola, "Brazil, IMF agree on Economic Framework," *Washington Post*, 5 February 1999.

11. IMF, "Memorandum of Economic Policies," 12 November 1999

12. International Labor Organization, "Laborsta [sic] on the Web."

13. ORIT (Organización Regional Interamericana de Trabajadores) website: www.ciosl-orit.org.

14. Luca Bonicini, ICFTU Online, 29 February 1999 (www.icftu.org).

15. *New York Times*, 21 February 2000.

16. UN Economic Commission for Latin America and the Caribbean (ECLAC), "Estudio económico de América Latina y el Caribe 1999–2000," August 2000.

17. ORIT website.

18. Laura Luz Ojeda, "La crisis de Brasil ya comenzó a dejar su marca en el empleo," *La Nación*, 17 February 1999.

19. Alexander Saldarriaga, "Brazil's 'Samba Effect' on Latin America," Standard New York Securities, 20 January 1999.

20. UN ECLAC, "Estudio económico," August 2000.

21. International Labor Organization, "Laborsta on the Web."

22. ORIT website, 12 March 1999.

23. "Ecuador on the Brink," *The Economist*, 15 January 2000.

24. UN ECLAC, "Estudio económico," August 2000.

25. AFL–CIO, "U.S. Workers Addressing the Global Crisis," Executive Council Statement, 14 October 1998. See also the following AFL–CIO documents: "New Rules for the Global Economy," (Resolution passed at the AFL–CIO's 23rd Biennial Convention, October 1999); "Equitable, Democratic, Sustainable Development," AFL–CIO Executive Council Statement, New Orleans, LA, 17 February 2000; and Thomas Palley, Elizabeth Drake, and Thea Lee, "The Case for Core Labor Standards in the International Economy: Theory, Evidence, and a Blueprint for Implementation," online at http://phantom-x.gsia.cmu.edu/IFIAC/.

26. ICFTU, "International Trade Union Statement on the Global Economic Crisis," Brussels, December 1998.

27. Council on Foreign Relations, "Safeguarding Prosperity in a Global Financial System," 16 September 1999, p. 61.

28. Cited in Jerome I. Levinson, "Separate Dissenting Opinion," March 2000, p. 10.

29. IMF, "Sweden: Staff Report for the 1999 Article IV Consultation," September 1999, p. 32.

30. "Separate Dissenting Statement of Jerome I. Levinson," March 2000, p.10.

31. Testimony of Treasury Secretary Lawrence Summers before the House Banking Committee, 23 March 2000.

32. James F. Smith, "Latin American Poverty Poses Threat to Globalization, Finance Group Warned," *Los Angeles Times*, 4 February 2000.

33. ICFTU, December 1998 statement, p. 2.

34. "A Call to Action: A Citizen's Agenda for Reform of the Global Economic System," with signatories of eighty organizations whose total membership includes over twenty-six million people, may be found at http://www.twnside.org.sg/title/ifgcall-cn.htm.

35. See Rita Bhatia, "Debt Standstill and Insolvency Procedures," Briefing Note: International Finance Network, Save the Children Fund, January 1999.

36. ICFTU, "Securing the Conditions for Reducing Poverty and Achieving Sustainable Growth," Statement by the International Confederation of Free Trade Unions (ICFTU), Trade Union Advisory Commission (TUAC) and the International Trade Secretariat (ITS) at the Spring 2000 meetings of the IMF and the World Bank.

37. Ibid.

38. U.S. Department of the Treasury, "Fast Track Commitments, U.S. Treasury Department Progress Report," 28 March 1999.

39. Elizabeth Drake, AFL–CIO Public Policy Department, memo dated 9 September 1999.

40. Jerome I. Levinson, "Separate Dissenting Statement," 9 March 2000.

41. Institute for Policy Studies and United for a Fair Economy, "CEOs Win, Workers Lose," fifth annual study of executive compensation, April 1998.

42. Sarah Anderson, ed., *Views from the South: The Effects of Globalization and the WTO on Third World Countries* (San Francisco: International Forum on Globalization, 1999).

43. John Eatwell and Lance Taylor, "International Capital Markets and the Future of Economic Policy," Paper prepared for the Ford Foundation project on International Capital Markets and the Future of Economic Policy, Center for Economic Policy Analysis, New York, 1998.

44. J. Tobin, "A Proposal for International Monetary Reform," *The Eastern Economic Journal*, July/October 1978.

45. Robert Kuttner, "A Tiny Tax Might Curb Wall Street's High Volatility," *Business Week*, 3 March 1997.

46. "Financial Globalisation Versus Free Trade: The Case for the Tobin Tax," *UNCTAD Bulletin*, January–February–March 1996, Geneva.

47. IMF, "Country Experiences with the Use and Liberalization of Capital Controls," 14 January 2000, p. 13.

48. Ibid., 17.

49. Barry Eichengreen and Charles Wyplosz, "Taxing International Financial Transactions to Enhance the Operation of the International Monetary System," in Mabub ul Haq, et al., *The Tobin Tax* (New York: Oxford University Press, 1996).

50. BankBoston Press Release, 14 March 1999.

51. Fernando Leiva, "Workers, the Global Financial Crisis and Agendas for Action," 20 October 1999, available online at www.laborrights.org.

52. For more information, see "Alternatives for the Americas: Building a Peoples' Hemispheric Agreement," available online at www.web.net/comfront.

53. Robert Blecker, *Taming Global Finance: A Better Architecture for Growth and Equity* (Washington, DC: Economic Policy Institute, 1999), 130.

54. Michael H. Shuman, *Going Local: Creating Self-reliant Communities in a Global Age* (New York: Free Press, 1998).

PART V

UNTANGLING THE WEBS OF THE PAST

10

Reckoning with Past Wrongs: A Normative Framework

David A. Crocker

Many nations and some international bodies today are deciding what, if anything, they should do about past violations of internationally recognized human rights. These abuses—which include war crimes, crimes against humanity, genocide, rape, and torture—may have been committed by a government against its own citizens (or those of other countries), by its opponents, or by combatants in a civil or international armed conflict.[1] Some of these societies are making a transition to democracy and some are not.

The challenge of "transitional justice," a term increasingly used, is how an incomplete and fledgling democracy (for example, South Africa, Guatemala, South Korea, the Philippines, Argentina, Chile, or El Salvador) should respond (or should have responded) to past evils without undermining its new democratic regime or jeopardizing its prospects for equitable and long-term development. This focus on new democracies has much to recommend it; it is important that new democratic institutions, where they exist, be protected and consolidated, and that reckoning with an evil past not imperil them.

However, nations other than new democracies also have occasion to decide what they "should do about a difficult past,"[2] and their choices are of intrinsic moral significance as well as relevant for new democracies. These countries, none of which is currently making a transition to democracy, can be roughly divided into three types: post–conflict societies (for example, Bosnia, Cambodia, and Rwanda) that aspire to make a democratic transition but are at present taken up with ongoing security issues following ethnic strife and massacres; authoritarian and conflict–ridden societies (for example,

Yugoslavia, Indonesia, and Peru) in which both an end to civil conflict and the beginning of democratization may depend on negotiated agreements between the government and its opposition with respect to treatment of human rights violators; and mature democracies (for example, United States, Germany, Japan, France, and Switzerland) reckoning with past evils that include slavery, war crimes, collaboration with the Nazi extermination efforts, or failures to prevent human rights abuses in their own or other countries.[3] The fashionable focus on new democracies tends to limit what such societies may learn from other attempts to reckon with past rights abuses and to diminish the moral challenge facing nondemocratic and mature democracies as they reckon with an unsavory past. Even in the context of societies making a democratic transition, the term "transitional justice" may be misleading. This is because, like the term "accountability," transitional justice singles out one morally urgent feature from a complex that has many pressing goals or obligations.

MEANS AND ENDS

Societies and international bodies have employed many means in reckoning with human rights abuses committed by a prior regime or its opponents. Many discussions assume that there are only two possible responses: trials and punishment or forgetting the past. For example, upon coming out of hiding and surrendering to the Cambodian government in late December 1998, Khieu Samphan, a former top leader of the Khmer Rouge, urged Cambodians to "let bygones be bygones." During its control of Cambodia from 1975 to 1979, the Khmer Rouge is estimated to have killed between 1.5 and 1.7 million people, including most of the educated class, and to have destroyed much of Cambodian culture. Although he was to backtrack a few days later, Cambodian Prime Minister Hun Sen initially agreed with Khieu Samphan and remarked that Khieu Samphan and another high–placed defector, Nuon Chea, should be welcomed back "with bouquets of flowers, not with prisons and handcuffs" and that "we should dig a hole and bury the past and look ahead to the 21st century with a clean slate."[4]

When trials are judged as impractical and forgetting as undesirable, truth commissions have been advocated (and in some twenty countries employed) as a third way. However, in addition to these three tools there are a variety of other measures, such as international (ad hoc or permanent) criminal tribunals; social shaming and banning of perpetrators from public office ("lustration"); public access to police records; public apology or memorials to victims; reburial of victims; compensation to victims or their families; literary and historical writing; and blanket or individualized amnesty (legal immunity from prosecution).

To decide among the diverse tools, as well as to fashion, combine, and sequence them, a society, sometimes in cooperation with international institutions, ideally should (1) consider what lessons it might learn from other societies, (2) examine its own capabilities and limitations, and (3) set clear objectives for its efforts. The first task is best accomplished by those who will be key actors in their nation's attempts to reckon with an evil past. The second responsibility most obviously falls to historians, social scientists, and legal scholars, who are adept at identifying a society's distinctive historical legacies, institutional strengths and weaknesses, and political constraints. The last task, that of identifying goals and standards of evaluation, must be taken up by philosophers and applied ethicists, but not by these alone; citizens, political leaders, policy analysts, and social scientists also have a responsibility to make moral judgments, engage in ethical analysis, and set forth ethically based recommendations.

Although philosophers and other ethicists have not entirely ignored the topic of reckoning with past wrongs, legal scholars, social scientists, policy analysts, and activists have made the most helpful contributions. It is understandable that much of the work on transitional justice has been of an empirical and strategic nature. Fledgling democracies need effective institutions and strategies for addressing prior human rights violations; establishing such arrangements and policies requires a grasp of what works and why. Legal and human rights scholars have focused on what national and international law permits and requires with respect to prosecuting gross human rights violations.[5] They have also reported and assessed the progress of the Bosnian and Rwandan international criminal tribunals, crafted the terms of an agreement on a permanent international criminal tribunal, and argued for the implementation of that agreement.[6] Investigative reporters have described what particular countries and the international community have done and failed to do in their efforts to reckon with past human rights abuses.[7] Principal actors or advisers have written about their experiences and assessed their achievements.[8] Historians and social scientists have addressed the issue of why certain countries decided on particular approaches and the motivations for and consequences of those choices.[9]

However, there are also large and pressing ethical questions. How should "success" be defined when reckoning with past wrongs? Are the ends that societies seek to achieve and the means they adopt to achieve them consistent and morally justified? Questions such as these should not be overlooked or swamped by legal or strategic considerations.

To be sure, moral concerns are often implicit in the existing work on transitional justice, and moral norms of various kinds underlie the institutions and policies that societies already have established to reckon with an evil past. Indeed, one task of ethical analysis with respect to past human rights abuses is to identify and clarify those operative values for which reasonable justification can be given. Michael Walzer's attempt to fashion a new moral theory (with historical illustrations) concerning just and unjust wars between nations can be adapted to the forging of a normative framework to assess what should be done when a society reckons with human rights violations.[10]

When political actors or scholars explicitly pose ethical questions with respect to addressing past wrongs, they usually do so in relation to only one goal—such as penal justice, truth, or reconciliation—or one tool—such as trials, truth commissions, or amnesties.[11] However, the full range of conceptual and moral issues underlying the many ends and means of transitional justice has not received the sustained analysis it deserves.[12]

CROSS-CULTURAL GOALS

To fashion and evaluate a tool to reckon with past evil in a particular society and to combine it with other tools requires not only knowledge of that society's historical legacies and current capabilities but also a grasp of morally important goals and standards of assessment. What goals and norms should be used, where should they come from, and how might they be promoted? In recent conference papers and writings, I have formulated eight goals that have emerged from worldwide moral deliberation on transitional justice. These goals, which may serve as a useful framework when particular societies deliberate about what they are trying to achieve and how they should go about doing so, are: (1) truth, (2) public platform for victims, (3) accountability and punishment, (4) rule of law, (5) compensation to victims, (6) institutional reform and long-term development, (7) reconciliation, and (8) public deliberation.[13]

In this chapter, my discussion of these goals helps to identify and clarify the variety of ethical issues that emerge in reckoning with past wrongs, frame widespread agreements about resolving each issue, offer leading options for more robust solutions of each issue, and determine ways to weigh or trade off the norms when they conflict. My aim is to show that there are crucial moral aspects in reckoning with the past and to clarify, criticize, revise, apply, and diffuse eight moral norms. The goals that I propose are not a recipe or "one-size-fits-all" blueprint but rather a framework for exploration by which societies confronting past atrocities can decide, through cross-cultural and critical dialogue, what is most important to accomplish and the morally best ways their goals might be achieved.

Before setting forth morally urgent ends, two opposing (but dialectically related) goals should be ruled out: vengeance, and disregarding the past in favor of the future. I will not repeat my arguments set forth elsewhere that countries should reject these goals.[14] However, remarks about both goals and a new example about implementing them are in order. First, various tools may be employed to realize each of these morally undesirable ends. Vengeance can be carried out privately (by individuals or groups) or officially (in reprisals and kangaroo courts). A nation can overcome an evil past and attempt to move to a better future by forgiving and forgetting (letting bygones be bygones), outright denial (for instance, that the Holocaust occurred), or rationalization of the past as a necessary evil. Second, attempts to realize each of these goals often lead, either precipitously or eventually, to efforts to achieve the other: the side that has wreaked revenge often attempts to protect itself from counter-revenge by calling for those offended to "forgive and forget"; silence about the past may incite revenge for both the original act and its burial.

Both tendencies are illustrated by the thousands of atrocities committed by Croat Nazis (Ustashi) against Serbs, Jews, and Gypsies during World War II, especially in the Jasenovac concentration camp. There is good reason to believe that the breakup of Yugoslavia and the Serb violation of Croat rights during the war between Croatia and Serbia in 1991–92 can be partially explained (not justified) by the genocidal practices of the Croats during World War II and by the failure of postwar Croats and the Tito government to hold either investigations or trials. Serbian philosopher Svetozar Stojanovi observes:

The communist victor [Tito] in Yugoslavia never seriously looked into Ustashi genocide as an issue or a problem. Instead of carrying out denazification through education . . . he limited himself to the liquidation of captured Ustashis. It is true that Pavelic and the other main criminals had, however, fled abroad, and the new authorities did not endeavor to organize their trial (at least in absentia) like the one in Nürnberg, although they more than deserved it. The karst pits into which Serbs were thrown alive by Ustashis in Herzegovina remained concreted over, and their relatives were not allowed to remove the bodies and bury them. These "concreted pits" have become a metaphor for the communist illusion that enforced silence is the best way to deal with terrible crimes among nations. Perhaps that was why, not only due to his personal nonchalance, Tito never visited Jasenovac.[15]

Truth

To meet the challenge of reckoning with past atrocities, a society should investigate, establish, and publicly disseminate the truth about them. What Alex Boraine calls "forensic truth" or "hard facts"[16] is information about whose moral and legal rights were violated, and by whom, how, when, and where. Given the moral significance of individual accountability, the identity of individual perpetrators, on the one hand, and of moral heroes who sacrificed personal safety to prevent violations, on the other, should be brought to light.

There is also what has been called "emotional truth"—knowledge concerning the psychological and physical impact on victims and their loved ones from rights abuses and the threat of such abuses. The constant threat of rights abuses, especially in contexts of physical deprivation, can itself cause overwhelming fear and, thereby, constitute a rights violation. David Rohde makes this point clearly in his agonizing account of the aftermath of the takeover of Muslim Srebrenica by General Ratko Mladic and his Bosnian Serb forces:

During the trek [the "Marathon of Death" in which thousands of male Bosnian noncombatants and a few soldiers fled Srebrenica], it quickly became clear that the threat to the column was as much psychological as it was physical. Shells abruptly whizzed overhead. Gunfire erupted with no warning. Corpses littered their route. A Serb mortar had landed ahead of them at 1 p.m. and killed five men. A human stomach and intestines lay across the green grass just below the intact head and torso of a man in his twenties. Mevludin [Oric, a Bosnian Muslim soldier] had seen such things before; the others hadn't. The image would slowly eat at their minds. Some men were already saying it was hopeless. It was better to kill yourself, they said, than be captured by the Serbs.[17]

Fear also had devastating consequences for the Muslim women and children, herded together in Srebrenica, whose husbands and fathers were taken away and tortured during the night of 12 July 1995:

She [Srebrenica resident Camila Omanovic] could see what was happening around her, but it was the sounds that haunted her. Screams suddenly filled the night. At one point, she heard bloodcurdling cries coming from the hills near the base. She later decided the Serbs must be playing recordings to terrorize them. Women gave birth or cried as their husbands were taken away. Men wailed and called out women's names. . . . Panic would grip the crowd. People would suddenly rise up and rush off in one direction. Then there would be silence until the cycle of screams and panic started all over again. Nearly hallucinating, Camila could not sleep. . . . But it was the fear that didn't let her sleep. A fear more intense than anything she had ever felt. A fear that changed her forever.[18]

Finally, there is less individualized and more general truth, such as plausible interpretations of what caused neighbors to brutalize neighbors, governments (and their opponents) to incite, execute, or permit atrocities, and other countries or international bodies to fail to act in time or in the right way.[19]

Knowledge about the past is important in itself. One way to make this point is to say that victims and their descendants have a moral right to know the truth about human rights abuses. Moreover, without reasonably complete truth, none of the other goals of transitional justice (to be discussed presently) is likely to be realized. Appropriate sanctions are impossible without reasonable certainty about the identity of perpetrators and the nature of their involvement. Public acknowledgment must refer to specific occurrences, while reparations presuppose the accurate identification of victims and the kinds of harm they suffered. If reconciliation in any of its several senses is to take place, there must be some agreement about what happened and why. Former enemies are unlikely to be reconciled if what count as lies for one side are verities for the other.

Yet truth, while important, sometimes must be traded off against other goods. Since the truth can harm people as well as benefit them, sometimes it is better that some facts about the past remain unknown. By deepening ethnic hostility, too much or the wrong kind of truth might impede democratization and reconciliation. Disclosures that satisfy a victim's need to know may incite violence when publicly revealed. The most effective methods for obtaining the truth might violate the rule of law, personal privacy, or the right not to incriminate oneself. Or such methods might be too costly in relation to other goals. Some truths about the past would be irrelevant to reckoning with past injustices. The general point is that apparently justified efforts in limiting the pursuit or the disclosure of truth imply the need to balance truth against other goals.

Even given that truth is one important good that can be traded off in relation to other goods, many issues remain to be resolved. First, can one plausibly argue that there is one truth about the past and, if so, how should we understand this ideal in relation to the frequently diverse views about the content of this truth? How should a truth commission address diverse interpretations of the past when they emerge in the commission's work or in public reaction to it? My own view is that disagreements should be reduced as much as possible, and those that remain should be clearly identified as topics for further public deliberation.[20] Second, to whom and at what cost should the truth be made known? Third, how should we assess truth commissions and other investigative bodies, investigative reporting and historical writing, national trials, international criminal tribunals, and the granting of public access to police files? Given their different standards of evidence and proof, how much and what sort of truth can be reasonably expected from each of these approaches? What are the merits of each method both in reducing disagreement and accommodating or respecting remaining differences? To what extent, if any, might a truth commission impede rather than promote international and domestic judicial determination of individual guilt and innocence? What ethical issues emerge from the various methods of collecting and interpreting information about past abuses?[21]

My general belief, which I cannot develop or defend within this chapter, is that there are many different but complementary ways of obtaining reasonable knowledge about the past and that no one means should be overemphasized. For example, owing to subpoena power and adversarial cross–examination, trials are usually superior to truth commissions in establishing truths relevant to the guilt or innocence of particular individuals; truth commissions tend to be better than trials in describing the larger institutional patterns contributing to rights violations; historical investigations—often with the advantage of fuller documentation, more ample opportunities to check sources, and greater hindsight than is possible in either trials or truth commissions—are best at sifting evidence and evaluating explanatory hypotheses. Not only can these tools complement each other, but each one can make use of others. Truth commissions often make recommendations about prosecuting suspects to legal proceedings. Historians provide expert testimony in trials and sometimes are members of truth commissions. Investigative reporters and forensic experts have been enormously important in uncovering atrocities and dispelling rumors and false propaganda.[22]

Public Platform for Victims

In any society attempting to reckon with an evil past, victims or their families should be provided with a platform to tell their stories and have their testimony publicly acknowledged. When victims are able to give their accounts and receive sympathy for their suffering, they are respected as persons with dignity rather than treated with the contempt they experienced previously. This respect enables those once humiliated as victims to become empowered as citizens. Those once reduced to screams or paralyzing fear now may share a personal narrative. The public character of the platform is essential, since secrecy about human rights abuses, enforced through violence and intimidation, was one of the conditions that made possible extensive campaigns of terror.

Among the unresolved questions that remain is the weight to be given to this goal when the public character of testimony would put former victims, perpetrators, or reporters at substantial risk. After disclosing to the press that the Argentine military did indeed kill some suspected "subversives" and their children by pushing them from airplanes into the sea, a military officer was brutally attacked and his face carved with the initials of the reporters to whom he revealed the truth. Another problem surfaces when a victim's public testimony is not followed up by efforts to heal wounds and compensate for harms.[23] Finally, unless there is independent investigation or cross–examination of accusers, alleged perpetrators may be treated unfairly and due process compromised.

Accountability and Punishment

Ethically defensible treatment of past wrongs requires that those individuals and groups responsible for past crimes be held accountable and receive appropriate sanctions or punishment. Punishment may range from the death penalty, imprisonment, fines, international travel restrictions, and the payment of compensation to economic sanctions on an entire society and public shaming of individuals and prohibitions on their holding public office.

Many questions about responsibility and punishment remain to be answered. How, for example, can accountability be explained and fairly assigned? How should we understand the degrees and kinds of responsibility with respect to the authorization, planning, "middle management," execution, provision of material support for, and concealment of atrocities? Consider also journalist Bill Berkeley's observation about a Hutu bourgmestre found guilty (by the International Tribunal for Rwanda) of "nine counts of genocide, crimes against humanity, and war crimes, including rape":

Jean-Paul Akayesu was neither a psychopath nor a simpleton. He was not a top figure like the former defense minister, Theonoste Bagasora, Rwanda's Himmler, who is now in custody [of the International Tribunal for Rwanda] in Arusha, nor a lowly, illiterate, machete-wielding peasant. He was, instead, the link between the two: an archetype of the indispensable middle management of genocide. He personified a rigidly hierarchical society and culture of obedience, without which killing on such a scale would not have been possible.[24]

Should those who actually commit minor abuses be ignored or pardoned in favor of holding their superiors accountable, or should the moral guilt and cumulative impact of those who "merely" followed orders also be recognized? What is needed is a theory—relevant to judging past rights abusers—that identifies those conditions that make an agent more or less blameworthy (and praiseworthy). Recent work suggests that a perpetrator's moral guilt is proportional to what he knew (or could reasonably know) and when he knew it; how much freedom (from coercion) or power (in a chain of command) he had to commit or prevent evil; and what personal risks he ran in performing or forgoing a rights violation.

For which crimes should people be held accountable when a country or the international community is reckoning with past evil?[25] Is it morally justifiable to hold people accountable either for an act that was not illegal at the time it was committed or for one that a government subsequently pardons?[26] Further, an ethics of reckoning with past wrongs would address violations such as war crimes, crimes against humanity, genocide, torture, and rape. This list implies both that Chile erred in restricting its official truth commission to investigating only killings and disappearances and that the International Criminal Tribunal for the Former Yugoslavia achieved moral progress when it convicted persons of rape in the wars in Croatia and Bosnia.

Should the list of human rights violations be extended further than "physical security rights"? Should it include civil and political rights, such as the right of free speech and the right not to be discriminated against on the basis of race, ethnicity, religion, or gender? And what about economic rights, such as the right not to be hungry or the right to employment? This chapter returns to this issue when it addresses what long–term economic and political development should aim for to protect against a recurrence of past atrocities.

Two additional questions with respect to accountability must be addressed. How should "sins of commission" be morally compared to "sins of omission"? How does the United Nations' failure to bomb the Serbs attacking Srebrenica in July 1995 compare with the atrocities committed by the Serbian forces? To what extent are groups—particular police units, political parties, religious bodies, professional associations (for example, of doctors or lawyers), independence movements (for example, the Kosovo Liberation Army), governments, and alliances (for example, the UN, NATO)—and not solely individuals responsible for rights violations?[27] Without a suitably nuanced and graded view of accountability or responsibility, a society falls into the morally objectionable options of, on the one hand, whitewash or social amnesia[28] or, on the other hand, the demonization of all members of an accused group.

Similar questions may be asked with respect to sanctions, whether criminal (punishment), civil, or non-legal (social shaming, individual lustration, or economic sanctions on an entire society). What types of sanctions are appropriate for what violations, and on what bases? Can justice be achieved through social shaming and moral censure rather than imprisonment? If trials and legal punishments are to be pursued, what purposes can or should they serve? Should a theory of criminal punishment include a retributive element and, if so, how should it be understood, and can retribution be distinguished from revenge?

Legal philosophers and scholars who have addressed reckoning with past political wrongs, such as Carlos Nino and Jaime Malamud–Goti, have tended to reject retributivism in favor of a deterrence or rehabilitation approach.[29] Retributivism, however, is having something of a revival, and I believe that it captures some important intuitions about penal justice. One task facing ethicists is to consider which retributive theory is best in itself and in reckoning with past atrocities. This inquiry would also consider whether the most reasonable approach to punishment would be a "mixed theory" in which a retributive principle, however understood, is coupled with other justifications or functions of punishment such as protection, deterrence, rehabilitation, and moral education.[30]

Rule of Law

As they reckon with past wrongs, democracies, whether new or mature, should comply with the rule of law, and societies (or their democratic oppositions) that aspire to become democratic should lay the groundwork now for eventual rule of law. The rule of law is a critical part of Nuremberg's complex legacy and is important for any society dealing with an evil past. I here follow David Luban's analysis of rule of law.[31]

The rule of law includes respect for due process, in the sense of procedural fairness, publicity, and impartiality. Like cases must be treated alike, and private revenge must be prohibited. Rule of law is especially important in a new and fragile democracy bent on distinguishing itself from prior authoritarianism, institutionalized bias, or the "rule of the gun."

Again, however, there is an ongoing debate about what the rule of law should mean and how it should be valued in relation to other goals. Can "victor's justice" be avoided and legal standards applied impartially to both sides in a former conflict? If so, at what cost? Can those suspected of rights abuses justifiably be convicted when their acts—even though prohibited by international law—were permitted by local law, covered by amnesty laws, or performed in obedience to higher orders? In what way, if any, does the ideal of procedural fairness apply to truth commissions when alleged per-petrators have no right to cross-examine their accusers? (In South Africa an investigative arm of the Truth and Reconciliation Commission determined the reliability of all testimony.) What if violations of due process result in fuller disclosures or more accurate assignment of responsibility?

Some advocates of due process, skeptical that victor's justice can be avoided, contend that the only ethically justified way to reckon with past political wrongs is to bury the past and move on to a better future.[32] But rule of law, like other ideals, is capable of more or less institutional embod-iment. Safeguards fairly protecting both defendants and victims have been developed in local and national jurisdictions and in jurisdictional decisions. Upon learning that one British Law Lord had failed to disclose a relationship to the human rights group Amnesty International, the British Law Lords set aside their initial decision to permit Pinochet's extradition to Spain to stand trial on charges of genocide and other rights abuses. The Pinochet case also shows the lack of both international and Chilean consensus on the issue of when, if ever, a court in one country has the moral or legal right to prosecute alleged human rights violators who are citizens or (former) leaders of other countries. Apart from the question of its impact on Chile's development achievements, international and Chilean opinion is divided about whether Chile's sovereignty would have been violated if Pinochet had been brought to justice in a foreign country.[33] This question cannot be answered merely by appealing to international law and therefore requires moral reflection, since international law points in different directions and is itself evolving in relation to the Pinochet case.

The International Criminal Tribunals for both Rwanda and the former Yugoslavia have slowly developed and improved the fairness of their pro-cedures. An enormous challenge in implementing the plan for a permanent international criminal court will be to devise fair procedures, including pro-cedures for determining whether international or national courts have juris-diction.

Compensation to Victims

Compensation, restitution, or reparation in the form of income, property, medical services, or educational and other opportunities should be paid to individuals and groups whose rights have been violated. One way of reckoning with past wrongs is by "righting" them—by restoring victims to something approaching their status quo ante.

But if compensation is pursued, pressing questions abound. Who should provide the compensation? Is it fair to use general taxes when, it can be argued, many citizens were not responsible for violations? Or does mere citizenship in a nation that violated rights imply liability? Do German (and U.S.) corporations that used slave labor during World War II owe compensation to the victims or their survivors? What moral obligations, if any, do foreign governments and international civil society have in making reparations to victims of rights abuses? Might requiring guilty perpetrators to provide reparations to their victims be a means for punishing perpetrators or promoting reconciliation between violator and victim? What form should reparation take and how should compensatory amounts be decided? Is compensation more justified in the form of cash, giving the victim the freedom to decide on its use, or as goods and services related to basic needs? Should compensation be the same for all, even though victims suffered in different degrees and ways, have different numbers of dependents, and have different access to services depending on where they live? Given the other goals of reckoning with past wrongs, what portion of public resources should be devoted to compensatory justice? What should be done about those victims (or their descendants) whose injuries, whether physical or psychological, do not become apparent until years after their rights have been violated?

Should groups—for instance, specific Mayan villages in Guatemala or Muslim villages in Bosnia's Drina Valley—as well as individuals be recipients of compensation? Is South Africa justified in considering public memorials such as museums and monuments or days of remembrance "symbolic compensation" for damage done to the entire South African society?[34]

Recent events suggest that nations and the international community are beginning to answer these questions. Following Chile's example, South Africa is implementing a nuanced "reparation and rehabilitation policy" that defends reparation on both moral ("restoration of dignity") and legal grounds and provides several types of individual and communal reparation. Individuals are compensated both through monetary packages that take into account the severity of the harm enacted, the number of the victim's dependents, and access to social services, and through services such as reburials and the provision of headstones.

There is widespread approval of recent agreements to compensate Holocaust victims and those who worked as slave laborers for German companies during World War II. Early in January 1999, two Swiss banks, but not the Swiss government, signed an agreement for $1.25 billion in payments to resolve all class action suits and individual claims against the banks. (To be sure, some Swiss claim that they are being unfairly singled out.) The fund will compensate Holocaust victims for a variety of harms, including the loss of bank deposits and insurance policies and the looting of assets by the Nazis.[35] Similarly, the German government has agreed to set up a "compensation fund" (the Remembrance, Responsibility and the Future fund) of $1.7 billion, to be financed by German banks and other corporations (and perhaps by the government), to compensate Holocaust survivors for the companies' role in stealing assets, financing the building of the Auschwitz concentration camp, or making use of slave labor.[36] While these agreements are also prudent ways for the banks and companies to terminate the legal claims against them, the basic principle of the agreements reflects considered judgments about compensatory justice. As German Chancellor Gerhard Schröder remarked, the fund is to fulfill "the moral responsibility of German firms with regard to such issues as forced laborers, Aryanization and other injustice during the Nazi regime." These cases illustrate "the quest," as journalist Roger Cohen puts it, "to find a balance between remembrance and forward-looking themes."[37]

Institutional Reform and Long-Term Development

An emerging democracy fails to make a sustainable transition unless it identifies the causes of past abuses and takes steps to reform the law and basic institutions—government, economic life, and civil society—in order to reduce the possibility that such violations will be repeated. In general, reckoning with past political wrongs requires that societies be oriented to the future as well as to the past and present; they must take steps to remedy what caused human rights violations and protect against their recurrence. Basic institutions include the judiciary, police, military, land tenure system, tax system, and the structure of economic opportunities. One temptation in post-conflict or post-authoritarian societies is to permit euphoria—which comes with the cessation of hostilities and the launching of a new democracy—to preempt the hard work needed to remove the fundamental causes of injustice and guard against their repetition.

In both Guatemala and South Africa, for example, among the fundamental causes of repression and human rights abuses were racism and deep disparities in economic and political power. A society, whether it already is or whether it aspires to be democratic, must try to remove such fundamental causes of human rights abuses in a way that will consolidate its democracy and promote equitable development in the future.

Questions remain, however, with respect to how democratic consolidation and economic development should be conceived. Are free and fair elections sufficient (or necessary) for the former?[38] Are increasing rates of per capita GNP necessary or sufficient for the latter? What should be the fundamental goals of economic and social development?[39] How might past injustices be addressed such that democratic and just development may be promoted and protected? What role, for example, might compensatory transfers to victims play in increasing social equity? When reckoning with past injustices does not coincide with or contribute to ameliorating present ones, how much should be spent on the former at the expense of the latter? Development ethicists should join scholars of transitional justice to explore the links between addressing past wrongs and advancing future rights.

Reconciliation

A society (or an international community) seeking to surmount its conflictual or repressive past should aim to reconcile former enemies. There are, however, at least three meanings of reconciliation, ranging from "thinner" to "thicker" conceptions. In the most minimal version, which almost everyone agrees is at least part of what should be meant by the term, reconciliation is nothing more than "simple coexistence,"[40] in the sense that former enemies comply with the law instead of killing each other. Although this modus vivendi is certainly better than violent conflict, transitional societies can and should aim for more: while former enemies may continue to disagree and even to be adversaries, they must not only live together nonviolently but also respect each other as fellow citizens. Mark J. Osiel calls this kind of reconciliation "liberal social solidarity,"[41] while Amy Gutmann and Dennis Thompson term it "democratic reciprocity."[42] Among other things, this implies a willingness to hear each other out, to enter into a give–and–take about matters of public policy, to build on areas of common concern, and to forge principled compromises with which all can live. The process of reconciliation, so conceived, may help prevent a society from lapsing into violence as a way to resolve conflict.

More robust conceptions of reconciliation have sometimes been attributed to the truth commissions of Chile and South Africa—reconciliation as forgiveness, mercy (rather than justice), a shared comprehensive vision, mutual healing, or harmony.[43] (Both of these commissions include the word "reconciliation" in their name.) Given the depth of hostility between past opponents and objections to coercing mutuality or contrition, these thicker conceptions of reconciliation are more difficult to defend than the thinner notions. An essential task of the ethics of transitional justice is to consider the advantages and disadvantages of going beyond the first or second conceptions of reconciliation to some version of the third notion.[44]

Public Deliberation

Any society reckoning with past atrocities should aim, I believe, to include public spaces, debate, and deliberation in its goals, institutions, and strategies. It is unlikely that in any given society there will be full agreement about the aims and means for dealing with past abuses. And, even if there were agreement, trade–offs would have to be made. All good things do not always go together; sometimes achieving or even approximating one end will come at the expense of (fully) achieving another. Legal sanctions against former human rights violators can imperil a potential or fragile democracy in which the military responsible for the earlier abuses still wields social and political power. In order to protect witnesses or secure testimony from alleged perpetrators, a truth commission's interrogation of witnesses or alleged perpetrators sometimes may have to take place behind closed doors. Testimony by victims and confessions by perpetrators may worsen relations among former enemies, at least in the short run.[45] What is spent on a truth commission or on high–profile trials and punishments will not be available to eradicate infrastructural causes (and effects) of rights violations. A truth commission's exchange of truth for amnesty may preclude achieving penal justice.

What can be aspired to, especially but not exclusively in a new democracy, is that disagreements about ends, trade–offs, and means will be reduced if not eliminated through public deliberation—both national and international—that permits a fair hearing for all and promotes both morally acceptable compromises and tolerance of remaining differences.[46] This public dialogue may be one of the ingredients in or conditions for social reform that replaces a culture of impunity with a culture of human rights. In nondemocratic Cambodia, for example, many citizens are disclosing what they suffered under Khmer Rouge tyranny, debating what should be done, and agreeing that Khmer leaders should be tried:

Countless unburdenings . . . are taking place among Cambodians today as the country seems to be embarking, spontaneously, on a long–delayed national conversation about its traumatic past. . . . The comments also suggest an emerging political assertiveness among people better informed and more aware of their rights. . . . The seemingly near–unanimous view is that Khmer Rouge leaders should be put on trial, if only to determine who is really to blame for the country's suffering—and even if any convictions are followed by an amnesty. . . . With popular emotions stirring, he [Kao Kim Hourn of the Cambodian Institute for Cooperation and Peace] said, "internal pressure on the government has begun to build up." He added: "National Reconciliation at all costs? Bury the past? Forgive and forget? No. I don't think that is the case now." . . . Despite the violent power politics that has persistently stunted the establishment of democracy and human rights, a fledgling civil society has begun to emerge, addressing everything from education to flood control.[47]

CONTEXTUALIZING GOALS AND TOOLS

Although each of the eight goals specified in this chapter has prescriptive content, each also allows considerable latitude in devising policies sensitive to specific historical and local facts. Different means may be justified for achieving particular ends, and the selection of means—constrained by local institutional capacities—will have consequences for the priority ranking that any given society assigns to the goals overall. In particular circumstances, the achievement of one or more of the goals would itself be a means (whether it be helpful, necessary, or the best) to the realization of one or more of the others. For instance, truth may contribute to just punishment, fair compensation, and even reconciliation. When perpetrators are judicially directed to compensate their former victims, steps may be taken toward both retribution and reconciliation.

In summary, I have employed the eight goals to identify the moral aspects of reckoning with past wrongs, the areas of emerging international agreement, and the topics for further cross–cultural reflection and deliberation. Moreover, I propose that the eight goals be employed—and in turn evaluated—as criteria for evaluating the general "success" of various tools for dealing with past wrongs[48] and for designing and assessing a package of tools for attaining transitional justice in particular countries.

Different local conditions have a crucial bearing on the best that can be done in particular contexts. For example, it matters what a given transition is from and what it is to. Were prior violations perpetrated or permitted by a dictatorship, or did they occur in the context of a civil war, ethnic conflict, or attempted secession? If one of the latter, has the previous conflict been brought to a negotiated end, or was one side unilaterally victorious? How long was the period of violations, and how many people were perpetrators and victims (or both)? Does the particular society have a history of democratic institutions, or was it a long–standing dictatorship? Does the emerging society perpetuate, albeit in a new form, the ruling party, judicial system, and military apparatus of the old regime? What are the strength and potential of democratic governance, the market, and civil society? What is the general level of well–being among citizens, and are there continuing ethnic conflicts or radical economic disparities between segments of society? Each of these factors highlights the dangers of supposing that there is a recipe or single set of policies for reckoning with past wrongs that will be ethically defensible and practically feasible. They also indicate that sometimes the best that can be done is to approximate one or more of the eight goals initially or postpone attempts to realize them until conditions are improved. And, at times, excruciatingly difficult trade–offs will have to be made.

CONCLUDING REMARKS

It might be claimed that, regardless of its structure and content, it is neither possible nor desirable to formulate a general, cross–cultural normative framework and that the best that a society can do is to generate various tactics of its own for reckoning with past evil. However, policies and strategies that are designed and implemented solely under the pressure of immediate circumstances and without proper attention to the relevant ethical questions are likely to be ad hoc, ineffective, inconsistent, and unstable. Moral questions have a habit of not going away. They may be trumped in the short term by certain strategic and prudential imperatives, and some measure of peace can be established without paying close attention to them. Long–term peace, however, cannot be realized if resentment, bitterness, and moral doubts about the just treatment of perpetrators and victims of human rights abuses linger in the minds of citizens. A general framework inspired and shaped by lessons learned from a variety of contexts can encourage each society reckoning with an atrocious past to realize in its own way as many as possible of the goals that international dialogue agrees are morally urgent.

It might also be argued that much more is needed than a normative framework or "vision." This is correct. But, while far from sufficient, it is essential to get clear on morally based objectives as we reckon with a society's past wrongs. The eminent Costa Rican philosopher Manuel Formosa nicely puts the general point: "It is clear that the new society will not come about just by thinking about it. But there is no doubt that one must begin by setting forth what is important; because, if we do not, we will never achieve it."[49]

NOTES

I am grateful to David P. Crocker, Stacy Kotzin, Mauricio Olavarria, and my colleagues at the Institute for Philosophy and Public Policy and the School of Public Affairs—especially Susan Dwyer, Arthur Evenchik, Peter Levine, Xiaorong Li, Judith Lichtenberg, and other participants in the Transitional Justice Project—for helpful comments on earlier versions of this essay. This chapter is a slightly updated version of an article that appeared in *Ethics & International Affairs*, 13 (1999): 43–64. Thanks to the journal's editors, Joel Rosenthal and Deborah Field Washburn, for permission to reprint the original article, which their suggestions improved, in the present context.

1. The best multidisciplinary collections on transitional justice are Neil J. Kritz, ed., *Transitional Justice: How Emerging Democracies Reckon with Former Regimes*, 3 vols. (Washington, DC: United States Institute of Peace Press, 1995); Naomi Roht–Arriaza, ed., *Impunity and Human Rights in International Law and Practice* (New York: Oxford University Press, 1995); and A. James McAdams, ed., *Transitional Justice and the Rule of Law in New Democracies* (Notre Dame: University of Notre Dame Press, 1997).

2. Timothy Garton Ash, "The Truth About Dictatorship," *New York Review of Books* 45 (19 February 1998): 35.

3. For these broader issues, see Ash's essay and Juan E. Méndez, "Accountability for Past Abuses," *Human Rights Quarterly* 19 (1997): 256–58, and "In Defense of Transitional Justice," in McAdams, ed., *Transitional Justice*, 22–23, n. 4.

4. Seth Mydans, "Under Prodding, Two Khmer Rouge Apologize for the Reign of Terror," *New York Times*, 30 December 1998, p. A1, and "Cambodian Leader Resists Punishing Top Khmer Rouge," *New York Times*, 29 December 1998, pp. A1, A8. See also David Chandler, "Will There be a Trial for the Khmer Rouge?" *Ethics & International Affairs* 14 (2000).

5. See Steven R. Ratner and Jason S. Abrams, *Accountability for Human Rights and Atrocities in International Law: Beyond the Nuremberg Legacy* (Oxford: Clar-

endon Press, 1997); and Aryeh Neier, *War Crimes: Brutality, Genocide, Terror and the Struggle for Justice* (New York: Times Books, 1998); Ruti G. Teitel, *Transitional Justice* (New York: Oxford University Press, 2000).

6. Ruth Wedgwood, "Fiddling in Rome," *Foreign Affairs* 77 (November–December 1998): 20–24.

7. Lawrence Weschler, *A Miracle, a Universe: Settling Accounts with Torturers* (New York: Pantheon, 1990); Roy Gutman, *Witness to Genocide* (New York: Macmillan, 1993); Tina Rosenberg, *The Haunted Land: Facing Europe's Ghosts After Communism* (New York: Random House, 1995) and "Defending the Indefensible," *New York Times Magazine*, 19 April 1998, pp. 45–69; David Rohde, *Endgame: The Betrayal and Fall of Srebrenica, Europe's Worst Massacre since World War II* (Boulder, CO: Westview Press, 1997); Marguerite Feitlowitz, *A Lexicon of Terror: Argentina and the Legacies of Torture* (New York: Oxford University Press, 1998); Roger Cohen, *Hearts Grown Brutal: Sagas of Sarajevo* (New York: Random House, 1997); Chuck Sudetic, *Blood and Vengeance: One Family's Story of the War in Bosnia* (New York: W. W. Norton, 1998); Bill Berkeley, "Aftermath: The Pursuit of Justice and the Future of Africa," *Washington Post Magazine*, 11 October 1998, pp. 10–15, 25–29; Philip Gourevitch, *We Wish to Inform You That Tomorrow We Will Be Killed with Our Families: Stories from Rwanda* (New York: Farrar, Straus & Giroux, 1998).

8. See, for example, the essays by Thomas Buergenthal, Carlos Nino, and José Zalaquett in Kritz, *Transitional Justice*, vol. 1. The authors took part respectively in attempts to reckon with past wrongs in El Salvador, Argentina, and Chile.

9. See McAdams, *Transitional Justice*; and Mark Osiel, *Mass Atrocity, Collective Memory, and the Law* (New Brunswick, NJ: Transaction Books, 1997).

10. See Michael Walzer, *Just and Unjust Wars: A Moral Argument with Historical Illustrations*, 2d ed. (New York: Basic Books, 1977), xxvii.

11. See, for example, Donald Shriver, *An Ethic for Enemies: Forgiveness in Politics* (New York: Oxford University Press, 1995); Pablo De Greiff, "Trial and Punishment, Pardon and Oblivion: On Two Inadequate Policies for the Treatment of Former Human Rights Abusers," *Philosophy and Social Criticism* 12 (1996): 93–111; "International Criminal Courts and Transitions to Democracy," *Public Affairs Quarterly* 12 (1998): 79–99; Lyn S. Graybill, "South Africa's Truth and Reconciliation Commission: Ethical and Theological Perspectives," *Ethics & International Affairs* 12 (1998): 43–62; and T. M. Scanlon, "Punishment and the Rule of Law," in Harold Hongju Koh and Ronald C. Slye, eds., *Deliberative Democracy and Human Rights* (New Haven and London: Yale University Press, 1999).

12. One exception to this judgment is Ash, "The Truth About Dictatorship." Although he neither clarifies nor defends his ethical assumptions and although his particular assessments can be disputed, Ash insightfully considers four general measures—forgetting, trials, purges, and historical writing—with lots of variations and examples, especially from East and Central European countries. See also Martha Minow, *Between Vengeance and Forgiveness: Facing History after Genocide and Mass Violence* (Boston: Beacon Press, 1998); and Tina Rosenberg, "Confronting the Painful Past," Afterword in Martin Meredith, *Coming to Terms: South Africa's Search for Truth* (New York: Public Affairs, 2000), 325–70.

13. David A. Crocker, "Transitional Justice and International Civil Society: Toward a Normative Framework," *Constellations* 5 (1998): 492–517; "Civil Society and Transitional Justice," in Robert Fullinwider, ed., *Civil Society, Democracy, and*

Civic Renewal (Lanham, MD: Rowman & Littlefield, 1999); and "Truth Commissions, Transitional Justice, and Civil Society," in Robert I. Rotberg and Dennis Thompson, eds., *Truth v. Justice: The Morality of Truth Commissions*" (Princeton, NJ: Princeton University Press, 2000); "Retribution and Reconciliation," *Report from the Institute for Philosophy & Public Policy* 20, no. 1 (Winter/Spring 2000): 16; "Can There Be Healing Through Justice," *Responsive Community* 11 (Spring 2001): 32–42; "Punishment, Reconciliation, and Democratic Deliberation," *Buffalo Criminal Justice Review* (forthcoming). My list of objectives has benefited from the work of Méndez and Zalaquett as well as from that of Margaret Popkin and Naomi Roht–Arriaza, who formulate and employ four criteria in "Truth as Justice: Investigatory Commissions in Latin America," *Law and Social Inquiry* 20 (1995): 79–116, especially 93–106.

14. Crocker, "Transitional Justice and International Civil Society," 495–496.

15. Svetozar Stojanovi, *The Fall of Yugoslavia: Why Communism Failed* (Amherst, N.Y.: Prometheus Books, 1997), 77–78; see also 89–92.

16. Alex Boraine, "The Societal and Conflictual Conditions That Are Necessary or Conducive to Truth Commissions" (Paper presented at the South African Truth and Reconciliation Commission Conference, World Peace Foundation, Somerset West, South Africa, 28–30 May 1998). See Alex Boraine, *A Country Unmasked: Inside South Africa's Truth and Reconciliation Commission* (Oxford: Oxford University Press, 2000).

17. Rohde, *End Game*, 226.

18. Ibid., 230–231.

19. For investigations of what the United States and other Western powers could and should have done to prevent the Holocaust, see Richard Breitman, *Official Secrets: What the Nazis Planned, What the British and Americans Knew* (New York: Hill and Wang, 1999); and Istvan Deak, "Horror and Hindsight," a review of *Official Secrets* by Richard Breitman, *The New Republic* (15 February 1999): 38–41. For consideration of the same issues with respect to the failure of the United States, the UN, and the European Union to intervene militarily in Croatia and Bosnia in 1991–1995, see Mark Danner, "The US and the Yugoslav Catastrophe," *New York Review of Books* 44 (20 November 1997): 56–64.

20. See Crocker, "Truth Commissions, Transitional Justice, and Civil Society."

21. See, for example, Patrick Ball, *Who Did What to Whom? Planning and Implementing a Large Scale Human Rights Data Project* (Washington, DC: American Association for the Advancement of Science, 1996); Patrick Ball, Paul Kobrak, and Herbert Spirer, *State Violence in Guatemala, 1960–1996: A Quantitative Reflection* (Washington, DC: American Association for the Advancement of Science, 1999).

22. See Mark Danner, "Bosnia: The Turning Point," *New York Review of Books* 45 (5 February 1998): 34–41, for a compelling argument that rejects Serb claims that it was Muslims themselves who were responsible for the mortar attack that killed sixty-eight Muslims in a Sarajevan market on 5 February 1994.

23. Suzanne Daly, "In Apartheid Injury, Agony Is Relived but Not Put to Rest," *New York Times*, 17 July 1997, A1, A10.

24. "Aftermath: Genocide, the Pursuit of Justice and the Future of Africa," *Washington Post Magazine*, 11 October 1998, pp. 14, 28.

25. See Michael Walzer, *Just and Unjust Wars: A Moral Argument with Historical Illustration* (New York: Basic Books, 1977), 304–327; Neier, *War Crimes*, 229–

245; Mark J. Osiel, "Obeying Orders: Atrocity, Military Discipline, and the Law of War," *California Law Review* 86 (October 1998): 943–1129.

26. Peter Quint, *The Imperfect Union: Constitutional Structures of German Unification* (Princeton: Princeton University Press, 1997), 194–215; cf. Anne Sa'adah, *Germany's Second Chance: Trust, Justice, and Reconciliation* (Cambridge: Harvard University Press, 1998).

27. Larry May and Stacey Hoffman, eds., *Collective Responsibility: Five Decades of Debate in Theoretical and Applied Ethics* (Lanham, MD: Rowman & Littlefield, 1991).

28. See Carlos Nino, *Radical Evil on Trial* (New Haven: Yale University Press, 1996), 210–228; Neier, *War Crimes*, 210–228; and Peter A. French, ed., *The Spectrum of Responsibility* (New York: St. Martin's Press, 1991).

29. Nino, *Radical Evil on Trial*, and "A Consensual Theory of Punishment," in A. John Simmons et al., eds., *Punishment: A Philosophy & Public Affairs Reader* (Princeton: Princeton University Press, 1995), 95–111; and Malamud–Goti, "Transitional Governments in the Breach: Why Punish State Criminals?" in Kritz, *Transitional Justice* 1: 193–202.

30. See, for example, Simmons et al., *Punishment*; Lawrence Crocker, "The Upper Limit of Punishment," *Emory Law Journal* 41 (1992): 1059–1110; and "A Retributive Theory of Criminal Justice" (unpublished ms.); Michael Moore, *Laying Blame* (Oxford: Clarendon Press, 1997); Jean Hampton, "The Moral Education Theory of Punishment," *Philosophy and Public Affairs* 13 (1984): 208, 238; Herbert Morris, "Persons and Punishment," *Monist* 52 (1968): 475–501; George Sher, *Desert* (Princeton: Princeton University Press, 1987); James Rachels, "Punishment and Desert," in Hugh LaFollette, ed., *Ethics in Practice: An Anthology* (Cambridge, MA and Oxford: Blackwell, 1997); and David A. Crocker, "Retribution and Reconciliation" and "Punishment, Reconciliation, and Democratic Deliberation."

31. David Luban, "The Legacies of Nuremberg," in *Legal Modernism* (Ann Arbor: University of Michigan Press, 1994), 335–78. He draws on Lon L. Fuller, *The Morality of Law*, rev. ed. (New Haven: Yale University Press, 1977), 33–39.

32. See, for example, Stephen Holmes, "The End of Decommunization," in Kritz, *Transitional Justice* 1: 116–120; and Jon Elster, "On Doing What One Can: An Argument Against Post–Communist Restitution and Retribution," in Kritz, *Transitional Justice* 1: 556–568.

33. Warren Hoge, "Law Lords in London Open Rehearing of Pinochet Case," *New York Times*, 19 January 1999, A1. Both the international and the Chilean consensus have evolved since this essay originally appeared in the spring of 1999. In January 2000, Pinochet was extradited from Britain to Chile, where he now has been charged in Chilean courts and has lost his immunity from prosecution. Even if Pinochet never stands trial in Chile, the effect of the Spanish and British actions has been to "establish that even former heads of state do not enjoy immunity for crimes against humanity, and may be tried outside the country where the crimes were committed." See "New Twist in the Pinochet Case," *New York Times*, 15 January 2000, A18.

34. *Report of the [South African] Truth and Reconciliation Commission*, vol. 5, chap. 5, para. 27–28 and 85–93.

35. David A. Sanger, "Gold Dispute with the Swiss Declared to Be at an End," *New York Times*, 31 January 1999, A1.

36. Roger Cohen, "German Companies Adopt Fund for Slave Laborers Under Nazis," *New York Times*, 17 February 1999, A1. Cohen observes that "since World War Two the German government has paid out about $80 billion in aid, most of it to Jews who survived concentration camps or fled."

37. Ibid. The best comprehensive historical study of approaches to restitution, reparation, and compensation is Elazar Barkan, *The Guilt of Nations: Restitution and Negotiating Historical Injustices* (New York: W. W. Norton, 2000).

38. See Robert A. Dahl, *Democracy and Its Critics* (New Haven: Yale University Press, 1989), especially chaps. 8, 17, and 18; and Larry A. Diamond, "Democracy in Latin America: Degrees, Illusions, Directions for Consolidation," in Tom Farer, ed., *Beyond Sovereignty: Collectively Defending Democracy in the Americas* (Baltimore: Johns Hopkins University Press, 1996), 52–104.

39. See, for example, David A. Crocker, "Development Ethics," in Edward Craig, ed., *Routledge Encyclopedia of Philosophy*, vol. 3 (London: Routledge, 1998), 39–44; Amartya Sen, *Development as Freedom* (New York: Alfred A. Knopf, 1999); and Martha C. Nussbaum, *Women and Human Development: The Capabilities Approach* (New York: Cambridge University Press, 2000).

40. Charles Villa–Vicencio, "A Different Kind of Justice: The South African Truth and Reconciliation Commission," *Contemporary Justice Review* (forthcoming).

41. Osiel, *Mass Atrocity, Collective Memory, and the Law* 17, n. 22; see also 47–51; 204, n. 136; and 263–265.

42. Amy Gutmann and Dennis Thompson, "Moral Foundations of Truth Commissions," in Rotberg and Thompson, *Truth v. Justice*.

43. See David Little, "A Different Kind of Justice: Dealing with Human Rights Violations in Transitional Societies," in *Ethics & International Affairs* 13 (1999): 65–80.

44. See Susan Dwyer, "Reconciliation for Realists," in *Ethics & International Affairs* 13 (1999): 81–98.

45. See Gilbert A. Lewthwaite, "In South Africa, Much Truth Yields Little Reconciliation," *Baltimore Sun*, 30 July 1998, p. 12; and Phylicia Oppelt, "Irreconcilable: The Healing Work of My Country's Truth Commission Has Opened New Wounds for Me," *Washington Post*, 13 September 1998, C1, C4.

46. See James Bohman, *Public Deliberation: Pluralism, Complexity, and Democracy* (Cambridge: MIT Press, 1996); and Amy Gutmann and Dennis Thompson, *Democracy and Disagreement* (Cambridge: Harvard University Press, 1996).

47. Seth Mydans, "20 Years On, Anger Ignites Against Khmer Rouge," *New York Times*, 10 January 1999, A1.

48. See, for example, Priscilla B. Hayner, "Past Truths, Present Dangers: The Role of Official Truth–Seeking in Conflict Resolution and Prevention," in National Research Council, *International Conflict Resolution: Techniques and Evaluation* (Washington, DC: National Research Council,) and *Unspeakable Truths: Confronting State Terror and Atrocity* (New York: Routledge, 2001).

49. Manuel Formosa, "La alternativa: Repensar la revolución," *Seminario Universidad*, Universidad de Costa Rica, San José, 23 October 1987, p. 5.

11

Wasted Opportunities: Conflictive Peacetime Narratives of Central America

Ana Patricia Rodríguez

In texts produced in Central America after the armed conflicts of the 1980s, the reconstruction of the isthmus is an underlying concern. Books such as *América Central hacia el 2000: Desafíos y opciones* (Central America Toward 2000: Challenges and Options), *Forjando la paz: El desafío de América Central* (Forging Peace: The Challenge of Central America), *De la locura a la esperanza: La guerra de 12 años en El Salvador* (From Insanity to Hope: The Twelve Year War in El Salvador), *Esquipulas, diez años después: ¿Hacia dónde va Centroamérica?* (Esquipulas, Ten Years Later: Where is Central America Headed?), and *Traspatio Florecido: Tendencias de la dinámica de la cultura en Centroamérica (1979–1990)* (Flourishing Ground: Tendencies in the Central American Cultural Dynamic [1979–1990])[1] not only assess the recent period of civil unrest in the region, but they also suggest that Central American nations are attempting to move forward into the twenty-first century. An extensive production of essays, monographs, and books invokes a past that is not easily erased, but upon which Central Americans must build new cultural-scapes given the context of recent economic and political realignments of Latin America. Indeed, as Julio Ramos suggests in his essay in this anthology, these texts are emblematic of new "articulations between the North and the South" and of reformulations of Latin and Central Americanist discourses. For Central Americans, as these texts imply, there is no starting from scratch, since Central America was indelibly marked by the recent wars and continues to be defaced by the onslaught of neo-liberal programs throughout the region.

In *Traspatio Florecido: Tendencias de la dinámica de la cultura en Cen-*

troamérica, Rafael Cuevas Molina explains that today there is an urgent need to examine the state of post-revolutionary cultural realities in Central America, as well as a need to forge a regional Central American cultural imaginary. For Cuevas Molina, the imperative is to bring to the fore connections between the peoples, histories, and societies of the isthmus and to underscore the differences among them. In his view, the wars of the last decades generated new heterogeneous cultural forms, which now offer other sites for critical study. In daily practice, however, there are limited cultural exchange and communication among Central Americans themselves. He explains, "Such neglect, even among intellectuals who are concerned with the issue of cultural identity, permits a lack of mutual awareness of what goes on in neighboring countries of the isthmus, of what is produced there, of what is published there, etc., to prevail. It also foments the reproduction of acritical stereotypes, myths, common sense prejudices against the other countries in the region."[2]

To offset these biases, the construction of cultures of peace in the region requires the promotion of mutual recognition among Central Americans and the production of an extended Central American imaginary, a project in which cultural texts are indispensable. The integration of Central American cultures into a regional imaginary, as suggested here, serves as a defense against further cultural memory loss and a front against cultural homogenization induced by the expansion of global (cultural and economic) capital in the region. As Cuevas Molina suggests, Central American communities would benefit from composing a regional cultural field,[3] which would promote awareness and co-existence of cultural differences, histories, and models throughout the region.

Indeed, Central American cultures today are not the national cultures imagined by nineteenth-century liberals and federalists, nor are they the revolutionary cultures projected in the last decades. Furthermore, they are no longer strictly located within national geographic boundaries. Central American cultures, in fact, have spilled over their national confines into other spaces in the South and the North. According to Cuevas Molina, regional and comparative studies of Central American cultures are necessary, as Central Americans share both a geographic region and similar historical developments. He suggests, however, that there is a near void in full-length studies of Central American regional cultures, with the exception of Sergio Ramírez Mercado's *Balcanes y volcanes y otros ensayos y trabajos* (Balkans and Volcanoes and Other Essays),[4] an overview of Central American cultural production from pre-Columbian times to the decade of the 1970s. More recently, Sergio Ramírez's *Hatful of Tigers: Reflections on Art, Culture and Politics* (1995)[5] offers a compilation of essays that examine the direct and subtle impact of revolutionary cultures on the region. Rafael Cuevas Molina's own *Traspatio Florecido* and Magda Zavala and Seidy Araya's *La his-*

toriografía literaria en América Central (1957–1987) (*Literary Histori-ography in Central America*)[6] have been important contributions to the field of comparative/regional Central American cultural studies. Occasioned by the opportunity to re-envision a regional imaginary for Central America, this essay examines the reconstruction, or recycling, of new and old narratives of peace in Central America.

POSTWAR CULTURAL PRODUCTION IN CENTRAL AMERICA

Following the noted apex of the *testimonio* and a critical break with the Marxist–Leninist revolutionary narrative of the 1980s,[7] contemporary Central American cultural production is located at the crossroads of discourses on Central American regional cultures. Postwar and reconstruction literature shows the signs of recent historical and discursive transformations. Grappling with the legacy of armed conflict, postwar literature in Central America is in the process of constructing peacetime narratives. Major strategies of this literature include, as Cuevas Molina's study suggests, the invention of a Central American imaginary across texts which propose both utopic and dystopic visions of the future and which seek to disrupt official peacetime narratives of the region. Many recent literary texts also interrogate the effects of neo-liberal politics and economies on the specific and diverse populations of the isthmus and offer critiques of the general devastation of the South, including Central America. Often they engage in a rethinking of alliances forged among Central Americans and their displaced refugee/immigrant populations (re)located in other sites in the North and the South.

Under neo-liberal regimes, all of the countries in Central America show the impact of similar economic, political, social, and cultural programs implemented throughout the South. The imaginary of Central America as the South is not limited to the confines of individual nation-states, but covers a wide expanse of sites across the world currently ruled by neo-liberal regimes that implement violent domestic policies and reforms. In this construction of a southern Central American imaginary, individual countries identify themselves as part of a larger Central American entity, and as part of the even larger economic composite of the South. Located in particular sites spread across the globe, the South might be understood as a location of cultures[8] produced under the heavy strain of the expropriation and accumulation of capital in the northern regions of the world. Jonathan R. Barton, in *A Political Geography of Latin America*,[9] offers a working definition of the region and the conditions of the South. According to Barton,

the South is a geographical reference within which the *majority* of countries share *similar* environmental, social, cultural, political and economic development contexts and conditions. . . . The South definition is neither precise, inclusive nor exclusive, and as such it reflects the heterogeneity of Latin American circumstances. Rather than attempting to justify the term, it is better to point out that there are many and various contradictions and ambiguities within this universalisation. The definition should continue that a recognition of the difference within the South is as important as a recognition of the difference between the North and the South. (Barton 6; emphasis in original text)

Spanning a vast terrain and various national territories, the South comprises two-thirds of the earth's surface, where three-and-a-half billion people or three-quarters of humanity often live in extreme degrees of impoverishment.[10] It encompasses the sites formerly and recently known as the Third World, the developing countries, and the peripheries.

Barton further notes that, "Within the globalised context of neocolonialism, the manipulation of armed forces is being replaced gradually by the manipulation of market force" (Barton, 3). Currently, Central Americans engage in a common struggle against the violent (economic) forces of the North. In the arena of the globalized state, as Barton points out, it is the firms, banks, agencies, and other organizations that determine domestic policies in specific countries. Under such conditions of selective expropriation of capital, Central America has gained a place among the impoverished states of the South, of which Latin America is a "key region" (Barton, 3).

In much current literature and photojournalism,[11] Central America is imagined as a site undergoing great socioeconomic and ecological devastation (the general condition of the South). The image of *garbage* or *waste* surfaces as the metaphor of Central American nations attempting to rebuild themselves from the rubble of armed conflict, while at the same time confronting the disruptive fallout of global capital. Waste also serves as the sign of the uncertain future of the isthmus, requiring critical readings of the devastation of the region throughout its long history of imperialism and intervention. Throughout the history of Central America, structures of power and attendant systems of thought have converted the region into raw material and terrain for the (mis)use of the North. In an act of reification, the same devastating effects produced in the South by the North come to represent Central America as a natural(ized) site of decomposition (underdevelopment), which requires regeneration by outside forces. Regeneration from the North comes to Central America in the form of imperialism, (neo)colonialism, and now neo-liberal programs.

In "Through the Tropical Looking Glass: The Motif of Resistance in U.S. Literature on Central America," Stephen Benz explains that the isthmus is imagined as a "deadly, diseased, disorderly, dissolute, and decadent" region, which must be brought to order by outside forces.[12] According to Benz, *tropicalism* (the southern version of Edward Said's Orientalism) is the underlying logic that informs many projects of imperialism, (neo)colonialism, and neo-liberalism that take root in Central America. Responding to this legacy of decomposition, the texts to be analyzed here pick at the garbage left behind by those structures imposed on Central America, and attempt to reconstruct narratives for the region out of the remains. These texts, moreover, trace the source of devastation of Central America directly to the North. Waste, in these Central American texts, is the premier sign of the degradation of the South, as produced by northern agents. In Carmen Naranjo's story "And We Sold the Rain" (1989),[13] Fernando Contreras Castro's *Única mirando al mar* (1994),[14] and Manlio Argueta's *Milagro de la Paz* (*Miracle of Peace*),[15] I examine the representation of communities living in the virtually wasted lands of Central America. Part of a wider post-revolutionary cultural politics and cultural production, these texts represent a general scene of devastation, which sets the ground for the construction of peace in Central America. The survival of Central America into the next millennium depends on the reconstruction of its societies and the reimagining of more equitable narratives of development and progress in the region. What follows, then, is a discussion of the construction of a Central American regional imaginary in postwar literature, where waste is a prime signifier of the contradictions of peacetime conditions and where the ambivalent f(r)iction of peace casts subjects into internal and external holding spaces of economic, material, and human expropriation.

CENTRAL AMERICA: THE PLACE CALLED *MILAGRO DE LA PAZ* (*MIRACLE OF PEACE*)

As formal peace agreements were institutionalized in subsequent policies over the last decades, the narrative of peace in Central America began to show its contradictions. At a most basic level, peace is defined by the Oxford English Dictionary as freedom from or cessation of hostilities and war; as a state of security, concord, and amity within a determined group or location; and as freedom from civil disorder, disturbance or perturbation, and dissension between parties. Peacetime is defined, moreover, as "a period when a country is not at war." [16] Following these definitions, and after the signing of peace accords across Central America, a narrative of peace was constructed for the region by political leaders, nongovernmental organizations, the media, and others. This fiction required the disarming of revolutionary sectors in order for countries to begin a multifaceted process of national socioeconomic reconstruction and recovery. Although the signing of the initial peace accords of Esquipulas II on 7 August 1987 promised new practices of peace in the region, these efforts often congealed into documents on peace,[17] discourses of peace,[18] and institutions of peace. (The University of la Paz, with campuses in Ciudad Colón, Costa Rica, and Managua, Nicaragua, is one such institution generated by regional peace processes.)[19]

In her discerning thesis entitled "Un plan de paz para Centroamérica" (1991),[20] Marlen Retana Guido sheds light on how the peace plans and accords of the last decade used the language of peace and drew from idealist intertextualities to mask the regional economic objectives behind the peace processes. Peace, according to Retana Guido, was presented as concomitant with the ideals of democracy, progress, and liberty, and served as a front for a market economy that up to then had been deterred from expanding by the conflict in the region. The production of peace would initiate the economic recovery of Central America. In this context, peace is constructed as a space of forced "interconnections" produced by North/South relations: peace provides the conditions that will make it possible for neo-liberal economies to take hold and thrive in the region. The imperative of peace thus begins to blur the line between fact and fiction, war and peace, and the rule and the exception in Central America.

A culture of peace that advocated development, progress, and capital growth under the tutelage of neo-liberal programs was almost immediately inscribed in the Central American imaginary after the 1980s. In the 1990s, Central America dealt not only with the lagging effects of the previous conflicts, but also with new crises produced in an ambivalent time of peace. Today, many Central Americans live in a peace that is often a continuation of previous crises. They find that peace does not immediately and necessarily translate into democracy, liberty, and development. For many, peacetime Central America is composed of many f(r)ictions that continue to tear families apart; push people into deeper levels of poverty, illiteracy, and hunger; pump up drug trafficking and criminal activity; induce migrations and scatter individuals throughout Central America and elsewhere; and finally, generate higher levels and new forms of violence. The wars of the 1980s may be over in most areas of Central America, but violence continues to spread: *El Diario de Hoy*, in El Salvador, for example, reported 800 kidnappings between January and August 1995; *La Nación*, of San José, noted on 2 June 1995 the sparking of political and economic tensions throughout Central America. Such news reports from the region project an image of "*alta tensión*,"[21] or high voltage, surging with continued human rights violations in Guatemala, catastrophic natural disasters in Honduras, institutional crisis in Nicaragua, contradictory peace processes in El Salvador, crippling programs of economic structural adjustment in Costa Rica, and escalating levels of poverty and "ungovernability" throughout the region.[22] As we enter the third millennium, unemployment, poverty, and lack of opportunities contribute to escalating levels of quotidian violence, especially among the youth of Central America.[23] As the rift between the narrative of peace and the practice of peace becomes wider, the f(r)ictions and contradictions of peace in the region become more apparent.

Producing a critical intervention into the hegemonic narrative of peace-building and national reconstruction, Manlio Argueta's *Milagro de la Paz* provides a disruptive testimony of peace. The novel represents the contradictions of peace as they are lived in a small, rural town that has been abandoned by the state and left to resume its history. The novel, moreover, offers a gendered history that focuses on female subjects who live out crises of peacetime in various dimensions and locations. William Rowe and Vivian Schelling in *Memory and Modernity: Popular Culture in Latin America* (1991)[24] note that popular sectors register and remember their versions of history through alternative modes that might include, in the case of El Salvador, *testimonios*, letters of combatants, artisan work, and finally, novels by authors such as Manlio Argueta. Produced under the pressure of hegemonic narratives—the institutional fictions of peace—these texts assume hybrid forms such as the testimonial novel to which Argueta repeatedly returns. Beyond recording the voices of marginal subjects, testimonial novels and documentary fiction (of which *Milagro de la Paz* is a late exponent) register the social contradictions produced out of the frictions and fictions of peace in the isthmus. Argueta's text participates in the struggles with and over the verbal fiction of history,[25] which has worked to erase resistant histories and subjects.

The postwar novel by Manlio Argueta is ironically yet appropriately entitled *Milagro de la Paz*, alluding to the long-awaited and deferred miracle of peace in El Salvador. This is the story of a family of women who have survived the Civil War in El Salvador, in which at least 80,000 Salvadorans lost their lives during the 1980s. The mother, Latina, as her name implies, is the allegorical figure of women across the Americas, a single mother who has kept her family together, despite the irresponsible paternity of the state, the institutions, and, in many cases, the male heads of household. She tells her daughter, "[Los hombres] se han inventado que son valientes, pero a la hora de la verdad son más cobardes que nosotras" [(The men) have imagined they are courageous, but in the end they are more cowardly than us] (15). This family of women continues to live through and beyond the crisis, the militarism, and the phallocratic violence that have ravaged parts of Latin America, especially Central America and, more particularly, El Salvador, during the last decades. Latina and her daughters, Magdalena and Crista, now live in a town called "Milagro de la Paz," which still awaits the miracle of peace. (The miracle, in this novel, is that the fictionalized Salvadorans have survived at all to tell their stories.) The war may have ended, but the conflicts that gave rise to it are very much present in this peacetime community. Impoverished further in the aftermath of the war, the general population works harder to subsist during peacetime. Latina sews clothing, Magdalena sells it in the streets, Crista takes care of the animals and the garden. The three live by the general law that "El que no trabaja no come" [S/he who does not work does not eat] (12).

In telling the story of the significant role of Salvadoran women in the history of their country,[26] *Milagro de la Paz* picks up where Argueta's other novels, *Un día en la vida* (*One Day in the Life*) and *Cuzcatlán donde bate la mar del sur* (*Cuzcatlán Where the South Sea Beats*), leave off. The wars have permeated the social fabric, disrupting traditional family and social structures. Women, in particular, have carried the weight of the prolonged war, and, as Argueta's novel would seem to indicate, their struggle is no less light in peacetime. Latina and her daughters, for example, are haunted by the *aullidos de los seres desconocidos* [the howls of unknown beings] who roam the night: "Andan muy cerca de nosotros y pueden atacar cualquier casa del barrio" [They are very near us and they could attack any house in the neighborhood](13). The text does not disclose if these are the cries of the war dead or the signals of the prowlers who now invade most areas of El Salvador. The reader becomes aware, however, of the acute levels of trauma and fear embedded in the characters after years of institutionalized violence against which there is little safeguard or protection.[27] The trauma of war crimes remains fresh in the minds of Salvadorans, as *Milagro de la Paz* indicates. *Milagro de la Paz*, in its critical intervention into the fiction of peace, writes the particular history of Salvadoran women into a hegemonic discourse that tends to erase them throughout the vast regions of the South.

NEO-LIBERAL REGIMES: THE EXCEPTION AND THE RULE

While it was once the exception to the rule of unrest in Central America and boasted the highest standards of living among the southern countries, Costa Rica in the 1990s joined the ranks of the South in Central America. Along with El Salvador, Nicaragua, Honduras, and Guatemala, Costa Rica is enmeshed in the narrative of "marginalization and impoverishment" and "a generalized public squalor that was already formidably wide,"[28] all of which are further compounded by higher levels of exploitation of labor and appropriation of capital by the industrialized countries. Costa Rica, along with the rest of Central America, is part of the larger f(r)ictions of peace, development, and progress in the era of neo-liberal reform. It lies within the domain of the South.

In her satirical short story entitled "And We Sold the Rain," the Costa Rican writer Carmen Naranjo narrates the fate of a small developing nation that has fallen into hard times of economic structural adjustments requiring a revamping of economic, social, and cultural systems. The story begins with the treasury minister summing up the predicament of his country: "This is a royal fuck-up" (149). The International Monetary Fund (IMF), playing a starring role, demands payment on the interest of the small country's loans, "stubbornly insisting that the country could expect no more loans until the interest had been paid up, public spending curtailed, salaries frozen, domestic production increased, imports reduced, and social programs cut" (149). Under pressure by the IMF, the ministers and the president rehearse a list of last resorts: Why not pray to the competing patron virgins of the country, *La Negrita* or the *Virgin of Ujarrás*? But even the *Virgen de los Angeles*, the patron mother of Costa Rica who sanctions Catholic national alliances, has stopped listening to the Costa Ricans. One by one, institutional icons are erased from popular memory, until even "the government had faded in the people's memory" (152). The country quickly falls apart: the president "had to dismiss civil servants, suspend public works, cut off services, close offices, and spread his legs somewhat to transnationals" (152); "hunger and poverty could no longer be concealed" (150). The poor could not even buy beans. Shantytowns spring up around the capital, while Mercedes and BMWs cruise the city, which is rapidly falling into decay and general disorder: "In the marketplace, robberies increased to one per second, and homes were burgled at the rate of one per half hour" (150). Capitalizing on an idea, as a last resource/recourse, the export minister agrees to sell the country's oversupply of rain to a country in the Middle East, which, with the help of French technicians, builds an aqueduct that siphons off the water. The Central American country is depleted of natural resources, economic means, and spiritual hope. Eventually, the people are forced to immigrate to the Arab nation to which their government has sold their last precious resource.[29] Equally indebted to the IMF (when petroleum prices fall), the Arab nation must hand over its water supply, and it, too, eventually runs dry.

An allegory of North/South relations, Naranjo's story foretells the role of multinational organizations in the depletion of weak economies, which are highly vulnerable to external forces and uneven flows of capital. The story also shows the effects of the abjectification[30] of subjects unmoored from the social pact and dislodged from the ideals of the model Central American republic (Costa Rica). These subjects have two options available for their survival. One, they could immigrate to other places where they would inevitably become second-class citizens, live in ghettos, and work in jobs tending to "coffee, sugar cane, cotton, fruit trees, and truck gardens" (156)—the diasporic condition of many who flee the South. Alternatively, they could move to one of the shantytowns springing up throughout the country.

As abject beings, the poor people of the small country live in conditions of waste and disorder. Within the order of hegemonic society, they are (to follow Julia Kristeva's notion of the abject) quite meaningless, or "fading away of all meaning" (Kristeva, 18). They become human degenerates, living in the putrid state of the decomposing nation. The human by-products and wasted bodies churned out by the devastating economies of neo-liberalism, they are, to push Kristeva's terms further, the "unassimilable alien" (11) and "jettisoned object" (2) that have lost their place in the order of society. Likewise, they have lost the capacity to produce meaning in the logocentric chain of the narratives of development and progress. Failing to generate the expected meaning of labor (exploitable human capital), they have been cast out or discarded by the nation, which runs on the production (and the logic) of late capitalism. Transformed into the most abject of materials, wasted bodies, the poor people in Naranjo's story are "what human life and culture exclude in order to sustain themselves."[31] Because waste and filth are among the most degraded products in the material and symbolic economy of the West, and are offensive and repulsive in many cultures, subjects living in such conditions disturb the sensibilities and order of a healthy body politic.[32] The garbage societies and shantytown dwellers of Naranjo's story disrupt the linear, orderly progression of development in the southern country of the story. The first paragraph of the story, in fact, shows the nation to be a mess, and the narrative of progress to be a myth:

"This is a royal fuck-up," was all the treasury minister could say a few days ago as he got out of the jeep after seventy kilometers of jouncing over dusty rutted roads and muddy trails. His advisor agreed: there wasn't a cent in the treasury, the line for foreign exchange wound four times around the capital, and the IMF was stubbornly insisting that the country could expect no more loans until the interest had been paid up, public spending curtailed, salaries frozen, domestic production increased, imports reduced, and social programs cut (Naranjo 149).

In Naranjo's story, the abject beings are "Poor people without umbrellas, without a change of clothes, they get drenched, people living in leaky houses, without a change of shoes for when they're shipwrecked" (151). Signifying the wreck left in the wake of the country's impoverishment and exploitation by industrialized nations, the people of this southern country are left to fend for themselves, to organize among themselves, and to look for alternatives outside of their religious, juridical, and political institutions. In a critique of the narratives of development and progress, the ending of Naranjo's story begs for an alternative to the fiction of progress in Central America and for the projection of different modes of development and modernization that rely on local resources and local knowledge, or what has been circulating in Central America as the desire for a sustainable economy, which political scientists have defined as "a development strategy that combines human development, growth, equity and technological change with a wiser and more creative use of local resources and knowledge."[33] The story suggests, in the metaphor of the selling of the rain, that ecological damage is irreversible, a plight faced by the isthmus as a whole. The prognosis of eminent economic and natural disasters in Central America serves as a warning to the region, which, like other countries of the South, is quickly losing many of its rain forests and natural resources, is doubling in population, and is on the brink of ecological disaster. These disasters, not natural at all but produced by inequitable exchanges of capital and unequal relations of power, are naturalized in the myths of progress of the region. Carmen Naranjo, in "And We Sold the Rain," thus implicitly makes the case for sustainable development that would meet the needs of generations of the poorest and most excluded Central Americans.[34] According to Naranjo's story, a society that sells its resources, as many developing countries are forced to do, seal and sell their future.

The novel *Única mirando al mar* (*Unica Watching the Sea*) by the Costa Rican writer Fernando Contreras Castro takes up Carmen Naranjo's narrative of the wasting away of Costa Rican society. Contreras Castro's text comments on the sociohistoric implications of a society that throws its citizens away into *el basurero*, the dumpsite or wasted land, once their productivity is spent. According to Margarita Rojas and Flora Ovares, in *100 años de literatura costarricense* (1995),[35] *Única mirando al mar* is part of the recent production of literature in Costa Rica which resuscitates the communicative value of literary discourse and proposes that the literary text may still serve as a vehicle for transmitting information and for denouncing social abuses (Rojas and Ovares 244). The social reality of Costa Rica, as represented in "And We Sold the Rain" and *Única mirando al mar*, has undergone great alterations and degradations over the last decades: the state in these texts has failed the nation and abandoned the founding principles, ideals, and values of the Costa Rican republic. Rojas and Ovares suggest that *Única mirando al mar* does not offer solutions to a "mundo [que] está condenado al fracaso" [a world condemned to failure] (244). Hence, at the end of the novel, the protagonist is left gazing into the sea of her despair and homelessness. The text, however, does destabilize those illusive principles, ideals, and values upon which Costa Rican exceptionalism are based: "El mundo armónico y familiar, propio del estereotipo costarricense, la representación del espacio nacional como lugar íntimo y conocido, sin conflictos, aparecen profundamente cuestionados en *Única mirando al mar*" [The harmonious and familiar world belonging to the stereotype of Costa Rica and the representation of the nation as an intimate and known space without conflicts are profoundly interrogated in *Única mirando al mar*] (244). Read as an allegory of the demythologized (de-idealized) republic of Costa Rica, the novel designates *el basurero* as an alternative imaginary space located within the deterioration of the nation-state. The dumpsite regenerates a community, while the country at large is in rapid decomposition, as Naranjo's story also shows.

Contreras Castro's novel is invested in representing a contemporary moment in Costa Rican and Central American history. *Única mirando al mar* follows the tradition of the social realist text, the thesis novel, and (along with Naranjo's story) the popular genre of social satire, which have been prime discursive vehicles of social criticism in Central American literature. This is a novel with recognizable referents, attempting to communicate a message about Central American realities in the late twentieth and early twenty-first centuries. It is part of a literature written to open a highly polemic discussion about the problem of the garbage, from the angles and perspectives of those who are dispossessed and disposed of within the general context of the decomposing nation-state. The site of enunciation in these novels is the dumpsite, from which those subjects most affected by the fallout of the decomposition of traditional Central American infrastructures speak. Contemporary Central American literary texts such as those examined here meet the new challenges of representing Central American realities within the conditions of the South. Contreras Castro's text, in using a social realist convention that is out of fashion in postmodernist literary and critical production, challenges many of the assumptions, definitions, and categories of literature that are fabricated, for the most part, in northern sites. Texts like *Única mirando al mar* attempt to address the discursive needs of Central American subjects by staying in touch, so to speak, with local realities.

In "Seis falsos golpes contra la literatura centroamericana" ("Six False Attacks Against Central American Literature"), Sergio Ramírez succinctly summarizes the main critiques made of Central American literature.[36] Ramírez proposes that Central American literature, contrary to literature written elsewhere, (1) still engages with referents and social realities; (2) produces rich imaginaries out of those referents and references; (3) thrives as an artistic enterprise despite the high levels of illiteracy in the region; (4) speaks out of Central American contexts using local vernacular sign systems; (5) shows literary texts to have a discursive, communicative and thus material function in society; and (6) claims that literature still has something to say, if not to denounce, in Central America.[37] The narratives of waste that are discussed here seem to respond to Ramírez's admonitions and theses on Central American literature with a brand of texts that are referent-based, address local social realities, and produce a pertinent contemporary imaginary of the region. In representing the post-revolutionary moment and the conflictive peacetime of Central America, these texts construct a highly contradictory image of the social realities of the region, which are encoded in the scene of waste.

THE DECOMPOSED AND RE-COMPOSED NATION

A composite of the larger debates in and about Central American literature, the novel *Única mirando al mar* is based on a series of prolonged discussions about finding a new dumpsite for the capital's solid waste, which took place in 1994 through 1995, between the president of Costa Rica, his government, and community leaders. At various times, former President of Costa Rica and Nobel Peace Prize recipient Oscar Arias critiqued the administration of then President José María Figueres (1994–1998) for stalling on the local problem of the garbage while attending to other issues such as the Costa Rican fiscal deficit and the privatization of public institutions. In *La Nación*, Arias commented on his own role "en un momento crucial, donde se luchaba por la paz y la igualdad de la mujer, y no 'por buscar donde botar la basura' " [at a crucial moment, when we fought for peace and the equality of women, and not 'where to throw away the garbage'] (*La Nación*, 2 June 1995). This debate over the ownership and management of the garbage is the context of Contreras Castro's novel.

Única mirando al mar is the story of Única Oconitrillo, her son El Bacán, and the stepfather Momboñombo Moñagallo. The threesome would seem to constitute the Costa Rican family. This family, however, lives in and off the garbage produced by San José. They literally make their residence within Río Azul, the massive dumpsite for the garbage of the Costa Rican capital. Every day, eight hundred tons of waste are deposited on these grounds, which the dump dwellers scout for recyclable goods, including their daily meals, their clothing, and other necessities and accessories. The text describes the *basurero* as the place where everything is turned upside down, where people eat garbage and dress in ripped clothing.[38] This is "el país de los buzos" (76), where people living on the margins of society, in the wasted lands, *bucean* (surf) the waves of garbage for their subsistence. Everyone living in the *basurero* has suffered a fall from society: Única, a former teacher, was forcibly retired at the age of forty, "por esa costumbre que tiene la gente de botar lo que aún podría servir largo tiempo . . ." [because of that custom that people have of throwing away what could still be useful for a long time] (14). Her meager pension forces her to retire to the newly opened dump, where she finds amid the rejected material a four-year-old boy whom she adopts. Later on, she finds another social outcast in the garbage, a fired security guard who, attempting to commit (as he calls it) *identicidio* (identicide, 24), throws himself into the garbage truck: ". . . a la hora que pasa el camión recolector, tomé la determinación de botarme a la basura . . ." [at the hour that the garbage truck came, I decided to throw myself into the garbage] (17). Upon finding himself resurrected in *el basurero*, rescued by Única, the old guard renames himself Momboñombo Moñagallo, giving up his former national and civic identity for a parodic one, as his name would seem to imply. Throughout the novel, Moñagallo does not disclose his original family name, but rather fabricates for himself an excessively and repetitively syllabic name. Indeed, "[t]he man elaborated a strange and grotesque name," one analogous to his extraneous and degenerating status in society (17). At the beginning of the novel, Moñagallo "had killed his identity, had gotten rid of his name, the home he had lived in for years, his identity card, his memories, everything, because the day he threw himself into the garbage was the last day that his income allowed him to simulate his life as a citizen."[39] Upon losing his job, or the sign of his material productivity and value, he loses all social standing and civil rights as a Costa Rican citizen, the text goes on to explain. Moñagallo's small pension, like Única's, relegates him to the margins of society, where he festers amid the rejected material of the nation. It is in Río Azul, however, that he is rescued by Única. He becomes *un humano reciclado* (recycled human being, 33) as well as a member of the community of dump dwellers (21), who form alternative families and organizations with their own local politics and daily rituals. The *basurero*, hence, becomes the habitus of what Moñagallo calls a life in decomposition (23), running on its own organic momentum rather than on the logic of official society. The dump citizens make their home in the rehabilitated and hospitable site, a new location of culture for the impoverished and the abject of the South. This marginal community, as the text shows, lives a sustainable existence, using rather than producing waste. They establish family bonds, and are loyal in their recycled love (86). Moñagallo eventually marries Única in a wedding ceremony conducted by a preacher invested by a bible and other religious paraphernalia found in the dump, and attended by everyone in their community of *buzos* (divers). The novel, in its ironic reassessment of hegemonic society, shows that "todo el país se estaba convirtiendo en un basurero" [the whole nation was turning into a dumpsite] (116).

In the novel, Costa Rica—the former "Switzerland of Central America"— is contaminated, degraded, and made violent by the forces of the neo-liberal regime. The novel reaches its climatic point when violence breaks out over the relocation of the dump: eight hundred riot policemen move in on the citizens of Esparza, living at a distance from the capital, when they protest against their city becoming the home of a new privatized dump. The armed police force shuts down a demonstration organized by the *buzos*, who will be turned out of their homes with the closure of Río Azul. One of the *buzos* claims that "hasta ahora nunca habíamos visto la policía utilizar esos métodos para dispersar la gente" [until now we had never seen the police use those methods to disperse the people] (105). Moñagallo wonders at the overall decomposition of Costa Rica, which prides itself on being a demilitarized, peaceful state since 1949 and in promoting the social welfare of its citizens. Momboñombo Moñagallo cannot be but astounded by the new society produced out of the rubble of economic structural adjustment programs. Even the garbage is to be appropriated by private industry (121), and the *buzos* will not be allowed to move to the new site. The novel ends with Momboñombo and Única, completely homeless, sitting on a bench overlooking the Pacific Ocean from the shore of Puntarenas. Their adopted son, *El Bacán*, has died from asthma produced by years of living in the dumpsite and exacerbated by the water with which the anti-riot police force flushed out the *buzos'* social movement. Única, in a catatonic state, is left *mirando al mar*, waiting for new rays of hope to descend upon the new refugees of Central American society.

WASTED OPPORTUNITIES FOR PEACE

In these texts of a wasted Costa Rica and an El Salvador wasting away in peacetime, Central America is represented as the underside of consumer capitalism. Costa Rica's city dump is overfilled with its own consumer waste, and El Salvador is recovering from an era of armament dumping that wasted away thousands of Salvadorans. Studying the image of waste in what she calls the "postnatural novel" of the 1980s in the United States,[40] Cynthia Deitering has suggested that in the North waste serves as a "cultural metaphor for a society's most general fears about its collective future and as expression of an ontological rupture in its perception of the Real" (197). The case might equally be made that garbage, in the texts analyzed here, expresses a collective fear of the uncertain future faced by many Central Americans today. Although the ideologeme of waste prevails in *Única mirando al mar*, "And We Sold the Rain," and *Milagro de la Paz*, the sign of waste is also open to more regenerative readings. It is suggested here that these texts do offer possibilities of other narrative resolutions and interpretations to the problem of the garbage at its symbolic and material levels. The texts project the possibility of resolutions onto the space of reception by readers, who must deal also with comparable problems as those represented in the texts. The texts leave their characters and readers suspended, in an interstitial space, where no definitive answers and resolutions are provided for the problem of the garbage, or for the conditions of the South. In the end, readers are invited to propose resolutions for Única who sits and waits at the shore, for the migrant workers in the Arab country who must relocate yet again, and for the women in *Milagro de la paz* who continue struggling for their survival.

The texts open a discussion on the current socioeconomic and political problems signified by the garbage. At the end of *Milagro de la Paz*, Latina and her daughters still have each other to face the next day of hardships: "Mañana será otro día común y corriente. Las cosas no habían mejorado pero estamos vivos" [Tomorrow will be another ordinary day. Things had not changed but we are alive] (Argueta, 188). The displaced people in Naranjo's "And We Sold the Rain" have found a temporary home in diaspora, where "[i]n a short time we were happy and felt as if these things too were ours, or at the very least, that the rain still belonged to us" (Naranjo, 156). And Única sits on a bench in Puntarenas, facing the sea of her and other Central Americans' discontent, a living testament to her displacement from hegemonic society. Out of the decomposition of Central American societies, these texts infer that garbage is also organic material that regenerates life. Manlio Argueta's novel about despoiled peace, and Carmen Naranjo's and Fernando Contreras Castro's texts about communities living in decomposing states (countries) project the necessity of imagining other narrative endings, if not alternative stories altogether, for Central America. All is not lost or turned to garbage in Central America, but the job of regenerating it and opening other directions belongs to Central Americans themselves.

Finally, in Gioconda Belli's futuristic novel *Waslala: Memorial del futuro* (*Waslala: Memorial of the Future*),[41] a Central American country in the third millennium receives (for pay) barges filled with toxic waste from the North.

The inhabitants of *Cineria*, the city of waste and the incinerator of the South, reclaim and recycle the throwaway goods they find in the garbage. Fantastic though it may seem, the exporting of waste to the South has a historical referent, as environmentalists Dana Alston and Nicole Brown explain in "Global Threats to People of Color." Identifying Central America as a growing site of environmental degradation,[42] Alston and Brown also verify the existence of an international waste trade in the North that "seeks alternative dump sites overseas" and exports wastes ("asbestos, incinerator ash, municipal wastes and sewage, and industrial chemical toxics," 183) to Central America, among other sites in the South. Read in this context, Cineria is the metaphorical phoenix of Central America.

It is in the garbage that Cinerians come to know directly and intimately "the underside of consumer capitalism."[43] They interpret the excesses of the North and come to some understanding of the widespread effects of the globalization of capital on the South. One of the garbage pickers in Gioconda Belli's novel explains the logic of garbage in Cineria: "esa basura, esa acumulación de objetos, eran como las huellas que un asesino deja tras de sí . . . Así es el sistema; cobra su precio. No hay desarrollo sin desperdicio." [That accumulation of objects was like the prints left behind by an assassin . . . That is how the system is; it has a price. There is no development without waste"] (165–166). In a mirroring effect, Cinerians recognize that their degradation is the North's gain. The waste they import is the sign of massive production, consumerism, and excess generated elsewhere. In *Waslala* and the other Central American narratives of garbage that have been analyzed here, waste circulates as the signifier of development and progress that happen elsewhere but that never come to these locations except in cruelly degraded and degrading forms such as the dumping of waste, cheap products, stockpiled armaments, and other contaminants. The inhabitants of Central America, like the Cinerians, are inundated with the waste of highly industrialized regions, and they are pushed to the limits of a world that becomes more and more inhospitable and inhumane. In Carmen Naranjo's "And We Sold the Rain," a Central American nation undergoing neo-liberal restructuring is turned into a massive shanty sprawl, its natural resources sold one by one and its populations pushed into labor migration. In Fernando Contreras Castro's *Única mirando al mar*, the discarded subjects of the nation commit acts of identicide by throwing themselves into a dumpsite where they live recycled lives. A bleak prognosis of the wasted opportunity for peace in the region, Manlio Argueta's *Milagro de la Paz* imagines a place of impoverishment that only survives because of the miraculous effort of the people of that southern community.

As these texts show, Central America is vital to understanding how world power and wealth are concentrated in the northern regions and expropriated from the South. The logic of tropicalism envisions Central America as a degraded and disorderly site requiring the aid, in this case, of agents skilled in the technologies of waste disposal. Following this imperative, the case is made that the South does not possess the capital and technology to refurbish its societies. The material and human potential of Central America is converted into expropriatable excess that can be recycled into profit. Contemporary Central American literature, therefore, represents societies robbed of their own productive (sustainable) means and potential. What remain are the impoverished shantytowns and depleted nations of Carmen Naranjo's story and Fernando Contreras Castro's novel, and the conflictive peacetime villages of Manlio Argueta's *Milagro de la Paz*, which have been abandoned by the state to the daily ingenuities and survival tactics of subjects shaped by the trauma of war. Looking back from the dystopic future of Central America, Gioconda Belli's novel *Waslala* suggests, however, that further economic, environmental, and human devastation of the region must be prevented today. These postwar and reconstruction texts, hence, set the scene for the production of creative alternatives to the conflictive narratives of progress, development, and peace that currently circulate in the isthmus.

NOTES

1. See Edelberto Torres-Rivas, comp., *América Central hacia el 2000: Desafíos y opciones* (Caracas: Editorial Nueva Sociedad, 1989); Richard Fagen, *Forjando la paz: El desafío de América Central*, trans. Carine Malfait (San José, Costa Rica: Editorial Departamento Ecuménico de Investigaciones, 1988); Comisión de la Verdad 1992–1993, *De la locura a la esperanza: La guerra de 12 años en El Salvador* (San José, CR: Editorial Departamento Ecuménico de Investigaciones, 1993); Jaime Ordoñez and Nuria Gamboa, eds. *Esquipulas, diez años después ¿Hacia dónde va Centroamérica?* (San José, CR: Editorial Universitaria Centroamericana, 1997); Rafael Cuevas Molina, *Traspatio Florecido: Tendencias de la dinámica de la cultura en Centroamérica (1979–1990)* (Heredia, CR: Editorial de la Universidad Nacional, 1993).

2. "Tal descuido permite que, incluso en círculos de intelectuales preocupados por la temática de la identidad cultural, prevalezca el desconocimiento mutuo de lo que ocurre en países vecinos del istmo, de lo que en ellos se produce, se publica, etc., y se reproduzcan, en formas bastante acrítica, estereotipos, mitos, prejuicios provenientes del sentido común respecto a los otros países de la región." Cuevas Molina, *Traspatio Florecido*, 13. All translations from this text into English are mine.

3. Based on Raymond Williams's work in *Marxism and Literature* (New York: Oxford University Press, 1977), Rafael Cuevas Molina defines "campo cultural" as "el sistema de relaciones (que incluye artistas, editores, marchantes, críticos, agentes, funcionarios, público) que determina las condiciones específicas de producción y circulación de sus productos. Dos elementos constituyen un campo: la existencia de un capital común y la lucha por su apropiación." Cuevas Molina, *Traspatio Florecido*, 14–15.

4. Sergio Ramírez, *Balcanes y volcanes y otros ensayos y trabajos* (Managua: Editorial Nueva Nicaragua, 1985). All translations from this text into English are mine.

5. Sergio Ramírez, *Hatful of Tigers: Reflections on Art, Culture and Politics*, trans. D.J. Flakoll (Willimantic, CT: Curbstone Press, 1995).

6. Magda Zavala and Seidy Araya, *La historiografía literaria en América Central (1957–1987)* (Heredia, CR: Editorial Fundación Universidad Nacional, 1995).

7. Daniel Camacho, "Latin America: A Society in Motion," ed. Ponna Wignaraja, *New Social Movements in the South: Empowering the People* (London: Zed Books, 1993), 36–58. Camacho claims that, for the most part, "[t]he change in revolutionary thought has occurred as a rupture with the authoritarian Hispanic or Caribbean culture and with the culture of a certain Marxism-Leninism (not simply Stalinism)," 39.

8. The term is borrowed from Homi K. Bhabha, *The Location of Culture* (New York: Routledge, 1994).

9. Jonathan R. Barton, *A Political Geography of Latin America* (New York: Routledge, 1997).

10. See Ponna Wignaraja, Preface, *New Social Movements in the South*, xv–xviii. Here, Wignaraja cites extensively from The South Commission's Report, *The Challenge to the South*.

11. See Larry Towell, *El Salvador*. Photographs by Larry Towell (New York: W.W. Norton & Company, Inc., 1997); *No hay guerra que dure cien años... El Salvador 1979—1992*, photographs by Iván C. Montecinos (San Salvador, ES: Equipo de Educación MAIZ, 1995); and *Solomon's House: The Lost Children of Nicaragua*, photographs and text by Henrik Saxgren (New York: Aperture Foundation, 2000).

12. Stephen Benz, "Through the Tropical Looking Glass: The Motif of Resistance in U.S. Literature on Central America," *Tropicalizations: Transcultural Representations of Latinidad*, ed. Frances R. Aparicio and Susana Chávez-Silverman (Hanover, NH: University Press of New England, 1997).

13. Carmen Naranjo, "And We Sold the Rain," trans. Jo Anne Engelbert, in *And We Sold the Rain: Contemporary Fiction from Central America*, ed. Rosario Santos (Peterborough: Ryan Publishing, 1989), 149–156.

14. Fernando Contreras Castro, *Única mirando al mar* (San José, CR: Ediciones FARBEN, 1994). All translations from this text into English are mine.

15. Manlio Argueta, *Milagro de la Paz* (San Salvador, El Salvador: Istmo Editores 1994). All translations from this text into English are mine.

16. *The Concise Oxford Dictionary of Current English*, 9th ed. (New York: Oxford University Press, 1995).

17. *Una hora para la paz* (San José: Imprenta Nacional, 1987). This document was signed by the presidents of El Salvador, Guatemala, Honduras, and Costa Rica.

18. Throughout the 1980s, former President of Costa Rica Oscar Arias played an important role in Central American peace negotiations. As mediator, Arias used a discourse of dialogue and negotiation.

19. See René Habachi, *Fundamentos filosóficos de una Universidad para la Paz* (San José: Editorial Universidad para la Paz, 1986) for a discussion of the philosophical tenets of the university, and the role that the United Nations and other global organizations play in promoting peace through the institution.

20. Marlen Retana Guido, "Un plan de paz para Centroamérica," Licentiate Thesis, Philology, Linguistics and Literature, University of Costa Rica, 1991.

21. "Crispación en Centroamérica," *La Nación* (San José, CR), 2 June 1995, 18A.

22. "Oscar Arias reprende a políticos," *La Nación* (San José, CR), 2 June 1995, 4A; Oscar Arias, "Los desafíos del siglo XXI desde América Latina" (Speech given at the National Theater, San José, 25 April 1995).

23. See Juanita Darling, "Mothers of the Banished," *Los Angeles Times Magazine*, 21 November 1999, pp. 20–21, 34–36; Juanita Darling, "El Salvador's War Legacy: Teen Violence," *Los Angeles Times*, 9 August, 1999, A1; Fen Montaigne, "Deporting America's Gang Culture," *Mother Jones* (July/August 1999), 44–51; Mike O'Connor, "A New U.S. Import in El Salvador: Street Gangs," *The New York Times International*, 3 July 1994; and José Miguel Cruz and Nelson Portillo Peña, *Solidaridad y violencia en las pandillas del gran San Salvador: Más allá de la vida loca* (San Salvador, ES: Universidad Centroamericana José Simeón Cañas Editores, 1998).

24. William Rowe and Vivian Schelling, *Memory and Modernity: Popular Culture in Latin America* (London: Verso, 1991).

25. Hayden White, "The Historical Text as Literary Artifact," *Tropics of Discourse: Essays in Cultural Criticism* (Baltimore: The Johns Hopkins University Press, 1978). In "The Historical Text as Literary Artifact," White uses the term *verbal fiction* to examine how historical and fictional narratives use similar literary devices and tropes to tell stories. History and fiction, according to White, are not exclusive terms but share "literary sensibilities" (99). White claims that there is a "fictive component in historical narratives" (87)—in other words, that there is as much fictionalization to history as there is historicity to fiction. The mutual emplotments of historical and literary discourses generate suggestive discussions on writing historical narratives, of which the texts analyzed here are variants.

26. See Ana Isabel García and Enrique Gomáriz, *Mujeres centroamericanas, Tomo II: Efectos del conflicto* (San José, CR: FLACSO, 1989). The authors note that Central American women suffered, in greater dimensions, the toll of institutionalized violence that intensified during the 1980s. Not only did they participate in direct logistic and combative work, but, more significant, they filled the ranks of displaced, refugee, and immigrant populations. Filling these tenuous social positions produced by war, they were dispersed internally within their own countries or externally across the globe (101–160). García and Gomáriz underscore the "feminization" of the displacement and immigration that occurred with the wars in Central America. These were wars waged against a gendered humanity, female subjects, whose presence is erased from the official record and relegated to "formal sub-registers" (145). Critical study of the effect and impact of war on women is often lacking or flawed. García and Gomáriz, furthermore, argue that half of the floating population of migratory and refugee Central Americans (recorded, in recent years, at 12 percent to 15 percent of the general population) is female.

27. The Peace Negotiation documents, signed in Chapultepec, Mexico City, on 16 January 1992, stipulated that the creation of the PNC (the National Civil Police) was fundamental for monitoring the process of peace. The signing of the final document, in fact, hinged on three significant issues: the cessation of the armed conflict, the economic and social recuperation of the country, and the founding of the PNC to ensure "safeguarding of peace, tranquillity, order and public security in urban and rural areas, under the control of civilian authorities." *El Salvador Agreements: The Path to Peace* (New York: The United Nations, 1992), 53.

28. James Dunkerley, *The Pacification of Central America: Political Change in the Isthmus 1987–1993* (London: Verso, 1994), 17.

29. See Dana Alston and Nicole Brown, "Global Threats to People of Color," *Confronting Environmental Racism: Voices from the Grassroots,* ed. Robert D. Bullard (Boston: South End Press, 1993). In their examination of current environmental scenarios in Central America, Alston and Brown discuss the marketing and selling of "plant materials for highly profitable biotechnology enterprises without any compensation to the source country" (190). Plants are being sold, and even patented, for "medicinal, industrial and agricultural use" by the pharmaceutical industry (191). The selling of natural resources is thus not as far fetched an idea as it would seem.

30. Julia Kristeva, *The Powers of Horror: An Essay on Abjection* (New York: Columbia University Press, 1982).

31. See the definition of the term "abjection" in *The Columbia Dictionary of Modern Literary and Cultural Criticism,* ed. Joseph Childers and Gary Hentzi (New York: Columbia University Press, 1995), 1.

32. For discussions of defilement and disease in various sociohistorical contexts, consult Mary Douglas, *Purity and Danger: An Analysis of Concepts of Pollution and Taboo* (London: Routledge, 1978); and Benigno Trigo, *Subject of Crisis: Race and Gender as Disease in Latin America* (Hanover, NH: University Press of New England, 2000). For the context of Central America, see Benz, "Through the Tropical Looking Glass."

33. Ponna Wignaraja, "Rethinking Development and Democracy," ed. Wignaraja, *New Social Movements in the South,* 4.

34. See Jorge Manuel Dengo Obregón, "Presentación," in *Desarrollo sostenible y políticas económicas en América Latina,* comp. Olman Segura (San José, CR: Editorial Departamento Ecuménico de Investigaciones, 1992), 11–12.

35. Margarita Rojas and Flora Ovares, *100 años de literatura costarricense* (San José, CR: Ediciones FARBEN, 1995). All translations from this text into English are mine.

36. Ramírez, "Seis falsos golpes contra la literatura centroamericana," *Balcanes y volcanes,* 117–128.

37. Ramírez asserts that "Política, ideología, represiones, heroísmos, masacres, fracasos, traiciones, luchas, frustraciones, esperanzas, son aún materia novelable en Latinoamérica y seguirán siéndolo porque la realidad no se agota; el novelista toma el papel de intérprete entre otros muchos que se arroga y quiere hablar en nombre de un inconsciente colectivo largamente silenciado y soterrado bajo un cúmulo de retórica falsa y pervertida. Y en esto, el escritor no puede dejar de cumplir un acto político, porque la realidad es política" [Politics, ideology, repression, heroism, massacre, defeat, betrayal, struggle, frustration, and hope are still subjects for novels in Latin America, and will continue to be so because reality has not exhausted itself. Among the many roles the novelist assumes, s/he becomes an interpreter and s/he desires to speak in the name of a collective unconscious that is largely silenced and buried under an accumulation of false and perverted rhetoric. Thus the writer cannot but act politically because reality is political] *Balcanes y volcanes,* 120.

38. ". . . donde todo se vuelve al revés, donde la gente come basura y se viste con lo roto." Contreras Castro, *Única mirando al mar,* 38. All translations from this text into English are mine. I have paraphrased the quote in English in the main text.

39. "Había matado su identidad, se había desecho de su nombre, de la casa donde vivió solo años de años, de su cédula de identidad, de sus recuerdos, de todo: porque el día que se botó a la basura fue el último día que sus prestaciones le permitieron

simular una vida de ciudadano." Contreras Castro, *Única mirando al mar*, 24. I have included the English translation of this quote in the main text.

40. Cynthia Deitering, "The Postnatural Novel: Toxic Consciousness in Fiction of the 1980s," *The Ecocriticism Reader: Landmarks in Literary Ecology*, ed. Cheryll Glotfelty and Harold Fromm (Athens, GA: The University of Georgia Press, 1996), 196–203.

41. Gioconda Belli, *Waslala: Memorial del futuro* (Managua: anamá ediciones, 1996). At this time, space does not permit me to examine this text in great detail. All translations from this text into English are mine.

42. See Dana Alston and Nicole Brown, "Global Threats to People of Color," in *Confronting Environmental Racism*, 179–194. According to these environmentalists, El Salvador is "[o]ne of the most ecologically deteriorated countries in the Americas," the result of decades of land scorching and bombings by military forces sponsored by the United States. They claim that "[b]y 1989, the Salvadoran air force had dropped more than 3,000 tons of U.S.-made bombs on the countryside" (180). In Guatemala, the population displaced by war destroyed much vegetation in their effort to seek cover, while the government used destructive scorch-land tactics against them as well. (181). In this article, the authors also discuss the global waste trade, which informs my own reading of Gioconda Belli's novel *Waslala*.

43. Deitering, "The Postnatural Novel," 197.

Bibliographic Essay

This bibliographic essay is meant to supplement the references provided by individual contributors in the notes to each of their chapters. It is divided into roughly chronological sections relating to the following (often overlapping) themes considered in this book: General Sources on U.S.–Latin American Relations; Intervention; Democracy; Human Rights; U.S.–Latin American Military Relations; Globalization; and Nongovernmental Organizations. A final section includes websites relevant to U.S.–Latin American relations.

GENERAL SOURCES ON U.S.–LATIN AMERICAN RELATIONS

Political scientists, historians, philosophers, journalists, sociologists, economists, and literary scholars and writers alike provide useful insights into the history of U.S.–Latin American relations. For general bibliographies on U.S.–Latin American relations, see John A. Britton, *The United States and Latin America: A Select Bibliography* (Lanham, MD: Scarecrow Press; Pasadena, CA: Salem Press, 1997); Michael C. Meyer, comp., *Supplement to a Bibliography of United States–Latin American Relations since 1910* (Lincoln: University of Nebraska Press, 1979); and David F. Trask, Michael C. Meyer, and Roger R. Trask, eds., *A Bibliography of United States–Latin American Relations since 1810* (Lincoln: University of Nebraska Press, 1968). A comprehensive historical reference work is David Shavit, *The United States in Latin America: A Historical Dictionary* (New York: Greenwood Press, 1992). The Hispanic Division of The Library of Congress, *Handbook of Latin American Studies*, available online at http://lcweb2.loc.gov/hlas/, provides an invaluable guide to select, annotated bibliographic references relating to ongoing scholarly production about Latin America.

Peter H. Smith, *Talons of the Eagle: Dynamics of U.S.–Latin American Relations*, 2nd. ed. (Oxford: Oxford University Press, 1999) provides a conceptual framework for analyzing the pattern of inter-American relations since the late eighteenth century. Lars Schoultz, *Beneath the United States: A History of U.S. Policy Toward Latin America* (Cambridge: Harvard University Press, 1998) explores the attitudes underlying U.S. policies toward Latin America from the early nineteenth century on. Although a bit dated, Federico G. Gil, *Latin American–United States Relations* (New York: Harcourt Brace Jovanovich, Inc., 1971) provides a comprehensive overview of the events, institutions, and issues that affected the course of U.S.–Latin American relations since Latin America secured its independence from Spain in the early nineteenth century until the period of the Alliance for Progress. Leopoldo Zea, *The Role of the Americas in History*, ed. Amy A. Oliver, trans. Sonja Karsen (Savage, MD: Rowman & Littlefield, 1992) offers a philosophical assessment that places the Americas within a broader international context. An eloquent literary text that links Latin American underdevelopment to the development of global capitalism over five centuries is Eduardo Galeano, *Las venas abiertas de América Latina* [*Open Veins of Latin America*] (México, DF: Siglo Veintiuno Editores, 1971). Robert H. Holden and Eric Zolov, *Latin America and the United States: A Documentary History* (New York: Oxford University Press, 2000) includes essential documents for the study of U.S.–Latin American relations. James D. Cockcroft, *Latin America: History, Politics, and U.S. Policy*, 2nd ed. (Chicago: Nelson-Hall Publishers, 1996) approaches the history of U.S.–Latin American relations from a variety of disciplines.

For the relationship of the Americas during their respective revolutionary periods of the eighteenth and nineteenth centuries, see Lester Langley, *Americas in the Age of Revolution, 1750–1850* (New Haven: Yale University Press, 1996); James E. Lewis, *The American Union and the Problem of Neighborhood: The United States and the Collapse of the Spanish Empire, 1783–1829* (Chapel Hill: University of North Carolina Press, 1998); and the well-researched Charles Carroll Griffin, *The United States and the Disruption of the Spanish Empire, 1810–1822* (New York: Columbia University Press, 1937). William R. Manning, ed., *Diplomatic Correspondence of the United States Concerning the Independence of the Latin American Nations*, 3 vols. (New York: Carnegie Endowment for International Peace, 1925) provides telling evidence of U.S. attitudes toward Latin America during the latter's efforts to achieve independence from Spain from 1809–1830. Thomas M. Leonard, ed., *United States–Latin American Relations, 1850–1903: Establishing a Relationship* (Tuscaloosa: University of Alabama Press, 1999) includes a series of essays that focus on the relationships between the United States and individual Latin American countries in the second half of the nineteenth century. Valerie J. Fifer, *United States Perceptions of Latin America, 1850–1930: A "New West" South of Capricorn?* (Manchester; NY: Manchester University Press; distr. St. Martin's Press; 1991) analyzes images of Latin America in the eighty years following the 1848 signing of the Treaty of Guadalupe Hidalgo, by which Mexico's north became the current southwest of the United States. On U.S. relations with Mexico in the nineteenth and twentieth centuries, see Clint E. Smith, *Inevitable Partnership: Understanding Mexico–U.S. Relations* (Boulder, CO: Lynne Rienner Publishers, 2000).

The end of the nineteenth century brought with it a realignment of relations between the North and South. Matthew Frye Jacobson, *Barbarian Virtues: The United States Encounters Foreign Peoples at Home and Abroad, 1876–1917* (New York: Hill and Wang, 2000) explores the linkages between immigration and empire building at that time. Walter LaFeber, *The New Empire: An Interpretation of American Expansion, 1860–1898* (Ithaca: Cornell University Press, 1963) provides an assessment of the economic interests favoring U.S. expansion overseas; and Emily S. Rosenberg, *Spreading the American Dream: American Economic and Cultural Expansion, 1890–1945* (New York: Hill and Wang, 1982) analyzes U.S. economic and cultural expansion in the late nineteenth and early twentieth century. Thomas Schoonover, *The United States and Central America, 1860–1911* (Durham, NC: Duke University Press, 1991) analyzes the early development of economic ties between the United States and Central America.

For overall assessments of U.S.–Latin American relations during the twentieth century, see Mark T. Gilderhus, *The Second Century: U.S.–Latin American Relations since 1889* (Wilmington, DE: Scholarly Resources, 2000); Ivan Musicant, *The Banana Wars: A History of United States Military Intervention in Latin America from the Spanish-American War to the Invasion of Panama* (New York: Macmillan Publishing Co., 1990); and Cole Blasier, *The Hovering Giant: U.S. Responses to Revolutionary Change in Latin America, 1910–1985*, rev. ed. (Pittsburgh: University of Pittsburgh Press, 1985). On the impact and legacy of U.S. policies in the Caribbean, see Lester D. Langley, *The United States and the Caribbean in the Twentieth Century* (Athens, GA: University of Georgia Press, 1980).

Several excellent collections of essays on twentieth century U.S.–Latin American relations focus on culture as a nexus and manifestation of U.S. imperialism. See especially Gilbert Joseph, Catherine LeGrand, and Ricardo Salvatore, eds., *Close Encounters of Empire: Writing the Cultural History of U.S.–Latin American Relations* (Durham, NC: Duke University Press, 1998); Amy Kaplan and Donald E. Pease, eds., *Cultures of United States Imperialism* (Durham, NC: Duke University Press, 1993); and James Dunkerley, *Warriors and Scribes: Essays on the History and Politics of Latin America* (New York: Verso, 2000). On Latin American cultural history in general, see Leslie Bethell, ed., *A Cultural History of Latin America: Literature, Music, and the Visual Arts in the 19th and 20th Centuries* (New York: Cambridge University Press, 1998).

General studies of U.S. policies toward Latin America at the end of the twentieth century abound, and many establish new frameworks for consideration of these relationships—via the perspective of human rights, the multiplicity of actors in the policy process, the exposure of covert relations, broadened definitions of national security, the increased integration of the hemisphere, and the effects of globalization. The end of the Cold War in the final decade of the twentieth century ushered in significant changes in U.S.–Latin American relations, which produced numerous volumes dedicated to reconceptualizing the relationship between the United States and Latin America. Jonathan Hartlyn, Lars Schoultz, and Augusto Varas, eds., *The United States and Latin America in the 1990s: Beyond the Cold War* (Chapel Hill: University of North Carolina Press, 1992) analyzes the impact of the new configuration of actors, issues, and international realities of the post-Cold War era on U.S. policies toward Latin America. Victor Bulmer-Thomas and James Dunkerley, eds., *The United States and Latin America: The New Agenda* (London: Institute of Latin American Studies and Cambridge, MA: David Rockefeller Center for Latin American Studies,

Harvard University, 1999) provides European perspectives on inter-American agendas on democracy, drugs, immigration, and trade policies. Inter-American Dialogue, *The Americas at the Millennium: A Time of Testing* (Washington, DC: IAD, 1999) analyzes the relationship between democratic politics and liberal economic policies at the end of the twentieth century. Don Coerver and Linda Hall, *Tangled Destinies: Latin America and the United States* (Albuquerque: University of New Mexico Press, 1999) analyzes the asymmetric economic, military, and political relations between the United States and its Latin American neighbors since the birth of the republics of the Western Hemisphere, with particular emphasis on more recent issues of intervention, debt, NAFTA, immigration, and drugs.

The 1980s were marked by a highly politicized debate over U.S. intervention in Latin America and support for repressive military regimes in the Southern Cone, as well as a debt crisis and recession felt throughout much of Latin America. Many books from these years analyzed U.S.–Latin American relations through the lens of democratic discourse and practices. Guy E. Poitras, *The Ordeal of Hegemony: The United States and Latin America* (Boulder, CO: Westview Press, 1990) analyzes the decline of U.S. hegemony in Latin America in the 1980s, particularly as it is related to questions of the foreign debt, Latin American assertiveness, and competition from external adversaries. Michael J. Kryzanek, *Leaders, Leadership, and U.S. Policy in Latin America* (Boulder, CO: Westview Press, 1992) treats U.S. policies regarding issues of drugs, debt, development, and intervention as they relate to different political regimes and leaders in Latin America.

INTERVENTION

The war of 1898 initiated a new paradigm for U.S.–Latin American relations in the twentieth century marked by intervention, often in the name of democracy and human rights. Numerous works were published in the wake of the 100-year anniversary of the war. The bibliography on the war itself is vast. See Louis A. Pérez, Jr., *The War of 1898: The United States & Cuba in History & Historiography* (Chapel Hill, NC: University of North Carolina Press, 1998); and the bibliographical essay in Virginia M. Bouvier, ed., *Whose America? The War of 1898 and the Battles to Define the Nation* (Westport, CT: Praeger, 2001). For cartoons of the war that provide images of and insights into national moods of the period, as well as the legacies of the war in contemporary artistic production, see Manuel Méndez Saavedra, *1898: La guerra hispanoamericana en caricaturas* (San Juan, PR: Comisión Puertorriqueña para la Celebración del Quinto Centenario del Descubrimiento de América y Puerto Rico [Gráfica Metropolitana], 1992); and *Cien años después . . . Cien artistas contemporáneos: reflexiones en torno a la presencia norteamericana* (San Juan, PR: Comité de los Cien, 1998).

A range of direct and indirect U.S. military, political, and economic interventions characterized U.S.–Latin American relations in the decades following the War of 1898. During this time, the United States gradually installed protectorate governments in Cuba, Panama, Nicaragua, Haiti, and the Dominican Republic, and intervened militarily to protect its investments in the region. See David Healy, *Drive to Hegemony: The United States in the Caribbean, 1898–1917* (Madison: University of Wisconsin Press, 1988); Dana G. Munro, *Intervention and Dollar Diplomacy in the*

Caribbean, 1900–1921 (Princeton: Princeton University Press, 1964); Lester D. Langley, *The Banana Wars: An Inner History of American Empire, 1900–1934* (Lexington, KY: University Press of Kentucky, 1983); and David Healy, *Gunboat Diplomacy in the Wilson Era: The U.S. Navy in Haiti, 1915–1916* (Madison: University of Wisconsin Press, 1976). On U.S. interventions in the Dominican Republic and the legacies of those interventions, see Bruce J. Calder, *The Impact of Intervention: The Dominican Republic During the U.S. Occupation of 1916–1924* (Austin: University of Texas Press, 1984). Juan José Arévalo, *The Shark and the Sardines,* trans. June Cobb and Raul Osegueda (New York: L. Stuart, 1961) is a powerful allegory by a Guatemalan intellectual and statesman. Arévalo uses U.S. intervention in Nicaragua at the beginning of this century as the basis for an engaging discussion of power politics, the nature of "democratic" institutions, and the political/economic context within which U.S. intervention in the Caribbean and the flouting of international conventions occurred.

For an analysis of the economic role of the United States in Latin America and the impact of American corporate culture on Latin American societies in the first part of the twentieth century, see Thomas O'Brien, *The Revolutionary Mission: American Enterprise in Latin America, 1900–1945* (New York: Cambridge University Press, 1996). Of special interest on the inter-war period is Michael L. Krenn, *U.S. Policy toward Economic Nationalism in Latin America, 1917–1929* (Wilmington, DE: SR Books, 1990), which examines economic interests and social movements in Latin America in the years between the two world wars. On U.S. policies toward Nicaragua in the period, see William Kamman, *A Search for Stability: United States Policy toward Nicaragua, 1925–1933* (Chicago: University of Notre Dame Press, 1968). For the same period on U.S.–Caribbean relations, see Dana G. Munro, *The United States and the Caribbean Republics, 1921–1933* (Princeton: Princeton University Press, 1974); and Hans Schmidt, *The United States Occupation of Haiti, 1915–1934* (New Brunswick: Rutgers University Press, 1971). On U.S.–Mexican relations, see Linda B. Hall, *Oil, Banks, and Revolution: Mexico and the United States, 1917–1924* (Austin: University of Texas Press, 1995); Lorenzo Meyer, *Mexico and the United States in the Oil Controversy, 1917–1942* (Austin: University of Texas Press, 1977); Lorenzo Meyer, *Los grupos de presión extranjeros en el México revolucionario, 1910–1940,* (Tlatelolco, Mex.: Secretaría de Relaciones Exteriores, 1973); and Robert E. Quirk, *An Affair of Honor: Woodrow Wilson and the Occupation of Vera Cruz* (New York: McGraw-Hill, 1962). On U.S.–Dominican relations, see Eric Paul Roorda, *The Dictator Next Door: The Good Neighbor Policy and the Trujillo Regime in the Dominican Republic, 1930–1945* (Durham, NC: Duke University Press, 1998).

U.S. intervention early in the twentieth century spawned an anti-imperialist movement in both the United States and Latin America. See Philip S. Foner and Richard C. Winchester, eds., *The Anti-Imperialist Reader: A Documentary History of Anti-Imperialism in the United States* (NY: Holmes & Meier Publishers, Inc., 1984); and Richard V. Salisbury, *Anti-Imperialism and International Competition in Central America, 1920–1929* (Wilmington, DE: SR Books, 1989). Erasmo Dumpierra, "El papel de las ligas antimperialistas en la lucha contra el imperialismo norteamericano," *Universidad de La Habana* [Cuba] 223 (1984): 212–26 examines the development and activities of anti-imperialist leagues in Latin America in the period between the two world wars, and their efforts to undermine U.S. hegemony in the region.

On the impact of World War II on U.S.–Latin American relations, see R.A. Humphreys, *Latin America and the Second World War, Volume One: 1939–1942* and *Latin America and the Second World War, Volume Two: 1942–1945* (London: Published for the Institute of Latin American Studies, University of London by Athlone; Atlantic Highlands, NJ: distr. Humanities Press, 1981, 1982); and Leslie Bethell and Ian Roxborough, eds., *Latin America between the Second World War and the Cold War, 1944–48* (New York: Cambridge University Press, 1992).

Within the literature on U.S.–Latin American relations, a number of excellent studies focus on notions and practices of intervention in the period since World War II. Martha L. Cottam, *Images and Intervention: U.S. Policies in Latin America* (Pittsburgh: University of Pittsburgh Press, 1994) considers the various worldviews of U.S. policymakers and uses case studies of intervention and nonintervention to theorize about the impact of images on the selection and timing of U.S. policies toward Latin America. She relates the various kinds of interventions prevalent from the 1950s to the 1980s to the dominant images U.S. policymakers held of Latin Americans, particularly in the context of shifting relations between the United States and the Soviet Union and increasing Latin American economic dependence. She analyzes the cases of Guatemala, the Bay of Pigs, Chile, Peru, and Central America, and discusses the range of military, political, and economic interventions considered, adopted, or rejected in each case. For a general, if somewhat dated, study of U.S. intervention, see C. Neale Ronning, ed., *Intervention in Latin America* (New York: Alfred A. Knopf, 1970); and the assessments in Peter J. Schraeder, ed., *Intervention in the 1980s: U.S. Foreign Policy in the Third World* (Boulder, CO: Lynne Rienner Publishers, 1989). For a broader discussion of the political, historical, and legal issues of intervention, see Laura W. Reed and Carl Kaysen, eds., *Emerging Norms of Justified Intervention* (Cambridge, MA: American Academy of Arts and Sciences, 1993).

The literature on particular interventions is abundant. On the U.S. overthrow of the Arbenz government in Guatemala in 1954, see Richard H. Immerman, *The CIA in Guatemala: The Foreign Policy of Intervention* (Austin: University of Texas Press, 1982); Piero Gleijeses, *Shattered Hope: The Guatemalan Revolution and the United States, 1944–54* (Princeton: Princeton University Press, 1991); and José M. Aybar de Soto, *Dependency and Intervention: The Case of Guatemala in 1954* (Boulder, CO: Westview Press, 1978). For a popularized journalistic account of the coup, the United Fruit Company, and U.S. corporate interests in Guatemala, see Stephen C. Schlesinger and Stephen Kinzer, *Bitter Fruit: The Untold Story of the American Coup in Guatemala* (Cambridge: Harvard University Press, 1999). See also Paul Dosal, *Doing Business with the Dictators: A Political History of United Fruit in Guatemala, 1899–1944* (Wilmington, DE: Scholarly Resources, 1993). On U.S. intervention in the Dominican Republic in 1965, see Piero Gleijeses, *The Dominican Crisis: The 1965 Constitutionalist Revolt and the American Intervention* (Baltimore: Johns Hopkins University Press, 1978); Jerome Slater, *Intervention and Negotiation: The United States and the Dominican Revolution* (New York: Harper & Row, 1970); and Abraham F. Lowenthal, *The Dominican Intervention* (1972; reprint, Baltimore: The Johns Hopkins University Press, 1995).

Central America, which U.S. academics had historically neglected, came into its own as a subject beginning in the 1980s, partially in answer to U.S. policies that consistently placed Latin America within a context of the hegemonic struggle for control between the USSR and the United States. As Central America claimed the attention and dollars of U.S. policymakers, a cohort of committed scholars sought to understand and document both the roots of conflict in Central America (which was increasingly seen as unrelated to the shadow of the Cold War) and the trajectory and consequences of U.S. policies in the region. Many of these studies pushed for changes in U.S. policies toward the region and analyzed the implications of U.S. intervention for democratic practices abroad and at home. For a discussion of the economic and social factors behind the revolutionary movements in Central America, see Walter LaFeber, *Inevitable Revolutions: The United States in Central America* (New York: W.W. Norton & Company, 1983); and John A. Booth and Thomas W. Walker, *Understanding Central America*, 3rd ed. (Boulder, CO: Westview, 1999). Cynthia Arnson, *Crossroads: Congress, the President, and Central America, 1976–1993*, 2nd. ed. (University Park: Pennsylvania State University Press, 1993) provides an invaluable look at policy-making and tensions inside and between different branches of the U.S. government, as does William M. LeoGrande, *Our Own Backyard: The United States in Central America, 1977–1992* (Chapel Hill: University of North Carolina Press, 1998). Other studies of this period of U.S.–Central American relations include Gabriel Aguilera, Abelardo Morales, and Carlos Sojo, *Centroamérica: de Reagan a Bush* (San José, Costa Rica: FLACSO, 1991); Adam Isacson, *Altered States: Security and Demilitarization in Central America* (Washington, DC: Center for International Policy, 1997); Robert Leiken and Barry Rubin, eds., *The Central American Crisis Reader* (New York: Summit Books, 1987); Morris Blachman, William M. LeoGrande, and Kenneth Sharpe, *Confronting Revolution: Security through Diplomacy in Central America* (New York: Pantheon Books, 1986); and Michael McClintock, *Instruments of Statecraft: U.S. Guerrilla Warfare, Counterinsurgency, and Counter-terrorism, 1940–1990* (New York: Pantheon Books, 1992). For the history of the Central American region, Ralph Lee Woodward, Jr., *Central America: A Nation Divided*, 3rd ed. (New York: Oxford University Press, 1999) continues to be a classic text. On the role of Central American intellectuals, see the special issue, "Communal Strategies and Intellectual Transitions: Central America Prepares for the 21st Century," *Latin American Perspectives* 24, no. 1 (March 1997).

Since the 1980s, many studies have been published on human rights, democracy, and U.S. policies toward individual Central American countries. On El Salvador, see The United Nations, *De la locura a la esperanza, la guerra de 12 años en El Salvador: Informe de la Comisión de la Verdad para El Salvador* (New York: United Nations, 1993); Mario Lungo Uclés, trans. Amelia F. Shogan, *El Salvador in the 1980s: Counterinsurgency and Revolution* (Philadelphia: Temple University Press, 1996); Michael McClintock, *The American Connection, Volume I: State Terror and Popular Resistance in El Salvador* (London: Zed Books, Ltd., 1985); Tommy Sue Montgomery, *Revolution in El Salvador: From Civil Strife to Civil Peace*, 2nd ed. (Boulder, CO: Westview Press, 1995); Marvin E. Gettleman [et al.], ed., *El Salvador: Central America in the New Cold War* (New York: Grove Press, 1987); The National Security Archive, *El Salvador: The Making of U.S. Policy, 1977–1984* (Washington, DC and Alexandria, VA: The National Security Archive and Chadwyck-Healey Inc., 1989); and Martha Doggett, *A Death Foretold: The Jesuit Murders in El Salvador* (Washington, DC: Georgetown University Press, 1993). On Honduras, see Donald E. Schulz and Deborah Sundloff Schulz, *The United States, Honduras, and the Crisis in Central America* (Boulder, CO: Westview Press, 1994); and Darío A. Euraque, *Reinterpreting the Banana Republic: Region and State in Honduras, 1870–1972* (Chapel Hill: University of North Carolina Press, 1996). On U.S. policies in Nicaragua, see Morris H. Morley, *Washington, Somoza, and the Sandinistas: State and Regime in U.S. Policy toward Nicaragua, 1969–1981* (New York: Cambridge University Press, 1994); and E. Bradford Burns, *At War in Nicaragua: The Reagan Doctrine and the Politics of Nostalgia* (New York: Harper & Row, 1987). On Costa Rica, see Martha Honey, *Hostile Acts: U.S. Policy in Costa Rica in the 1980s* (Miami: University Press of Florida, 1994); and John A. Booth, *Costa Rica: Quest for Democracy* (Boulder, CO: Westview, 1999). On Guatemala, see Annette Baker Fox, *Guatemala, Human Rights, and U.S. Foreign Policy* (Philadelphia, PA: PEW Case Studies Center, 1989); Comisión para el Esclarecimiento Histórico (CEH), *Guatemala: Memoria del Silencio* (Guatemala City: CEH, 1999); Jennifer Schirmer, *The Guatemalan Military Project: A Violence Called Democracy* (Philadelphia: University of Pennsylvania Press, 1998); Washington Office on Latin America (WOLA), *Military Intelligence and Human Rights in Guatemala: The Archivo and the Case for Intelligence Reform* (Washington, DC: WOLA, March 1995); and [Proyecto Interdiocesano de] Recuperación de la Memoria Historica (REMHI), *Guatemala: Nunca Más* (Guatemala City: Oficina de Derechos Humanos del Arzobispado de Guatemala, 1998).

U.S. academic literature on Chile and the Southern Cone also flourished in the wake of U.S. interventions which brought to power or supported Latin American military regimes that unabashedly flouted their power. On the military coup in Uruguay in 1973, see Servicio Paz y Justicia-Uruguay, *Uruguay Nunca Más: Human Rights Violations, 1972–1985* (Philadelphia: Temple University Press, 1992); Washington Office on Latin America, *From Shadow into Sunlight: A Report on the 1984 Uruguayan Electoral Process* (Washington, DC: Washington Office on Latin America, 1985); and A. J. Langguth, *Hidden Terrors* (New York: Pantheon Books, 1978). Iain Guest, *Behind the Disappearances: Argentina's Dirty War Against Human Rights and the United Nations* (Philadelphia: University of Pennsylvania Press, 1990) is an exposé of collaboration between the Reagan administration and the Argentine government to prevent the United Nations from investigating military abuses in Argentina during the 1980s. On Argentina, see also Marguerite Feitlowitz, *A Lexicon of Terror: Argentina and the Legacies of Torture* (New York: Oxford University Press, 1998); and Alison Brysk, *The Politics of Human Rights in Argentina: Protest, Change, and Democratization* (Stanford: Stanford University Press, 1995). On Chile, see Armando Uribe Arce, *The Black Book of American Intervention in Chile*, trans. Jonathan Casart (Boston: Beacon Press, 1975); Cathy Schneider, *Shantytown Protest in Pinochet's Chile* (Philadelphia: Temple University Press, 1995); John Dinges and Saul Landau, *Assassination on Embassy Row* (New York: Pantheon Books, 1980); and Human Rights Watch, *When Tyrants Tremble: The Pinochet Case*, 11, no. 1 (B) (October 1999). On Brazil, see Kenneth P. Serbin, *Secret Dialogues: Church–State Relations, Torture, and Social Justice in Authoritarian Brazil* (Pittsburgh: University of Pittsburgh Press, 2000); and Phyllis R. Parker, *Brazil and the Quiet Intervention, 1964* (Austin: University of Texas Press, 1979). On Paraguay, see Virginia M. Bouvier, *Decline of the Dictator: Paraguay at a Crossroads* (Washington, DC: WOLA, 1988). On the legacies of dictatorships in the Southern Cone, see Mario Sznajder and Luis Roniger, *The Legacy of Human Rights Violations in the Southern Cone: Argentina, Chile, and Uruguay* (New York: Oxford University Press, 1999).

HUMAN RIGHTS

For overviews on human rights in Latin America, see Margaret E. Crahan, *Human Rights and Basic Needs in the Americas* (Washington, DC: Georgetown University Press, 1982); and Edward L. Cleary, *The Struggle for Human Rights in Latin America* (Westport, CT: Praeger, 1997). For an excellent study of the role of human rights in U.S. policy debates on Latin America, particularly during the Carter years, see Lars Schoultz, *Human Rights and United States Policies Toward Latin America* (Princeton: Princeton University Press, 1981). On the expansion of human rights to include women's rights, see Rebecca J. Cook, *Human Rights of Women: National and International Perspectives* (Philadelphia: University of Pennsylvania Press, 1994). Marjorie Agosín, ed., *A Map of Hope: Women's Writings on Human Rights: An International Literary Anthology* (New Brunswick, NJ: Rutgers University Press, 1999) includes essays, poems, memoirs, and excerpts on the topic from novels and diaries of prominent women writers such as Claribel Alegría, Isabel Allende, Rosario Castellanos, Carolina María de Jesus, Matilde Mellibovsky, Angelina Muñiz-Huberman, Ana Pizarro, and Luisa Valenzuela. On issues of cultural relativism and human rights, see Rhoda Howard, *Human Rights and the Search for Community* (Boulder, CO: Westview Press, 1995).

Within the human rights literature, a new genre of studies emerged in the 1990s dealing with the international and ethical legacies of earlier civil wars and dirty wars in Latin America. An excellent study of truth commissions with substantial information relevant to Latin America is Priscilla Hayner, *Unspeakable Truths: Confronting State Terror and Atrocity* (New York: Routledge, 2001). Ruti G. Teitel, *Transitional Justice* (New York: Oxford University Press, 2000) provides a legal framework for a discussion of the scope of remedies available for societies undergoing transitions from military to civilian rule. Complementary case studies may be found in Neil J. Kritz, ed., *Transitional Justice: How Emerging Democracies Reckon with Former Regimes,* 3 vols. (Washington, DC: United States Institute of Peace Press, 1995). See also A. James McAdams, ed., *Transitional Justice and the Rule of Law in New Democracies* (Notre Dame: University of Notre Dame Press, 1997); Martha Minow, *Between Vengeance and Forgiveness: Facing History after Genocide and Mass Violence* (Boston: Beacon Press, 1998); Aryeh Neier, *War Crimes: Brutality, Genocide, Terror and the Struggle for Justice* (New York: Times Books, 1998); Mark Osiel, *Mass Atrocity, Collective Memory, and the Law* (New Brunswick, NJ: Transaction, 1997); Steven R. Ratner and Jason S. Abrams, *Accountability for Human Rights and Atrocities in International Law: Beyond the Nuremberg Legacy* (Oxford: Clarendon Press, 1997); and Robert I. Rotberg and Dennis Thompson, eds., *Truth v. Justice: The Moral Efficacy of Truth Commissions in South Africa and Beyond* (Princeton, NJ: Princeton University Press, forthcoming).

Numerous other resources are available that place Latin America within a broader context of international human rights laws, frameworks, and practices. For studies of the growing international consensus on human rights issues, see Paul Gordon Lauren, *The Evolution of International Human Rights: Visions Seen* (Philadelphia: University of Pennsylvania Press, 1998); David P. Forsythe, *The Internationalization of Human Rights* (Lexington: Lexington Books, 1991); Jack Donnelly, *International Human Rights,* 2nd ed. (Boulder, CO: Westview Press, 1998). David P. Forsythe,

Human Rights in International Relations (New York: Cambridge University Press, 2000); and James W. Nickel, *Making Sense of Human Rights: Philosophical Reflections on the Universal Declaration of Human Rights* (Berkeley: University of California Press, 1987) provide excellent overviews of the foundations and implementation of human rights standards in international relations. For a history of the concept of human rights, see Michael Palumbo, *Human Rights: Meaning and History* (Malabar, FL: Robert E. Krieger Publishing Company, 1982); and Henry J. Steiner and Phillip Alston, eds., *International Human Rights in Context: Law, Politics, Morals* (New York: Clarendon Press, 1996). Micheline R. Ishay, ed., *The Human Rights Reader: Major Political Essays, Speeches, and Documents From the Bible to the Present* (London: Routledge, 1997) provides a selection of key human rights texts. Jack Donnelly, *Universal Human Rights in Theory and Practice* (Ithaca: Cornell University Press, 1989) summarizes the evolution of human rights regimes. Human Rights Watch, *Indivisible Human Rights: The Relation of Political and Civil Rights to Survival, Subsistence, and Poverty* (New York: Human Rights Watch, 1992) explores the re-lationship between the various political, social, and economic rights. For a discussion of humanitarian interventions, see Oliver Ramsbotham and Tom Woodhouse, *Humanitarian Intervention in Contemporary Conflict* (Cambridge: Polity Press, 1996); Lori Fisler Damrosch, ed., *Enforcing Restraint: Collective Intervention in Internal Conflicts* (New York: Council on Foreign Relations Press, 1993); and Thomas J. Weiss and Cindy Collins, *Humanitarian Challenges and Intervention: World Politics and the Dilemmas of Help* (Boulder, CO.: Westview Press, 1996).

On the United Nations, see Philip Alston, ed., *The United Nations and Human Rights: A Critical Appraisal* (Oxford: Clarendon Press, 1995); William J. Durch, *The Evolution of UN Peacekeeping: Case Studies and Comparative Analysis* (New York: St. Martin's Press, 1993); Adam Roberts and Benedict Kingsbury, eds., *United Nations, Divided World: The UN's Role in International Relations* (New York: Oxford University Press, 1993); Richard B. Lillich, ed., *Humanitarian Intervention and the United Nations* (Charlottesville, VA: University Press of Virginia, 1979); David J. Scheffer, Richard N. Gardner, and Gerald B. Helman, *Three Views on the Issue of Humanitarian Intervention: Post–Gulf War Challenges to the UN Collective Security System* (Washington, DC: United States Institute of Peace, 1992); and Thomas G. Weiss, David P. Forsythe, and Roger A. Coate, *The United Nations and Changing World Politics* (Boulder, CO: Westview Press, 1997). For a critique of United Nations' human rights activities, see Human Rights Watch, *The Lost Agenda: Human Rights and UN Field Operations* (New York: Human Rights Watch, 1993).

On the International Labor Organization, see Hector G. Bartolomei de la Cruz, Geraldo von Potobsky, and Lee Swepston, *The International Labor Organization: The International Standards System and Basic Human Rights* (Boulder, CO: West-view Press, 1996). Lance A. Compa and Stephen F. Diamond, eds., *Human Rights, Labor Rights, and International Trade* (Philadelphia: University of Pennsylvania Press, 1996) provides a solid overview of the issues. For studies of the OAS, see Francisco Villagrán de León, *The OAS and Democratic Development* [microform] (Washington, D.C.: United States Institute of Peace, 1992); and Viron P. Vaky and Heraldo Muñoz, *The Future of the Organization of American States* (New York: Twentieth Century Fund, 1993).

DEMOCRACY

A number of books analyze the nature of democratic practices and policies as they relate to Latin America. Thomas Farer, ed., *Beyond Sovereignty: Collectively Defending Democracy in the Americas* (Baltimore: Johns Hopkins Press, 1996) contains case studies on Chile, El Salvador, Haiti, Peru, Cuba, and Mexico by prominent scholars and policy experts and explores the ways in which, with increased frequency and tolerance, external actors—including governments, regional organizations, the United Nations, financial institutions, and nongovernmental institutions—are affecting democratic transitions and consolidation in Latin America and the Caribbean. Mark Peceny, *Democracy at the Point of Bayonets* (University Park: Pennsylvania State University Press, 1999) argues that both liberal ideals and security concerns have served as motives for U.S. military interventions in Latin America. Lars Schoultz, *Security, Democracy and Development in U.S.–L.A. Relations* (Coral Gables, FL: University of Miami, North–South Center Press; distr. Lynne Rienner, 1998); and Lars Schoultz, *National Security and United States Policy toward Latin America* (Princeton: Princeton University Press, 1987) are provocative studies of the shifting U.S. notions of democracy and national security and their implications for U.S. policies toward Latin America. Already slightly dated, but still relevant are Abraham F. Lowenthal, ed., *Exporting Democracy: The United States and Latin America, Themes and Issues* (Baltimore: Johns Hopkins University Press, 1991); and Thomas Carothers, *In the Name of Democracy: U.S. Policy toward Latin America in the Reagan Years* (Berkeley: University of California Press, 1991). Richard Newfarmer, *From Gunboats to Diplomacy: New U.S. Policies for Latin America* (Baltimore: Johns Hopkins University Press, 1984); and Harold Molineu, *U.S. Policy toward Latin America: From Regionalism to Globalism*, 2nd. ed. (Boulder, CO: Westview Press, 1990) analyze the shifting contours of U.S. policies over time. Laurence Whitehead, ed., *The International Dimensions of Democratization: Europe and the Americas* (Oxford: Oxford University Press, 1996) provides comparative material from a European perspective.

In the 1980s, much of the literature on democracy was explicitly or implicitly linked to economic questions concerning the foreign debt. On this topic, see Robert A. Pastor, ed., *Latin America's Debt Crisis* (Boulder, CO: Lynne Rienner, 1987); Stephany Griffith-Jones, *International Finance and Latin America* (New York: St. Martin's Press, 1984); Robert Wesson, ed., *Coping with the Latin American Debt* (Westport, CT: Praeger, 1988); Paul W. Drake, ed., *Money Doctors, Foreign Debts, and Economic Reforms in Latin America from the 1890s to the Present* (Wilmington: Scholarly Resources, 1994). On U.S. economic aid to Latin America, see Francis Adams, *Dollar Diplomacy: United States Economic Assistance to Latin America* (Burlington, VT: Ashgate, 2000).

Studies that link democratic paradigms and conditions in Latin America to U.S. policies and policy prescriptions from a variety of different political perspectives include Sidney Weintraub, *Development and Democracy in the Southern Cone: Imperatives for U.S. Policy in South America* (Washington, DC: Center for Strategic and International Studies, 2000); Howard J. Wiarda, *Democracy and its Discontents: Development, Interdependence, and U.S. Policy in Latin America* (Lanham, MD: Rowman & Littlefield Publishers, 1995); and James F. Petras, *América Latina: Pobreza de la democracia y democracia de la pobreza* (Rosario, Argentina: Ediciones Homo

Sapiens, 1995). Jorge I. Domínguez, *Authoritarian and Democratic Regimes in Latin America* (New York: Garland Pub., 1994) contains a variety of useful case studies. See also Jorge I. Domínguez, ed., *Constructing Democratic Governance: Latin America and the Caribbean in the 1990s* (Baltimore, MD: Johns Hopkins University Press, 1996); and Jorge I. Domínguez, ed., *International Security and Democracy: Latin America and the Caribbean in the Post-Cold War Era* (Pittsburgh: University of Pittsburgh Press, 1998). Sara Steinmetz, *Democratic Transition and Human Rights: Perspectives on U.S. Foreign Policy* (Albany: SUNY Press, 1994) analyzes U.S. foreign policies toward states in transition, including Nicaragua, Iran, and the Philippines.

On the history of democratic practice in Latin America, see Jonathan Hartlyn and Arturo Valenzuela, *Democracy in Latin America since 1930* (Durham, NC: Duke–University of North Carolina Program in Latin American Studies, 1994); and Scott Mainwaring and Arturo Valenzuela, *Politics, Society, and Democracy. Latin America* (Boulder, CO: Westview Press, 1998). Juan J. Linz and Arturo Valenzuela, eds., *The Failure of Presidential Democracy: The Case of Latin America,* vol. 2 (Baltimore: Johns Hopkins University Press, 1994) looks at regime type and democratic stability in varying political contexts in Latin America and is particularly concerned with the institutional dimensions of democratic stability. Roderic A. Camp, ed., *Democracy in Latin America: Patterns and Cycles* (Wilmington, DE: SR Books, 1996) explores the links between politics and development, the current economic integration between the United States and Latin America, and the cyclical history of democracy in Latin America. John Peeler, *Building Democracy in Latin America* (Boulder, CO: Lynne Rienner, 1998) studies the democratic transitions in the 1980s. On the disenchantment with democratic politics in the 1990s, see Rodolfo Cerdas Cruz, Juan Rial, and Daniel Zovatto, eds., *Elecciones y democracia en América Latina 1992–1996: urnas y desencanto político* (San José, Costa Rica: IIDH/CAPEL, 1998).

On the transitions from military to civilian rule, see Peter Lambert and Andrew Nickson, eds., *The Transition to Democracy in Paraguay* (Houndmills, Basingstroke, Hampshire [England] : Macmillan Press; New York: St. Martin's Press, 1997); and Edy Kaufman, *Uruguay in Transition: From Civilian to Military Rule* (New Brunswick, NJ: Transaction Books, 1979).

Studies of the peace negotiations between rebel and government forces in Central America are analyzed in Susanne Jonas, *Of Centaurs and Doves: Guatemala's Peace Process* (Boulder, CO: Westview Press, 2000); Cynthia Arnson, ed. *Comparative Peace Processes in Latin America* (Washington, DC: Woodrow Wilson Center Press; Stanford: Stanford University Press, 1999); The Aspen Institute, *Honoring Human Rights and Keeping the Peace: Lessons from El Salvador, Cambodia and Haiti* (Washington, DC: The Aspen Institute, 1995); and Edelberto Torres–Rivas and Gabriel Aguilera Peralta, *Desde el Autoritarismo a la Paz* (Guatemala: FLACSO, 1998).

On the future of democracy in Latin America, see Felipe Aguero and Jeffrey Stark, *Fault Lines of Democracy in Post-transition Latin America* (Coral Gables, FL: North–South Center Press/University of Miami, 1998); and Scott Mainwaring and Timothy R. Scully, eds., *Building Democratic Institutions: Party Systems in Latin America* (Stanford, CA: Stanford University Press, 1995). Other studies include Jorge I. Domínguez and Clarence Dillon, *The Future of Inter-American Relations* (New York: Routledge, 2000); and Jorge Nef, *América Latina frente al siglo XXI : la reestructuración del encuadre mundial y regional: las relaciones interamericanas frente al siglo*

XXI, 1st ed. (Quito, Ecuador: Facultad Latinoamericana de Ciencias Sociales, Sede Ecuador, 1994).

U.S.–LATIN AMERICAN MILITARY RELATIONS

Consideration of the Latin American military is essential in any study of the evolution of relationships across national borders. Edwin Lieuwen, *Arms and Politics in Latin America* (New York: Frederick A. Praeger, 1961) provides a good overview on the status of the Latin American armed forces and the history of U.S. policies toward the Latin American military. For a longer term vision on the military's role in Latin America, see Will Fowler, ed., *Authoritarianism in Latin America Since Independence* (Westport, CT: Greenwood Press, 1996); and Robert Wesson, *The Latin American Military Institution* (NY: Praeger, 1986).

A number of studies analyze the shifting role of the military within Latin American societies during the twentieth century. See especially Karen L. Remmer, *Military Rule in Latin America* (Boston: Unwin Hyman, 1989); David Collier, ed., *The New Authoritarianism in Latin America* (Princeton: Princeton University Press, 1979); John J. Johnson, *The Military and Society in Latin America* (Stanford, CA: Stanford University Press, 1964); and John Child, *Unequal Alliance: The Inter-American Military System, 1938–1979* (Boulder, CO: Westview Press, 1980). On the role of the military in Latin American politics, see Thomas L. Pearcy, *We Answer Only to God: Politics and the Military in Panama, 1903–1947* (Albuquerque: University of New Mexico Press, 1998); Brian Loveman, *For la Patria: Politics and the Armed Forces in Latin America* (Wilmington, DE: Scholarly Resources, 1998); Alain Rouquié, *The Military and the State in Latin America,* trans. Paul E. Sigmund (Berkeley: University of California Press, 1987); and Brian Loveman and Thomas M. Davies, Jr., eds., *The Politics of Anti-Politics: The Military in Latin America* (Lincoln: University of Nebraska Press, 1978).

On the relationships between the United States, Latin American military regimes, and political ideologies, see David F. Schmitz, *Thank God They're on Our Side: The United States and Right-Wing Dictatorships, 1921–1965* (Chapel Hill: University of North Carolina Press, 1999); Michael T. Klare and Peter Kornbluh, eds. *Low Intensity Warfare: Counterinsurgency, Proinsurgency, and Antiterrorism in the Eighties* (New York: Pantheon Books, 1988); and Michael T. Childress, *Effectiveness of U.S. Training Efforts in Internal Defense and Development: The Cases of El Salvador and Honduras* (Santa Monica, CA: Rand, 1995).

On the Latin American military's relationship to democratic transitions, see Bruce W. Farcau, *The Transition to Democracy in Latin America: The Role of the Military* (Westport, CT: Praeger, 1996); Richard L. Millet and Michael Gold-Biss, eds., *Beyond Praetorianism: The Latin American Military in Transition* (Miami: University of Miami, North–South Center Press; distr. Lynne Rienner, 1998); Gabriel Marcella, ed., *Warriors in Peacetime: The Military and Democracy in Latin America, New Directions for U.S. Policy* (Ilford, England; Portland, OR: F. Cass, 1994); and Louis Goodman, Johanna Mendelson, and Juan Rial, eds., *The Military and Democracy: The Future of Civil–Military Relations in Latin America* (Lexington, MA: Lexington Books, 1990).

A theme within the U.S.–Latin American military relations that merited special attention at the end of the twentieth and beginning of the twenty-first centuries was drugs and the militarization of the drug war in Latin America. Peter H. Smith, ed., *Drug Policy in the Americas* (Boulder, CO: Westview Press, 1992) contains articles on a variety of national, regional, and international policy perspectives (including sections on the OAS and UN roles) regarding drug production, usage, and abuse. See also Bruce M. Bagley and William O. Walker, eds., *Drug Trafficking in the Americas* (Coral Gables, FL: University of Miami, North–South Center; distr. Lynne Rienner, 1996); Bruce M. Bagley and J.G. Tokatlian, *Droga y dogma: La narcodiplomacia entre Estados Unidos y América Latina en la década de los ochenta y su proyección para los noventa*, Documentos Ocasionales C.E.I., no. 23 (September–October 1991); Eva Bertram, Morris Blachman, Kenneth Sharpe, and Peter Andreas, *Drug War Politics: The Price of Denial* (Berkeley: University of California Press, 1996); Elizabeth Joyce and Carlos Malamud, eds., *Latin America and the Multinational Drug Trade* (New York: St. Martin's Press, 1998); Michael C. Desch, Jorge I. Domínguez, and Andres Serbin, ed., *From Pirates to Drug Lords: The Post-Cold War Caribbean Security Environment* (Albany: State University of New York Press, 1998); and Carlos O. Suárez, *Globalización y "narcoterrorismo" en América Latina* (Buenos Aires: Ediciones de Nuestra América, 1996).

GLOBALIZATION

Numerous new studies focus on the challenges and dangers for Latin America presented by the diversification of economic and political ties. Noam Chomsky and Heinz Dieterich, *Latin America: From Colonization to Globalization* (New York: Ocean Press, 1999) analyzes globalization as a historical process which involved Latin America since it was "discovered" by Columbus, continued with U.S. domination of Latin America throughout the twentieth century, and deepened over time, as seen in Latin America's susceptibility to the Asian economic crisis of the 1990s. See also Joseph S. Tulchin and Ralph H. Espach, eds., *Latin America in the New International System* (Boulder, CO: Lynne Rienner, 2000); Gordon Mace and Jean-Philippe Thérien, eds., *Foreign Policy and Regionalism in the Americas* (Boulder, CO: Lynne Rienner, 1996); Charles Oman, *Globalisation and Regionalisation: The Challenge for Developing Countries* (Paris: OECD, 1994); Maurice Schiff and L. Alan Winters, *Regional Integration as Diplomacy*, World Bank Policy Research Paper no. 1801 (Washington, DC: World Bank, 1997); Joseph S. Tulchin and Ralph H. Espach, *Security in the Caribbean Basin: The Challenge of Regional Cooperation* (Boulder, CO: Lynne Rienner, 2000); and G. Pope Atkins, *Latin America and the Caribbean in the International System*, 4th ed. (Boulder, CO: Westview Press, 1998).

Max J. Castro, ed., *Free Markets, Open Societies, Closed Borders?: Trends in International Migration and Immigration Policy in the Americas* (Coral Gables, FL: North–South Center Press, 1999) includes essays analyzing the impact of immigration and immigration policies on both North–South and South–South relations, particularly in an era of free-trade agreements and hemispheric integration. Likewise, Frank Bonilla, ed., *Borderless Borders: U.S. Latinos, Latin Americans, and the Paradox of Interdependence* (Philadelphia: Temple University Press, 1998) contains a provocative selection of essays on the relationships between Latin Americans and Latinos, particularly with regard to immigration, identity, and globalization. On

Latino immigrants in the United States, see also Jorge Ramos, *La otra cara de América: Historias de los inmigrantes latinoamericanos que están cambiando a Estados Unidos* (México, DF: Grijalbo, 2000); and Marc R. Rosenblum, *At Home and Abroad: The Foreign and Domestic Sources of U.S. Immigration Policy* (Ph.D. diss., University of California, San Diego, 2000).

On the relationship between globalization and workers' rights in the Caribbean Basin, see Henry J. Frundt, *Trade Conditions and Labor Rights: U.S. Initiatives, Dominican and Central American Responses* (Miami: University Press of Florida, 1998). Ellen Meiksins Wood, Peter Meiksins, and Michael Yates, *Rising from the Ashes? Labor in the Age of "Global" Capitalism* (New York: Monthly Review Press, 1998) analyzes the changing composition of the working class, patterns of work under contemporary capitalism, and the relationship of race and gender to class.

Much of the analysis coming from Latin America questions the globalization paradigms and the excessive optimism regarding the effects of globalization. See Rosa María Marrero, *Las trampas de la globalización: paradigmas emancipatorios y nuevos escenarios en América Latina* (La Habana, Cuba; Galfisa: Editorial José Martí, 1999); Arturo Léon, *¿Globalización para quién?: ¡por un desarrollo global incluyente!* (México: Universidad Autónoma Metropolitana Xochimilco, 1999), which contains the papers from the 1998 Latin American Congress on Rural Sociology; Fabio López de la Roche and Hugo Fazio, *Globalización: incertidumbres y posibilidades: política, comunicación, cultura* (Santafé de Bogotá, Colombia: Tercer Mundo Editores; IEPRI, 1999); Klaus Liebig, *Will Globalization Help or Harm Latin America's Less Developed Countries?* (Göttingen: Ibero-Amerika-Institut für Wirtschaftsforschung, 1998), discussion paper no. 73; David Gertner, Paulo F. Bocater, and Ricardo P.C. Leal, *Regionalism and Globalization in Latin America, a Contradiction?* (Rio de Janeiro: Business Association of Latin American Studies, 1997); William Perry and Peter Wehner, eds., *The Latin American Policies of U.S. Allies: Balancing Global Interests and Regional Concerns* (New York: Praeger, 1985); Augusto Varas, *Latin American and Post-Cold War Globalization* (Madison: Global Studies Research Program, University of Wisconsin-Madison, 1993); Manfred Mols, Hengstenberg, Kohut, Sandner, Sangmeister, eds., *Cambio de paradigmas en América Latina: Nuevos impulsos, nuevos temores* (Caracas: Asociación Alemana de Investigación sobre América Latina; Fundación Friedrich Ebert; Editorial Nueva Sociedad, 1994); Eduardo Saxe Fernández, *El "globalismo democrático neoliberal" y la crisis latinoamericana* (Heredia, Costa Rica: Departamento de Filosofía and Escuela de Relaciones Internacionales, Universidad Nacional, 1996); and Jacques Chonchol, *¿Hacia dónde nos lleva la globalización? Reflexiones para Chile* (Santiago: LOM Ediciones: Universidad Arcis, 1999). Latin American Society of Studies on Latin America and the Caribbean, *América Latina e Caribe e os desafios da nova ordem mundial* (São Paulo, Brazil: Programa de Pós-Graduação em Integração de América Latina da Universidade de São Paulo, 1998) includes essays in Portuguese and Spanish on the challenges of globalization for Latin America and the Caribbean.

Juan E. Méndez, Guillermo O'Donnell, and Paulo Sérgio Pinheiro, eds., *The (Un)Rule of Law and the Underprivileged in Latin America* (Chicago: University of Notre Dame Press, 1999); and Víctor E. Tokman and Guillermo O'Donnell, eds., *Poverty and Inequality in Latin America: Issues and New Challenges* (Chicago: University of Notre Dame Press, 1998) include thought-provoking essays on the impact of globalization on poverty and inequality by scholars and activists from a range of disciplines, as does Douglas A. Chalmers, ed., *The New Politics of Inequality in Latin America: Rethinking Participation and Representation* (New York: Oxford University Press, 1997). William M. Loker, ed., *Globalization and the Rural Poor in Latin America* (Boulder, CO: Lynne Rienner, 1998) includes nine anthropological essays on the impact of globalization on different rural working communities in Latin America. John Sheahan, *Patterns of Development in Latin America: Poverty, Repression, and Economic Strategy* (Princeton, NJ: Princeton University Press, 1987) analyzes the persistence of poverty and economic inequality in Latin America, the nature of the relationship between Latin American countries and the global economy, and the relationship between the move toward market-oriented economic systems and political repression. Nancy Birdsall and Augusto de la Torre with Rachel Menezes, *Washington Contentious: Economic Policies for Social Equity in Latin America* (Washington, DC: The Carnegie Endowment for International Peace and The Inter-American Dialogue, 2001) analyzes current Latin American economic policies that address issues of poverty reduction and equity.

Studies of the economic, political, and social impact of globalization on Latin America include also Philip Oxhorn and Graciela Ducatenzeiler, eds., *What Kind of Market? What Kind of Democracy? Latin America in the Age of Neoliberalism* (University Park: Pennsylvania State University Press, 1998); Robert N. Gwynne, ed., *Globalization and Modernity* (New York: Oxford University Press, 1999); William C. Smith and Roberto Patricio Korzeniewicz, eds., *Politics, Social Change and Economic Restructuring in Latin America* (Miami: North–South Center Press; distr. Lynne Rienner, 1998); Jorge A. Lawton, *Privatization Amidst Poverty: Contemporary Challenges in Latin American Political Economy* (Coral Gables, FL: North–South Center, University of Miami, 1995); and Victorio Taccetti, *Constelación sur: América Latina frente a la globalización* (Buenos Aires: Fondo de Cultura Económica, 1997).

On the relationship between regionalization and globalization, see Arie Marcelo Kacowicz, *Regionalization, Globalization, and Nationalism: Convergent, Divergent, or Overlapping?* Working paper, no. 262 (Notre Dame, IN: The Helen Kellogg Institute for International Studies, 1988). On the globalization of trade, see Armando Di Filippo, *Regional Integration in Latin America, Globalization and South–South Trade* (Santiago, Chile: United Nations, 1998); Riordan Roett, ed., *Mercosur: Regional Integration, World Markets* (Boulder, CO: Lynne Rienner, 1999); and Rogelio Frigerio, *La integración regional: la nación, la región y la globalización* (San Salvador de Jujuy, Argentina: Universidad Nacional de Jujuy, 1997).

On regionalism and economic integration, see Richard L. Bernal, *Trade Blocks: A Regionally Specific Phenomenon or a Global Trend?* (Washington, DC: National Policy Association, 1997); William R. Cline and Enrique Delgado, *Economic Integration in Central America* (Washington, DC: Brookings Institution, 1978); George Irvin and Stuart Holland, *Central America: The Future of Economic Integration* (Boulder, CO: Westview Press, 1989); Francisco Rojas Aravena, ed., *Argentina, Brasil y Chile: integración y seguridad* (Caracas, Venezuela: Editorial Nueva Sociedad, 1999); and Richard Feinberg and Delia M. Boyulan, *Modular Multilateralism: North–South Economic Relations in the 1990s*, Policy Essay I (Washington, DC: Overseas Development Council, 1991).

Satya R. Pattnayak, ed., *Globalization, Urbanization, and the State: Selected Studies on Contemporary Latin America* (Lanham, MD: University Press of America, 1996) analyzes the relationships between economic growth, political legitimacy, and social development, and questions the capacity of economic globalization to foster free markets or democracy. Ernesto López, *Globalización y democracia* (Buenos Aires: Página 12: Red de Editoriales de Universidades Nacionales, 1998) explores the relationship between political culture and globalization. In the cultural realm, see José Rivero, *Educación y exclusión en América Latina: reformas en tiempos de globalización* (Lima: Tarea, 1999); and Roberto Donoso Torres, *Mito y educación: el impacto de la globalización en la educación en Latinoamérica* (Buenos Aires: Espacio, 1999).

A number of books examine the ramifications of the end of the Cold War and the impact of the emerging world order on developing nations, including those in Latin America. See Louise L'Estrange Fawcett and Yazid Sayigh, *The Third World Beyond the Cold War: Continuity and Change* (New York: Oxford University Press, 1999); and Francis Adams, Satya Dev Gupta, and Kidane Mengisteab, *Globalization and the Dilemmas of the State in the South* (New York: St. Martin's Press, 1999). Ippei Yamazawa, *Developing Economies in the Twenty-first Century: The Challenges of Globalization: Papers and Proceedings of the International Symposium on Developing Economies in the 21st Century* (Tokyo: Institute of Developing Economies, Japan External Trade Organization, 2000) includes a chapter on the challenges and dilemmas of globalization for Latin America, as well as comparative insights from Asian, African, and Middle East experiences. Björn Hettne, András Inotai, and Osvaldo Sunkel, eds., *The New Regionalism and the Future of Security and Development* (New York: St. Martin's Press, 2000) contains several chapters that deal with regional integration, security, and collective diplomacy in Latin America.

On Latin America's role in the world economy, see Alessandro Bonanno et al., *From Columbus to ConAgra: The Globalization of Agriculture and Food* (Lawrence, KS: University Press of Kansas, 1994), which includes essays on the globalization of the food system and the ramifications for Latin America's agricultural sector; Susan Kaufman Purcell and Françoise Simon, eds., *Europe and Latin America in the World Economy* (Boulder, CO: Lynne Rienner, 1994); and Peter Smith, ed., *The Challenge of Integration: Europe and the Americas* (New Brunswick, NJ: Transaction Publishers, 1993). John H. Coatsworth and Alan M. Taylor, eds., *Latin America and the World Economy Since 1800* (Cambridge, MA: Harvard University, David Rockefeller Center for Latin American Studies, 1998) includes a series of essays on Latin American development through the lens of economic analysis.

NONGOVERNMENTAL ORGANIZATIONS

The emergence of nongovernmental organizations and the "neo-globalized solidarity" began to be the focus of greater scholarly attention in the 1990s. For general studies on the role of the NGO sector in Latin America, see Carrie A. Meyer, *The Economics and Politics of NGOs in Latin America* (Westport, CT: Praeger, 1999); Charles Reilly, *New Paths to Democratic Development in Latin America: The Rise of NGO-Municipal Collaboration* (Boulder, CO: Lynne Rienner, 1995); and The Inter-American Foundation, *A Guide to NGO Directories: How to Find Over 20,000 Nongovernmental Organizations in Latin America and the Caribbean*, 2nd ed. (Arlington, VA: The Inter-American Foundation, 1995). A good overview of the issues facing NGOs may be found in Susanne Jonas and Edward J. Jonas, *Latin*

America Faces the Twenty-first Century: Reconstructing a Social Justice Agenda (Boulder, CO: Westview Press, 1994).

A burgeoning scholarship is developing that analyzes the relationship of the NGO sector to democratization in Latin America. See Geraldine Lievesley, *Democracy in Latin America: Mobilization, Power, and the Search for a New Politics* (Manchester; NY: Manchester University Press; New York: distr. St. Martin's Press, 1999); Arturo Escobar and Sonia E. Alvarez, eds., *The Making of Social Movements in Latin America: Identity, Strategy, and Democracy* (Boulder, CO: Westview Press, 1992); Elizabeth Jelin and Eric Hershberg, eds., *Constructing Democracy: Human Rights, Citizenship, and Society in Latin America* (Boulder, CO: Westview Press, 1996); and Richard E. Fineberg and Robin L. Rosenberg, eds., *Civil Society and the Summit of the Americas: The 1998 Santiago Summit* (Coral Gables, FL: North–South Center Press at the University of Miami, 1999). See also Tania Palencia Prado, *Peace in the Making: Civil Groups in Guatemala* (London: Catholic Institute for International Relations, 1996); Chetan Kumar, *Building Peace in Haiti* (Boulder, CO: Lynne Rienner, 1999); and Christopher Welna, *Reform of Justice and the Proliferation of Human Rights: Non-governmental Organizations in Mexico (1977–1994)* (México, DF: División de Estudios Internacionales, Centro de Investigación y Docencia Económicas, 1997). For more general studies, see Margaret E. Keck and Kathryn Sikkink, *Activists Beyond Borders: Advocacy Networks in International Politics* (Ithaca: Cornell University Press, 1998); and Jackie Smith, Charles Chatfield, and Ron Pagnucco, eds., *Transnational Social Movements and Global Politics: Solidarity Beyond the State* (Syracuse: Syracuse University Press, 1997).

On the role of women within these sectors, see Jane S. Jaquette et al., "Women and the Transition to Democracy: The Impact of Political and Economic Reform in Latin America" (Washington, DC: Latin American Program, Wilson Center, 1994); Jane S. Jaquette and Sharon L. Wolchik, *Women and Democracy: Latin America and Central and Eastern Europe* (Baltimore, MD: Johns Hopkins University Press, 1998); Adriana Santa Cruz, Viviana Erazo, Graciela Torricelli, and Tete Valdovinos, *Mujer y democracia* (Santiago, Chile: Instituto Latinoamericano de Estudios Transnacionales, Unidad de Comunicación Alternativa de la Mujer, [1985?]); and Dorrit K. Marks, ed., *Women and Grass Roots Democracy in the Americas* (New Brunswick, NJ: Transaction Publishers, 1993). On indigenous sectors and the state, see Donna Lee Van Cott, ed., *Indigenous Peoples and Democracy in Latin America* (New York: St. Martin's Press in association with the Inter-American Dialogue, 1994).

On the development of NGO networks in the United States, see David F. Ronfeldt and Cathryn L. Thorup, *North America in the Era of Citizen Networks: State, Society, and Security* (Santa Monica, CA: RAND, 1995). On NGOs in Europe, see Christian Freres, ed., *La co-operación de las sociedades civiles de la Unión Europea con América Latina* (Madrid: AIETI, 1998).

On NGOs and human rights, see Thomas G. Weiss and Leon Gordenker, eds., *NGOs, the UN, and Global Governance* (Boulder, CO: Lynne Rienner, 1996); William Korey, *NGOs and the Universal Declaration of Human Rights: A Curious Grapevine* (New York: St. Martin's Press, 1998). On the peacemaking role of NGOs, see Emily MacFarquar, Robert I. Rotberg, and Martha A. Chen, *Non-governmental Organizations, Early Warning, and Preventive Diplomacy* (Cambridge, MA: World Peace Foundation, 1995); Kevin M. Cahill, ed., *Preventive Diplomacy: Stopping Wars Before They Start* (New York: Basic Books, 1996); Henry J. Steiner, *Diverse Partners:*

Non Governmental Organizations and the Human Rights Movement (Cambridge, MA: Harvard Law College, 1991); and Ernst A. Haas, *Human Rights and International Action* (Stanford: Stanford University Press, 1970). Tommie Sue Montgomery, ed., *Peacemaking and Democratization in the Western Hemisphere: Multilateral Missions* (Boulder, CO: Lynne Rienner, 2000) includes a multitude of case studies of multilateral electoral, political, military, and peacemaking and peace-building missions in Latin America and the Caribbean. Howard J. Tolley, Jr., *The International Commission of Jurists: Global Advocates for Human Rights* (Philadelphia: University of Pennsylvania Press, 1994) analyzes the role of that Geneva-based NGO. On NGOs and the UN, see Peter Willets, ed., *"The Conscience of the World": The Influence of Non-Governmental Organizations in the UN System* (Washington, DC: Brookings, 1996).

WEB RESOURCES

One of the consequences of globalization has been the increased accessibility of a wide range of organizational resources that can now be found online. Web pages of interest are available for the following human rights and non-governmental organizations: Amnesty International (http://www.amnesty.org/); Human Rights Watch (http://open.igc.org//hrw/home.html); International Committee of the Red Cross (http://www.icrc.ch/); El Grupo de Trabajo Latinoamericano (http://www.igc.apc.org/lawg/); Washington Office on Latin America (http://www.wola.org); Lawyers Committee for Human Rights (http://www.lchr.org/); Center for International Policy (http://www.us.net/cip/index.htm); Institute for Policy Studies (http://www.ips-dc.org/); North American Congress on Latin America (gopher://gopher.igc.apc.org:70/11/pubs/nacla.gopher); Human Rights Quarterly Online Journal (http://muse.jhu.edu/demo/human_rights_quarterly); The Americas Society (http://www.americas-society.org); and the Council of the Americas (http://www.counciloftheamericas.org). The Latin American Working Group's invaluable guide to the U.S. foreign aid process, *Just the Facts: A Civilian's Guide to U.S. Defense and Security Assistance to Latin America and the Caribbean*, is available online at http://www.ciponline.org/facts.htm. Many of the reports of the national Latin American Truth Commissions are available at the United States Institute of Peace Library website at www.usip.org/library/truth.html.

Additional statistical information and analysis may be found at sites for Amnesty International country reports (http://www.oil.ca/amnesty/ailib/countries/); the Almanac for the Latin American Air Forces (http://www.cdsar.af.mil/almanac/almanac.html); DIANA–International Human Rights Database (http://www.law.uc.edu:81/Diana/index.html); Geographic Guide to Latin American Regional Security Resources (http://cfcsc.dnd.ca/links/milorg/indexa.html); Heads of State and Cabinet (gopher://summit.fiu.edu:70/11/Background/Heads); International Economic Development Resources (http://www.contact.org/intdev.htm); Latin American Statistical Sources (http://latino.lib.cornell.edu/latstat2.html); Military Expenditure Figures, SIPRI (http://www.sipri.se/projects/Milex/Introduction.html); North America Project: International Bills of Rights (http://worldpolicy.org/americas/); Summit of the Americas Center (http://summit.fiu.edu/); Summit Conference on Sustainable Development Bolivia (http://www.oas.org/EN/

PROG/BOLIVIA/summit.htm); and World Crime Survey Data United Nations (http://www.ifs.univie.ac.at/uncjin/wcs.html).

The Latin American Network Information Center at the Institute of Latin American Studies of the University of Texas (http://lanic.utexas.edu/) provides extensive links to news and analysis from Latin America, as well as to the Association of Research Libraries (ARL) Latin Americanist Research Resources Project's searchable Web database (http://lanic.utexas.edu/project/arl/) with access to the tables of contents of more than 500 journals published in Latin America. A political database of the Americas managed by the Georgetown University Center for Latin American Studies with the collaboration of the Organization of American States is available at http://www.georgetown.edu/pdba/. For economic information on Latin America, see the Economic Commission on Latin America's site at http://www.eclac.org/. Links to position and background papers relating to U.S. policies on Latin America may be found at websites for The Inter-American Dialogue (http://www.iadialog.org/main.html); the Heritage Foundation (http://www.heritage.org/); the Woodrow Wilson International Center for Scholars (http://wwics.si.edu/); and the University of California at Berkeley's Center for Latin American Studies (http://garnet. berkeley.edu:7001/).

For international organizations that deal with Latin America, see the web pages of the Inter-American Development Bank (http://www.iadb.org/); the Junta Interamericana de Defensa (http://www.jid.org/); the International Monetary Fund (http://www.imf.org/); the Organization of American States (http://www.oas.org); PeaceNet: Directory of Human Rights Resources (http://www.igc.org/igc/peacenet); The Embassy Page (http://www.embpage.org/); The World Bank Group: Latin America and the Caribbean (http://www.worldbank.org/html/extdr/lac.htm); and the United Nations Development Programme (http://www.undp.org/).

Links to press information on Latin America may be found at El Nuevo Herald Diario de Miami (http://www.diariolasamericas.com/); Newspapers Online (http://www.newspapers.com/); Publicaciones de América Latina, España, y Portugal (http://www.cyberus.ca/sudameris/ezines-l.htm). The electronic *Wall Street Journal* contains brief news reports in Spanish at http://interactive.wsj.com/americas/resources/documents/sp-amer.htm.

The following U.S. government sites contain information concerning relations with Latin America: the General Accounting Office (http://gao.gov); Promoting Democracy USAID Gopher (gopher://gaia.info.usaid.gov:70/11/promoting_demo); U.S. White House (http://www.whitehouse.gov/); U.S. State Department (http://www.state.gov); U.S. Government Links Page (http://geocities.com/Pentagon/3076); U.S. Southern Command (SOUTHCOM) Fact File (http://www.dtic.dla.mil/defenselink/factfile/chapter1/southcom.html); U.S. Congress (http://thomas.loc.gov); U.S. Information Agency (http://www.usia.gov); U.S. House of Representatives (http://www.house.gov); the U.S. Senate (http://www.senate.gov); the Inter-American Foundation (http://www.iaf.gov/iaf1.htm); and the Library of Congress (http://www.loc.gov).

Index

About the Contributors

SARAH ANDERSON is the Director of the Global Economy Program at the Institute for Policy Studies, a multi-issue research and education center founded in 1963. Anderson has published dozens of studies and articles on the impact of trade and investment liberalization on communities, workers, the poor, and the environment. Most recently, she co-authored (with John Cavanagh and Thea Lee) *Field Guide to the Global Economy* (NY: New Press, 2000). Anderson is on the steering committee of the Alliance for Responsible Trade and is a board member of the Coalition for Justice in the Maquiladoras. She also served on the staff of the International Financial Institutions Advisory Commission, which presented their recommendations for World Bank and IMF reform to the U.S. Congress in March 2000.

VIRGINIA M. BOUVIER is research director and consultant for a project on women in foreign and economic policy-making for the Women's Leadership Conference of the Americas. She is the author of *Women and the Conquest of California, 1542–1840: Codes of Silence* (Tucson: University of Arizona Press, 2001); editor of *Whose America? The War of 1898 and the Battles to Define the Nation* (Westport, CT: Praeger, 2001); and author of numerous monographs and articles on U.S.–Latin American relations. Her research interests center around human rights and justice issues, women and gender in Latin America, and imperial encounters in the Americas.

JOHN CAVANAGH is Director of the Washington-based Institute for Policy Studies. He co-authored (with Sarah Anderson and Thea Lee) *A Field*

Guide to the Global Economy (NY: New Press, 2000); (with Richard J. Barnet) *Global Dreams: Imperial Corporations and the New World Order* (NY: Simon & Schuster, 1994); and (with Robin Broad) *Plundering Paradise: The Struggle for the Environment in the Philippines* (Berkeley: University of California Press, 1994).

MARGARET E. CRAHAN is the Dorothy Epstein Professor of Latin American History at Hunter College of the City University of New York. From 1982–1994, she was the Henry R. Luce Professor of Religion, Power, and Political Process at Occidental College and from 1993 to 1994, the Marous Professor at the University of Pittsburgh. She has served on the Executive Council of the Latin American Studies Association and the Pacific Coast Council on Latin American Studies, as well as on the board of directors of the Inter-American Institute of Human Rights, For CHILDREN, Inc., and the Kellogg Institute of the University of Notre Dame. Among her publications are more than sixty articles and books, including *Africa and the Caribbean: Legacies of a Link* (Baltimore: Johns Hopkins, 1979), *Human Rights and Basic Needs in the Americas* (Washington: Georgetown University Press, 1982), and *The City and the World: New York's Global Future* (New York: Council on Foreign Relations, 1997).

DAVID A. CROCKER is Senior Research Scholar at the Institute for Philosophy and Public Policy and the Maryland School of Public Affairs (MSPA) at the University of Maryland, where he specializes in sociopolitical philosophy, international development ethics, and transitional justice. Dr. Crocker received three graduate degrees (M. Div., M. A., Ph.D.) from Yale University. Crocker's writings include *Praxis and Democratic Socialism: The Critical Social Theory of Markovic and Stojanovic* (Atlantic Highlands, NJ: Humanities Press, 1983) and *Florecimiento humano y desarrollo internacional: La nueva ética de capacidades humanas* (San Jose, Costa Rica: Editorial de la Universidad de Costa Rica, 1998). He co-edited (with Toby Linden) *Ethics of Consumption: The Good Life, Justice, and Global Stewardship* (Lanham, MD: Rowman and Littlefield, 1998). He has completed a manuscript entitled "Well-being, Capability, and Development: Essays in International Development Ethics" and is working on a book on the ethics of reckoning with past wrongs. He is a founder and the current president of the International Development Ethics Association (IDEA).

EDGAR J. DOSMAN is Senior Research Fellow at the Centre for International and Security Studies, York University (Toronto, Canada) and Professor in the Department of Political Science. Current research interests include Canadian foreign policy and defense policy, the evolution of Western Hemisphere relations, and Cuban foreign policy and defense policy with special reference to the war in Angola. Dosman is the co-editor (with Jean Daudelin) of *Beyond Mexico* (Ottawa: Carleton University Press, 1995). He is the author of "Canadian–Latin American Relations: the New Look," *International Journal* (Summer 1992); "Adjusting the Sights: the Post-Miami Dynamic in Canadian–Latin American Relations," in *Canada Among Nations* (New York: Oxford University Press, 1998); and *The Rise and Fall of the Americas* (Montreal and Buffalo, NY: McGill-Queen's University Press, forthcoming 2001).

DOUGLAS FARAH was named the West Africa Bureau Chief for the *Washington Post* in 2000. From 1992 to 1997 he served as Central America and Caribbean Bureau Chief and, from 1997 to 2000 as International Investigative Correspondent for the *Post*. Farah recently published an essay on Colombia that appeared in Roy Gutman, ed., *Crimes of War: What the Public Should Know* (NY: W.W. Norton & Co., 1999).

CARRIE A. FOSTER is an Associate Professor of History at Miami University in Ohio. She is the author of *The Women and the Warrior: The U.S. Section of the Women's International League for Peace and Freedom, 1915–1946*, Peace and Conflict Resolution series (Syracuse: Syracuse University Press, 1995). Her recent research interests have expanded to focus on such colorful issues as conspiracies and assassinations, as exemplified by the latest course she has created for her undergraduate students, "Assassinations in U.S. History."

JULIO RAMOS is Professor of Spanish and Portuguese at the University of California, Berkeley. He is the author of *Divergent Modernities: Culture and Politics in Nineteenth-Century Latin America*, trans. John D. Blanco (Durham, NC: Duke University Press, 2001); *Desencuentros de la modernidad en América Latina: literatura y política en el siglo XIX* (México: Fondo de Cultura Económica, 1989); *Paradojas de la letra* (Caracas and Quito: Excultura Editores and Universidad Andina Simón Bolívar, 1996); and has published extensively in Latin America and the United States on Latin American literature, politics, and culture. He is the editor of *Amor y anarquía: Los escritos de Luisa Capetillo* (San Juan: Ediciones Huracán, 1992).

ANA PATRICIA RODRÍGUEZ is Assistant Professor of U.S. Latina/o Literatures in the Department of Spanish and Portuguese at the University of Maryland, College Park. She received a Ph.D. in literature from the University of California, Santa Cruz, in 1998. She is completing a book entitled *Dividing the Isthmus: Central American Cultural Politics and Literature*, which examines metaphors of economic, symbolic, and human excess across various Central American and Central American immigrant texts. Her research focuses on the transnational cultures of U.S. Latinos, particularly Central American populations in the isthmus and in the United States. She was born in El Salvador and grew up in the San Francisco Bay Area.

LARS SCHOULTZ has been William Rand Kenan, Jr., Professor of Political Science at the University of North Carolina at Chapel Hill since 1991. He is author of *Human Rights and United States Policy toward Latin America* (Princeton: Princeton University Press, 1981); *The Populist Challenge: Argentine Electoral Behavior in the Postwar Era* (Chapel Hill: The University of North Carolina Press, 1983); *National Security and United States Policy toward Latin America* (Princeton: Princeton University Press, 1987); and *Beneath the United States: A History of United States Policy toward Latin America* (Cambridge: Harvard University Press, 1998). He served as president of the Latin American Studies Association from 1991 to 1992.

MICHAEL SHIFTER is a Senior Fellow and Program Director at the Inter-American Dialogue. Since 1993, Mr. Shifter has also taught Latin American politics at Georgetown University's School of Foreign Service. His recent articles on U.S.–Latin American relations and hemispheric affairs, democracy and human rights, multilateralism, drug policy, security issues, press freedom, and Colombian and Peruvian politics have appeared in *Foreign Affairs, Foreign Policy* (Global/Spanish edition), *Current History,* the *Los Angeles Times,* the *Journal of Democracy, Harvard International Review*, as well as in periodicals in many Latin American and Caribbean countries.

MOLLY TODD received her M.A. degree in Latin American Studies from the University of Texas at Austin, and is now pursuing her doctoral studies in Latin American History at the University of Wisconsin in Madison. Her current research explores grassroots organizing in rural El Salvador prior to and during the country's civil war, and the post-war, intergenerational transfer of historical memories of the war within the country's repopulated communities. Ms. Todd's work has appeared in a variety of publications, including *NACLA Report on the Americas,* the *Nation,* and the *Allegheny Review.*